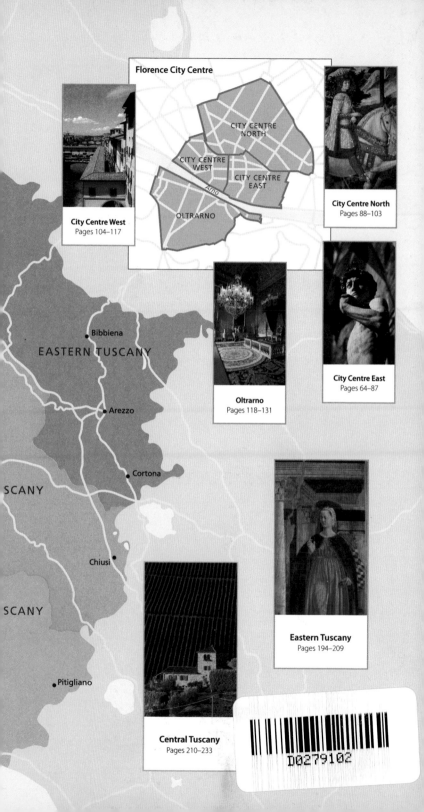

Florence City Centre

CITY CENTRE
NORTH

CITY CENTRE
WEST

CITY CENTRE
EAST

OLTRARNO

Arno

City Centre West
Pages 104–117

City Centre North
Pages 88–103

City Centre East
Pages 64–87

Oltrarno
Pages 118–131

Bibbiena

EASTERN TUSCANY

Arezzo

Cortona

SCANY

Chiusi

SCANY

Pitigliano

Eastern Tuscany
Pages 194–209

Central Tuscany
Pages 210–233

D0279102

EYEWITNESS TRAVEL

FLORENCE & TUSCANY

EYEWITNESS TRAVEL

FLORENCE
& TUSCANY

Main Contributor **Christopher Catling**

LONDON, NEW YORK,
MELBOURNE, MUNICH AND DELHI
www.dk.com

Project Editor Shirin Patel

Art Editor Pippa Hurst

Editors Maggie Crowley,
Tom Fraser, Sasha Heseltine

Designers Claire Edwards,
Emma Hutton, Marisa Renzullo

Map Co-Ordinators Simon Farbrother, David Pugh

Contributors
Anthony Brierley, Kerry Fisher,
Tim Jepson, Carolyn Pyrah

Maps
Jan Clark, James Mills-Hicks
(Dorling Kindersley Cartography)

Photographers
Philip Enticknap,
John Heseltine, Kim Sayer

Illustrators
Stephen Conlin, Donati Giudici Associati Srl,
Richard Draper, Robbie Polley

Printed and bound by South China Printing Co. Ltd., China

First published in the UK in 1994 by
Dorling Kindersley Limited
80 Strand, London WC2R 0RL

14 15 16 17 10 9 8 7 6 5 4 3 2 1

Reprinted with revisions 1994 (twice), 1996, 1997, 1999, 2000, 2001, 2002,
2003, 2004, 2005, 2006, 2007, 2009, 2011, 2013, 2015

Copyright 1994, 2015
© Dorling Kindersley Limited, London
A Penguin Random House Company

A CIP catalogue record is available from the British Library.

ISBN 978-1-40936-919-6

Floors are referred to throughout in accordance with European usage;
ie the "first floor" is the floor above ground level

MIX
Paper from
responsible sources
FSC™ C018179

**The information in this
DK Eyewitness Travel Guide is checked regularly.**
Every effort has been made to ensure that this book is as up-to-date as possible
at the time of going to press. Some details, however, such as telephone numbers,
opening hours, prices, gallery hanging arrangements and travel information, are
liable to change. The publishers cannot accept responsibility for any consequences
arising from the use of this book, nor for any material on third party websites, and
cannot guarantee that any website address in this book will be a suitable source of
travel information. We value the views and suggestions of our readers very highly.
Please write to: Publisher, DK Eyewitness Travel Guides, Dorling Kindersley,
80 Strand, London, WC2R 0RL, UK, or email: travelguides@dk.com.

Front cover main image: The Duomo, Florence

◀ View of Florence's Duomo from the towering Campanile

Contents

Brunelleschi's door panel, Bargello

Introducing Florence and Tuscany

Piazza della Repubblica, Cartona

Florence's oldest bridge, Ponte Vecchio, stretching over the Arno

Flowering courgettes at the market

Abbey church of Sant'Antimino

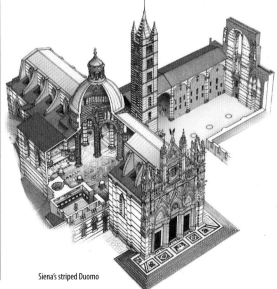
Siena's striped Duomo

HOW TO USE THIS GUIDE

This guide helps you get the most from your stay in Florence and Tuscany. It provides both expert recommendations and detailed practical information. *Introducing Florence and Tuscany* maps the region and sets it in its historical and cultural context. *Florence Area by Area* and *Tuscany Area by Area* describe the important sights, with maps, pictures and detailed illustrations. Suggestions for food, drink, accommodation and shopping are in *Travellers' Needs*, and the *Survival Guide* has tips on everything from the Italian telephone system to getting to Tuscany and travelling around the region.

Florence Area by Area

The historic centre of the city has been divided into four sightseeing areas. Each has its own chapter, which opens with a list of the sights described. All the sights are numbered and plotted on an *Area Map*. The detailed information for each sight is presented in numerical order, making it easy to locate within the chapter.

Sights at a Glance lists the chapter's sights by category: Churches; Museums and Galleries; Historic Buildings, Streets and Piazzas.

All pages relating to Florence have the same coloured tabs.

A locator map shows where you are in relation to other areas of the city centre.

1 Area Map
For easy reference, the sights are numbered and located on a map. The sights are also shown on the Florence Street Finder on pages 144–51.

2 Street-by-Street Map
This gives a bird's-eye view of the heart of each sightseeing area.

A suggested route for a walk covers the more interesting streets in the area.

3 Detailed information on each sight
All the sights in Florence are described individually. Addresses, telephone numbers, opening hours and information on admission charges and wheelchair access are also provided.

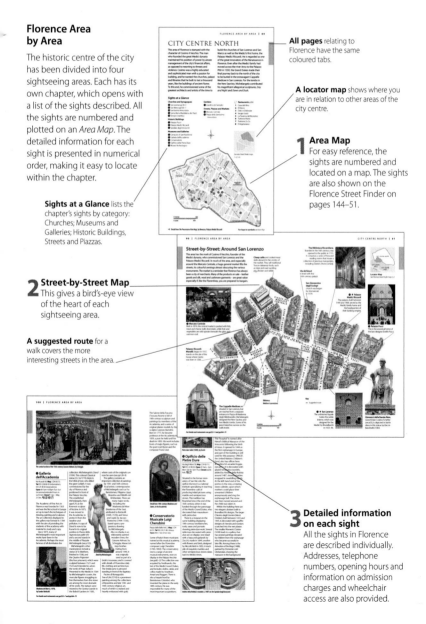

Tuscany Area by Area

In this book, Tuscany has been divided into five regions, each of which has a separate chapter. The most interesting sights to visit have been numbered on a *Regional Map*.

Each area of Tuscany can be quickly identified by its colour coding.

1 Introduction
The landscape, history and character of each region is described here, showing how the area has developed over the centuries and what it offers the visitor today.

2 Regional Map
This shows the road network and gives an illustrated overview of the whole region. All the sights are numbered and there are also useful tips on getting around the region by car, bus and train.

3 Detailed information on each sight
All the important towns and other places to visit are described individually. They are listed in order, following the numbering on the *Regional Map*. Within each town or city, there is detailed information on important buildings and other sights.

Stars indicate the best features and works of art.

For all the top sights, a Visitors' Checklist provides the practical information you will need to plan your visit.

4 The top sights
These are given two or more full pages. Historic buildings are dissected to reveal their interiors; museums and galleries have colour-coded floorplans to help you locate the most interesting exhibits.

INTRODUCING FLORENCE AND TUSCANY

DISCOVERING FLORENCE AND TUSCANY

The following itineraries have been designed to take in as many of Tuscany's highlights as possible, while allowing plenty of time for spontaneous diversions. First come two-, three- and five-day tours of Florence, each designed to cover the main sights and give you a taste of the city's life and colour. These are followed by a ten-day tour of Central Tuscany, which includes many of the region's famous art towns, such as Lucca, Pisa, San Gimignano and Siena.

It also includes a selection of historic towns and villages known for their wines, with a tour of Chianti and stops at Montepulciano and Montalcino. Finally, the Southern Tuscany tour takes visitors off the beaten tourist track to the region's coast, offshore islands and Etruscan heartland. These itineraries could easily be spliced together for anyone with three or more weeks to spare, or you may wish to simply dip in and draw inspiration.

The Bay of Talamone
The village of Talamone lies on a rocky promontory just south of the Maremma. The area around the bay featured in the 2008 James Bond film *Quantum of Solace*.

A Week in Southern Tuscany

- Tuck into delicious seafood at the workaday fishing port of **Livorno**.

- Soak up the stunning coastal views between **Talamone** and the estuary of the great river Ombrone.

- Meander through the narrow medieval streets of **Pitigliano**, perched high atop a sheer cliff face.

- Join Italy's intelligentsia in the pretty hilltop town of **Capalbio**.

- Explore the Argentario and catch a boat to the remote islands of **Giglio** and **Giannutri**.

- Wallow and splash in the thermal springs of **Saturnia**.

- Marvel at the art of the Etruscans in **Volterra**'s Museo Guarnacci.

- Visit the beautifully kept 13th-century town of **Massa Marittima**.

- Look out for wildlife on a walk through **Parco Naturale dell'Uccellina**.

Lucca

Pisa

Arno

Elsa

Livorno

Volterra

Cecina

Massa Marittima

Golfo di Follónica

Mar Tirreno

Giglio

0 kilometres 20

0 miles 20

Florence from the South Bank
A riverside stroll in the Oltrarno district offers spectacular views of the river Arno, the city and the surrounding Tuscan hills.

Ten Days in Central Tuscany

- Wander along **Pisa**'s elegant riverbank to discover there is more to the town than the **Leaning Tower**.

- Join the civilized residents of **Lucca** in an evening stroll around the ramparts, or past the Liberty shop fronts of pretty Via Fillungo.

- Eat and drink your way around the picture-postcard wine villages, towns and estates of **Chianti**.

- Marvel at **Siena**'s tiger-striped Duomo and discover *panforte*, the town's chewy fruit-and-nut cake.

- See the noble Renaissance centre of sleepy **Pienza**, planned by, and named after, Pope Pius II.

- Take in the surreal pool-piazza of **Bagno Vignoni**.

- Head out to **Arezzo**, **Sansepolcro** and **Monterchi** on the trail of artist Piero della Francesca.

Key

▬ A Week in Southern Tuscany
▬ Ten Days in Central Tuscany

Countryside in Chianti
Set amid rolling Tuscan hills, Chianti's wine estates and villages are truly beautiful. They offer plenty of opportunities for tasting too.

Two Days in Florence

- **Arriving** Arrive and depart from Pisa or Florence airport.

- **Transport** This itinerary can be followed entirely on foot, but the journey to San Miniato al Monte is best made by bus. For more information on buses in Florence, *see p302*.

- **Booking Ahead** Call ahead to reserve tickets for the Uffizi and Galleria dell'Accademia.

Day 1
Morning Start with the stunning **Duomo, Campanile and Baptistry** *(pp68–9)*. Climb to the top of the Campanile for a crow's-eye view of Florence. Back on firm ground, visit the Gothic Baptistry to see copies of the bronze East doors dubbed "the Gates of Paradise" by Michelangelo.

Walk down Via dei Calzaiuoli to **Piazza della Signoria** *(pp80–81)*, which is dominated by crenellated Palazzo Vecchio and several instantly recognizable statues. Cross the Arno via medieval **Ponte Vecchio** *(pp110–11)* to take a stroll around the **Boboli Gardens** *(pp128–9)*.

Afternoon Lunch in atmospheric **Piazza di Santo Spirito** *(p122)*, then walk to the **Brancacci Chapel** *(pp130–31)* to see the famous *Life of St Peter* frescoes. Head back to the centre of town and visit the **Uffizi** *(pp84–7)*, at its least crowded after 4:30pm. Wind down with a touch of designer window-shopping along **Via de' Tornabuoni** *(p109)*.

Ghiberti's bronze Baptistry doors, known as the "Gates of Paradise"

Day 2
Morning Visit the church of **Santa Croce** *(pp76–7)*, with its peaceful cloisters and the signature Cappella de' Pazzi by Brunelleschi. Move on to the **Bargello** *(pp72–3)*, a former prison housing Renaissance sculptures, such as Giambologna's exquisite *Mercury* and Donatello's androgynous *David*. Devote the rest of the morning to sublime frescoes by Fra Angelico at **San Marco** *(pp100–1)*, and to Michelangelo's muscled tomb statuary in the Cappelle Medicee at **San Lorenzo** *(pp94–5)*.

Afternoon See more of Michelangelo at the **Galleria dell'Accademia** *(pp98–9)*, then take bus 12 from the train station to the delicate church of **San Miniato al Monte** *(pp134–5)*. Soak up splendid views and enjoy the jewel-like interior, with its frescoes, mosaics and an inlaid marble floor. If it is nice weather, walk back downhill into town, ending up at the Ponte Vecchio. Enjoy an aperitif along the Arno before dinner.

Three Days in Florence

- **Arriving** Arrive and depart from Pisa or Florence airport.

- **Transport** This itinerary can be followed entirely on foot.

- **Booking Ahead** Call ahead to reserve tickets at the Uffizi and Galleria dell' Accademia.

Day 1
Morning Begin the day with the **Duomo, Campanile and Baptistry** *(pp68–9)*. The Duomo is so huge that the only way of seeing the entire building is to tackle the 414 steps that climb to the top of the Campanile, also the best vantage point for admiring the iconic cupola. The dome's layers of cantilevered brick rings make it entirely self-supporting, an ingenious construction. Designed by Brunelleschi, the dome is best appreciated by climbing to the top (463 steps). Walk right around the octagonal Gothic Baptistry, and then admire Ghiberti's use of perspective on copies of his famous bronze East doors.

Pass by **Orsanmichele** *(p71)*, and then stroll around **Piazza della Signoria** *(pp80–81)* to admire Palazzo Vecchio and statues by Giambologna, Cellini and Michelangelo. Break for lunch.

Afternoon Cross medieval **Ponte Vecchio** *(pp110–11)* for a stroll in the **Boboli Gardens** *(pp128–9)*, then explore the shops of the historic centre – for designer clothes target **Via de' Tornabuoni** *(p109)*. Finish your day at **Santa Maria Novella** *(pp114–15)*. Admire the façade by Alberti and frescoes by Masaccio before heading to the Santa Maria Novella pharmacy *(p277)*, founded by Dominican friars in the 16th century.

Day 2
Morning Head to the church of **San Lorenzo** *(pp94–5)* to see monumental tombs by Michelangelo in the Cappelle Medicee and the marvellous staircase he designed for the Biblioteca. Move on to **San**

Jewellers' shops and workshops overhang the Arno on the iconic Ponte Vecchio

For practical information on travelling around Florence and Tuscany, see pp298–307

Marco *(pp100–1)* and admire Fra Angelico's exquisite pastel frescoes. Relax in the **Giardino dei Semplici** *(p93)*, then take a look at **Spedale degli Innocenti** *(p99)* on Piazza della Santissima Annunziata. This former orphanage is decorated with delicate blue-and-white-glazed terracotta roundels of swaddled babies by Andrea della Robbia.

Afternoon After lunch, visit the **Galleria dell'Accademia** *(pp98–9)* to see Michelangelo's renowned *David*. Walk or take a bus over to the Oltrarno, where you can view the rhythmic Renaissance architecture of **Santo Spirito** *(see p122)* before walking down to the **Brancacci Chapel** *(pp130–31)* to see frescoes by Masolino and his pupil, Masaccio. Cross the Arno at the Ponte Santa Trinità, and take a stroll around the shops and cafés of Borgo Santi Apostoli and Via Porta Rossa.

Day 3
Morning Begin with a tour of celebrity sculptures by Donatello, Michelangelo and Giambologna at the **Bargello** *(pp72–3)*. If the weather is good, follow the walk to **San Miniato** *(pp134–5)*. If it is raining, spend the rest of the morning visiting Palazzo Vecchio.

Afternoon See the works of Botticelli, Titian, Leonardo da Vinci and many other celebrated artists at the **Uffizi** *(pp84–7)*, and then shop for gifts by Piazza della Signoria and Santa Croce. Pay your respects to Machiavelli, Michelangelo and Galileo at the church of **Santa Croce** *(pp76–7)* before going for a final aperitif near the Duomo.

Clipped box hedges and lush flower beds in the Boboli Gardens

Five Days in Florence

- **Arriving** Arrive and depart from Pisa or Florence airport.
- **Transport** There is a regular bus from Florence to Fiesole *(see p136)*. The rest of the tour can be followed on foot.
- **Booking Ahead** Call ahead to reserve tickets at the Uffizi and Galleria dell'Accademia.

Day 1
Morning Start with the **Duomo** *(pp68–9)*, and drop by **Museo dell'Opera del Duomo** *(p71)* to see the original "Gates of Paradise" and Michelangelo's masterpiece, *Pietà*. Visit **Orsanmichele** *(p71)*, where a copy of Donatello's *St George* is set in the niche for which it was created, then wander over to **Piazza della Signoria** *(pp80–81)* and have lunch in one of the cafés.

Afternoon After lunch, see the bloodier side of Florence's history in the **Palazzo Vecchio** *(pp82–3)*, then take a stroll through historic streets to **Via de' Tornabuoni** *(p109)* to begin the evening with a Prosecco.

Day 2
Morning Devote the morning to the **Uffizi** *(pp84–7)*. Follow with a stroll from Ponte Vecchio to **Santa Croce** *(pp76–7)* and up to the lively Sant'Ambrogio market.

Afternoon Follow the **San Miniato** walk *(pp134–5)*. On your return, pop into the church of **Santa Felicita** *(p123)* to see the extraordinary candy-coloured

Deposition by Pontormo. Treat yourself to an aperitif on **Piazza di Santo Spirito** *(p122)*.

Day 3
Morning Enjoy the company of Michelangelo and the Medici at **San Lorenzo** *(pp94–5)*. Then see some Fra Angelico frescoes at **San Marco** *(pp100–1)*. Finish up by looking at some extraordinary marble craftsmanship at the **Opificio delle Pietre Dure** *(p99)*.

Afternoon Marvel at masterpieces in the **Galleria dell' Accademia** *(pp98–9)*, and then visit **Santa Maria Novella** *(pp114–15)*. Afterwards, window-shop on **Via de' Tornabuoni** *(p109)*.

Day 4
Morning Begin your day with the Renaissance sculptures of the **Bargello** *(pp72–3)*, including Donatello's nervy *St George*.

Afternoon Take bus number 7 out to the hill town of **Fiesole** *(pp136–7)* and explore the romantic delights of Florence's popular summer retreat.

Day 5
Morning Head down to **Santo Spirito** *(p122)* for its market and striking church, then walk over to the **Brancacci Chapel** *(pp130–31)* to see Masaccio's *Expulsion of Adam and Eve*.

Afternoon Explore the **Palazzo Pitti** *(pp124–7)* and its earthy paradise, the **Boboli Gardens** *(pp128–9)*, a quintessential example of Renaissance landscaping. Then enjoy a final stroll through the historic centre.

The exterior of the Uffizi, built as a suite of offices in 1560–80

Ten Days in Central Tuscany

- **Arriving** Arrive and depart from Pisa or Florence airport.
- **Transport** There are good bus and train connections between the main towns in Tuscany, but you will need a car to explore the back roads.
- **Booking ahead** It is best to book accommodation and dinner in advance, especially during high season.

Day 1: Pisa

Arrive in **Pisa** *(pp160–64)*. Instead of heading straight to the **Campo dei Miracoli**, take in the ambience of Pisa slowly, with a visit to the market on Piazza delle Vettovaglie – a good lunch spot – and a walk by the languid Arno. After seeing the Campo, drive to **Lucca** *(pp180–86)*, and begin the evening with a stroll down Via Fillungo, lined with wonderful Art Nouveau shop fronts. Finish up at **San Frediano** *(p186)*, its façade shimmering with mosaics.

Day 2: Lucca

Begin with Lucca's Duomo, **San Martino** *(pp184–5)*. Marvel at its elaborate black-and-white-striped façade and the interior, which houses a wooden image of Christ, said to have been carved as he hung on the cross. Take a walk around the **Ramparts** *(p183)* and climb the **Torre dei Guinigi** *(p181)* to see one of Tuscany's highest roof gardens. Head down to **Piazza del Mercato**, originally built around a Roman amphitheatre *(p182)*. End the day with a visit to **Puccini's house** *(p183)*. Stay in Lucca or Florence.

Days 3–5: Florence

See the Three-Day Florence itinerary on pp12–13.

Day 6: Monteriggioni to San Gimignano

Drive south from Florence into the heart of Tuscany, pausing for lunch in the perfectly preserved medieval town of **Monteriggioni** *(p214)*. Then double back to **San Gimignano** *(pp216–19)*, its medieval towers and imposing crenellated buildings evidence

of a belligerent past. Don't miss the humbug-striped interior of the **Collegiata** *(p218)*, nor the evocative Piazza della Cisterna.

Day 7: Chianti region

Take a tour of the most inviting villages of the Chianti Classico wine region. Start with castle-crowned **Castellina in Chianti**, and then make a diversion up the S222 to **Greve in Chianti**, a diminutive medieval town devoted to wine and food. Follow signs to the hamlet of **Volpaia** and on to **Radda in Chianti**. East of Radda (SP2), more workaday **Gaiole in Chianti** has superb wine estates on its fringes, including **Badia a Coltibuono** (a winery and villa in a former Romanesque abbey). Head to Siena for the night.

Day 8: Siena

Wander around Siena's **Piazza del Campo** *(p222)*, climbing the **Torre del Mangia** *(p222)* for splendid views before heading down to the tiger-striped **Duomo** *(pp224–5)*. Inside, look out for Nicola Pisano's pulpit panels and the astonishing inlaid marble floor. After lunch, head to the pretty ruined abbey of **San Galgano** *(p228)* before driving back for a final night in Siena.

Day 9: Siena to Montalcino

Leave Siena along the Asciano road, passing through the surreal clay bluffs known as the Crete. Make a stop at the sleepy village of **Pienza** *(p230)* to see its elegant Renaissance centre, created by Pope Pius II in an attempt to transform his birthplace into a

The ruined nave of the monumental abbey of San Galgano

model Renaissance town. Have lunch in **Montepulciano** *(p231)*, famous for its Vini Nobile wines, before crossing the Val d'Orcia to **Montalcino** *(p228)* for the night. This august medieval village produces Brunello di Montalcino, a prestigious, punchy red.

Day 10: Montalcino to Florence or Pisa

Begin the morning with a stroll around **Montalcino**, then drive out to the Benedictine abbey of **Sant'Antimo** *(p232)*, one of the finest Romanesque churches in Tuscany. Start your journey back north, making a stop to see the extraordinary main square of **Bagno Vignoni** *(p230)* – instead of cobbles it has a large thermal spa pool (now off limits). Drive back to Florence or Pisa airport.

> **To extend your trip...**
> Fans of artist Piero della Francesca should visit his frescoes in **Arezzo** *(pp202–5)*, **Sansepolcro** *(p200)* and **Monterchi** *(p201)*.

Lucca's Torre dei Guinigi, now home to a pleasant roof garden

A Week in Southern Tuscany

- **Arriving** Arrive and depart from Pisa.

- **Transport** A car is recommended. If considering following the itinerary on public transport, allow several additional days.

- **Booking ahead** It is essential to book hotel accommodation along the coast in the summer. In other areas of southern Tuscany, it is advisable to make advance restaurant and accommodation bookings between Easter and October.

Boats moored in the pretty harbour at Porto Ercole

Day 1: Livorno to Volterra

Drive to the bustling fishing port of **Livorno** *(pp166–7)*, and visit one of its many typical trattorias for a hearty lunch of *cacciucco* (Livorno's answer to bouillabaisse). Follow with a stroll around the Renaissance Piazza Grande, one of few parts of town to survive World War II. Continue to historic **Volterra** *(pp170–71)*, where you can delve into Tuscany's Etruscan past at the stupendous **Museo Etrusco Guarnacci** *(p170)*. Don't miss the *Ombre della Sera* (Shadow of the Evening), an eerie elongated bronze which had a profound impact on 20th-century sculptor Alberto Giacometti. Spend the night in Volterra.

Day 2: Talamone to Massa Marittima

The most beautiful stretch of Tuscan coastline lies between the fishing village of **Talamone** *(p244)* and the estuary of the river Ombrone. This area is protected by a nature reserve, the **Parco Naturale dell'Uccellina** *(pp240–41)*. There are waymarked trails and a beach area at Marina di Alberese, where migratory and resident birds (and occasionally wild boar) can often be spotted. **Massa Marittima** *(p238)*, inland, is a marvellously preserved 13th-century town rarely visited by tourists. The Romanesque Duomo is particularly interesting. Return to Talamone for supper.

Day 3: Capalbio to Monte Argentario

Capalbio *(p245)* is a perfectly preserved picture-postcard hill village and a popular summertime escape for Italy's left-wing politicians and intelligentsia. There are wonderful places to eat, so time your arrival to coincide with lunch. Wander through the medieval streets and enjoy stunning views from the village's crenellated walls, then make your way to the nearby **Giardino dei Tarocchi**. Inspired by Tarot cards, this bizarre sculpture park features huge figures covered in brightly coloured mosaic. Afterwards, drive to **Monte Argentario** *(p244)*, a mid-sea mountain connected to the mainland by causeways. There are two main settlements here: chic Porto Ercole and the rather more down-to-earth Porto Santo Stefano. Both are home to excellent fish restaurants. Find a spot by the harbour and look out for the luxury yachts.

The thermal waterfalls of the Cascate del Gorello in Saturnia

Day 4: Monte Argentario

Spend the morning on the beach, swimming off rocky coves or trekking up the mountain (635 m/2000 ft). If it rains, take a drive along the coastal road known as the Strada Panoramica and enjoy breathtaking views of the Tuscan Archipelago. In good weather, take a boat trip to the tranquil islands of **Giglio** and **Giannutri** *(p244)*. Both are home to wild, rugged landscapes and pristine beaches with crystal-clear water. Return to Monte Argentario, or stay overnight on Giglio (in which case add an extra day to the itinerary).

Day 5: Saturnia to Pitigliano

Back on the mainland, head to **Saturnia** *(p242)* to enjoy the simple pleasure of splashing about in the pools and cascades of the Cascate del Gorello. Spend an afternoon exploring enchanting **Sovana** *(p242)*, its fish-bone paved Via di Mezzo lined with medieval palazzo and churches. **Pitigliano** *(p243)*, clamped to a tufa ridge, has narrow medieval streets, dizzying views and a small but fascinating museum devoted to the history of the Jewish community that lived in the town until World War II. Sleep in Pitigliano or nearby Sorano.

Day 6 and 7: Pisa

Drive north to **Pisa** *(pp160–64)*, and spend a day sightseeing at Lucca and Pisa before flying home *(see Day One of the Central Tuscany tour on p14)*.

Putting Florence and Tuscany on the Map

Tuscany lies in central Italy, bordered by the regions of Emilia-Romagna, Marche, Umbria and Lazio. Along with Elba, several islands in the Ligurian Sea also form part of Tuscany. A region of rolling hills, mountains and rugged coastlines, Tuscany covers an area of 22,992 sq km (8,875 sq miles), and has a population of more than 3.5 million. There are international airports at Pisa and Florence. Florence is about 2½ hours by train from Rome (1½ hours on Eurostar) and about 3 hours from Milan.

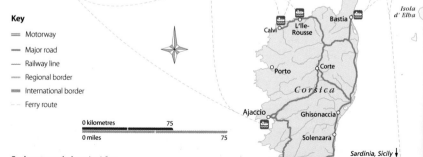

SWITZERLAND

Chur

San Bernardino
Locarno
Chiavenna
Colico
Verbania
Como
Lecco
Bergamo
Monza
Milano (Milan)
LOMBARDIA
Lodi
Novara
Pavia
Lodi
A1
Piacenza

Aosta
VALLE D'AOSTA
Biella
Ivrea

Grenoble
Modane
Susa
Torino (Turin)
PIEMONTE
Asti
Alessandria
Tortona
Marsaglia

Briançon

Gap
Carmagnola
Alba

Barcelonnette
Argentera
Cuneo
Mondovì
Carcare
Savona
LIGURIA
Genova (Genoa)
Pontremoli
La Spezia

FRANCE
Digne-les-Bains
Calizzano
Entrevaux
Tende
Albenga
Imperia

Escragnolles
Nice
Monaco
Sanremo
Cannes
Antibes
Fréjus

Toulon

Ligurian Sea

Isola di Gorgona

Arcipelago

Isola d' Elba

Barcelona, Tangier, Tunis

Centuri

Bastia

Calvi
L'Ile-Rousse

Porto
Corte

Corsica

Ajaccio
Ghisonaccia

Solenzara

Sardinia, Sicily

Key

— Motorway
— Major road
— Railway line
— Regional border
— International border
--- Ferry route

| 0 kilometres | 75 |
| 0 miles | 75 |

For keys to symbols *see back flap*

Greater Florence

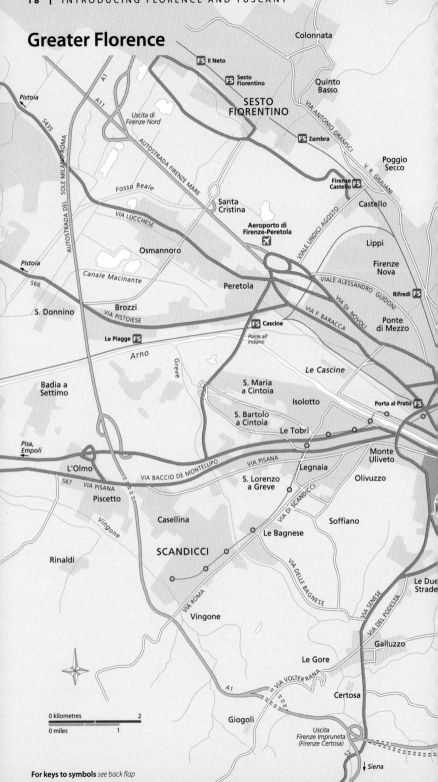

Colonnata

FS Il Neto

FS Sesto
Fiorentino

Quinto
Basso

VIA ANTONIO GRAMSCI

**SESTO
FIORENTINO**

Pistoia

A11

A11

S435

Uscita di
Firenze Nord

AUTOSTRADA FIRENZE MARE

FS Zambra

V. R. GIULIANI

Poggio
Secco

AUTOSTRADA DEL SOLE MILANO-ROMA

Fosso Reale

Santa
Cristina

**Firenze
Castello** **FS**

Castello

VIA LUCCHESE

**Aeroporto di
Firenze-Peretola** ✈

VIALE UNDICI AGOSTO

Lippi

Firenze
Nova

Pistoia

S66

Osmannoro

Canale Macinante

Peretola

VIALE ALESSANDRO GUIDONI

Rifredi **FS**

VIA DI NOVOLI

Ponte
di Mezzo

S. Donnino

VIA PISTOIESE

Brozzi

VIA F. BARACCA

FS Cascine

Le Piagge **FS**

Ponte all'
Indiano

Arno

Greve

Le Cascine

Badia a
Settimo

S. Maria
a Cintoia

Isolotto

Porta al Prato **FS**

S. Bartolo
a Cintoia

Le Tobri

Pisa,
Empoli

VIA PISANA

Legnaia

Monte
Uliveto

L'Olmo

S67

VIA BACCIO DE MONTELUPO

S. Lorenzo
a Greve

Olivuzzo

VIA PISANA

Piscetto

VIA DI SCANDICCI

Soffiano

Casellina

Le Bagnese

Vingone

SCANDICCI

VIA DELLE BAGNESE

Le Due
Strade

Rinaldi

VIA SENESE

VIA ROMA

Vingone

VIA DEL PODESTA

Galluzzo

Le Gore

A1

VIA VOLTER RANA

Certosa

Giogoli

Uscita
Firenze Impruneta
(Firenze Certosa)

↓ Siena

0 kilometres   2

0 miles   1

For keys to symbols *see back flap*

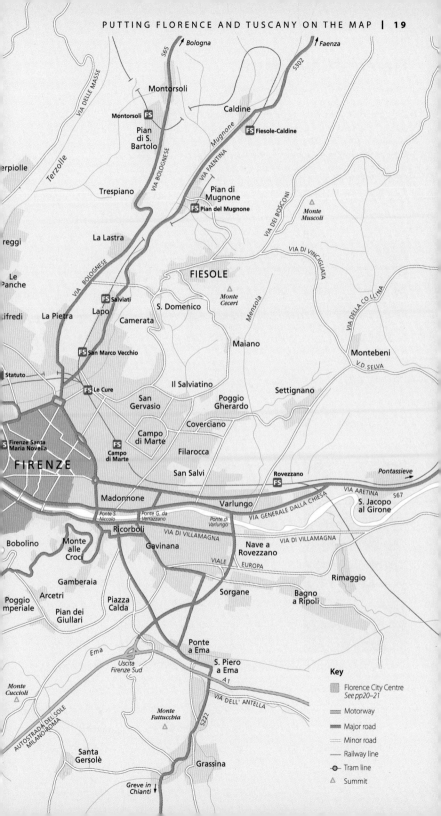

↑ *Bologna*
↑ *Faenza*

S65

S302

VIA DELLE MASSE

Montorsoli

Montorsoli **FS**

Caldine

FS Fiesole-Caldine

Pian
di S.
Bartolo

VIA BOLOGNESE

Mugnone

VIA FAENTINA

Terzolle

erpiolle

Trespiano

Pian di
Mugnone

FS Pian del Mugnone

VIA DEI BOSCONI

△ Monte
Muscoli

La Lastra

VIA DI VINCIGLIATA

reggi

Le
Panche

FIESOLE

ifredi

La Pietra

VIA BOLOGNESE

FS Salviati

S. Domenico

Monte
Ceceri

Mensola

VIA DELLA COLLINA

Lapo

Camerata

Maiano

Montebeni

V.D. SELVA

FS San Marco Vecchio

Il Salviatino

Settignano

Statuto

FS Le Cure

San
Gervasio

Poggio
Gherardo

S Firenze Santa
Maria Novella

FIRENZE

Coverciano

Campo
di Marte

FS Campo
di Marte

Filarocca

San Salvi

Rovezzano

FS

Pontassieve →

VIA ARETINA

S67

Madonnone

Varlungo

VIA GENERALE DALLA CHIESA

S. Jacopo
al Girone

Ponte S.
Niccolò

Ponte G. da
Verrazzano

Ponte di
Varlungo

Bobolino

Monte
alle
Croci

Ricorboli

VIA DI VILLAMAGNA

Gavinana

Nave a
Rovezzano

VIA DI VILLAMAGNA

Rimaggio

Gamberaia

VIALE   EUROPA

Poggio
mperiale

Arcetri

Piazza
Calda

Sorgane

Bagno
a Ripoli

Pian dei
Giullari

Ema

Ponte
a Ema

Monte
Cuccioli
△

Uscita
Firenze Sud

S. Piero
a Ema

A1

AUTOSTRADA DEL SOLE
MILANO-ROMA

Monte
Fattucchia
△

VIA DELL' ANTELLA

S222

Santa
Gersolè

Grassina

↓ Greve in
Chianti

Key

▢ Florence City Centre
See pp20–21

▭ Motorway

▬ Major road

▦ Minor road

— Railway line

⊸ Tram line

△ Summit

Florence City Centre

Florence's best sights are encompassed within such a compact area that the city seems to reveal its treasures at every step. The sights described in this book are grouped within four areas, each of which can be easily explored on foot. In the centre is the massive Duomo, providing a historical as well as geographical focus to the city. Santa Croce to the east and San Marco to the north, with Santa Maria Novella to the west and the Palazzo Pitti in Oltrarno, mark the outlying areas.

City Centre West *(see pp104–117)*: Ponte Santa Trinità, with Ponte Vecchio behind

Oltrarno *(see pp118–31)*: taking a break in Piazza di Santo Spirito

City Centre North *(see pp88–103)*: fountain in Piazza della Santissima Annunziata

VIALE SPARTACO LAVAGNINI

V. D. S. CATERINA D'ALESSANDRIA

VIA BONIFACIO LUPI

VIA CAVOUR

VIA ALFONSO LA MARMORA

VIALE GIACOMO MATTEOTTI

PIAZZA DELL'
DIPENDENZA

VIA XXVII APRILE

VIA PIER ANTONIO MICHELI

PIAZZA
ISIDORO

VIA G. LA PIRA

San
Marco

GIARDINO
DEI
SEMPLICI

VIA GINO CAPPONI

GUELFA

VIA DEGLI
ARAZZIERI

PIAZZA
DI SAN
MARCO

GIARDINO
DELLA
GHERARDESCA

VIA C. BATTISTI

VIA GIUSEPPE PINTI

PIAZZA DEL
MERCATO
CENTRALE

VIA CAVOUR

PIAZZA DELLA
SANTISSIMA
ANNUNZIATA

BORGO GIUSTI

VIALE ANTONIO GRAMSCI

ppelle
edicee

San
Lorenzo

PIAZZA
DI SAN
LORENZO

VIA RICASOLI

VIA DEGLI ALFANI

VIA DELLA COLONNA

PIAZZA
MASSIMO
D'AZEGLIO

V. PIETRO
GIORDANA

iblioteca
Aediceo-
aurenziana

V. DE'
MARTELLI

VIA DE' PUCCI

VIA DEI SERVI

PIAZZA FILIPPO
BRUNELLESCHI

PINTI

P. VIA DE' PILASTRI

VIA DELLA MATTONAIA

V. ALESSANDRO
MANZONI

BRUNELLESCHI

VIA DEL PROCONSOLO

VIA MAURIZIO BUFALINI, V. S. EGIDIO

Duomo

PIAZZA
DEL DUOMO

VIA DEI

VIA ROMA

PIAZZA
DELLA
UBBLICA

VIA CALZAIUOLI

VIA DELL'ORIUOLO

BORGO

PESSA

CALIMALA

VIA DEL CORSO   BORGO DEGLI ALBIZI

PIAZZA
GAETANO
SALVEMINI

VIA PIETRAPIANA   BORGO LA CROCE

PIAZZA DEI
CIOMPI

V. D. CONDOTTA

Bargello

PIAZZA
DI SAN
FIRENZE

V. GIUSEPPE VERDI

PIAZZA
D. SIGNORIA

Palazzo
Vecchio

VIA DE' MACCI

VIA GHIBELLINA

Uffizi

V. DE CASTELLANI

PIAZZA DI
S. REMIGIO

VIA DE' BENCI

PIAZZA DI
SANTA CROCE

L-GO PIERO
BARGELLINI

Ponte
Vecchio

PIAZZA DI
ANTA MARIA
SOPRARNO

PIAZZA
MENTANA

Santa
Croce

V. D. S.
GIUSEPPE

COSTA

LUNG. GEN. DIAZ

LUNG. DELLE GRAZIE

PIAZZA DEI
CAVALLEGGERI

Ponte
alle
Grazie

DI SAN

LUNG. TORRIGIANI LUNG. SERRISTORI

DE' BARDI

PIAZZA DE'
MOZZI

V. D. S. NICCOLÒ

V. GIORGIO

0 metres   500

0 yards   500

City Centre East *(see pp64–87)*: main entrance to Palazzo Vecchio

A PORTRAIT OF TUSCANY

Tuscany is renowned throughout the world for its art, history and beautiful landscape. Here, the past merges with the present to a remarkable degree, for its people pride themselves on their heritage. Independent and combative, they have for centuries preserved their surroundings and traditions, in which lie much of Tuscany's eternal fascination for the outsider.

The people of Tuscany are fiercely proud of their ancestry, which they trace back to the Etruscans. Geneticists have even found gene segments that are uniquely Tuscan: there are strong similarities between the faces carved on Etruscan cremation urns (see pp46–7) and those of the people on the streets of modern Tuscany.

Florence and its surroundings were occupied by the Germans during World War II, and memories of the disgrace suffered under Fascism are still strong. As a result, people in this area have a fierce love of democracy and a strong sense of obligation to vote and participate in politics, even at grass-roots levels, through referendums on such issues as whether to ban traffic from the centre of Florence, for example. Florentines will, however, take the law into their own hands, as they did when they fought the police in 1990 to prevent the closure of San Lorenzo market. The Tuscan love of home has resulted in a

strong *campanilismo*: a form of parochialism that is named after the sound of the local church bell (in the campanile, or belltower). Social anthropologists see this regional character trait as the lasting legacy of intercity conflicts that took place in medieval times. It can be observed at many a Tuscan festival when, beneath the pageantry, there is a serious rivalry between a city's different quarters.

Even the working day of many Tuscans echoes that of their ancestors centuries ago. For people who work out in the fields, the day begins at sunrise, as early as 4:30am in summer. Farm and vineyard labourers will have completed a day's work by noon, when they retire indoors to eat and rest.

Until the 1950s, most Tuscans were familiar with this pattern of life: the region still relied on a feudal system, *mezzadria*, whereby peasants working on the land without payment took a share of the

A timeless view and way of life: peaceful old age in Casole d'Elsa

◀ Brilliant, medieval-style pageantry before Siena's Palio (see p226)

A rare sight today – farming with oxen near Pienza

crops as their reward. Today, agricultural produce remains an important ingredient in the Tuscan economy, but less than 20 per cent of Tuscans now work in agriculture. Many farming families left the land in favour of a stable income and a shorter working day as factory hands. Town dwellers had a much easier way of life, but vestiges of the old rhythms continue to prevail even today. In smaller villages, many shops and sights still close for a few hours each afternoon. Wise travellers soon learn that it pays to follow the same pattern, rising early to join the

A cheese stall in Florence

café throng, before heading out to study ancient frescoes in peace. In the middle of Florence there are several lively early-morning markets where you can buy fresh, local produce *(see p279)*. Bargain-hunters and food-loving Tuscans frequent them, but by 1pm the stallholders will have packed up.

Churches open at 8am, and, except on Sunday when mass is held, there will be few other people to disturb your thoughts if you stray into one. Today, very few Tuscans go regularly to church and Sunday is spent visiting friends, watching sport or enjoying family lunch. After the burst of activity that marks the beginning of the day, Tuscan towns adopt a more sedate pace. New building is prohibited inside their walls, so many people of school or working age travel out, by bus or car, to schools, offices or factories in the suburbs, leaving the old centres to visitors.

Some of the larger towns, particularly Pisa, Lucca, Florence and Siena, have resisted this tide, determined not to become museum cities given over

Clerics in conversation, Colle di Val d'Elsa

entirely to tourism. They have thriving service sectors, testimony to the same Tuscan flair for banking, insurance and accountancy that made the Medici family and the "Merchant of Prato" *(see p192)* some of the richest people in their time. It is, however, the lucky few who work in such beautiful towns. They practise as lawyers, architects, conservationists or designers and are often graduates of the renowned local universities: Pisa, Siena and Florence. For the great majority of Tuscans, however, the working day is spent in purpose-built suburbs, such as the one linking Prato to the Firenze Nuova (New Florence) suburbs west of the city.

The grape harvest in Chianti

Craft and Economy

The Tuscan economy remains firmly rooted in craft traditions. Top designers from Milan use the textile factories of Prato and Florence for the execution of their designs. Leather products made in Tuscany are considered among the best in the world, and factories in the town of Santa Croce sull' Arno, across the Arno from San Miniato, account for a large proportion of Italy's export market. Gold-working is not confined to the Ponte Vecchio workshops in Florence – Arezzo produces jewellery that is sold throughout Europe.

Tourism is, of course, hugely important to the Tuscan economy, and within Italy, only the region of Venice and the Veneto has higher visitor numbers. Tuscans are well aware of the role tourism plays in funding the preservation of its monuments. As a result, you will find most are very welcoming to visitors.

Glass, marble and motorcycles are among Tuscany's most important industrial products, while its olive oil and wine are exported worldwide. This explains why Livorno, Tuscany's port, is the second busiest in Italy, while Pisa's Galileo Galilei airport is rapidly becoming a major air-freight distribution centre.

Individual Tuscan artistry can best be admired in the heart of any Tuscan town during the evening promenade – the *passeggiata*. One moment the streets are empty, the next they are filled with elegant people strolling and chatting. The skill of *fare bella figura* ("looking good") is so prized that visitors will be judged by the same standard. It is an opportunity for you to join in the inherently Tuscan aspiration to create a civilized world.

The hour for relaxing in Cortona

Italian chic, or *bella figura*

A Tuscan Town Square

The main square, or piazza, of nearly every Tuscan town is the focus for much of the town's activities. It is here that the townsfolk gather, at around 6–7pm, for the daily *passeggiata*, the traditional evening stroll, or to participate in local festivals and rallies. In most towns, there are certain religious and civic buildings that are usually grouped around the piazza. Many of these buildings, you will notice, have standard features, such as the campanile, the *cortile* or the loggia, each of which fulfils a specific function. And often you will find that many of these buildings are still in use today, performing the same function for which they were originally built during the 13th–16th centuries.

Wellhead
Water was a valuable resource that was protected by strict laws to prevent pollution.

Marble or hard sandstone paving

A palazzo is any town house of stature. It is usually named after its owner.

Cortile
The arcaded courtyard, or *cortile*, of a palazzo served as an entrance hall shielded from the outside; it also provided a cool retreat.

There are three floors in most palazzi. Public reception rooms were on the middle floor, the *piano nobile*.

The ground floor was used for storage and workshops. Today, many ground floors are let to businesses, while the owners live above.

Baptismal font

Stemmae
Stone-carved coats-of-arms, belonging to citizens who served as councillors and magistrates, are often seen on public buildings.

The Baptistry, usually octagonal, was a separate building to the west of the church. After baptism, the infant was carried ceremoniously into the church for the first time.

Festival in the Piazza
The prestigious buildings of the main piazza often form an appropriate backdrop to costumed tournaments involving jousting, archery and horsemanship, recalling the medieval arts of war.

Fishtail battlements

Loggia
Many loggias, built to provide shelter from the sun or rain, now harbour colourful street markets.

The Palazzo del Comune
(town hall) often houses the Museo Civico (town museum) and the Pinacoteca (art gallery).

Wide central nave, with narrower side aisles

Loggia, or colonnade

The Duomo (from Latin *Domus Dei*, or House of God) is the cathedral, the focal point of the piazza. A smaller parish church is called a *pieve*.

The campanile rose high so that the town bells could be heard far and wide. The bells were rung to announce public meetings or mass, to sound the curfew, or, when rung furiously *(a stormo)*, to warn of impending danger.

Side Chapel
Wealthy patrons paid for ornate tombs, paintings and frescoes in their own private chapels to commemorate their dead.

Understanding Architecture in Tuscany

The survival of so many fine Gothic and Renaissance buildings is part of Tuscany's immense appeal. Whole streets and squares, such as the Piazza dei Priori in Volterra *(see p171)* and the streets around the Mercato Nuovo in Florence, and even towns, such as San Gimignano, have scarcely changed since the 16th century. Simple clues, such as the shape of arches, windows and doorways, reveal the style of the building and when it was built.

Gothic palazzi in Cortona

Romanesque (5th to Mid-13th Centuries)

The Tuscan Romanesque style developed from late Roman architecture. Early Tuscan churches, such as Sant'Antimo *(see pp48–9)*, have round arches, Roman-style columns and arcades. Profuse surface decoration was introduced in the 12th century, resulting in the jewel-like church façades of Pisa and Lucca.

A twisted knot

Interlace and knots are typical motifs.

Capitals are carved with animal and human heads.

Gables often have three tiers of arcading.

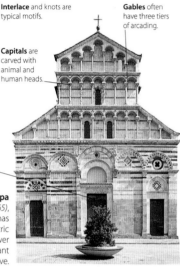

The central portal is flanked by smaller side doors.

Pisa's San Paolo a Ripa d'Arno *(see p165)*, begun in 1210, has restrained geometric patterns on the lower façade and exuberant arcades above.

Marble patterning on stonework

Gothic (13th to Mid-15th Centuries)

Pointed arches are the key feature of Gothic architecture. The style was introduced to Tuscany by French Cistercian monks, who built the abbey of San Galgano in 1218 *(see p228)*. Siena then made this style its own, using it for the city's Duomo, palazzi and civic buildings, such as Palazzo Pubblico *(see pp222–7)*.

Pinnacles, like miniature spires, bristle from the roofline.

Pointed gables

Gabled niches, sheltering statues of saints or Apostles, are a Gothic innovation.

The crockets are shaped like leaves and flowers.

Santa Maria della Spina (1230–1323), with its pointed gables and spikey pinnacles *(see p165)*, is a typical example of Pisan Gothic architecture.

St Luke, from Orsanmichele

Renaissance (15th and 16th Centuries)

Brunelleschi, the father of Renaissance architecture, was inspired by the purity and simplicity of Classical Roman buildings. This style is reflected in his first true Renaissance work, the loggia of the Spedale degli Innocenti in Florence (1419–24) *(see p99)*, with its elegant lines and simple arched bays. The style he created was adopted with enthusiasm by his fellow Florentines, who saw their city as the "new" Rome.

Arch with tear-drop keystone

Courtyard, Spedale degli Innocenti

Classical cornices are moulded in Roman style.

String courses define each floor.

Wedge-shaped masonry around semi-circular window arches is characteristic of Renaissance buildings.

Palazzo Strozzi *(see p109)* is typical of many Tuscan Renaissance buildings. The rusticated stonework gives an impression of strength and stability.

Baroque (Late-16th and 17th Centuries)

The theatrical Baroque style, much favoured by the popes in Rome, largely passed Tuscany by. Although a few churches in Florence were given new façades in the 17th century, the Florentine version of the Baroque style is very Classical in spirit and not as bold or as exuberant as elsewhere in Italy.

Curved pediments are typical of the Baroque style.

Baroque architects liked to use intricate mouldings.

Scroll

Swag

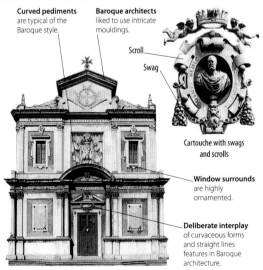

Cartouche with swags and scrolls

Window surrounds are highly ornamented.

Santo Stefano dei Cavalieri *(see p160)* has columns and pilasters on its Baroque façade, which give the illusion of depth.

Deliberate interplay of curvaceous forms and straight lines features in Baroque architecture.

Understanding Art in Tuscany

Tuscany was the scene of one of the most influential and sustained artistic revolutions in history. Its masterpieces record the transition from the stylized charm of medieval art to the Classical beauty and richness of the High Renaissance.

No detailed setting or background

Idealized figures

Medieval Art

Medieval art served as an aid to prayer and contemplation. The Virgin, patron saint of many Tuscan cities, including Siena, was often depicted as the Queen of Heaven, surrounded by adoring angels and saints.

Gold, symbolizing purity, was used lavishly.

Lack of spatial depth

Unifying flow of drapery

Maestà (1308–11)
The stylized figures in this detail from Duccio's huge altarpiece for Siena cathedral are painted with great delicacy.

The figures form a triangle, symbolizing the Holy Trinity. The viewer's eye is drawn upwards to the figures of Christ and God the Father, at the apex.

The Virgin and St John are depicted as real people, rather than idealized figures.

Lorenzo Lenzi, Masaccio's patron, kneels opposite his wife.

The Trinity (c.1427)
Masaccio pioneered perspective in painting, using architectural illusion to create a three-dimensional effect (see p114).

Renaissance Art

The artistic revolution known as the Renaissance, which spread throughout Europe from the 15th century onwards, had its roots in Tuscany. Inspired by ancient Roman art, sculptors and painters brought about a "rebirth" of Classical ideals.

They were supported by wealthy and cultured patrons, themselves fascinated by the works of such Classical authors as Plato and Cicero. Nudes, landscapes, portraits, and scenes from mythology and

Timeline of Great Tuscan Artists

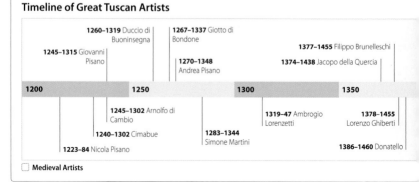

1260–1319 Duccio di Buoninsegna
1245–1315 Giovanni Pisano
1267–1337 Giotto di Bondone
1377–1455 Filippo Brunelleschi
1270–1348 Andrea Pisano
1374–1438 Jacopo della Quercia

1200 — **1250** — **1300** — **1350**

1245–1302 Arnolfo di Cambio
1240–1302 Cimabue
1283–1344 Simone Martini
1319–47 Ambrogio Lorenzetti
1378–1455 Lorenzo Ghiberti
1223–84 Nicola Pisano
1386–1460 Donatello

☐ Medieval Artists

Mannerist Art

Mannerist artists used "hot" colours, elongated forms and deliberately contorted poses, often within complicated, large-scale compositions.

The twisted pose and vivid colours of Michelangelo's *Holy Family (see p85)* established the key features of the style. Few artists could match the monumental scale of his work, but Bronzino, Pontormo and Rosso Fiorentino brought new life to traditional biblical subjects by their skilful and dramatic composition.

Statues of Roman gods reflect a direct debt to Classical art.

Writhing figures create a sense of dramatic tension.

Flesh and musculature are painted in subtle gradations of light and shade.

The Martyrdom of St Lawrence *(1569)*
With Mannerist bravura, Bronzino shows the human body in numerous poses *(see p94)*.

everyday life became legitimate subjects for art.

Rejecting the stylized art of the medieval era, Renaissance artists studied anatomy in order to portray the human body more realistically, and strove to develop innovations to please their patrons. They learned how to apply the mathematics of linear perspective to their art, to create the illusion of spatial depth. Painters set figures against recognizable landscapes or city backgrounds, and flattered their patrons by including them as onlookers or protagonists of the scene.

The greatest Renaissance artists also added another dimension – that of psychological realism.

It is evident in Donatello's sculpture *La Maddalena*, which vividly conveys the former prostitute's grief and penitence. Even when painting traditional subjects, they often tried to express the complexities of human character and emotion. The religious elements of the Virgin and Child theme gave way, for example, to an exploration of the mother-child relationship, as in the *Madonna and Child* (c.1455) by Fra Filippo Lippi *(see p86)*.

La Maddalena (1438), by Donatello

Pallas, symbolizing wisdom, tames the centaur, representing brute animal impulse.

Pallas and the Centaur
Botticelli's allegory (1485) typifies the Renaissance interest in pagan myth.

1400–82 Luca della Robbia	1449–94 Ghirlandaio	1483–1520 Raphael	
1401–28 Masaccio	1452–1519 Leonardo		1511–92 Bartolomeo Ammannati
1406–69 Fra Filippo Lippi	1457–1504 Filippino Lippi	1486–1531 Andrea del Sarto	1524–1608 Giambologna
1410–92 Piero della Francesca			
1400	**1450**	**1500**	**1550**
1397–1475 Paolo Uccello	1445–1510 Botticelli	1477–1549 Sodoma	1511–74 Giorgio Vasari
1396–1472 Michelozzo	1435–88 Verrocchio	1475–1564 Michelangelo	1503–72 Agnolo Bronzino
c.1395–1455 Fra Angelico	1421–97 Benozzo Gozzoli	1494–1556 Jacopo Pontormo	1500–71 Benvenuto Cellini
			1495–1540 Rosso Fiorentino

☐ Renaissance Artists   ☐ Mannerist Artists

Renaissance Frescoes

Frescoes decorate the walls of churches, public buildings and private palaces throughout Tuscany. Renaissance artists, in particular, favoured the medium of fresco painting for decorating new buildings. The word *fresco*, meaning "fresh", refers to the technique of painting on to a thin layer of damp, freshly laid plaster. Pigments are drawn into the plaster by surface tension and the colour becomes fixed as the plaster dries. The pigments react with the lime in the plaster to produce very strong, vivid colours. As the colours do not lie on the surface, restorers are able to remove the superficial soot and grime that have accumulated over the years to reveal the original, embedded colours *(see pp60–61)*.

Chiaroscuro
This is a subtle method of contrasting light and dark for dramatic effect.

Jewel-like Colours
Artists used rare, costly minerals to create bright, striking pigments. The blue of Mary's robe in Piero della Francesca's *Madonna del Parto* (c.1460) *(see p201)* is made from lapis lazuli.

Earth colours, such as reds and browns, came from clay-based paints containing iron.

White pigment was used for important highlights because it reflects light.

Use of Sinopia
The outlines of the fresco were drawn on to the plaster undercoat using a red pigment called *sinopia*. This layer was visible through the final plaster coat, guiding the artist as he painted in the details *(see p160)*.

The Giornata
Once the final plaster coat was applied, artists had to work quickly before it dried. This meant painting a small area of plaster each day (the *giornata*, or daily portion). Joins between the sections were often concealed in borders, columns and frames.

Masons left the bare wall surface uneven.

The bare wall was covered with coarse plaster, called *arriccio*, made of clay, hair, sand and lime.

The artist either sketched his design on to the *arriccio* using the pigment *sinopia*, and then painted directly on to the plaster, or he prepared a charcoal drawing on paper which was copied onto the wall.

The final fresco was painted on to a top coat of fine, lime-based plaster called *intonaco*.

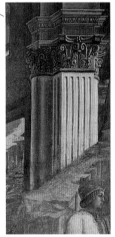

Workshops
The master artist worked in tandem with apprentices employed in his workshop. The master concentrated on important features, such as faces and expressive gestures.

Apprentices
While learning their trade, apprentices painted drapery, backgrounds and architectural details in the style of their master.

What to Buy in Tuscany

As a centre for high fashion and quality antiques, Florence is expensive but hard to beat. Bargains also abound, especially in leather goods and shoes. For food-lovers, there is a wide variety of wines, olive oils and preserves. Away from Florence, small farm estates in Tuscany sell their produce, such as honeys, liqueurs and wines, direct to the public, while many Tuscan towns have their own craft and food specialities. *(see also pp276–81).*

Desk tidy made of traditional hand-marbled paper

Marbled-paper notebook and box of pencils

Colourful Stationery

Marbled paper is a Florentine speciality. You can buy it in sheets and notebooks, or shaped into carnival masks and even birds and flowers.

Greetings Cards
Beautifully illustrated cards are sold at bookshops and museums.

Soap made to an ancient recipe

Flower-scented air freshener

Hand-made Perfumes and Toiletries

The products in Florentine pharmacies have often been made to ancient formulas by monks and nuns.

Hand-painted majolica

Terracotta and ceramic bowl

Alabaster figurine from Volterra

Ceramics and Reproductions

Tuscan potters produce highly decorative pieces, from modern originals *(artistiche)* and Renaissance copies *(reproduzioni)* to attractive kitchenware. You can also buy copies of your favourite sculptures.

Reproductions of Renaissance ceramics

Woven leatherwork handbag

Elegant document case

Small coin purse

Quality Leather Goods

Fine leather handbags, wallets and jackets are all remarkably good value, but fake designer brands are also sold by street traders and market stalls.

Hand-crafted men's footwear

Belt with distinctive Gucci buckle

Beautifully made lady's shoe

Luxury charm bracelet

Designer silk scarf

Fashionable Footwear

Even Hollywood filmstars come to Florence to buy shoes from boutiques such as Ferragamo.

Fashion Accessories

Florence has all the top names in fashion, including homegrown couturiers like Gucci.

Sunflower honey from Montalcino

Chocolate and biscuit cake

Red-wine vinegar and fine olive oil

Tuscan Delicacies

Lovers of good food will want to visit an *alimentari* (grocer's) to choose from the fascinating range of stock available. Tuscan products to sample and take back home include bottled antipasti, fruity olive oils, delicious honeys and a wide variety of confectionery.

Artichoke hearts with peppers and olives

Sun-dried tomatoes in sunflower oil

Peppers preserved in olive oil

The Landscape of Tuscany

Tuscany is rich in wildlife, especially flowers and the insects that feed on them, including bees, crickets, cicadas and grasshoppers, whose songs are heard during the summer months. For years, Tuscan farmers were too poor to afford modern intensive, agricultural methods, so the region was, until recently, still farmed by traditional methods. As a result, rural areas have remained relatively unspoiled, a safe haven for many species of flora and fauna – with the exception of the songbird, which has fallen victim to the Tuscan passion for hunting.

Cypress Trees
The flame-shaped cypress is often planted as a windbreak in fields and along roadsides.

Building on hilltops ensures a cooling wind in summer.

The Crete
The clay landscape south of Siena is one of bare hillocks and ravines, denuded of topsoil by heavy rain.

Terracing
The steep hillsides are farmed by cutting terraces and holding the soil in place with stone walls.

Tuscan Farmland
A typical Tuscan farm will combine olive groves and vineyards with fields of maize and barley to feed the cattle and chickens.

Garfagnana Landscape
Much of this region is an unspoilt national park, where deer, boar, martens and eagles are protected.

Viticulture
Many families make their own wine and every spare plot is planted with vines.

Olives
The olive tree, with its silver-backed leaves, is widely cultivated. Many farms sell home-produced olive oil.

Tuscan Wildlife

The best time to see the Tuscan countryside is in May and June, when all the flowers are in bloom. Autumn rains bring a second burst of flowering later in the year, and then cyclamen carpets the woodland floors. Even winter has its flowers, such as hellebores and snowdrops.

Animals, Birds and Insects

Hummingbird hawk moths hover in front of brightly coloured flowers, feeding with their long tongues.

Swifts perform aerial acrobatics at dusk, flying high above the city rooftops and towers.

The green lizard feeds on grasshoppers and basks on walls in the sunlight.

Wild boars are abundant but very shy, as they are hunted for their tasty meat.

Wayside Flowers

The blue chicory plant flowers all summer and is used as animal fodder.

Pink, white and red flowering mallows are a valuable food plant for bees.

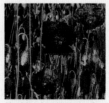

The blood-red poppy often grows alongside bright-white oxeye daisies.

The almond-scented bindweed attracts a variety of different insects.

FLORENCE AND TUSCANY THROUGH THE YEAR

Tuscany is most beautiful in May, when meadows and waysides are carpeted with the same bright flowers that Botticelli's Flora blithely scatters in *Primavera*, his celebration of spring *(see p86)*. Autumn is equally colourful, when the beech and chestnut woods turn a glorious blaze of seasonal red and gold.

The best months for escaping the heat and the crowds are May, September and October. Easter should be avoided, as well as July and August, because of the long queues outside major museums. During August, when Tuscans head for the sea, you will find shops, bars and restaurants closed. To see traditional festivities, like the Palio in Siena or Arezzo's Joust of the Saracen, you will need to book accommodation a year ahead, but there are many other local festivals to enjoy. For information, enquire at main tourist offices *(see p291)*.

Spring

Tuscany begins to wake from winter as Easter approaches. The hillsides are vibrant with the soft green of new leaves and the scent of fresh growth. Even in the cities there is a sense of renewal, as hanging baskets and window boxes are displayed outside from April onwards, and wisteria and iris bloom in the public gardens.

Instead of winter's heavy game dishes, asparagus – a speciality of the Lucca area – begins to feature on restaurant menus, along with tender young beans, usually served in lemon juice and oil.

Except at Easter time, the streets and main sights are rarely overcrowded, but the weather can be unpredictable and unseasonably wet.

A window box in bloom: the first sign of spring in Cortona

"Explosion of the Carriage" festival

March

Carnevale *(four Sundays leading to Lent and Shrove Tuesday)*, Viareggio *(see p42)*.

Scoppio del Carro, or the Explosion of the Carriage *(Easter Sunday)*, Piazza del Duomo, Florence. An 18th-century gilded cart is pulled to the cathedral doors by white oxen, and a dove-shaped rocket swoops down a wire from above the High Altar inside to ignite fireworks in the cart. Ostensibly a celebration of the Resurrection, the ceremony has roots in pagan fertility rites. Many Tuscans still believe that a successful firework display means a good harvest.

Festa degli Aquiloni, or Kite Festival *(first Sunday after Easter)*, San Miniato *(see p167)*. Kite-lovers perform aerial acrobatics on the Prato della Rocca, the grassy common above San Miniato.

April

Sagra Musicale Lucchese, *(April–early July)* Lucca *(see pp180–83)*. This extensive festival of sacred music is held in the city's numerous Romanesque churches.

Mostra Mercato Internazionale dell'Artigianato, or Exhibition of Crafts *(last week)*, Fortezza da Basso, Florence. An important European exhibition of the work of artists and artisans.

May

Maggio Musicale, Florence. This is the city's major arts festival and it now lasts until late June, with concerts by the Orchestra Regionale Toscana, directed by Zubin Mehta, and other international performers. The festival has been extended to include dance (from classical ballet to experimental work) and fringe events.

Festa del Grillo, or the Cricket Festival *(first Sunday after Ascension Thursday)*, Le Cascine, Florence. The huge park to the west of Florence, where Shelley wrote *Ode to the West Wind*, is the setting for this event, a celebration of the joys of spring. Stallholders used to sell live crickets, which were then released to bring good luck. These days the festival is celebrated with handmade crickets.

Il Balestro del Girifalco, or Falcon Contest *(first Sunday after 20 May)*, Massa Marittima *(see p43)*.

Average Daily Hours of Sunshine

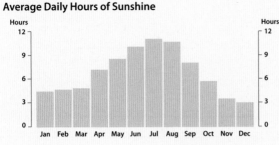

Hours

12											
9											
6											
3											
0											
Jan	Feb	Mar	Apr	May	Jun	Jul	Aug	Sep	Oct	Nov	Dec

Sunshine Chart
Tuscany has been praised for its light, which has a clear golden quality most noticeable when the intensely sunny days of high summer begin to shorten. Spring and autumn days are still warm, with plenty of hours of sunshine to enjoy.

Summer

From June onwards, Tuscany's festive calendar becomes increasingly crowded. There are scores of small-town festivals, many of them taking place around Midsummer Day, the feast of John the Baptist, on 24 June. These provide an opportunity to sample local food and wine and soak up the atmosphere, or to seek out some of the bigger set-piece festivals.

A glorious crop of sunflowers in high summer

June

Calcio in Costume, or Football in Costume *(24 June and two other days in June)*, Florence *(see p42)*.
Estate Fiesolana, or Fiesole Summer *(mid-June to end August)*, Fiesole *(see p136)*. Festival of music, arts, drama, dance and film. Many events are staged in the amphitheatre.
Regata di San Ranieri *(17 June)*, Pisa *(see p160)*. Boat races in costume and processions of colourfully decorated boats on the river Arno. After dark, its bankside buildings are illuminated by tens of thousands of flaming torches.
Gioco del Ponte, or Game of the Bridge *(last Sunday in June)*, Pisa. A ritual battle played out on a bridge *(see p42)*.

Celebrating a local saint's day on the streets of Siena

July

Corsa del Palio *(2 July and 16 August)*, Siena. Tuscany's most famous event *(see p226)*.
Pistoia Blues *(early July)*, Piazza del Duomo, Pistoia *(see pp190–91)*. Famous international festival of blues music, lasting for a week.
Settimana Musicale Senese *(dates vary)*, Siena *(see pp220–27)*. Throughout this "Musical Week", chamber music and classical concerts are performed in splendid settings, such as the Palazzo Chigi-Saraceni.

Italian ice cream, a feast for all ages

August

Festival Pucciniano *(late July–all August)*, Torre del Lago Puccini *(see p179)*. Performances of the composer's operas in an open-air theatre by the lake where he lived.
Rodeo della Rosa *(15 August)*, Alberese. Cowboys of the Maremma *(see pp240–41)* demonstrate cattle herding.
Cantiere Internazionale d'Arte *(late July–early August)*, Montepulciano *(see p231)*. Directed by the composer Hans Werner Henze, this is an important festival of new work by leading composers, dramatists and choreographers.
Festa della Bistecca *(15 August)*, Cortona *(see pp208–9)*. The Festival of the Beefsteak – a local speciality.
Il Baccanale *(penultimate Saturday)*, Montepulciano *(see p231)*. Feast of wine, food and song to celebrate the local Vino Nobile *(see p262)*.

Average Monthly Rainfall

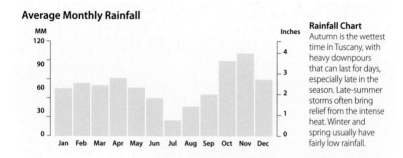

Rainfall Chart
Autumn is the wettest time in Tuscany, with heavy downpours that can last for days, especially late in the season. Late-summer storms often bring relief from the intense heat. Winter and spring usually have fairly low rainfall.

Autumn

Autumn is the season of the *vendemmia*, the grape harvest. Visitors should watch for public notices of the many *sagre*, or festivals, that take place throughout the region. These are family-orientated events that typically feature a single local speciality that is in season, such as *funghi porcini* (porcini mushrooms). The first frosts will occur any time from the end of October, and at this point, the great tracts of woodland all over Tuscany begin to turn brilliant shades of red and gold.

Autumn in the Val d'Orcia, in southern Tuscany

Grape-picking by hand in a Chianti vineyard

September
Giostra del Saracino, or the Joust of the Saracen *(first Sunday)*, Arezzo *(see p43)*.
Festa della Rificolona *(7 September)*, Piazza della Santissima Annunziata, Florence. Children from all over the city carry candlelit paper lanterns to honour the eve of the birth of the Virgin.
Palio della Balestra, or Crossbow Festival *(second Sunday)*, Sansepolcro *(see pp200–1)*. Costume parades and flag-throwing accompany a crossbow competition between Sansepolcro and the Umbrian town of Gubbio.
Luminara di Santa Croce *(13 September)*, Lucca *(see p184)*. The city's famous relic, the *Volto Santo*, a wooden statue of Christ, is paraded around by torchlight.
Rassegna del Chianti Classico *(second week)*, Greve in Chianti. The biggest Tuscan celebration of local wines.
Mostra Mercato Internazionale dell'Antiquariato *(Sep–Oct, in odd-numbered years)*, Florence. A major biennial antiques fair.

October
Amici della Musica *(Oct–Apr)*, Florence. The "Friends of Music" concert season begins.
Sagra del Tordo, or Festival of the Thrush *(last Sunday)*, Montalcino *(see p43)*.

Participant in the Joust of the Saracen festival in Arezzo

Average Monthly Temperature

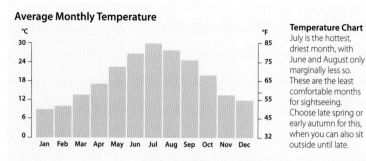

Temperature Chart
July is the hottest, driest month, with June and August only marginally less so. These are the least comfortable months for sightseeing. Choose late spring or early autumn for this, when you can also sit outside until late.

November
Festival dei Popoli *(Nov–Dec)*, venues throughout Florence show films in their original language, with Italian subtitles.
Florence Queer Festival *(end Nov–early Dec)*. Vibrant film and arts festival celebrating gay lifestyles.

Winter
This can be a good time to visit Florence and enjoy the city's museums and churches in tranquillity. It can be bitterly cold, but the skies are blue and the city is often bathed in golden sunlight, making this many photographers' favourite season. All over Tuscany, town squares are filled with the aroma of roasting chestnuts, and in December, the last of the olive crop is being harvested in the southernmost parts.

December
Fiaccole di Natale, or Festival of Christmas Torches *(Christmas Eve)*, Abbadia di San Salvatore, near Montalcino *(see p228)*. Carols and torchlight processions in memory of the shepherds from the first Christmas Eve.

January
Capodanno. New Year's Day is celebrated with gusto all over Tuscany. There are firework displays, and volleys from hunters firing into the air and from exploding firecrackers: all are part of a ritual to frighten away the ghosts and spirits of the old year and welcome in the new.

Roasting chestnuts, Montalcino

Pitti Immagine Uomo *(throughout January)*, Fortezza da Basso, Florence. At this prestigious fashion show, Italian designers and international couturiers gather to present their spring and summer collections for men. Children's collections (Pitti Bimbo) are sometimes presented in January too.

February
Carnevale *(Sundays before Lent, Shrove Tuesday)*, Viareggio *(see p179)*. A festive event renowned for its parades, competitions and amusing floats, often inspired by topical themes *(see p42)*.

There are many other opportunities to enjoy pre-Lent celebrations, such as the equally splendid carnival festivities that take place in San Gimignano and Arezzo.

Public Holidays

New Year's Day (1 Jan)

Epiphany (6 Jan)

Easter Sunday & Monday

Liberation Day (25 Apr)

Labour Day (1 May)

Republic Day (2 Jun)

Ferragosto (15 Aug)

All Saints' Day (1 Nov)

Immaculate Conception (8 Dec)

Christmas Day (25 Dec)

Santo Stefano (26 Dec)

Florence's Piazza di Santo Spirito in winter – serene and free of crowds

Festivals in Tuscany

Many Tuscan festivals celebrate battles and historical events that took place centuries ago; others have their origins in medieval tournaments. Yet they are not merely a pastiche of history, put on for the benefit of tourists. They are living festivals, mounted with an amazing degree of skill and commitment to authenticity and perfection. This can be seen in such details as the embroidery on the costumes worn by the participants and in the exhilarating displays of horsemanship, jousting and archery. Here is a selection of Tuscany's best.

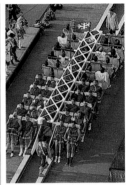

Pisa's Game of the Bridge

Football in Costume at fever pitch

Florence

Calcio in Costume, or Football in Costume (a festival held over three days in June), is a combination of football and rugby. Each of the four medieval quarters of the city (Santo Spirito, Santa Croce, San Giovanni and Santa Maria Novella) fields a team of 27 men. The games are usually held in Piazza Santa Croce, and always attract a lively crowd. There is fierce rivalry among the teams, and play can be quite violent. The final prize is a live cow. Before the game, the players and other characters in sumptuous 14th-century dress parade through the city.

The final often takes place on 24 June, the feast of John the Baptist, the patron saint of the city. These events are celebrated by a firework display, best seen from the north bank of the Arno, between Ponte Vecchio and Ponte alle Grazie, or from Fiesole.

Western Tuscany

The last Sunday in June is the occasion for the Gioco del Ponte, or Game of the Bridge, in Pisa *(see pp160–61)*. This battle, in Renaissance costume, takes place between the Pisans who live north of the river Arno and those who live south. Arranged into teams, they attempt to push a seven-tonne carriage over the historic Ponte di Mezzo (literally, the Middle Bridge), which divides the city. On the actual day, the river's banks are crowded with thousands of onlookers. This event probably has its roots in pre-Renaissance times, when there was no regular army and all citizens had to be trained and ready for war.

Some of the participants wear suits of antique armour that date from the 15th and 16th centuries, and their shields bear the colours of the city's different districts. This regalia is kept in the Museo Nazionale di San Matteo *(see p161)* when it is not in use.

Northern Tuscany

Carnevale (Carnival) in Viareggio *(see p179)*, on Shrove Tuesday and the four Sundays leading to it, is famous for its imaginative floats. These carry elaborate satirical models of politicians and other public figures. After courting controversy in recent years, however, this celebration is now more of a family event, but there is still an abundance of pointed visual jokes that can be appreciated by those in the know. The designers of the floats enjoy much flattery and prestige, and their creations remain on view all year. As elsewhere, the occasion is one of merrymaking, and it combines ancient pagan rituals and Christian values.

One of the spectacular floats from the Viareggio Carnival

Knights waiting to charge at the Joust of the Saracen in Arezzo

Eastern Tuscany

The Piazza Grande in Arezzo *(see p202)* is the scene of the Giostra del Saracino, or Joust of the Saracen. Held on the first Sunday in September, this tournament dates back to the Crusades in the Middle Ages, when all Christendom dedicated itself to driving the North African Arabs (the Moors) out of Europe.

There are lively and colourful processions to precede the event, in which eight costumed knights charge towards a wooden effigy of the Saracen. The aim is to try to hit the Saracen's shield with lances and then avoid a cat-of-three-tails swinging back and unseating them. Each pair of knights represents one of Arezzo's four rival *contrade* (districts), and their supporters occupy a side each of Piazza Grande. They are quiet when their own *contrada* knights are jousting, but make as much noise as is possible to distract the opposition. The winner receives a gold lance.

Central Tuscany

The most important festival in this region is Siena's Palio *(see p226)*, but the Sagra del Tordo, or Festival of the Thrush, is also a great attraction. It takes place in Montalcino *(see pp228–9)* on the last Sunday in October. The 14th-century Fortezza (castle) is the setting for an archery contest that is fought in traditional costume by members of the town's four *contrade*. This is accompanied by considerable consumption of the local red Brunello wine and, much to the horror of many bird-lovers, of charcoal-grilled thrush.

Archery at the Festival of the Thrush in Montalcino

The festival is essentially an excuse for gastronomic overindulgence, and a celebration of the thriving local economy, which is based on olive oil and wine production. Brunello is widely regarded as one of the finest of Italian wines.

Visitors are welcome to participate, and more conventional specialities, such as *porchetta* (roast suckling pig), are available for those who prefer not to eat songbirds. Archery competitions are also held in Montalcino during August to mark the beginning of the hunting season.

Southern Tuscany

Il Balestro del Girifalco, or the Falcon Contest, takes place in Massa Marittima *(see p238)* on the first Sunday after the feast of San Bernardino (20 May) and again on the second Sunday in August. It is preceded by a long procession through the town of people in dazzling Renaissance costume, accompanied by flag-waving and music. The contest itself is a test of ancient battle skills and the teams represent the town's three traditional historic divisions, which are known as *terzieri*, or thirds. Marksmen come forward and try to shoot down a mechanical falcon, tethered on a wire, with their crossbows. Great precision is required to hit the target and the whole contest is imbued with intense *terzieri* rivalry.

Renaissance finery at the Falcon Contest in Massa Marittima

THE HISTORY OF FLORENCE AND TUSCANY

Tuscany is rich in historical monuments. Etruscan walls encircle many of the region's hilltop towns and the streets within are lined with medieval and Renaissance palazzi, town halls testifying to the ideals of democracy and self-government, and churches built on the ruins of ancient pagan temples. The countryside, too, is dotted with castles and fortified villages, symbols of the violence and intercommunal strife that tore Tuscany apart for so many years during the medieval period. Typical of these is the hilltop town of San Gimignano (see pp216–19), with its defensive towers.

Some of the most imposing castles, such as the Fortezza Medicea in Arezzo (see p202), bear the name of the Medici family. Their coat of arms, found all over Tuscany, is a reminder of the role they played in the region's history. They presided over the simultaneous birth of Humanism and the Renaissance and, later, when they were Grand Dukes of Tuscany, patronized eminent scientists and engineers, such as Galileo. Tuscany has also played a part in wider events: Napoleon was exiled to Elba, and Florence served briefly as capital of the newly united Italy (1865–71).

Much damage was done to Tuscany's art and monuments by World War II bombing and the floods of 1966. However, major restoration projects undertaken as a result have stimulated research into scientific methods to aid art conservation. In this way, Tuscany's artistic heritage continues to inspire contemporary life – something it has always done for the many creative people who live and work here and for its endless trail of admiring visitors.

16th-century map of Italy, showing Pisa and the river Arno leading to Florence

◄ San Gimignano, held by its patron saint – little has changed in the town since it was painted by Taddeo di Bartolo (1362–1422)

Etruscan and Roman Tuscany

The Etruscans migrated to Italy from Asia Minor around 900 BC, attracted to the area they called Etruria (now in Tuscany, Lazio and Umbria) by its mineral wealth. This they exploited to produce weapons, armour, tools and jewellery to trade with Greece. After a fierce war with Rome in 395 BC, the Etruscan civilization was eclipsed by Roman rule. Many aspects of Roman religion can be attributed to the Etruscans, including animal sacrifice and divination – reading the will of the gods in animal entrails or cloud patterns. Everyday Etruscan life and the preoccupation with the afterlife are reflected in detailed carved cremation urns and tombs like those at Volterra *(see pp170–71)*.

Wax writing tablets were used to keep household accounts.

A covered wagon carved on the urn shows the Etruscans were skilled at carpentry.

Bronze Chimera (4th century BC)
The wounded chimera (part goat, lion and serpent) is a dramatic example of Etruscan bronze casting.

Athletic Games
Tomb paintings depicting chariot races, dancing and athletics suggest that the Etruscans had festivals similar to the Olympic Games of the ancient Greeks.

Etruscan Cremation Urn

Much of what is known about the Etruscans comes from studying the contents of their tombs. This 1st-century BC terracotta cremation urn from Volterra is carved with scenes from Etruscan domestic life.

The relief depicts the last journey of the deceased into the underworld.

9th century BC Earliest evidence of Etruscans on Elba

508 BC Lars Porsena, Etruscan ruler of Chiusi, leads an unsuccessful attack on Rome

474 BC Etruscans defeated in Asia Minor by their commercial rivals; trade with Greece suffers and Etruscan ports such as Populonia begin to decline

900 BC	800	700	600	500	400	300

7th century BC Beginning of extensive maritime trade with Greece and the Near East

6th century BC Founding of the Dodecapolis, a confederation of the 12 most powerful Etruscan cities

Coin from Populonia

395 BC Rome captures Veii in Lazio, signalling the end of Etruscan independence

Circular Chandelier
Sixteen oil lamps decorate the rim of this bronze chandelier, made around 300 BC.

The family of the deceased watches the funeral cortège.

Statue of Venus
Under Roman rule, the Etruscans adopted new deities like Venus, goddess of beauty.

Lead Tablet
Etruscan priests recorded details of their prayers and religious rites on lead tablets. However, their language has not yet been fully deciphered, and many of their beliefs and traditions are not yet understood.

Where to See Ancient Tuscany

The famous bronzes of the *Chimera* and the *Orator* are in Florence's Museo Archeologico *(see p103)*. Good museum collections are in Fiesole *(pp136–7)*, Volterra *(p170)*, Chiusi *(p232)*, Cortona *(p208)* and Grosseto *(p242)*. There are tombs at Sovana *(p242)*, and the ruins of an Etruscan town have been excavated near Roselle *(p245)*.

Etruscan Rock-cut Tomb
The tombs in Sovana date from the 3rd century BC *(p242)*.

Roman Theatre
The bath and theatre complex excavated in Volterra was built after Rome conquered the city in the 4th century BC *(p171)*.

205 BC All Tuscany now under Roman control; the Etruscans forced to pay tribute in bronze, grain and iron

90 BC Etruscans granted Roman citizenship, marking the end of their existence as a distinct culture

AD 250 Christianity brought to Florence by Eastern merchants; St Minias martyred in the city

AD 313 Constantine grants official status to Christianity

| 200 | 100 | AD 1 | 100 | 200 | 300 | 400 |

Bronze of a Roman Orator c.300 BC

20 BC Military colony of Saena (Siena) founded

59 BC Florentia (Florence) founded as a town for retired Roman army veterans

AD 405 Flavius Stilicho defeats the Ostrogoths besieging Florence

Early Medieval Tuscany

The church kept the flame of learning alive during the dark years when Tuscany was under attack from Teutonic tribes, such as the Goths and Lombards. Charlemagne, responding to the pope's request for help, drove the Lombards out of Tuscany in the 8th century. He was crowned Holy Roman Emperor as his reward, but this was soon to spark off a long conflict between church and emperor about who should rule Italy.

Early churches have simple wooden joists.

The capitals are carved with biblical scenes.

Mosaic Madonna
A 12th-century mosaic of the Virgin from Cortona *(see p208)* is typical of the Byzantine-influenced art of the early-medieval period.

Knight on Horseback
This 11th-century carving from Sovana's cathedral symbolizes the conflict between pope and emperor over control of the church.

Priests' quarters

Chapel of Sant'Agata
Like most early churches in Tuscany, the 12th-century octagonal brick chapel in Pisa, with its pyramid-shaped roof, was built on the grave of a Christian saint martyred by the Romans *(see p165)*.

Semi-circular chapels
with limpet-shell roofs are a typical feature of the period.

552 Totila the Goth attacks Florence

570 Lombards conquer northern Italy

Carts used by Charlemagne's army in battle

500	600	700	800

774 Charlemagne, King of the Franks, begins a campaign to subjugate the Lombards

7th-century Lombardic gold crown in the Bargello Museum, Florence (see pp72–3)

800 Charlemagne crowned Holy Roman Emperor

The bells in the campanile were rung to call the village to church and prayer.

Countess Matilda
Matilda, the last of the Margraves, ruled Tuscany in the 11th century and built many churches in the area.

Where to See Early Medieval Tuscany

Well-preserved early-medieval churches are found throughout Tuscany: in San Piero a Grado (*see p165*); Barga (*p178*); Lucca (*pp184–5*); San Quirico d'Orcia (*p229*); Massa Marittima (*p238*); Sovana (*p242*); San Miniato al Monte in Florence (*p134*); and in Fiesole (*p136*).

Castello di Romena
The 11th-century tower near Bibbiena was built by the Guidi family, who dominated the area.

Baptismal Font
Scenes taken from the lives of Moses and Christ adorn the 12th-century font at San Frediano, Lucca (*see p186*).

Santi Apostoli in Florence
Founded in 786, the church includes columns from ancient Roman baths (*see p113*).

Sant'Antimo

Founded, according to legend, by Charlemagne in 781, the shape of the church demonstrates the influence of the Roman basilica (law court) on the design of early churches; the altar occupies the position of the magistrate's chair (see p232).

The ambulatory ran behind the altar and was used for processions.

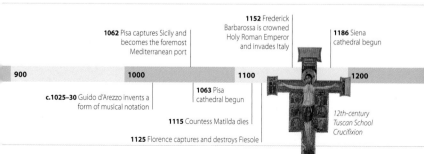

1062 Pisa captures Sicily and becomes the foremost Mediterranean port

1152 Frederick Barbarossa is crowned Holy Roman Emperor and invades Italy

1186 Siena cathedral begun

900   **1000**   **1100**   **1200**

c.1025–30 Guido d'Arezzo invents a form of musical notation

1063 Pisa cathedral begun

1115 Countess Matilda dies

1125 Florence captures and destroys Fiesole

12th-century Tuscan School Crucifixion

Late-Medieval Tuscany

During the 13th century, Tuscany grew rich on textile manufacturing and trade. Commercial contact with the Arab world led the Pisan mathematician Fibonacci to introduce Arabic numerals to the West; a new understanding of geometry followed, and Tuscan architects began to build ambitious new buildings. At the same time, Tuscan bankers developed the book-keeping principles that still underlie modern accountancy and banking practice. It was also an age of conflict. Cities and factions fought ruthlessly and incessantly to secure wealth and power.

Defensive towers protected the city.

Contented citizens had time for leisure.

Condottieri (mercenaries) were hired to settle conflicts.

Dante's Inferno
Dante *(in blue)* was caught in the Guelph-Ghibelline conflict and was exiled from Florence in 1302. He took revenge in his poetry, describing his enemies' torments in Hell.

Petrarch and Boccaccio
Petrarch and Boccaccio *(top and bottom left)*, like Dante, wrote in the Tuscan dialect, not Latin. Petrarch's sonnets and Boccaccio's tales were very popular.

Good Government
Ambrogio Lorenzetti's early 14th-century allegorical fresco in Siena's Palazzo Pubblico (see p222) shows thriving shops, fine buildings and dancing citizens, symbolizing the benefits of good government. Another fresco, Bad Government, *shows rape, murder, robbery and ruin.*

1215 Start of conflict between Guelph supporters of the pope and Ghibelline supporters of the Holy Roman Emperor

1252 First gold florin minted

1260 Siena defeats Florence at Montaperti

1278 Campo Santo begun in Pisa

| **1200** | **1220** | **1240** | **1260** | **1280** |

1220 Frederick II of Germany is crowned Holy Roman Emperor and lays claim to Italy

1224 St Francis receives the "stigmata" (the wounds of Christ) at La Verna

1284 Pisan navy defeated by Genoa; the beginning of Pisa's decline as a port

Florin stamped with the lily of Florence

Wool Traders' Emblem
Luca della Robbia's roundel depicts the Lamb of God, symbol of the Calimala (wool importers), whose trade guild was the most powerful in Florence.

Where to See Late-Medieval Tuscany

San Gimignano's spectacular towers *(see pp216–19)* show what most Tuscan cities must have looked like during the Middle Ages. Siena has the best surviving late-medieval town hall *(p222)*, and Pisa's Leaning Tower, Duomo and Baptistry *(pp162–4)* reflect the willingness of architects of this period to experiment with new styles.

A building boom resulted from increased prosperity.

Medieval building techniques
Circular putlock holes show where medieval builders placed their scaffolding timbers.

St Francis (1181–1226)
From monasteries founded in Tuscany by St Francis, the Franciscans brought about a major religious revival in reaction to the excesses of the church.

Lucignano
Some of Tuscany's best-preserved medieval architecture, including several defensive towers, can be seen in Lucignano *(p207)*.

Bankers in Siena
Tuscan banks provided loans to popes, monarchs and merchants. Many bankers were ruined when Edward III of England defaulted on his debts in 1342.

1294 Work begins on Florence's cathedral

1300 Giovanni Pisano carves pulpit for Pisa's cathedral

1350 Pisa's Leaning Tower completed; Boccaccio begins writing *The Decameron*

1377 Sir John Hawkwood appointed Captain General of Florence

| 1300 | 1320 | 1340 | | 1380 |

1302 Dante begins writing *The Divine Comedy*

1345 Work begins on Florence's Ponte Vecchio

1299 Work begins on Palazzo Vecchio in Florence

1348–93 Black Death carries off half the Tuscan population

Sir John Hawkwood, English mercenary

1374 Death of Petrarch

The Renaissance

Under astute Medici leadership, Florence enjoyed a period of peace and prosperity. Rich bankers and merchants invested in fine palaces to replace their cramped tower houses, and paid for the adornment of churches. The result was an outpouring of art and architecture, remarkable for its break with the Gothic past and its conscious attempt to give "rebirth" to Classical values. The rediscovery of works by ancient philosophers, such as Cicero and Plato, profoundly influenced the intellectual preoccupations of the day. Their ideas inspired the Humanists, who emphasized the role of knowledge and reason in human affairs.

Textile Market
The thriving Florentine textiles industry allowed the textile guilds and merchants, such as the dye importer Rucellai *(see p108)*, to become patrons of the arts.

Terracotta roundels of babies in swaddling bands, added by Andrea della Robbia in 1487, reflect the building's function as an orphanage.

Classical arches illustrate the Florentine passion for ancient Roman architecture.

Battle of San Romano (1456)
Florence hired *condottieri* (mercenaries) to fight its battles. Its citizens were therefore free to concentrate on making the city wealthy. Uccello's striking depiction of the Florentine victory over Siena in 1432 is an early attempt to master perspective.

Spedale degli Innocenti

The archetypal Renaissance building, Brunelleschi's colonnade (1419–26) for the Spedale degli Innocenti (see p99) is a masterpiece of restrained Classical design. Europe's first orphanage, the Spedale is also a major social monument. Today UNICEF, the United Nations Children's Fund, has its offices here.

1402 Florence Baptistry doors competition *(see p70)*

1416 Donatello completes his *St George (see p71)*

1425–7 Masaccio paints *The Life of St Peter* frescoes in Santa Maria del Carmine *(see pp130–31)*

1436 Brunelleschi completes dome for Florence cathedral *(see pp68–9)*. Work starts on San Marco *(see pp100–1)*

| 1400 | 1410 | 1420 | | 1440 |

1406 Pisa falls to Florence

1419 Work begins on the Spedale degli Innocenti

Cosimo il Vecchio

1434 Cosimo il Vecchio returns from exile

Grey sandstone and white plaster contrasts radically with the rich surface ornamentation of late-medieval architecture.

Humanist Scholars
By studying a broad range of subjects, from art to politics, the Humanists fostered the idea of Renaissance man, equally skilled in many activities.

Classical Corinthian capital

Where to See Renaissance Tuscany

Most of Florence was rebuilt during the Renaissance. Highlights include San Lorenzo (*see pp94–5*), Masaccio's frescoes in the Brancacci Chapel (*pp130–31*), many paintings in the Uffizi (*pp84–7*) and the sculptures at the Bargello (*pp72–3*).

Pienza Duomo (1459)
Pope Pius II's plans for a model Renaissance city at Pienza (*p230*) were never fully realized.

David (1475)
A favourite Florentine subject, David looks youthful and vulnerable in Verrocchio's bronze.

San Marco Cloister (1437)
Cosimo il Vecchio paid for Michelozzo's cloister (*pp100–1*) and used it as a retreat.

Pazzi Family Emblem
The wealthy Pazzi were disgraced after trying to assassinate Lorenzo the Magnificent and seize control of Florence in 1478.

1454–66 Piero della Francesca's *The Legend of the True Cross* (see pp204–5)

1480 Botticelli's *Primavera*. The villa at Poggio a Caiano begun (see p169)

Lorenzo the Magnificent

| 1450 | 1460 | 1470 | 1480 | 1490 |

1464 Death of Cosimo il Vecchio

1469 Lorenzo the Magnificent comes to power

1478 Pazzi conspiracy

1485 Botticelli's *The Birth of Venus*

1492 Death of Lorenzo the Magnificent

The Medici of Florence

The Medici family held power in Florence almost continuously from 1434 until 1743. Their rule began discreetly enough with Cosimo il Vecchio, son of a self-made man, Giovanni di Bicci. For years, Cosimo and his descendants directed policy with popular support, but without ever being voted into office. Later generations gained titles and power, but ruled by force. Two were elected pope and, after the Republic (see pp56–7), the decadent Alessandro took the title Duke of Florence. From him, control passed to Cosimo I, who was crowned Grand Duke of Tuscany.

Giovanni di Bicci
An astute merchant banker, he founded the Medici fortune.

Lorenzo the Magnificent
A poet and statesman, Lorenzo was the model Renaissance man. One of his greatest achievements was to negotiate peace among the cities of northern Italy.

Giovanni di Bicci
(1360–1429)

① Cosimo il Vecchio
(1389–1464)

② Piero the Gouty
(1416–69)

③ Lorenzo the
Magnificent
(1449–92)

Giuliano
(1453–78)

Giulio, Pope Clement VII
(1478–1534)

④ Piero
(1472–1503)

⑤ Giovanni, Pope
Leo X
(1475–1521)

⑦ Giuliano,
Duke of Nemours
(1479–1516)

⑥ Lorenzo,
Duke of Urbino
(1492–1519)

⑧ Alessandro, Duke of Florence
(1511–37: parentage uncertain)

Catherine, Duchess of
Urbino m Henry II of
France (1519–89)

Catherine of France
Catherine married Henri II of France in 1533. She is shown with two of her sons, who both became French kings: Charles IX and Henri III. Yet another son became Francis II of France.

Pope Leo X
Elected pope when only 38, Leo made corrupt plans to fund the rebuilding of St Peter's in Rome, which triggered a furious reaction that led to the birth of the Protestant movement.

Medici Patronage

As one of the most powerful families in Florence, the Medici were responsible for commissioning some of the greatest works of the Renaissance. Many artists flattered their patrons by placing them prominently in the foreground of their paintings. In Botticelli's *Adoration of the Magi* (1475), the grey-haired king, who is pictured kneeling at the feet of the Virgin, is Cosimo il Vecchio. The kneeling figure in the white robe is his grandson, Giuliano. The young man holding a sword, on the far left of the painting, is thought to be a rather idealized portrait of Lorenzo the Magnificent, Cosimo's other grandson.

Adoration of the Magi (1475) by Botticelli

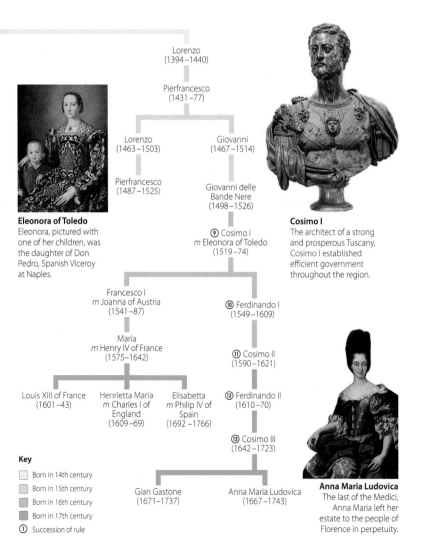

Lorenzo
(1394–1440)

Pierfrancesco
(1431–77)

Lorenzo
(1463–1503)

Giovanni
(1467–1514)

Pierfrancesco
(1487–1525)

Giovanni delle
Bande Nere
(1498–1526)

⑨ Cosimo I
m Eleonora of Toledo
(1519–74)

Eleonora of Toledo
Eleonora, pictured with one of her children, was the daughter of Don Pedro, Spanish Viceroy at Naples.

Cosimo I
The architect of a strong and prosperous Tuscany, Cosimo I established efficient government throughout the region.

Francesco I
m Joanna of Austria
(1541–87)

⑩ Ferdinando I
(1549–1609)

Maria
m Henry IV of France
(1575–1642)

⑪ Cosimo II
(1590–1621)

Louis XIII of France
(1601–43)

Henrietta Maria
m Charles I of
England
(1609–69)

Elisabetta
m Philip IV of
Spain
(1692–1766)

⑫ Ferdinando II
(1610–70)

⑬ Cosimo III
(1642–1723)

Key

Born in 14th century

Born in 15th century

Born in 16th century

Born in 17th century

① Succession of rule

Gian Gastone
(1671–1737)

Anna Maria Ludovica
(1667–1743)

Anna Maria Ludovica
The last of the Medici, Anna Maria left her estate to the people of Florence in perpetuity.

The Florentine Republic

In 1494, when Piero de'Medici abandoned Florence to the invading troops of Charles VIII of France, the city was declared a Republic. Under the leadership of the religious fundamentalist Girolamo Savonarola, the people were encouraged to believe that God was their only ruler. After his execution in 1498, the Republic survived 32 years of constant attack. Finally, in 1530, the Medici Pope Clement VII and the Holy Roman Emperor Charles V of Spain combined forces and returned the city to Medici rule.

Palazzo Vecchio Frieze
The inscription, "Christ is King", on this Republican frieze implies that no mortal ruler has absolute power.

Present-day Boboli Gardens

Charles VIII Enters Siena
When the French invaded Tuscan cities in 1494, Savonarola claimed it was God's punishment for the Tuscan obsession with profane books and art. He ordered such objects burned in bonfires of "vanity".

Judith and Holofernes
Donatello's statue of the virtuous Judith slaying the tyrant Holofernes was placed in front of the Palazzo Vecchio in 1494 to symbolize the end of Medici rule.

The Siege of Florence (1529–30)
Besieged by 40,000 papal and imperial troops, the citizens of Florence held out for ten months before starvation and disease led to their surrender. Vasari's fresco in the Palazzo Vecchio shows the full extent of the city's defences and the scale of the enemy assault.

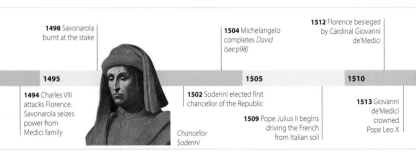

1498 Savonarola burnt at the stake

1504 Michelangelo completes *David* (see p98)

1512 Florence besieged by Cardinal Giovanni de'Medici

1495

1505

1510

1494 Charles VIII attacks Florence. Savonarola seizes power from Medici family

1502 Soderini elected first chancellor of the Republic

1509 Pope Julius II begins driving the French from Italian soil

Chancellor Soderini

1513 Giovanni de'Medici crowned Pope Leo X

Execution of Savonarola
Savonarola was an inspirational orator who commanded great popular support. His political enemies had him executed for heresy in 1498.

Where to See Republican Tuscany

A plaque in Piazza della Signoria (see pp80–81) marks the spot where Savonarola was executed; his cell can be seen in San Marco (pp100–1). Michelangelo's *David* (p98) symbolizes the victory of the youthful Republic over tyranny. The Republican council met in the Salone dei Cinquecento (p80).

All roads out of Florence were blocked.

Tower of San Miniato
This was reinforced in 1530 as a gun platform (p135)

Artillery platform

Troops camped to the south.

Niccolò Machiavelli
The author of *The Prince*, a treatise on the ruthless skills required to be a successful politician, was the last Republican chancellor.

Michelangelo's Sketches
During the siege of 1530, Michelangelo worked in the safety of the Cappelle Medicee (pp94–5).

Crystal casket belonging to Pope Clement VII

1527 Florentine Republic reconstituted when Rome is sacked by imperial troops

1531 Alessandro de' Medici becomes first Duke of Florence

1515

1525

1530

1520 Michelangelo begins work on Medici tombs (see p95)

1521 Giulio de'Medici crowned Pope Clement VII and Medici rule restored in Florence

1530 Siege of Florence by combined forces of pope and emperor

1532 Posthumous publication of Machiavelli's *The Prince*

The Grand Duchy

Cosimo I was created Grand Duke of Tuscany in 1570, having forced Tuscany into a state of political unity for the first time. A period of prosperity followed, in spite of the corrupt and debauched nature of Cosimo's heirs. When the Medici line ended in 1737, the Grand Duchy was inherited by the Austrian Dukes of Lorraine. They were removed from power in 1860 during the Risorgimento, when the Italian people joined forces to overthrow their foreign rulers. From 1865–70, Florence was the nation's capital. With the final unification of Italy in 1870, however, the centre of power returned to Rome.

Leopoldo and Family
Leopoldo I, later Emperor Leopold II of Austria, introduced many reforms, including abolition of the death penalty.

Galileo explains his theory of gravity.

The Church rejected Galileo's discoveries.

Livorno Harbour
Livorno became a free port in 1608: ships from every nation were granted equal docking rights, and the resulting influx of Jewish and Moorish refugees contributed to the city's prosperity.

The Old Market
Florence's Old Market was knocked down in 1865, when the city was briefly the Italian capital. In its place is the triumphal arch of the Piazza della Repubblica (see p116).

The Age of Science

Galileo was one of several brilliant scientists who benefited from Medici patronage during the 17th century, making Tuscany a centre of scientific innovation. His experiments and astronomical observations laid the foundations for modern empirical science, but led to his persecution for contradicting the teachings of the Roman Catholic Church.

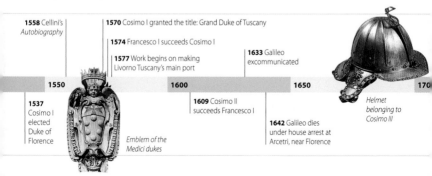

1558 Cellini's *Autobiography*

1570 Cosimo I granted the title: Grand Duke of Tuscany

1574 Francesco I succeeds Cosimo I

1577 Work begins on making Livorno Tuscany's main port

1633 Galileo excommunicated

1550

1600

1650

170

1537 Cosimo I elected Duke of Florence

Emblem of the Medici dukes

1609 Cosimo II succeeds Francesco I

1642 Galileo dies under house arrest at Arcetri, near Florence

Helmet belonging to Cosimo III

The Grand Tour

It became fashionable for wealthy 18th-century European aristocrats to visit Tuscany. This detail from Zoffani's *Tribuna* (1770) shows a tour of the Uffizi.

Where to See Grand Duchy Tuscany

The Uffizi art collection *(see pp84–7)* was assembled by the Medici at this time, along with the collections in the Palazzo Pitti *(pp124–7)*, the building from which the Grand Dukes ruled Tuscany for more than 300 years. The story of Galileo and his contemporaries is told in the Museo Galileo in Florence *(p78)*. The frescoes of the Sala del Risorgimento, in the Palazzo Pubblico, Siena *(p222)*, depict the events that preceded the final unification of Italy.

Galileo conducted
his experiments using specially designed equipment *(see p78)*.

Cosimo II gave refuge to Galileo after the Church accused him of heresy.

Palazzo dei Cavalieri
Francavilla's statue of Cosimo I (1596) marks the entrance to Vasari's ornate Palazzo *(p160)*.

National Rule

Florence ran up huge debts while serving as the Italian capital. This cartoon shows a protest against the seat of power (the Palazzo Vecchio) being transferred to Rome.

Napoleon's Bathroom
Napoleon never used this bathroom (1790–99), built for him at the Palazzo Pitti *(pp124–7)*.

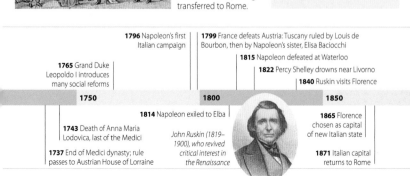

The Modern Era

The 20th century has seen many threats to Florence's fragile artistic heritage. The city's historic bridges, except for the Ponte Vecchio, were destroyed during World War II, and worse was to come in 1966 from devastating floods. Traffic and pollution have also taken their toll, leading to tough environmental controls aimed at preserving the historic city centre. Fortunately, the city has energetically risen to these challenges. It continues to thrive both on its proud heritage as a tourist destination and as a living, working city with a robust commercial and industrial base.

Traffic Control
In 1988, Florence banned cars from the city centre.

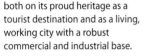

La Bohème (1896)
This popular opera by Puccini, Tuscany's greatest composer, often features in the region's music festivals (see p39).

Firenze Nuova
Florentine commerce and industry are moving to the suburb of "New Florence", leaving the city centre free for cultural and creative enterprises.

Art Restoration

Great pride is taken in Tuscany's artistic heritage, and modern scientific methods are used to analyse frescoes, such as The Procession of the Magi *(see p88 and p93), before restoration. These methods include computer-aided mapping of the pigments and plotting any structural damage.*

DOMENICO TIBURZI

Domenico Tiburzi, folk hero and notorious Maremman bandit

1896 First performance of Puccini's *La Bohème*

1922 Mussolini heads Italy's first Fascist government

1940 Italy enters World War II, on the side of the Germans

1943 Fall of the Fascists

1890	1900	1910	1920	1930	1940

1915 Italy enters World War I on the side of the Allies (France, Britain and Russia)

1896 Domenico Tiburzi is caught and shot after 24 years on the run

1944 Many historic structures in Tuscany are damaged by Allied bombing or retreating Nazis

1946 Italy become a republi

The 1966 Floods
On 4 November, floodwater from the Arno rose to 6 m (19.5 ft) above street level. Many art treasures were ruined; some are still in restoration.

Where to See Modern Florence
The shops of Via de' Tornabuoni and Via della Vigna Nuova *(see p109)* sell the best in Florentine fashion. Exhibitions of photographs at the Museo Alinari *(p117)* illustrate the city as it has developed during the 20th century. Cimabue's ruined *Crucifixion (p76)*, in the museum of Santa Croce, is displayed as a reminder of the 1966 floods.

A scanned image lets restorers trace existing outlines and reconstruct damaged areas.

Fashion
Many Florentine designers have become household names. These include Pucci, who invented the "Palazzo Pyjamas", Gucci, Ferragamo *(see p276)* and, more recently, rising stars like Daelli and Coveri.

Railway station (1935)
The Functionalist station is one of the city centre's few notable modern buildings *(see p117)*.

Commands for operating the computer program

Tourism
Florence and Tuscany have long been popular destinations for tourists. Florence now receives some 5 million visitors each year.

San Giovanni Battista (1964)
Giovanni Michelucci's modern church stands near Amerigo Vespucci airport.

1966 Floods in Florence

1987 The Sorpasso: Italian economy outstrips that of France and the UK

1999 Italy joins the single European currency

2010 Line 1 of the tram system opens, linking Santa Maria Novella station with the Scandicci district

950   1960   1990   2000   2010   2020

1957–65 Italian industrial boom

Bomb damage at the Uffizi

1993 The Uffizi is damaged in a terrorist explosion

2005 After a 26-year reign Pope John Paul II dies on 2 April. He is succeeded by Pope Benedict XVI on 19 April

Ceiling of the Galleria in the Palazzo Medici Riccardo, decorated by Luca Giordano, 1683 ▶

DVLCE

FLORENCE AREA BY AREA

CITY CENTRE EAST

The dominant building in this part of Florence is the magnificent Duomo, the first place most people will visit when they arrive in the city. Traffic is now banned in the Piazza del Duomo, which makes it easier to appreciate the immensity of this great building. It is, in fact, so large that a comprehensive view is impossible from such close quarters. As you wander the streets to the south, you will continually catch glimpses of its multicoloured marble cladding.

The area's other major church, Santa Croce, containing the tombs and monuments of many great Florentines, sits at the centre of the traditional artisans' quarter. These streets have few prestigious palaces, but there is a lively and attractive sense of community. It is here that you will find characterful neighbourhood shops and restoration workshops where specialists continue to repair the many books and works of art damaged in the 1966 floods *(see pp60–61)*.

Sights at a Glance

Museums and Galleries

❷ Museo dell'Opera del Duomo
❹ Casa di Dante
❻ The Bargello pp72–3
❼ Palazzo Nonfinito
❿ Casa Buonarroti
⓬ Museo Horne
⓭ Museo Galileo
⓱ Palazzo Vecchio pp82–3
⓲ The Uffizi pp84–7

Churches

❶ Duomo, Campanile and Baptistry pp68–9
❸ Orsanmichele
❺ Badia Fiorentina
⓫ Santa Croce pp75–7
⓮ Santo Stefano al Ponte

Historic Streets and Piazzas

❽ Piazza di Santa Croce
⓰ Piazza della Signoria pp80–81

Shops

⓯ Erboristerie Spezierie

Ice-Cream Parlours

❾ Bar Vivoli Gelateria

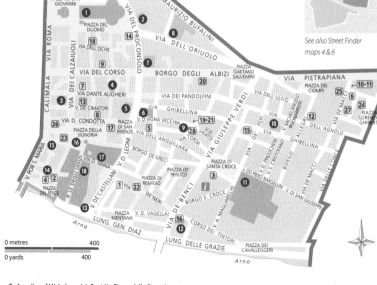

See also Street Finder maps 4 & 6

◀ A replica of Michelangelo's *David* in Piazza della Signoria

For keys to symbols *see back flap*

Street-by-Street: Around the Duomo

Much of Florence was rebuilt during the Renaissance, but the eastern part of the city retains a distinctly medieval feel. With its confusing maze of tiny alleyways and hidden lanes, it would still be recognizable to Dante. His house, the Casa di Dante, still stands near the parish church where he first glimpsed his beloved, Beatrice Portinari *(see p74)*. He would also recognize the Bargello and, of course, the Baptistry. One of the oldest streets is the Borgo degli Albizi. Now lined with Renaissance palaces, it follows the line of the ancient Roman road to Rome.

The dome, completed in 1436, was designed by Brunelleschi to dwarf even the great buildings of ancient Greece and Rome.

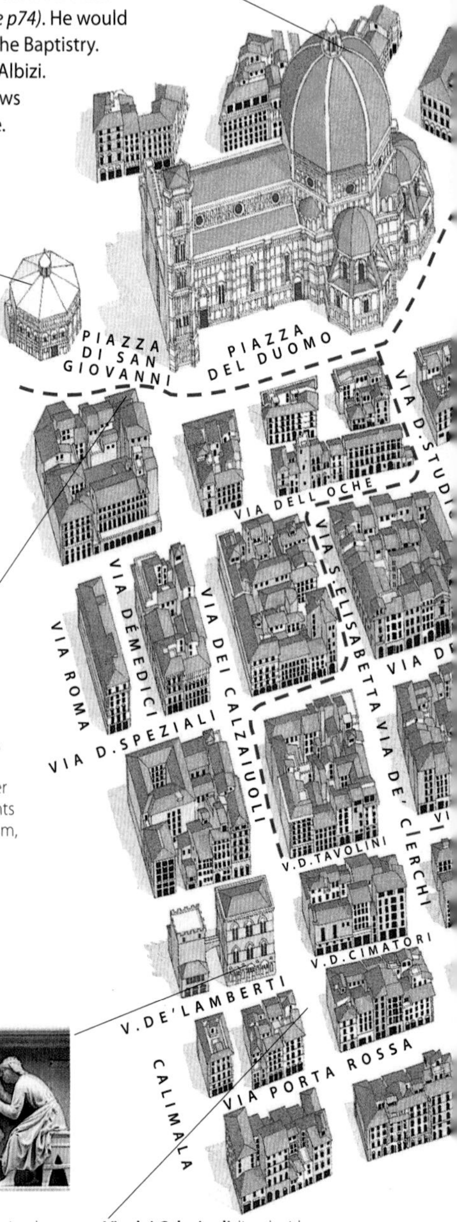

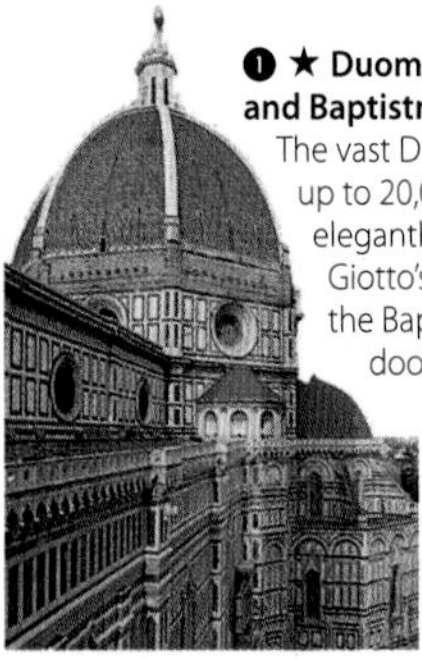

❶ ★ **Duomo, Campanile and Baptistry**
The vast Duomo holds up to 20,000 people. It is elegantly partnered by Giotto's campanile and the Baptistry, whose doors demonstrate the artistic ideas that led to the Renaissance.

The Loggia del Bigallo was built for the Misericordia by Alberto Arnoldi in 1358. During the 15th century, abandoned children were displayed here for three days. If, after this time, their parents had not claimed them, they were sent to foster homes.

❸ ★ **Orsanmichele**
The carvings on the walls of this Gothic church depict the activities and patron saints of the city's trade guilds, such as the Masons and Carpenters.

Via dei Calzaiuoli, lined with smart shops, is the focus of the *passeggiata*, the traditional evening stroll.

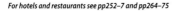

❷ ★ Museo dell'Opera del Duomo
Works removed from the Duomo, Campanile and Baptistry, like this panel by Verrocchio, are displayed here.

CITY CENTRE NORTH
CITY CENTRE EAST
Arno
OLTRARNO

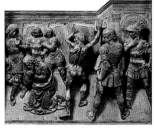

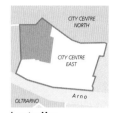

Locator Map
See Florence Street Finder map 6

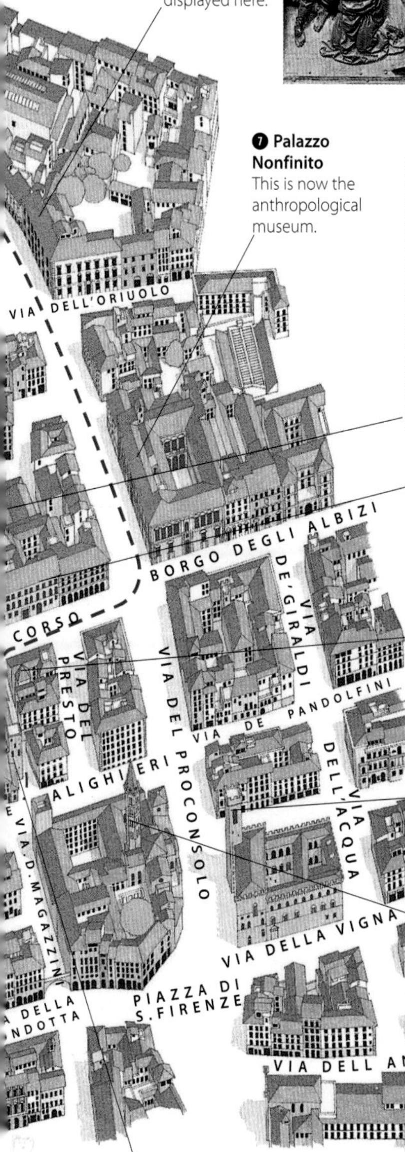

VIA DELL'ORIUOLO
BORGO DEGLI ALBIZI
CORSO
VIA DE' GIRALDI
VIA DEL PRESTO
VIA DEL PROCONSOLO
VIA DE PANDOLFINI
ALIGHIERI
VIA DELL'ACQUA
VIA D. MAGAZZINI
VIA DELLA VIGNA VECCHIA
PIAZZA DI S. FIRENZE
DELLA
NDOTTA
VIA DELL ANGUILLARA

❼ Palazzo Nonfinito
This is now the anthropological museum.

PEGNA
DROGHERIA

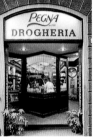

Pegna, a mini-supermarket tucked away in the Via dello Studio, sells a range of gourmet treats, including chocolate, honey, wine, balsamic vinegar and olive oil *(see p280)*.

Palazzo Salviati, now the head office of the Banca Toscana, has 14th-century frescoes in the main banking hall.

Santa Margherita de' Cerchi is where Dante married Gemma Donati in 1285.

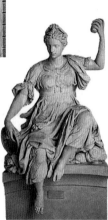

❻ ★ Bargello
The city's old prison is home to a rich collection of applied arts and sculpture, like this figure by Cellini (1500–71).

❺ Badia Fiorentina
The Badia's bell regulated daily life in medieval Florence.

0 metres 100
0 yards 100

❹ Casa di Dante
This medieval house is a museum devoted to Dante's life and work.

Key
— Suggested route

❶ Duomo, Campanile and Baptistry

Set in the heart of Florence, Santa Maria del Fiore – the Duomo, or cathedral, of Florence – dominates the city with its enormous dome. Its sheer size was typical of Florentine determination to lead in all things, and to this day, no other building stands taller in the city. The Baptistry, with its celebrated doors *(see p70)*, is one of Florence's oldest buildings, dating back to perhaps the 4th century. In his capacity as city architect, Giotto designed the Campanile in 1334; it was completed in 1359, 22 years after his death.

The Campanile
At 85 m (278 ft), the Campanile is 6 m (19 ft) shorter than the dome. It is clad in white, green and pink Tuscan marble.

★ **Baptistry Ceiling**
Colourful 13th-century mosaics illustrating the Last Judgment are set above the large octagonal font where many famous Florentines, including Dante, were baptized.

Steps to Santa Reparata
The crypt contains the remains of the 4th-century church of Santa Reparata, demolished in 1296 to make way for the cathedral.

Main entrance

KEY

① **South Doors**

② **The terracotta panels** with bas-reliefs are by Andrea Pisano.

③ **The Neo-Gothic marble façade** echoes the style of Giotto's Campanile, but was only added in 1871–87.

④ **Gothic windows**

⑤ **The top of the dome** offers spectacular views over the city.

⑥ **Bricks of varying size** were set in a self-supporting herringbone pattern – a technique Brunelleschi copied from the Pantheon in Rome.

⑦ *Last Judgment* **frescoes** are by Vasari.

⑧ **The octagonal marble sanctuary** around the High Altar was decorated by Baccio Bandinelli.

VISITORS' CHECKLIST

Practical Information
Piazza del Duomo. **Map** 2 D5
(6 D2). Duomo: **Tel** 055 230 28 85.
Open 10am–5pm Mon–Sat (to
3:30 Thu, to 4:45 Sat), 1:30–4:45pm
Sun. 🕇 7:30am, 8am, 8:30am,
9:30am, 6pm Mon–Sat; 5pm Sat
(English); 7:30am, 9am, 10am,
10:30am, noon, 5:30pm, 6pm Sun.
♿ 🔲 Dome: **Open** 8:30am–
6:20pm Mon–Sat (to 5pm Sat).
Crypt: **Open** 10am–5pm Mon–Sat
(to 4:45pm Sat, earlier closing Thu).
Campanile: **Open** 8:30am–6:50pm
daily. Baptistry: **Open** 11:15–
6:30pm Mon–Sat (Jun–Sep until
10:30pm Thu–Sat), 8:30am–
1:30pm Sun. 🕇 🔲 All: **Closed**
1 Jan, 15 Aug & relig hols. 🔲 combined or separate (Duomo free).
🌐 **ilgrandemuseodelduomo.it**

Transport
🚌 1, 6, 14, 17, 23.

★ Brunelleschi's Dome
Brunelleschi's revolutionary achievement was to build the largest dome of its time without scaffolding. As you climb the 463 steps to the top, you can see how an inner shell provides a platform for the timbers that support the outer shell.

Chapels at the East End
The three apses house five chapels each and are crowned by a miniature copy of the dome. The 15th-century stained glass is by Lorenzo Ghiberti and other artists.

Entrance to steps to the dome

Marble Pavement
As you climb up to the dome, you can see that the 16th-century marble pavement is laid out as a maze.

4th–5th centuries The Baptistry and Santa Reparata church built

1403–24 Ghiberti's North Doors added

1338 Andrea Pisano's South Doors added

Panel from South Doors

1425–52 Ghiberti's East Doors, the "Gates of Paradise", added

1887 Long-delayed completion of the cathedral façade

400	600	800	1000	1200	1400	1600	1800

897 First documented record of the Baptistry

11th–13th centuries Baptistry re-clad in green and white marble

1209 Zodiac pavement laid in Baptistry

1271 *The Last Judgment* completed on Baptistry ceiling

1436 Dome completed

1359 Giotto's Campanile completed

1296 Arnolfo di Cambio begins the new cathedral on the site of Santa Reparata

The East Doors of the Baptistry

Lorenzo Ghiberti's celebrated doors were commissioned in 1401 to mark Florence's deliverance from the plague. Ghiberti was chosen after a competition involving seven leading artists, including Donatello and Brunelleschi. Ghiberti's and Brunelleschi's trial panels *(see p73)* are so different from Florentine Gothic art of the time that they are often regarded as the first products of the Renaissance.

Ghiberti's winning panel

The "Gates of Paradise"
Having spent 21 years on the North Doors, Ghiberti worked on the East Doors from 1424 to 1452. Michelangelo enthusiastically dubbed them the "Gates of Paradise". The original panels are in the Museo dell'Opera del Duomo; those on the Baptistry are copies.

The jagged rocks, symbolizing Abraham's pain, are carefully arranged to emphasize the sacrificial act.

Abraham and the Sacrifice of Isaac

Architecture is used to create the illusion of spatial depth. Ghiberti was a master of perspective.

Joseph Sold into Slavery and Recognized by his Brothers

Key to the East Doors

1	2
3	4
5	6
7	8
9	10

1 Adam and Eve are Expelled from Eden
2 Cain Murders his Brother, Abel
3 The Drunkenness of Noah and his Sacrifice
4 Abraham and the Sacrifice of Isaac
5 Esau and Jacob
6 Joseph Sold into Slavery
7 Moses Receives the Ten Commandments
8 The Fall of Jericho
9 The Battle with the Philistines
10 Solomon and the Queen of Sheba

❶ Duomo, Campanile and Baptistry

See pp68–9.

❷ Museo dell'Opera del Duomo

Piazza del Duomo 9. **Map** 2 D5 (6 E2). **Tel** 055 230 28 85. **Open** 9am–6:50pm Mon–Sat; 9am–1pm Sun & public hols. **Closed** 1 Jan, Easter Sun, 25 Dec.

The Museo dell'Opera del Duomo is undergoing a major renovation, expanding into the theatre space next door. The museum is expected to re-open in autumn 2015. In the mean-time, it is still possible to see Michelangelo's masterpiece *Pietà* and the original "Gates of Paradise". The following description refers to the layout prior to the current renovation.

The main room is reached through open spaces containing Etruscan and Roman reliefs, carvings and sarcophagi.

The main ground-floor room contains statues from the workshop of Arnolfo di Cambio, which were once placed in the cathedral's niches. Some are by Arnolfo himself, including the Gothic *Madonna of the Glass Eyes*.

Pulley used to build Brunelleschi's dome

Nearby, visitors can see Nanni di Banco's *St Luke,* Bernardo Ciuffagni's *St Matthew* and, most striking of all, Donatello's *St John.* The three were carved between 1408 and 1415. A side room contains 14th–15th century religious paintings and a number of reliquaries, one of which contains the finger of San Giovanni.

The hooded figure of Nicodemus by Michelangelo is widely believed to be a self-portrait. That Mary Magdalene is the inferior work of a pupil is strikingly obvious.

The first room on the upper floor is dominated by two choir lofts, dating to the 1430s, by

Carving from della Robbia's choir loft in the Museo dell'Opera del Duomo

Donatello and Luca della Robbia. Carved in crisp white marble and decorated with coloured glass and mosaic, both depict children playing musical instruments and dancing. But while della Robbia's figures seem innocent, Donatello's look like frenzied participants in some primitive ritual.

Among a number of works by Donatello in this room are his statue of *La Maddalena* (1455) *(see p31)* and several Old Testament figures, including the prophet Abakuk (1423–5), affectionately known by Florentines as *lo zuccone* (marrow-head).

The room to the left contains an exhibition of the tablets that used to decorate the bell tower, some by Andrea Pisano and della Robbia.

A lower level houses examples of the tools used by Brunelleschi's workmen, and a copy of di Cambio's original cathedral façade.

In the courtyard, are some of the original panels of doors of the baptistry, as well as the exit.

❸ Orsanmichele

Via dell'Arte della Lana. **Map** 3 C1 (6 D3). **Tel** 055 28 49 44. **Open** 10am–5pm Tue–Sun. **Closed** August, 1 Jan, 1 May, 25 Dec. Sculpture museum: **Open** 10am–5pm Mon.

The name is a corruption of *Orto di San Michele*, a former monastic garden. Orsanmichele was built in 1337 as a grain market, but was soon turned into a church. The open arcades became windows, and though these are now bricked in, the original Gothic tracery can still be seen. The outside walls have 14 niches, each holding a statue of the patron saint of one of Florence's major *Arti* (guilds).

The interior has two parallel naves. To the right is an extraordinary 1350s altar by Andrea Orcagna. It is covered in cherubs and carved reliefs and encrusted with coloured marble and glass. Close by is Bernardo Daddi's *Virgin and Child* (1348), its frame beautifully carved with angels. Upstairs is a small museum dedicated to statuary. Continue up another flight for great views.

St George on the façade of Orsanmichele

❻ Bargello

Built in 1255 as the city's town hall, the Bargello is the oldest seat of government surviving in Florence. In the 16th century, it was the residence of the chief of police and a prison: executions took place here until 1786. After extensive renovation, it became one of Italy's first national museums in 1865. The Bargello houses a superb collection of Florentine Renaissance sculpture, with rooms dedicated to the work of Michelangelo, Donatello, Verrocchio, Giambologna and Cellini, as well as a collection of Mannerist bronzes and examples from the decorative arts.

Arms and Armour Collection

Mercury
Giambologna's famous 1564 bronze shows the athletic youth poised for flight.

Ivory Collection

Magdalen Chapel

Gallery Guide

To the right of the entrance hall, the Michelangelo Room is presided over by Bacchus (1497). The courtyard staircase leads up to the Upper Loggia, filled with statues of birds by Giambologna. To the right is the Donatello Room, which contains the panels for the Baptistry doors competition of 1401. The Magdalen Chapel and Islamic Collection are also on the first floor. The Verrocchio Room, the Andrea and Giovanni della Robbia rooms, the Arms and Armour Collection and the Room of the Small Bronzes are on the second floor.

Carrand Collection

The courtyard
was once the place of execution.

★ Bacchus
The Roman god of wine with a small satyr was Michelangelo's first major work (1497). The modelling is Classical, but the unsteady, drunken posture mocks the poise of ancient works.

Michelangelo Room

The tower dates to the 12th century.

Entrance

Lady with a Posy
This bust (1474), attributed to Andrea Verrocchio (1435–88), may have been done in collaboration with Leonardo da Vinci.

Room of the Small Bronzes

VISITORS' CHECKLIST

Practical Information
Via del Proconsolo 4.
Map 4 D1 (6 E3).
Tel 055 238 86 06; bookings: 055 294 883. **Open** 8:15am–1:50pm daily. **Closed** 2nd & 4th Mon & 1st, 3rd & 5th Sun of each month; 1 Jan, 1 May, 25 Dec. 🖼 ✉ ♿ 📷

Transport
🚌 14, A.

Ivory Saddle
Made for the Medici, this saddle inlaid with ivory was used during jousts in 15th-century Florence.

Upper Loggia

★ David
This famous bronze by Donatello (1450) was the first nude statue by a Western artist since Classical times.

Donatello Room

Islamic Collection

★ Baptistry Doors Competition Panel
Brunelleschi's bronze panel depicting Abraham about to slay Isaac was made in 1401 for the Baptistry doors competition (see p70).

The Bargello has a daunting and heavily fortified façade.

Key

- ☐ Ground floor
- ☐ First floor
- ☐ Second floor
- ☐ Temporary exhibitions
- ☐ Non-exhibition space

Bargello Prison

Among the notorious figures executed here was Bernardo Baroncelli. He went to the gallows in 1478 for his part in the failed attempt to assassinate Lorenzo the Magnificent in the Pazzi conspiracy (see p53). Baroncelli's body, hanging from a window in the Bargello as a warning to other anti-Medici conspirators, was sketched by Leonardo da Vinci.

❹ Casa di Dante

Via Santa Margherita 1.
Map 4 D1 (6 E3). **Tel** 055 21 94 16.
Open 10am–5pm Tue–Sun.
Closed last Sun of the month. 🖼

It is uncertain whether the poet
Dante Alighieri (1265–1321)
was actually born
here, but at least the
house looks the part.
In 1911, the remains of
a 13th-century tower
house were restored
to give the
building its
rambling
appearance.

Just a short
stroll north of
the house is the
parish church of
Santa Margherita de' Cerchi,
built during the 11th century.
It is here that Dante is said to
have first caught sight of
Beatrice Portinari, whom
he idolized in his poetry.
The church, which is often
used for Baroque chamber
music and organ recitals,
contains a fine altarpiece
by Neri di Bicci (1418–91).

*Bust of Dante on the façade of
Casa di Dante*

❺ Badia Fiorentina

Via del Proconsolo. **Map** 4 D1
(6 E3). **Tel** 055 234 45 45.
Church: **Open** 8am–6pm Tue–Sat.
Cloister: **Open** 3–6pm Mon. 🖼

The abbey, one of Florence's
oldest churches, was founded in
978 by Willa, the widow
of Count Uberto of Tuscany.
Their son, Count Ugo, was
buried inside the church in
1001. His splendid tomb was
carved by Mino da Fiesole
and dates from 1469–81.
Mino also carved the altarpiece
and, in the right transept, the
tomb of Bernardo Giugni,
the Florentine statesman,
with its fine effigy of Justice.

Filippino Lippi's *The Virgin
Appearing to St Bernard* (1485)
also enlivens an otherwise
drab and solemn interior. Its
remarkable detail, particularly
in the landscape, makes it
one of the most artistically
significant works of the
15th century. The peaceful

Chiostro degli Aranci ("cloister
of the orange trees") is a little
hard to find. Look for a door
to the right of the altar. Sadly,
the orange trees that the
monks used to cultivate
here are no longer present.
The two-tier cloister, built by
Rossellino in 1435–40,
has a well-preserved
fresco cycle showing
scenes from the life of
St Benedict. Dating from
the 15th century,
it was restored as
recently as 1973.
An early fresco
by Bronzino
(1503–72) can
also be seen in
the north walkway.
Excellent views of
the hexagonal campanile,
which is mentioned by Dante
in the *Paradiso* section of *The
Divine Comedy*, can be enjoyed
from the cloister.

In the 14th century, a series
of readings and lectures
devoted to Dante's work were
given at the Badia by the poet
Boccaccio. In keeping with the
spirit of these meetings, the
abbey is today often used for
talks and concerts.

❻ Bargello

See pp72–3.

❼ Palazzo Nonfinito

Via del Proconsolo 12.
Map 2 D5 (6 E2). **Tel** 055 239
64 49. **Open** 9am–1pm Thu–Tue
(to 5pm Sat). **Closed** 1 Jan, 25 Apr,
Easter Sun, 1 May, 24 Jun, 15 Aug,
8 Dec, 25–26 Dec, 31 Dec. 🖼 🖼

The Palazzo Nonfinito
(Unfinished Palace) was
begun by theatrical designer,
architect and military engineer
Buontalenti in 1593 and was
still incomplete when it became
Italy's first museum of anthro-
pology and ethnology in 1869.
The most striking architectural
feature is an imposing inner
courtyard usually attributed to
Cigoli (1559–1613).

The operating hours are a
little inconvenient with, barring
Saturdays, the museum only
open on occasional mornings.
However, it's worth making the
effort to see the collection of
art from Italy's former African
colonies, and material carried
away by Captain Cook, the
18th-century British explorer,
on the last of his Pacific voyages.

The Virgin Appearing to St Bernard (1485), by Filippino Lippi

Façade of Palazzo dell'Antella, Piazza di Santa Croce

❽ Piazza di Santa Croce

Map 4 E1. 🚌 C, 14, 23.

Located in central Florence, the Piazza di Santa Croce is one of the largest and most impressive piazzas in the city. It provides the setting for the stunning Gothic Basilica di Santa Croce, which contains the tombs of Michelangelo and Galileo *(see pp76–7)*. The piazza is also home to some interesting palazzi and shops, and hosts numerous markets.

Lying on the south side of the square is the Palazzo dell'Antella, a long medieval building. During the years 1619 and 1620, the façade was decorated with frescoes by Giovanni da San Giovanni. The façade's design incorporates an interesting optical illusion intended to make it appear more impressive. Towards the end of the building closest to the Basilica di Santa Croce, the windows are set increasingly closer together; when seen from the church steps they appear to be equally spaced and the building appears wider. Today, the ground floor of the Palazzo dell'Antella is home to restaurants and shops, and the upper floors have been converted into luxury rental apartments.

Piazza di Santa Croce is often the chosen venue for the Calcio Fiorentino games that take place in early summer *(see p42)*, played out on a giant sandpit arena between teams from the four medieval quarters of Florence.

❾ Bar Vivoli Gelateria

Via Isola delle Stinche 7r. **Map** 4 D1 (6 F3). **Tel** 055 29 23 34. **Open** 7:30am–1am Tue–Sat, 9:30am–1am Sun. **Closed** three weeks in Jan & three weeks in Aug. 🆆 vivoli.it

This tiny ice-cream parlour attracts large crowds and long queues for its rich iced concoctions. Vivoli claims to make the "best ice cream in the world", and the walls of the bar

Bar Vivoli Gelateria

are covered in press clippings from ice-cream connoisseurs that strongly support this view.

The bar stands at the heart of the colourful Santa Croce district, with its narrow alleys and tiny squares. Here, you will find small shops that serve the local community, rather than cater for tourists, and scores of little workshops where craftsmen make picture frames or mend furniture. Via Torta is typical of the area.

❿ Casa Buonarroti

Via Ghibellina 70. **Map** 4 E1. **Tel** 055 24 17 52. **Open** 9:30am–2pm Wed–Mon. **Closed** 1 Jan, Easter Sun, 25 Apr, 1 May, 15 Aug, 25 Dec. 🎨 ✉ ♿

Michelangelo (whose surname was Buonarroti) lived briefly in this group of three houses, which he bought as an investment in 1508. Subsequent generations of his descendants added what they could to a significant collection of his works.

Among these is his earliest known work, the *Madonna della Scala*, a marble *tavoletta*, or rectangular relief, carved in 1490–92. There is also a relief from 1492 showing *The Battle of the Centaurs*, and the design, never used, for the façade of San Lorenzo, shown in a wooden model.

⓫ Santa Croce

The magnificent Gothic church of Santa Croce (1294) contains the tombs of many famous Florentines, including Michelangelo and Galileo. The spacious, airy interior is enhanced by the radiant frescoes of Giotto and his gifted pupil, Taddeo Gaddi, painted early in the 14th century. The Arnolfo and Brunelleschi Cloisters provide visitors with fine examples of Renaissance architectural precision, and a moment of peace and tranquillity during their tour. The rest of the monastic buildings ranged around the cloister form a museum of religious painting and sculpture.

Galileo's Tomb
Condemned by the church in 1633, Galileo was denied a Christian burial until 1737, when this tomb, by Giulio Foggini, was erected.

Michelangelo's Tomb
Michelangelo never completed the *Pietà* he planned for his own tomb *(see p71)*. This monument was designed in 1570 by Vasari. The figures are Painting, Architecture and Sculpture.

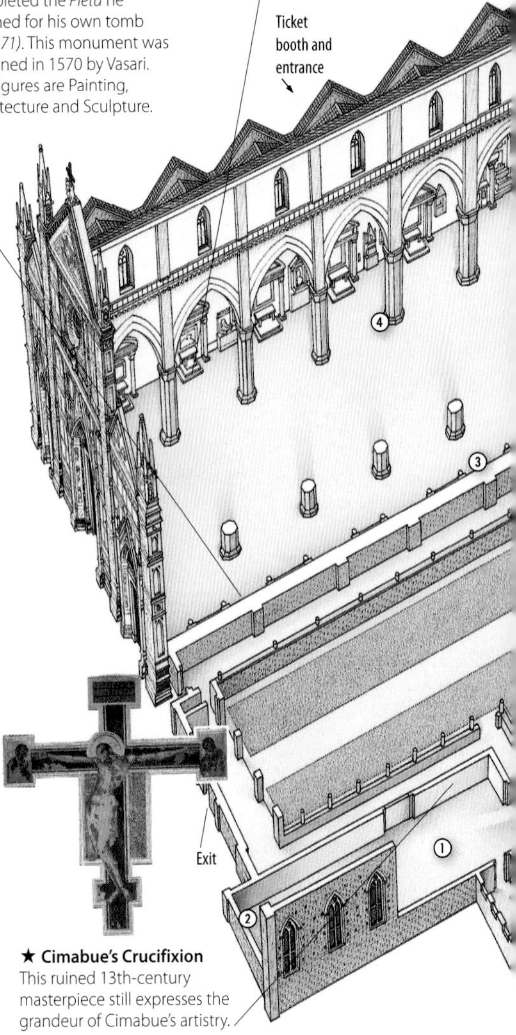

Ticket booth and entrance

KEY

① **Reflectory**

② *Tree of Life* by Taddeo Gaddi

③ **Machiavelli** *(see p57)* was buried here in 1527. His monument, by Innocenzo Spinazzi, was erected in 1787.

④ **Lorenzo Ghiberti** (1378–1455), creator of the magnificent doors of Florence's Baptistry *(see p70)*, is buried here, along with his sons and assistants, Vittorio and Lorenzo.

⑤ **Donatello's Crucifix** (1425) is found in the Bardi di Vernio Chapel. The perfect balance in its form and its subtle play of light and shadow fill it with drama and realism. It is one of the most beautiful works of Florentine humanism.

⑥ **The Neo-Gothic campanile** was added in 1842, after the original was destroyed in 1512 by lightning.

⑦ **In the Bardi and Peruzzi Chapels**, Giotto's frescoes depict scenes from the lives of St Francis, St John the Baptist and St John the Evangelist.

⑧ **Sacristy**

⑨ **This second cloister** was designed by Brunelleschi, and offers a peaceful spot to absorb the atmosphere.

Exit

★ **Cimabue's Crucifixion**
This ruined 13th-century masterpiece still expresses the grandeur of Cimabue's artistry.

The façade was reclad with coloured marble in 1863, paid for by an English benefactor, Francis Sloane.

VISITORS' CHECKLIST

Practical Information
Piazza di Santa Croce.
Map 4 E1 (6 F4). **Tel** 055 24 46 19.
Open 9:30am–5pm daily (from 2pm Sun). Ticket office closes at 5pm. No visits during mass.
🕆 8am, 9am (not Aug), 6pm Mon–Sat; 8am, 9:30am, 11am, noon, 6pm Sun and relig hols.

Transport
🚌 C, 14, 23.

★ Fresco by Gaddi, Baroncelli Chapel
This image of an angel appearing to sleeping shepherds (1338) was the first true night scene depicted in fresco.

Tomb of Leonardo Bruni
Rossellino's effigy (1447) of the great Humanist, depicted in serene old age, is a triumph of realistic portraiture.

★ Cappella de'Pazzi
Brunelleschi designed this domed chapel in 1430. Delicate grey stonework frames white plaster inset with Luca della Robbia's terracotta roundels of the Apostles.

Museo Horne

⓫ Santa Croce

See pp76–7.

⓬ Museo Horne

Via de'Benci 6. **Map** 4 D1 (6 F4).
Tel 055 24 46 61. **Open** 9am–1pm
Mon–Sat. **Closed** 1 Jan, Easter Sun,
Easter Mon, 25 Apr, 1 May, 15 Aug,
1 Nov, 25–26 Dec. 🖼

The museum's small collection
of paintings, sculpture and
decorative arts was left to the
city by Herbert Percy Horne
(1844–1916), the English art
historian. It is housed in a
splendid example of a Renaissance *palazzino* (small town
house), built in 1489 for the
wealthy Alberti family.

The arrangement of rooms,
with a working and storage area
at ground level and grander
apartments above, is typical of
many Renaissance houses. The
Alberti family, who grew wealthy
from the city's thriving cloth
trade, had wool-dyeing vats
in the basement and drying
racks in the courtyard.

Most of the museum's major
artifacts, for instance a number
of important 17th- and 18th-
century drawings, are now
housed in the Uffizi. However,
the collection still boasts at
least one major exhibit: Giotto's
13th-century *St Stephen*
polyptych (an altarpiece with
more than three panels). There
is also a *Madonna and Child*
attributed to Simone Martini
(1283–1344) and *Madonna* by
Bernardo Daddi (c.1312–48).

The kitchen, which was built
on the top floor to stop fumes
passing through the entire
house, now contains Horne's
superb collection of
Renaissance pots, artisan tools
and cooking utensils.

⓭ Museo Galileo

Piazza de'Giudici 1. **Map** 4 D1 (6 D4).
Tel 055 26 53 11. 🚌 B, 23. **Open**
9:30am–6pm daily (to 1pm Tue).
Closed 1 Jan, 25 Apr, 1 May, 24 Jun,
15 Aug, 8, 25 & 26 Dec. 🖼 ♿ ♿

This small museum is something of a shrine to the Pisa-
born scientist Galileo Galilei
(1564–1642). Exhibits include
his telescopes and the lens he
used to discover the largest
moons of Jupiter.

The museum also features
large-scale reconstructions of
his experiments into motion,
weight, velocity and acceleration.
These are sometimes demon-
strated by the attendants.

In 1657, in memory of Galileo,
Florence founded the world's
first ever scientific institution,
the Accademia del Cimento
(Academy for Experimentation).
Some of the academy's
inventions, such as early
thermometers, hygrometers
and barometers are on show
here. Of equal interest
are the huge
globes

made during the 16th and
17th centuries to illustrate the
motion of the planets and stars.

Also look out for the map
of the world dating from 1554,
created by Portuguese cartographer Lopo Homem, and the
nautical instruments invented
by Sir Robert Dudley, the
Elizabethan marine engineer.
He was employed by the
Medici dukes to build the
harbour at Livorno from
1607–21 (*see p166*).

Galileo Galilei (1564–1642), court
mathematician to the Medici

⓮ Santo Stefano al Ponte

Piazza Santo Stefano al Ponte.
Map 3 C1 (6 D4). **Tel** 055 012 46 45.
Open 2–6pm Mon–Fri.

St Stephen "by the bridge",
dating from 969, is so
called because
of its close

Armillary sphere of 1564, used to map the stars and planets

Mapping the World

The same preoccupation with space that made Florentine artists such masters of perspective also made them excellent navigators and mapmakers. Florentine cartographers based their maps on the observations and navigational records of early explorers. That is how America came to be named after the Florentine Amerigo Vespucci, rather than Christopher Columbus. When Columbus returned from his transatlantic voyage, King Ferdinand of Spain hired Vespucci, an expert navigator, to check whether Columbus really had discovered a new route to the Indies. Vespucci was the first to realize that Columbus had discovered a new continent, and he described his own voyage in a series of letters to Piero de'Medici. As soon as the letters were made public, Florentine cartographers rushed out revised maps of the world based on Vespucci's account. Out of loyalty to a fellow Florentine, they named the New World Amerigo, which was later corrupted to America.

Tip of South America still unmapped

Argentina mapped for the first time

Africa and Arabia well-mapped thanks to centuries of trading

The Antipodes were yet to be "discovered"

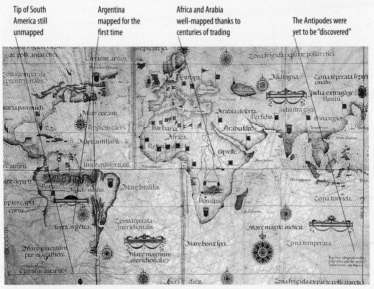

16th-century map by the Portuguese cartographer Lopo Homem, in the Museo Galileo

proximity to the Ponte Vecchio. The Romanesque façade, dating from 1233, is its most important architectural feature. Florentines, however, know the church better as a venue for some top-quality orchestral concerts.

⓰ Erboristerie Spezierie

Via Vacchereccia 9r. **Map** 3 C1 (6 D3). **Tel** 055 239 60 55. **Open** 9am–7:30pm Mon–Sat, first & last Sun of month. **Closed** 1 Jan, 1 May, 25 & 26 Dec. 🅦 spezieriepalazzovecchio.it

This little herbalist's shop, Erboristerie Spezierie di Palazzo Vecchio, is hidden among the pavement cafés lining Via Vaccherecia, off Piazza della Signoria. Several such shops in

Florence sell herbal soaps, potpourri, cosmetics and fragrances made to ancient recipes by monks and nuns in various parts of Tuscany. Another is the Erboristeria della Antica Farmacia del Cinghiale (Herbalist at the Old Boar Pharmacy), just around the corner at Calimala 4r, which takes its name from the famous bronze boar statue in the Mercato Nuovo opposite *(see p116)*.

⓰ Piazza della Signoria

See pp80–81.

⓱ Palazzo Vecchio

See pp82–3.

⓲ The Uffizi

See pp84–7.

Arno façade of the Uffizi with the Vasari Corridor *(pp110–11)* above

⑯ Piazza della Signoria

The piazza is a unique outdoor sculpture gallery and, with the Palazzo Vecchio *(see pp82–3)*, has been at the heart of Florentine politics since the 14th century. Citizens gathered here when called to a *parlamento* (a public meeting) by the Palazzo's great bell. The statues, some copies, commemorate major events in the city's history. Many are linked to the rise and fall of the Florentine Republic *(see pp56–7)*, during which the religious leader Girolamo Savonarola was executed here.

Salone dei Cinquecento
This vast council chamber, built in 1495, is decorated with Vasari's frescoes on the history of Florence.

Grand Duke Cosimo I
Giambologna's equestrian statue (1595) celebrates the man who subjugated all Tuscany under his military rule *(see pp58–9)*.

★ Neptune Fountain
Ammannati's Mannerist fountain (1575) of the Roman sea god surrounded by water nymphs commemorates Tuscan naval victories.

VISITORS' CHECKLIST

Practical Information
Map 4 D1 (6 D3).

Transport
🚌 A, B. Pedestrian area.

Pageantry
For centuries, the piazza has been the city's venue for public rallies and festivities, as shown in this 18th-century engraving.

★ **Perseus**
Cellini's bronze statue (1554) of Perseus holding Medusa's head was meant to warn Cosimo I's enemies of their probable fate. The original of the base it rests on is in the Bargello.

★ **The Rape of the Sabine Women** (1583)
The writhing figures in Giambologna's famous statue were carved from a single block of flawed marble.

KEY

① **The Marzocco** is a copy. The original of Donatello's heraldic lion is in the Bargello.

② **Palazzo Vecchio**

③ **Campanile**

④ **The Uffizi café**, on the roof of the Loggia dei Lanzi, offers fine views over the piazza.

⑤ **The Loggia dei Lanzi** (1382) is named after Cosimo I's bodyguards, the Lancers. Also known as Loggia di Orcagna, after the architect, it is lined with ancient Roman statues.

⑥ *Hercules and Cacus* (1533), by Bandinelli

★ **David**
The original of Michelangelo's celebrated statue of David was moved from its initial location in the Piazza della Signoria into the Accademia in 1873 *(see p98)*. A replica now stands in the piazza.

⓱ Palazzo Vecchio

The Palazzo Vecchio ("Old Palace") still fulfils its original role as Florence's town hall. It was completed in 1322 when a huge bell, used to call citizens to meetings or warn of fire, flood or enemy attack, was hauled to the top of the imposing bell tower. The palazzo has retained its medieval appearance, but much of the interior was remodelled for Duke Cosimo I when he moved into the palace in 1540. Leonardo and Michelangelo were asked to redecorate the interior, but it was Vasari who finally undertook the work. His many frescoes (1563–5) glorify Cosimo and his creation of the Grand Duchy of Tuscany.

★ **Sala dei Gigli (Room of the Lilies)**
Gold fleurs-de-lis, emblems of Florence, cover the walls in between Ghirlandaio's frescoes (1485) of Roman statesmen.

Palace Guide

A monumental staircase leads to the first-floor Salone dei Cinquecento, with its frescoed walls and marble statues. Above this is a suite of decorated rooms once used by the rulers of Florence. Parts of the Salone dei Cinquecento, the Studiolo of Francesco I, the Treasury of Cosimo I and the staircase of the Duke of Athens are only accessible by tour. The tours follow the "secret routes" made for the rulers.

Heraldic Frieze
Shields on the façade symbolize episodes in Florentine history. The crossed keys represent Medici papal rule.

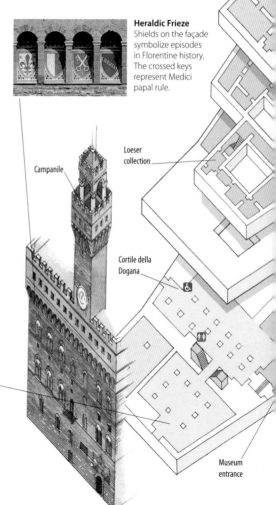

Loeser collection

Campanile

Cortile della Dogana

Museum entrance

★ **Cortile and Putto Fountain**
A copy of Verrocchio's Putto Fountain was placed in the courtyard by Vasari in 1565.

Key to Floorplan

- ⬜ Ground floor
- ⬜ First floor
- ⬜ Mezzanine floor
- ⬜ Second floor
- ⬜ Temporary exhibition space
- ⬜ Non-exhibition space

Eleonora di Toledo's Rooms
Cosimo I's wife had a suite
of rooms decorated with
scenes of virtuous women.
Penelope, wife of the Greek
hero Odysseus, is shown
waiting faithfully for her
husband to return.

The Map
Room

**The Quartiere degli
Elementi** contains
Vasari's allegories of
Earth, Fire, Air and Water.

Putto with Dolphin
Verrocchio's bronze fountain
head (1470) is displayed in the
Terrazzo di Giunone. The small
room next door has fine views
of San Miniato al Monte.

Pope Leo X's rooms

**The Salone dei
Cinquecento**
was a meeting
place for the
leaders of the
Florentine
Republic
(see pp56–7).

Cappella di Eleonora
Egyptian soldiers in pursuit of Moses drown in the
Red Sea in the biblical frescoes (1540–45) by
Bronzino in Eleonora di Toledo's chapel.

The Treasury
of Cosimo I

★ Victory by Michelangelo
Michelangelo's nephew presented this
statue (1533–4), intended for the tomb
of Pope Julius II, to Cosimo I in 1565,
following the Duke's military triumph
over Siena.

⑱ The Uffizi

The Uffizi was built in 1560–80 as a suite of offices (*uffici*) for Duke Cosimo I's new administration (*see p54*). The architect Vasari used iron reinforcement to create an almost continuous wall of glass on the upper storey. From 1581, Cosimo's heirs used this well-lit space to display the Medici family art treasures, creating what is now the oldest gallery in the world.

Corridor ceilings are frescoed in the "grotesque" style of the 1580s, inspired by Roman grottoes.

Second floor

The Loggia dei Lanzi terrace merits a visit for its unusual views of the Piazza della Signoria (*see pp80–81*).

Bar

First floor

Boy Removing a Thorn from his Foot
This ancient Roman statue is, like many of the collection's antique sculptures, based on a Greek original.

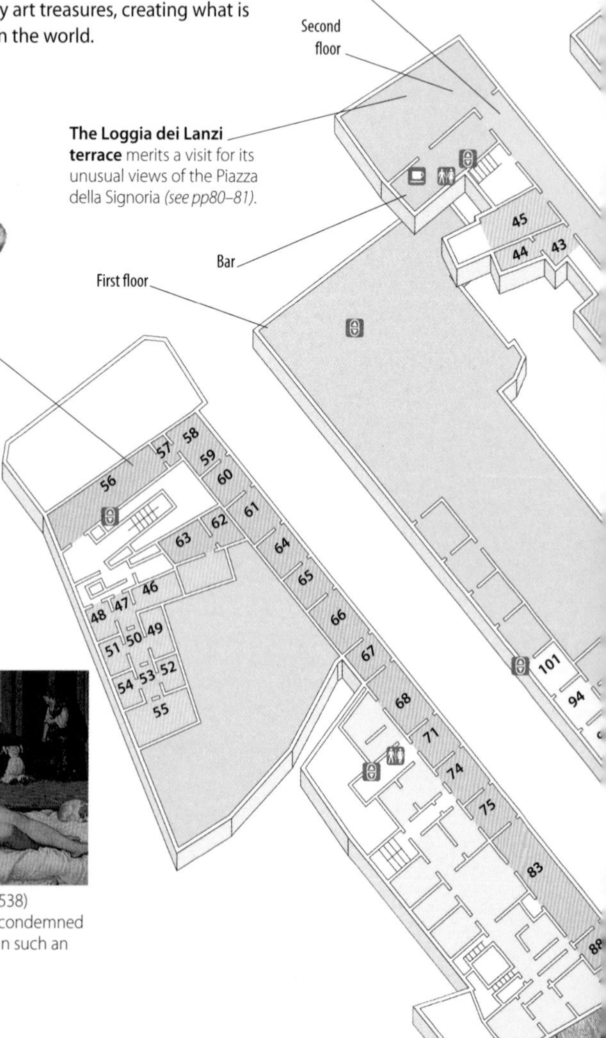

★ **The Venus of Urbino** (1538)
Titian's sensuous nude was condemned for portraying the goddess in such an immodest pose.

Gallery Guide

The paintings are hung in a series of rooms to show the development of Florentine art from Gothic to Renaissance and beyond. The earliest works are on the second floor – start here to explore the collection in a broadly chronological order. There are many well-known Early Renaissance paintings in rooms 7–18. Ancient Greek and Roman sculptures are in the second-floor corridor, as well as room 56 on the first floor. Some familiar High Renaissance masterpieces, by artists such as Titian and Raphael, are hung on the first floor, and masters from other European countries are in rooms 44–55. To avoid queues, book your ticket and visiting time in advance.

Main staircase

★ The Duke and Duchess of Urbino (1460)
Piero della Francesca's panels are among the first true Renaissance portraits. He even recorded the Duke's hooked nose – broken by a sword blow.

The Tribune, decorated in red and gold, contains the works that the Medici valued most.

Buontalenti staircase

The Ognissanti Madonna
Giotto's grasp of spatial depth in this altarpiece (1310) was a milestone in the mastery of perspective.

★ The Birth of Venus
(1485)
Botticelli's captivating image shows the Roman goddess of love, born in a storm in the Aegean sea. Blown ashore by the winds, she is greeted by nymphs, ready to wrap her in a cloak.

Entrance to the Vasari Corridor (see pp110–11).

★ The Holy Family
(1506)
Michelangelo's painting, the first to break with the convention of showing Christ on the Virgin's lap, inspired Mannerist artists through its expressive handling of colour and posture (see p31).

Vasari's Classical Arno façade

Key to Floorplan

- East Corridor
- West Corridor
- Arno Corridor
- Gallery Rooms 1–45
- 17th–18th-century painting in Europe
- 17th-century painting in Italy
- 16th-century painting in Italy
- Sculpture gallery
- Temporary exhibitions
- Non-exhibition space

Exploring the Uffizi's Collection

The Uffizi offers an unrivalled opportunity to see some of the greatest works of the Renaissance. The collection was born from the immense wealth of the Medici family *(see pp54–5)*, who commissioned work from many great Florentine masters. Francesco I housed the family collection at the Uffizi in 1581. His descendants added to it until 1737, when Anna Maria Ludovica, the last of the Medici, bequeathed it to the people of Florence.

Gothic Art

Rooms 2 to 6 of the gallery are devoted to Tuscan Gothic art from the 12th to the 14th century. Giotto (1266–1337) introduced a degree of naturalism that was new in Tuscan art. The angels and saints in his *Ognissanti Madonna* (1310), in room 2, express a range of human emotions, from awe and reverence to puzzlement. The throne in this painting and the temple in Lorenzetti's *Presentation in the Temple* (1342), in room 3, show a concern for three-dimensional depth quite at odds with the flatness of much Gothic art.

Giotto's naturalism extends throughout the works in room 4. One of the key examples is the *Pietà* (1360–65), attributed to Giottino: look at the difference between the characters' expressions, their medieval, rather than Biblical, style of dress and the blood, still fresh on the cross. You can see the restored Ognissanti cross in the city's Ognissanti church.

Early Renaissance

A better understanding of geometry and perspective allowed Renaissance artists to create an illusion of space and depth in their works. Paolo Uccello (1397–1475) was obsessed with perspective; witness his nightmarish *The Battle of San Romano* (1456) *(see p52)* in room 7.

Two panels by Piero della Francesca (1410–92), depicting the Duke and Duchess of Urbino on one side and representations of their virtues on the other, are in room 8. Painted between 1465 and 1470, these are two of the first Renaissance portraits.

If these works seem coldly experimental, Fra Filippo Lippi's *Madonna and Child with Angels* (1455–66), also in room 8, is a masterpiece of warmth and humanity. Like so many Renaissance artists, Lippi uses a religious subject to celebrate earthly delights, such as feminine beauty, sumptuous fabrics and the Tuscan landscape.

Madonna and Child with Angels (1455–66), by Fra Filippo Lippi

Botticelli

The Botticelli paintings in rooms 10–14 are the highlight of the Uffizi's collection. The brilliant colours and crisp draughtsmanship of, for instance, *The Birth of Venus* (about 1485) *(see p85)* are a reminder that Renaissance artists often experimented

Primavera (1480), by Botticelli

with new pigments to achieve striking colour effects. The subject of this painting, the Roman goddess Venus, is also significant. By painting Venus instead of the Christian Virgin, Botticelli expressed the fascination with Classical mythology common to many Renaissance artists.

The same is true of his other famous work, *Primavera* (about 1480). It breaks with the tradition of Christian religious painting by illustrating a pagan rite of spring. Other works to see here include the *Adoration of the Magi* (about 1475), a thinly disguised Medici family portrait *(see p55)*.

Leonardo da Vinci

Room 15 contains works attributed to the young Leonardo. Still under the influence of his tutor Andrea del Verrocchio, the artist he collaborated with on *The Baptism of Christ* (1470–75), he was already developing his own highly naturalistic style in *The Annunciation* (1472–5) and in his first independent commission, the unfinished *Adoration of the Magi* (1481).

Detail from *The Annunciation* (1472–5), by Leonardo da Vinci

High Renaissance and Mannerism

Michelangelo's *The Holy Family* (1506–8), in room 35, is striking for its vibrant colours and the unusually twisted pose of the Virgin *(see p85)*. This painting proved to be enormously influential with the next generation of Tuscan artists, notably Bronzino (1503–72), Pontormo (1494–1556) and Parmigianino

Madonna of the Goldfinch (1506), by Raphael

(1503–40). The latter's *Madonna of the Long Neck* (about 1534) in room 74 on the first floor, with its contorted anatomy and bright colours, is a remarkable example of what came to be known as the Mannerist style.

Room 66 on the first floor is dedicated to Raphael. The tender *Madonna of the Goldfinch* (1506) still shows signs of earthquake damage dating from 1547. Works by Titian (1488–1576) are in room 83, including *The Venus of Urbino* (1538), said to be one of the most beautiful nudes ever painted.

European Art

The works in room 45 show how the naturalism pursued by Northern European masters, such as Dürer (1471–1528) and Cranach (1472–1553), had a profound influence on Renaissance painters such as Pietro Perugino (1446–1523) and Jacopo da Sallaio (1441–1493). A selection of works by Flemish painter Hans Memling (1430–94) is also displayed in room 43.

Later Flemish paintings, including those by Rubens (1577–1640) and Van Dyck (1599–1641), are in room 55. Dutch paintings of the 17th and 18th century, including a number of Rembrandt self-portraits, are in room 49. Paintings by Spanish masters El Greco (1541–1624), Velázquez (1599–1660) and Goya (1746–1828) are on display in room 46.

Later Italian Paintings

Rooms 90 to 93 are dedicated to Caravaggio (1571–1610) and his legacy in the early 17th century. There are works by several of his followers, including Gerard van Honthorst (1592–1656), a Dutch artist renowned for his depictions of artificially lit scenes, and Artemisia Gentileschi (1593–1656), a celebrated female painter perhaps best known for her brutal masterpiece *Judith Slaying Holofernes* (1611–12).

The Tribune

The octagonal tribune was designed in 1584 by Buontalenti so that Francesco I could display all his favourite works from the Medici collection in one room.

Notable paintings include Bronzino's portrait (1545) of Eleonora di Toledo with her son, Giovanni *(see p55)*, and the same artist's portrait of Bia, Cosimo I's illegitimate daughter. It was painted just before her early death in 1542.

Portrait of *Bia* (1542), by Bronzino

Sculptures

The ancient Roman sculptures displayed along the corridors and in room 56 were mainly collected by the Medici during the 15th century. Their anatomical precision and faithful portraiture were much admired and copied by Renaissance artists, who saw themselves as giving rebirth to Classical perfection in art.

CITY CENTRE NORTH

This area of Florence is stamped with the character of Cosimo il Vecchio. The man who founded the great Medici dynasty maintained his position of power by astute management of the city's financial affairs, as opposed to resorting to threats and violence. Cosimo was a highly educated and sophisticated man with a passion for building, and he wanted the churches, palazzi and libraries that he built to last a thousand years, like the buildings of ancient Rome. To this end, he commissioned some of the greatest architects and artists of the time to

build the churches of San Lorenzo and San Marco as well as the Medici's first home, the Palazzo Medici Riccardi. He is regarded as one of the great innovators of the Renaissance in Florence. Even after the Medici family had moved across the river Arno to the Palazzo Pitti in 1550, the Grand Dukes made their final journey back to the north of the city to be buried in the extravagant Cappelle Medicee in San Lorenzo. For the tombs in the New Sacristy, Michelangelo contributed his magnificent allegorical sculptures, *Day and Night* and *Dawn and Dusk*.

Sights at a Glance

Churches and Synagogues
2 San Lorenzo pp 94–5
6 San Marco pp100–1
13 Santissima Annunziata
15 Santa Maria Maddalena dei Pazzi
16 Tempio Israelitico

Historic Buildings
3 Palazzo Pucci
4 Palazzo Medici Riccardi
11 Spedale degli Innocenti

Museums and Galleries
5 Cenacolo di Sant'Apollonia
8 Galleria dell'Accademia
9 Conservatorio
10 Opificio delle Pietre Dure
14 Museo Archeologico

Gardens
7 Giardino dei Semplici

Streets, Piazzas and Markets
1 Mercato Centrale
12 Piazza della Santissima Annunziata

☐ **Restaurants** *p266*
1 Casa del Vino
2 Il Desco
3 Dolci e Dolcezze
4 Sergio Gozzi
5 La Taverna del Bronzino
6 Trattoria Mario
7 Trattoria Za Za
8 Il Vegetariano

See also Street Finder maps
1–2, 5–6

0 metres 300
0 yards 300

◀ Detail from *The Procession of the Magi*, by Benozzo, Palazzo Medici Riccardi

For keys to symbols *see back flap*

Street-by-Street: Around San Lorenzo

This area has the mark of Cosimo il Vecchio, founder of the Medici dynasty, who commissioned San Lorenzo and the Palazzo Medici Riccardi. In much of the area, and especially around the Mercato Centrale, a huge general market fills the streets, its colourful awnings almost obscuring the various monuments. The market is a reminder that Florence has always been a city of merchants. Many of the products on sale – leather goods and silk, wool and cashmere garments – are great value especially if, like the Florentines, you are prepared to bargain.

Cheap cafés and cooked-meat stalls abound in the vicinity of the market. They sell traditional Tuscan takeaway foods, such as tripe and roast suckling pig, chicken and rabbit.

❶ Mercato Centrale
Built in 1874, the central market is packed with fish, meat and cheese stalls downstairs, while fruit and vegetables are sold upstairs beneath the glass and cast-iron roof.

Palazzo Riccardi-Manelli, begun in 1557, stands on the site of the house where Giotto was born in 1266.

The Cappelle Medicee are situated in San Lorenzo, but are reached from a separate entrance in Piazza di Madonna degli Aldobrandini. Michelangelo designed the New Sacristy and two Medici tombs. Some of his pencil sketches survive on the walls inside.

Biblioteca Mediceo-Laurenziana

0 metres 100
0 yards 100

The Biblioteca Riccardiana, founded in the 16th century, was opened to the public in 1715. It comprises a series of frescoed reading rooms that house a collection of precious manuscripts, including Dante's *Divine Comedy*.

Locator Map
See Florence Street Finder maps 5, 6

Via de'Ginori is lined with fine 16th-century palazzi.

San Giovannino degli Scolopi church was begun by Ammannati in 1579.

❹ ★ Palazzo Medici Riccardi
The palazzo, built between 1444 and 1464, served as the Medici family home and the headquarters of their banking empire.

❸ Palazzo Pucci
This is the ancestral home of the late designer Emilio Pucci.

Key

— Suggested route

❷ ★ San Lorenzo
The unfinished façade belies the noble interior, which was designed for the Medici by Brunelleschi in 1425–46.

Giovanni delle Bande Nere, Grand Duke Cosimo I's father *(see p55)*, is depicted in battle dress in this statue by Baccio Bandinelli (1540).

❶ Mercato Centrale

Via dell'Ariento 10–14. **Map** 1 C4 (5 C1).
Tel 055 239 97 98. Ground-floor food
market: **Open** 7am–2pm Mon–Sat.
First floor: **Open** 10am–midnight daily.
w mercatocentrale.it

Florence's busiest food market,
the bustling Mercato Centrale,
is housed in a vast two-storey
building made of cast iron and
glass, built in 1874 by Giuseppe
Mengoni. A major renovation of
the market in 2014 was a
cornerstone in the rejuvenation
of the San Lorenzo neighbourhood, which had become a
tawdry, touristy and rather
neglected area of the city.
Many of the market stalls that
were squeezed into the historic
streets and ran all the way down
to Piazza di San Lorenzo have
been shut down. The remaining
stalls, selling touristy nick-nacks
and everyday items from cheap
clothes to lentils, are now

Iron girders and contemporary design on the first floor of the Mercato Centrale

concentrated in the streets
to the north of the market.
At night, this area is still somewhat seedy, despite improve-
ments to lighting.

In the grand market building
itself are dozens of stalls selling
meat, fish, cheese and typical
Tuscan takeaway foods, such as
porchetta (roast suckling pig).
The first floor has been

transformed into a modern
light-filled space where visitors
are welcome to eat their
purchases from the ground
floor and order a glass of wine if
they so wish. Numerous food
stands here offer high quality
meals and snacks, and there's a
beer stand, a Chianti tasting bar,
a bookshop and a cooking
school, too.

If you're after quality goods
such as leather luggage or
table linens, head to the
shops neighbouring the
market rather than the stalls
to the north.

❷ San Lorenzo

See pp94–5.

❸ Palazzo Pucci

Via de'Pucci 6. **Map** 2 D5 (6 E1).
Tel 055 28 30 61. **Closed** to the public.

The Palazzo Pucci is the
ancestral home of clothes
designer Emilio Pucci, Marchese
di Barsento. The Pucci family,
traditionally friends and allies of
the Medici, feature prominently
in Florence's history, and this
large palace was built in the
16th century to designs by
Bartolomeo Ammannati.

Emilio Pucci's boutique can
be found at Via de'Tornabuoni
22r. In the past, haute couture
clients were fitted out in palatial
rooms above the showroom.
Pucci is most famous for smart
but casual clothes, and
designed the stylish blue
uniforms worn by Florentine
traffic police, the *vigili urbani*
(see p292).

The rooftops of San Lorenzo, dominated by the church's dome

❹ Palazzo Medici Riccardi

Via Cavour 1. **Map** 2 D5 (6 D1).
Tel 055 276 03 40. Cappella dei Magi:
Open 9am–6pm Thu–Tue (last adm
5pm. **Closed** 1 May, 25 Dec. 🏛
Booking is advisable in busy periods.
📧 ♿

Home of the Medici for 100
years from 1444, the palazzo
was later acquired by the
Riccardi family and now
houses government offices.
It was built to an austere
design by Michelozzo for
Cosimo il Vecchio, who rejected
Brunelleschi's original plans
as being too flamboyant –
Cosimo did not want to flaunt
his wealth. The windows on
either side of the entrance
were added in 1517 and
designed by Michelangelo.

Through the main door, the
courtyard walls are covered in
ancient Roman masonry
fragments. The roundels above
the arcade show scenes copied
from antique intaglios now on
display in the Museo degli
Argenti *(see p127)*. Donatello's
statue of David (now in the
Bargello, *see pp72–3*) used to
be here, but today the place of
honour is given to Bandinelli's
marble statue of *Orpheus*.

Only a few rooms in the palazzo
are open to the public. In the
Cappella dei Magi is a colourful
fresco of *The Procession of the
Magi* painted in 1459–60 by
Benozzo Gozzoli. It depicts
several members of the Medici
dynasty *(see pp54–5)*. The Sala di
Luca Giordano is named after the

The Last Supper (1445–50), by Andrea del Castagno, in Sant'Apollonia

Neapolitan artist who painted
its walls with *The Apotheosis of
the Medici* in High Baroque style
in 1683. A selection of marble
sculptures from the Medici
Riccardi collection is also on
display. The palazzo often plays
host to temporary art exhibitions, for which there is an
additional admission charge.

❺ Cenacolo di Sant'Apollonia

Via XXVII Aprile 1. **Map** 2 D4.
Tel 055 238 86 07. **Open** 8:15am–
1:50pm daily. **Closed** 1st, 3rd & 5th
Sun, 2nd & 4th Mon of the month. ♿

The cloister and refectory of
what was originally a convent
for the Camaldolite order of
nuns are now used by the
students of Florence University.
On the main wall of the
refectory is a fresco of *The Last
Supper*, painted in 1445–50, one
of the few surviving works by
Andrea del Castagno. He was a
pupil of Masaccio and among
the first Renaissance artists to
begin to experiment with
perspective. Here, Judas sits
isolated in the foreground of the
picture, disrupting its balance
and breaking up the long white
strip of tablecloth. He is shown
in profile with the face of a satyr:
a mythological creature, half-
man, half-goat, often used in
Renaissance paintings to
represent evil.

❻ San Marco

See pp100–1.

❼ Giardino dei Semplici

Via Micheli 3. **Map** 2 E4. **Tel** 055 275
74 02. **Open** 9am–7pm Sun–Fri (until
5pm in winter), 9am–1pm Sat. **Closed**
1 Jan, 6 Jan, 25 Apr, Easter Sun & Mon,
1 May, 13–17 Aug, 1 Nov, 24–26 Dec,
31 Dec. ♿ 🏛

The word "Semplici" refers to the
raw ingredients, "simples", used
by medieval apothecaries in
preparing medicine – thus the
Giardino dei Semplici was
where medicinal herbs were
grown and studied. It was set
up in 1545 by Niccolò Tribolo for
Cosimo I in the area between Via
Micheli, Via Giorgio la Pira and Via
Gino Capponi. The garden retains
its original layout, but now the
collection includes tropical plants
as well as flora native to Tuscany.

Around the garden are small
specialist museums: a geology
collection includes fossils; a
mineralogy section shows the
geological structure of Elba,
whose ores attracted bronze
traders in the 10th century BC.
The botanical museum has
specimens of rare plants.

Statuary in the garden of the Palazzo
Medici Riccardi

Giardino dei Semplici

❷ San Lorenzo

San Lorenzo was the parish church of the Medici family, and they lavished their wealth on its adornment. Brunelleschi rebuilt the church in Renaissance Classical style in 1419, although the façade was never completed. In 1520, Michelangelo began work on the Medici tombs and designed the Biblioteca Mediceo-Laurenziana in 1524 to house the manuscripts collected by the Medici. In both the New Sacristy and the Cappella dei Principi, extensive scaffolding has been erected (for an indefinite period) to protect visitors from falling marble.

★ **Cappella dei Principi**
The marble decoration of the Medici mausoleum, begun in 1604 by Matteo Nigetti, was not completed until 1962.

★ **Michelangelo's Staircase**
The Mannerist *pietra serena* sandstone staircase to the Biblioteca is one of Michelangelo's most innovative designs. It was built by Ammannati in 1559.

KEY

① **The formal cloister garden** is planted with clipped box hedges, pomegranate and orange trees.

② **Michelangelo** designed the desks and ceiling of the Biblioteca, which is entered from Manetti's graceful, tiered cloister, built in 1462.

③ **The Old Sacristy** was designed by Brunelleschi (1420–29) and painted by Donatello.

④ **The huge dome** by Buontalenti echoes that of Brunelleschi's Duomo (*see pp68–9*).

⑤ **Six Grand Dukes** are buried in the Cappella dei Principi.

⑥ **The campanile** was built in 1740.

⑦ **A simple stone slab** marks the unostentatious grave of Cosimo il Vecchio (1389–1464), founder of the Medici dynasty.

⑧ **Michelangelo** submitted several designs for the façade of San Lorenzo, but it remains unfinished.

The Martyrdom of St Lawrence
Bronzino's huge Mannerist fresco of 1569 is a masterly study of the human form in various contorted poses (*see p31*).

★ Medici Tombs
Michelangelo's monumental funerary figures, symbolizing Night, Day, Dawn and Dusk, are among his greatest works.

VISITORS' CHECKLIST

Practical Information
Piazza di San Lorenzo (Basilica and Biblioteca), Piazza di Madonna degli Aldobrandini (Cappelle Medicee).
Map 1 C5 (6 D1).
Basilica: **Tel** 055 21 66 34.
Open 10am–5:30pm Mon–Sat (Mar–Oct also 1:30–5:30pm Sun).
🕇 8am, 9:30am, 6pm Mon–Sat, 9:30am, 11am, 6pm Sun & religious hols. 🈺 📨 Biblioteca: **Tel** 055 21 07 60. **Open** to readers 8am–2pm Fri–Mon & Wed, 8am–5:30pm Tue & Thu. **Closed** public hols. 🈺 📨 Cappelle Medicee: **Tel** 055 238 86 02 (055 29 48 83 to book). **Open** 8:15am–1:50pm daily. **Closed** 1st, 3rd & 5th Mon, 2nd & 4th Sun of the month. 🈺

Transport
🚌 many routes.

Donatello's Pulpits
Donatello was 74 when he began work on the bronze pulpits in the nave in 1460; they depict Christ's Passion and Resurrection.

St Joseph and Christ in the Workshop
Pietro Annigoni (1910–88) is one of the few modern artists whose work is seen in Florentine churches.

Entrance to church

Street-by-Street: Around San Marco

The buildings in this part of Florence once stood on the fringes of the city, serving as stables and barracks. The Medici menagerie, including lions, elephants and giraffes, was housed here. Today it is the student quarter and, in termtime, Piazza di San Marco is filled with young people waiting for lectures at the university or at the Accademia di Belle Arti. Based on an academy set up in 1563 *(see p98)*, this is the world's oldest art school.

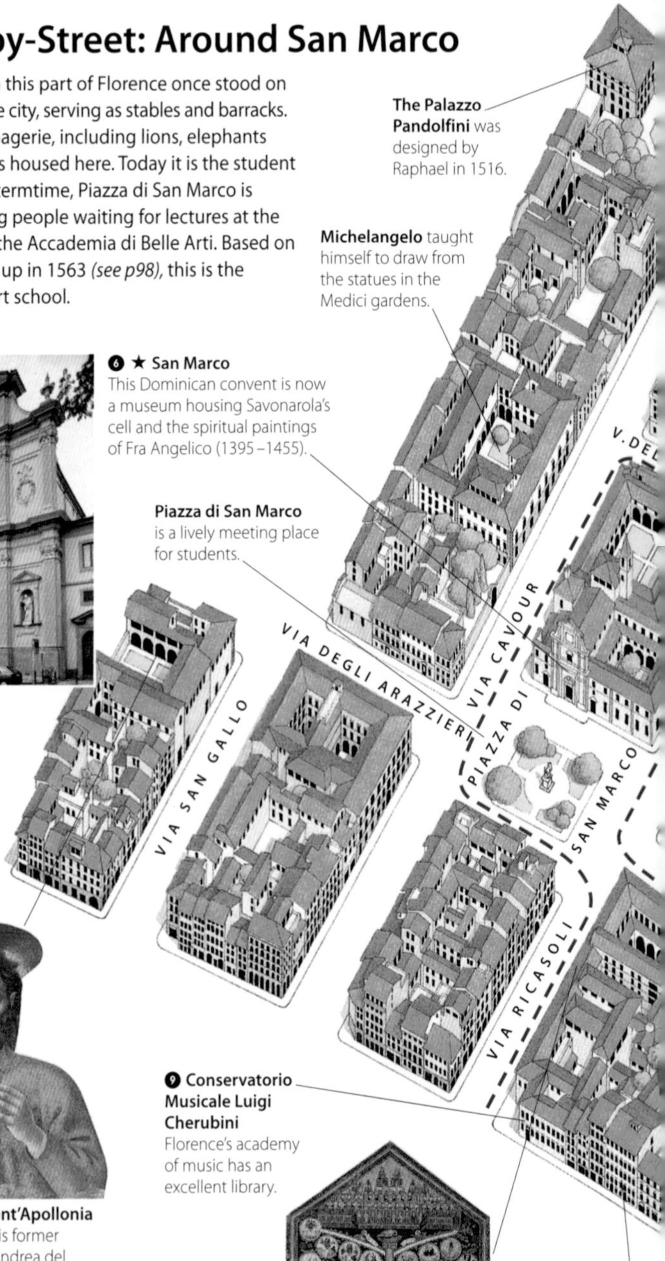

The Palazzo Pandolfini was designed by Raphael in 1516.

Michelangelo taught himself to draw from the statues in the Medici gardens.

❻ ★ San Marco
This Dominican convent is now a museum housing Savonarola's cell and the spiritual paintings of Fra Angelico (1395–1455).

Piazza di San Marco is a lively meeting place for students.

V. DEL

VIA DEGLI ARAZZIERI

VIA CAVOUR

PIAZZA DI

SAN MARCO

VIA SAN GALLO

VIA RICASOLI

❾ Conservatorio Musicale Luigi Cherubini
Florence's academy of music has an excellent library.

❺ Cenacolo di Sant'Apollonia
The refectory of this former convent features Andrea del Castagno's *The Last Supper* (1450).

❿ Opificio delle Pietre Dure
Precious mosaics are restored here.

Key

— Suggested route

❽ ★ Galleria dell' Accademia
This gallery, famous for Michelangelo's *David*, also contains Bonaguida's *Tree of the Cross* (1330).

⑬ Santissima Annunziata
The Medici funded the rebuilding of this church, begun in 1444 by Michelozzo. The atrium was frescoed by Andrea del Sarto.

Locator Map
See Florence Street Finder map 2

❼ Giardino dei Semplici
Research into plant remedies has been undertaken here since 1543.

⑪ ★ Spedale degli Innocenti
The city orphanage *(see pp52–3)* was Brunelleschi's first completed Classical design. Andrea della Robbia added cameos of swaddled infants in the 1480s, as an inspiration to charity.

⑭ Museo Archeologico
Etruscan vases and bronzes form part of this major collection.

Grand Duke Ferdinando I
was Giambologna's last statue and was cast by Tacca in 1608, using the bronze from cannons captured as battle trophies by the Tuscan navy.

0 metres 50
0 yards 50

⊙ San Marco

The convent of San Marco was founded in the 13th century and enlarged in 1437 when Dominican monks from nearby Fiesole moved here at the invitation of Cosimo il Vecchio. He paid a considerable sum to have the convent rebuilt by his favourite architect, Michelozzo, whose simple cloisters and cells are the setting for a remarkable series of devotional frescoes (c.1438–45) by Fra Angelico.

Cells 38 and 39 were reserved for Cosimo il Vecchio when he retreated to the convent to find spiritual sustenance and peace.

The Mocking of Christ, Fra Angelico's beautiful allegorical fresco (c.1440), represents Jesus being blindfolded and struck by a Roman guard.

Cells 12 to 15 contain relics of the religious fanatic Savonarola, made prior of San Marco in 1491 (see pp56–7).

An ancient cedar stands in Michelozzo's Sant'Antonino cloister.

Entrance to the church (Chiesa di San Marco)

Entrance to Museo di San Marco

Sant'Antonino cloister

The Deposition (1435–40)
This poignant scene of the dead Christ, and other works by Fra Angelico and his school, are displayed in the former Pilgrims' Hospice.

Key to Floorplan

- ☐ Ground floor
- ☐ First floor
- ☐ Non-exhibition space

For hotels and restaurants see pp252–7 and pp264–75

The dormitory cells contain scenes from *The Life of Christ*, intended to inspire prayer and contemplation.

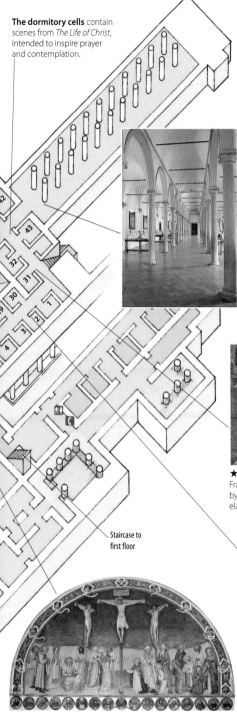

42

43

32

31

30

29

3

2

1

4

3

2

1

C

Staircase to first floor

★ **Library**
Michelozzo designed Europe's first public library, in a light and airy colonnaded hall, for Cosimo il Vecchio in 1441.

★ **The Annunciation** (c.1440)
Fra Angelico shows his mastery of perspective by placing Gabriel and the Virgin in an elaborate loggia, inspired by Michelozzo.

The Entombment
Fra Angelico's tender fresco (c.1442) in Cell 2 shows Mary Magdalene and St John mourning Christ.

★ **The Crucifixion** (1441–42)
Fra Angelico was moved to tears as he painted this image of the Crucifixion of Christ in the Chapter House.

The central section of the 15th-century *Cassone Adimari*, by Scheggia

❽ Galleria dell'Accademia

Via Ricasoli 60. **Map** 2 D4 (6 E1).
Tel 055 238 86 09 (information);
055 29 48 83 (reservations).
Open 8:15am–6:50pm Tue–Sun
(occasional extended hours in
summer). **Closed** 1 Jan, 1 May,
25 Dec. 🅿 ✉ ♿ 📷

The Academy of Fine Arts in
Florence was founded in 1563
and was the first school in Europe
set up to teach the techniques of
drawing, painting and sculpture.
The art collection displayed in
the gallery was formed in 1784
with the aim of providing the
students of the academy with
material to study and copy.

Since 1873, many of
Michelangelo's most important
works have been in the
Accademia. Perhaps the most
famous of all dominates the

Madonna del Mare (c.1470),
by Sandro Botticelli

collection: Michelangelo's *David*
(1504). This colossal Classical
statue (5.2 m/17 ft) depicts
the biblical hero who killed
the giant Goliath. It was
commissioned by the
city of Florence and
positioned in front of
the Palazzo Vecchio.
This established
Michelangelo, then
aged 29, as the
foremost sculptor
of his time. In 1873,
it was moved to
the Accademia, to
protect it from the
weather and
pollution. A copy of
David is now to be
found in its original
position in Piazza della
Signoria (see pp80–81)
and a second stands in
the middle of Piazzale
Michelangelo (see p135).

Michelangelo's other
masterpieces include a
statue of St Matthew,
finished in 1508, and
the *Quattro Prigionieri*
(the four prisoners), which were
sculpted between 1521 and
1523 and intended to adorn
the tomb of Pope Julius II.
Presented to the Medici in 1564
by Michelangelo's cousin, the
muscular figures struggling to
free themselves from the stone
are among the most dramatic
of his works. The statues were
moved to the Grotta Grande in
the Boboli Gardens in 1585,

David by Michelangelo

where casts of the originals can
now be seen (see pp128–9).

The gallery contains an
important collection of paintings
by 15th- and 16th-century
local artists: contemporaries
of Michelangelo such as Fra
Bartolomeo, Filippino Lippi,
Bronzino and Ridolfo del
Ghirlandaio. There are
many major works,
including the
Madonna del Mare
(Madonna of the Sea),
attributed to Botticelli
(1445–1510), and *Venus
and Cupid*, by Jacopo
Pontormo (1494–1556),
based upon a pre-
paratory drawing
by Michelangelo.

Also on display is an
elaborately painted
wooden chest, the
Cassone Adimari, by
Scheggia, Masaccio's
step-brother.
Dating from
around 1440, it
was originally
used as part of a
bride's trousseau, and is covered
with details of Florentine daily
life, clothing and architecture.
The bridal party is pictured
standing in front of the Baptistry.

Pacino di Bonaguida's
Tree of Life (1310) is a prominent
painting among the collections
of Byzantine and late 13th- and
14th-century religious art,
much of which is stylized and
heavily embossed with gold.

The Salone della Toscana (Tuscany Room) is full of 19th-century sculpture and paintings by members of the Accademia, and a series of original plaster models by the sculptor Lorenzo Bartolini. Born in 1777, he became professor at the Accademia in 1839, a post he held until his death in 1850. His work includes busts of major figures, such as the poet Lord Byron and the composer Franz Liszt.

Detail from 14th-century *Madonna and Saints*, in the Accademia

❾ Conservatorio Musicale Luigi Cherubini

Piazza delle Belle Arti 2. **Map** 2 D4 (6 E1). **Tel** 055 29 21 80. Library: **Open** Mon–Sat; times vary.

Some of Italy's finest musicians trained at this musical academy, named after the Florentine composer Luigi Cherubini (1760–1842). The conservatory owns a range of ancient musical instruments, now on display in the Palazzo Vecchio (*see pp82–3*). The collection was acquired by Ferdinando, the last of the Medici Grand Dukes, and includes violins, violas and cellos made by Stradivari, Amati and Ruggeri. There is also a harpsichord by Bartolomeo Cristofori, who invented the piano in the early 18th century. He was responsible for many of the most important acquisitions.

The conservatory has one of the best music libraries in Italy, holding many original manuscripts by composers like Monteverdi and Rossini.

Pietre dure table (1849), by Zocchi

❿ Opificio delle Pietre Dure

Via degli Alfani 78. **Map** 2 D4 (6 F1). **Tel** 055 24 98 83. **Open** 8:15am– 2pm Mon–Sat (to 7pm Thu). **Closed** public hols.

Situated in the former monastery of San Niccolò, the *opificio* (factory) is a national institute specializing in teaching the Florentine craft of producing inlaid pictures using marble and semiprecious stones. This tradition has flourished since the end of the 16th century, when it was funded through the patronage of the Medici Grand Dukes, who decorated their mausoleum with *pietre dure*.

There is a museum in the same building displaying 19th-century workbenches, tools, vases and portraits showing *pietre dure* work. Several table tops decorated with *pietre dure* are on display: one inlaid with a harp and garlands by Zocchi, made in 1849, another with flowers and birds, designed by Niccolò Betti in 1855. A stockpile of exquisite marbles and other semiprecious stones dates back to Medici times.

⓫ Spedale degli Innocenti

Piazza della Santissima Annunziata 12. **Map** 2 D4 (6 F1). **Tel** 055 249 17 08. **Open** 9am–4pm Mon–Fri, 11am– 5pm Sat; last adm 30 mins before closing. **Closed** 1 Jan, Easter, 25 Dec.

This "hospital" is named after Herod's biblical Massacre of the Innocents following the birth of Jesus. It opened in 1444 as the first orphanage in Europe, and part of the building is still used for this purpose. UNICEF, the United Nations Children's Fund, also has offices here. Brunelleschi's arcaded loggia (*see pp52–3*) is decorated with glazed terracotta roundels, added by Andrea della Robbia around 1487, showing babies wrapped in swaddling bands. At the left-hand end of the portico is the *rota*, a rotating stone cylinder, upon which mothers could place their unwanted children anonymously and ring the orphanage bell. The stone was then turned around and the child was taken in.

Within the building there are two elegant cloisters built to Brunelleschi's designs. The larger Chiostro degli Uomini (Men's Cloister), built between 1422 and 1445, is decorated with *sgraffito* designs of cherubs and roosters scratched into the wet plaster. The smaller Women's Cloister (1438) leads to a gallery that has several paintings donated by children from the orphanage who became successful in later life. Among these is the *Adoration of the Magi* (1488), painted by Domenico del Ghirlandaio, showing the massacre in the background.

Andrea della Robbia's roundels (c.1487) on the Spedale degli Innocenti

Mannerist fountain by Pietro Tacca in Piazza della Santissima Annunziata

⓬ Piazza della Santissima Annunziata

Map 2 D4.

The delicate nine-bay arcade on the eastern side of this elegant square was designed by Brunelleschi in 1419 and forms the façade to the Spedale degli Innocenti (see p52). Brunelleschi's round arches gave rise to the Classical style widely copied by Renaissance architects. In the centre of the square is an equestrian statue of Duke Ferdinando I, started by Giambologna towards the end of his career. It was finished in 1608 by his assistant, Pietro Tacca, who also designed the two stylized Mannerist bronze fountains in the square.

A fair is held annually in the piazza on the feast of the Annunciation, 25 March, when homemade sweet biscuits called brigidini are sold from the stalls.

⓭ Santissima Annunziata

Piazza della Santissima Annunziata.
Map 2 E4. **Tel** 055 26 61 81. **Open** 7:30am–12:30pm, 4–6:30pm daily. 🖼

The Church of the Holy Annunciation was founded by the Servite order in 1250 and later rebuilt by Michelozzo between 1444 and 1481. There is a series of early 16th-century frescoes in the atrium by Mannerist artists Rosso Fiorentino, Andrea del Sarto and Jacopo Pontormo, but many of these frescoes have suffered from damp and are fading. The most celebrated are The Journey of the Magi (1511) and The Birth of the Virgin (1514), by del Sarto.

The interior is dark and heavily decorated, with a frescoed ceiling, completed by Pietro Giambelli in 1669.

The church also boasts one of the most revered shrines in Florence, a painting of the Virgin Mary, begun in 1252 by a monk. Devout Florentines believe it was finished by an angel, and many newly wed couples

traditionally come here after their wedding ceremony to present a bouquet of flowers to the Virgin and pray for a long and fruitful marriage. Nine chapels radiate from the sanctuary. The central one was reconstructed by Giambologna to use as his tomb, and contains bronze reliefs and a crucifix sculpted by him.

Through the door in the north transept of the church is the Chiostro dei Morti (Cloister of the Dead), so called because it was originally used as a burial ground and is packed with memorial stones. The fresco above the entrance porch is by Andrea del Sarto. Painted in 1525, it shows the Holy Family resting on their flight to Egypt and is usually known as La Madonna del Sacco, since Joseph is depicted leaning on a sack.

The Cappella di San Luca, off the cloister, has been owned by the Accademia delle Arti del Disegno since 1565 and a special service dedicated to artists is held here every year on St Luke's day (which falls on 18 October). Benvenuto Cellini is among the artists buried in the vault below.

The Birth of the Virgin (1514), by Andrea del Sarto

The François Vase, covered in figures from Greek mythology

⓮ Museo Archeologico

Via della Colonna 36. **Map** 2 E4. **Tel** 055 23 57 50. **Open** 8:30am–7pm Tue–Fri; 8:30am–2pm Sat–Mon. **Closed** 1 Jan, 1 May, 25 Dec. 🅿️ ♿

The Archaeological Museum is in a palazzo built by Giulio Parigi for the Princess Maria Maddalena de'Medici in 1620. It now exhibits outstanding collections of Etruscan, Greek, Roman and ancient Egyptian artifacts.

A section on the second floor is dedicated to Greek vases, with a room given over to the François Vase, found in an Etruscan tomb at Fonte Rotella near Chiusi *(see p232)*. Painted and signed in 570 BC, it is decorated with six rows of black and red figures depicting scenes from Greek mythology. The Etruscan collection was very badly damaged by the 1966 floods in Florence *(see p61)*, so since then restoration work has been carried out on the pieces.

In addition to the splendid series of bronze Etruscan statues, on the first floor of the museum there are two famous bronzes. The *Chimera (see p46)*, sculpted in the 4th century BC, is a mythical lion with a goat's head imposed on its body and a serpent for a tail, shown here cowering in terror. It was ploughed up in a field near Arezzo in 1553 and presented to Cosimo I

Bronze Etruscan warrior

de'Medici by Giorgio Vasari, the artist, author and critic. The *Arringatore* (Orator) was found c.1566 near Lake Trasimeno in central Italy and is inscribed with the name of an Etruscan aristocrat, Aulus Metullus. The sculpture dates from the 1st century BC, and the figure, splendidly dressed in a Roman toga, appears to be addressing his audience.

Part of the Egyptian collection was acquired during a joint French and Tuscan expedition in 1829. It is especially rich in wooden, cloth and bone artifacts, which were well preserved in the dry atmosphere of the desert tombs in which they were found. They include a near-complete chariot of bone and wood found in a tomb near Thebes (dating from c.15th century BC), along with textiles, hats, ropes, furniture, purses and baskets.

⓯ Santa Maria Maddalena dei Pazzi

Borgo Pinti 58. **Map** 2 E5. **Tel** 055 247 84 20. Church and chapter house: **Open** 9am–noon, 3–7pm daily. **Closed** for mass 5:30–6pm.

This former convent has been restored following the floods of 1966. Originally run by the Cistercian order, it was taken over by Carmelites in 1628, and Augustinian monks have lived here since 1926. The chapterhouse contains the famous *Crucifixion and Saints* fresco, painted in 1493–6 by Perugino (his real name was Pietro Vannucci), who was one of the founders of the Umbrian school of artists. This beautiful and well-preserved fresco is regarded as a masterpiece, bearing all Perugino's trademarks, most notably the background, which is a detailed landscape of wooded hills and winding streams painted in soft blues and greens.

The main chapel, decorated with coloured marble by Ciro Ferri (1675), is one of the best examples of the High Baroque style in a Florentine church. In 1492, Giuliano da Sangallo designed the church's unusual and striking portico, with its square-topped, Ionic-style arcades.

Interior of the Tempio Israelitico

⓰ Tempio Israelitico

Via Farini 4. **Map** 2 F5. **Tel** 055 24 52 52. Synagogue and Museum: **Open** Oct–May: 10am–5:30pm, Sun–Thu, 10am–3pm Fri; Jun–Sep: 10am–6:30pm Sun–Thu, 10am–5pm Fri. Last adm 45 mins before closing. **Closed** Jewish hols. ✉️

The green copper-covered dome of Florence's main synagogue stands out on the horizon as you look down on the city from the surrounding hills. As elsewhere in Europe, Jews in Florence were alternately welcomed and persecuted over the years. In the early 17th century, they flocked to Livorno and then to Florence when it was freed from its strong political ties with Spain by Grand Duke Ferdinando I (1549–1609).

In the Inquisition, Grand Duke Cosimo III (1642–1723) passed laws forbidding Christians to work for Jewish families and businesses. In the 1860s, the Jewish ghetto was cleared to make way for the Piazza della Repubblica *(see p116)*. The synagogue was built by Marco Treves in 1874–82 in Spanish-Moorish style. It has a museum of ritual objects dating from the 17th century.

CITY CENTRE WEST

At one end of this part of Florence is the main railway station – a rare example of modern architecture in the city centre. At the other end, a magnet for visitors and Florentines alike, is the Ponte Vecchio, the city's oldest bridge. It is lined with jewellers' shops, here from 1593, and presents a scene that has changed little since.

Between these two focal points there is something to interest most people, from the frescoes of Santa Maria Novella and Santa Trinità to the luxurious 14th-century interiors of the Palazzo Davanzati and the awe-inspiring scale of Palazzo Strozzi. Nearby is

Piazza della Repubblica, originally laid out as part of the grandiose plans to remodel Florence when it was briefly the nation's capital. Most locals may consider it an eyesore, but the cafés here have always been very popular. This is also the part of Florence in which to shop, from the leather goods, silks and woollens of the Mercato Nuovo to the elegant showrooms of the top couturiers in Via della Vigna Nuova and Via de' Tornabuoni. In the smaller streets off these, local artisans continue Florence's proud tradition of craftsmanship, from stonecutting to restoration work.

Sights at a Glance

Museums and Galleries
1 Museo Marino Marini
   (San Pancrazio)
10 Palazzo Davanzati
16 Museo Nazionale Alinari
   della Fotografia

Churches
7 Santa Trinità
8 Santi Apostoli
17 Ognissanti
18 Santa Maria Novella
   pp114–15

Historic Buildings
2 Palazzo Rucellai
5 Palazzo Strozzi
11 Palazzo di Parte Guelfa
14 Palazzo Antinori
19 Stazione di Santa
   Maria Novella

Historic Streets and Piazzas
3 Via della Vigna Nuova
4 Via de' Tornabuoni
6 Piazza di Santa Trinità
13 Piazza della Repubblica
15 Via dei Fossi

Bridges
9 Ponte Vecchio
   pp110–11

Markets
12 Mercato Nuovo

☐ Restaurants pp266–7
1 Cacio Vino Trallallà
2 Caffè Giocosa Roberto Cavalli
3 Cantinetta Antinori
4 Coco Lezzone
5 Colle Bereto
6 Da il Latini
7 Florian
8 Gilli
9 Paskowski
10 Procacci
11 Obika
12 Oliviero

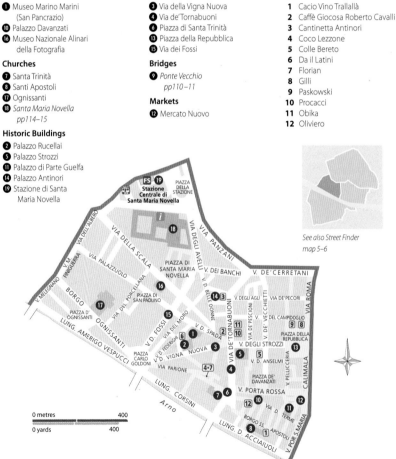

See also Street Finder
map 5–6

0 metres   400
0 yards   400

◀ The Corridoio Vasariano, running between the Uffizi and the Ponte Vecchio   For keys to symbols see back flap

Street-by-Street: Around Piazza della Repubblica

Underlying the street plan of modern Florence is the far older pattern of the ancient Roman city founded on the banks of the Arno. Nowhere is this more evident than in the rectilinear grid of narrow streets in the western half of the city centre. Here, the streets lead north from the river Arno to the Piazza della Repubblica, once the site of the forum, the main square of the ancient Roman city. It later became the city's main food market (*see p58*), until the authorities decided to tidy it up in the 1860s, building the triumphal arch that now stands in today's café-filled square.

❺ Palazzo Strozzi
This monumental palazzo dominates the square.

❻ Piazza di Santa Trinità
The square is marked by an ancient Roman column.

❼ ★ Santa Trinità
Ghirlandaio's frescoes, *The Life of St Francis* (1483), depict scenes that took place in this area. Here, a child is restored to life, after falling from the Palazzo Spini-Ferroni.

Palazzo Spini-Ferroni, a medieval palazzo featured in Ghirlandaio's frescoes in Santa Trinità, now houses the fashion boutique of Salvatore Ferragamo (*see p112*).

The statues of the Four Seasons decorating the approaches to Ponte Santa Trinità were erected in 1608 to celebrate the wedding of Cosimo I.

❽ Santi Apostoli
A plaque claims Charlemagne as founder.

⑬ ★ Piazza della Repubblica
The Roman-style triumphal arch celebrates Florence's stint as Italy's capital (1865–71).

Locator Map
See Florence Street Finder maps 5, 6

⑫ Mercato Nuovo
Designed as a covered general market in 1547, Mercato Nuovo is full of expensive souvenir stalls.

⑩ Palazzo Davanzati
Frescoes with exotic birds decorate the Sala dei Papagalli, which was once the dining room of this 14th-century palazzo.

⑨ ★ Ponte Vecchio
Giotto's pupil, Taddeo Gaddi, designed this medieval bridge in 1345. It is the oldest – and most popular – of Florence's bridges and retains many of its original features.

⑪ Palazzo di Parte Guelfa
This was the head quarters of the Guelphs, the dominant political party of medieval Florence.

Key

— Suggested route

| 0 metres | 200 |
| 0 yards | 200 |

❶ Museo Marino Marini (San Pancrazio)

Piazza San Pancrazio. **Map** 1 B5 (5 B2).
Tel 055 21 94 32. **Open** 10am–5pm
Mon, Wed–Sat. **Closed** public hols.
♿ 🚻 🌐 museomarinomarini.it

The former church of San Pancrazio has been turned into a museum devoted to the work of Italy's best-known abstract artist, Marino Marini (1901–80). Marini was born in Pistoia, where more of his work can be seen in the Palazzo del Comune and in the Centro Marino Marini *(see p190)*. Marini studied art in Florence before moving on to teaching in Monza and at the prestigious Brera Academy in Milan. He sought to reinterpret Etruscan and medieval art forms and is noted for rugged and elemental bronzes. Many of these are on the theme of the horse and rider, expressing a range of moods and experiences, from sombre weariness to joyous eroticism.

San Pancrazio itself is one of the oldest churches in Florence. It was founded in

Bronze statue *Cavaliere* (1949), by Marini, in the Museo Marino Marini

the 9th century, though its most attractive features are from the Renaissance period, including a graceful Classical façade and porch (1461–7) by Leon Battista Alberti.

San Pancrazio was the parish church of the wealthy merchant Giovanni Rucellai. Inside, in the Cappella di San Sepolcro, built by Alberti in 1467, is Rucellai's tomb, which is modelled on the Holy Sepulchre in Jerusalem (the tomb of Christ).

❷ Palazzo Rucellai

Via della Vigna Nuova 16. **Map** 1 C5
(5 B2). 🌐 palazzorucellai.org

Built in 1446–51, this is one of the most ornate Renaissance palaces in the city. It was commissioned by Giovanni Rucellai, whose wealth derived from the family business, the import of a rare and costly red dye made from a lichen found only on Majorca. The dye was called *oricello*, from which the name Rucellai is derived.

Giovanni commissioned several buildings from the architect Leon Battista Alberti, who went on to write an influential architectural treatise called *De Re Aedificatoria* (Concerning Architecture) in 1452. Alberti designed the Palazzo Rucellai almost as a textbook illustration of the major Classical orders. In ascending order of complexity, the pilaster strips on the ground floor are Doric, those above are Ionic and those on the top floor are Corinthian. The construction of the palace combined eight medieval houses into one structure.

Two symbols are carved into the entablature: the Rucellai's billowing sails of Fortune and the ring symbol of the Medici family. The ring is a reminder that Bernardo Rucellai formed an alliance with the Medici in the 1460s by marrying Lorenzo de'Medici's sister, Lucrezia. The Loggia del Rucellai, opposite the palace, was most likely built to commemorate the marriage. The Loggia is now a shop, but it is still possible to see the architrave.

Today, the Palazzo remains the property of the Rucellai family. It is located on a prominent shopping street and is within easy walking distance of several main sights and the Stazione di Santa Maria Novella. Part of the building is used as an educational center, the Institute at Palazzo Rucellai, which provides a liberal-arts study-abroad programme for students of North American colleges. On site are fully-equipped classrooms, a library and a fine-art studio for classes and student exhibitions.

19th-century view of Lungarno degli Acciaiuoli, from Palazzo Rucellai

❸ Via della Vigna Nuova

Map 3 B1 (5 B3).

Reflecting its associations with wealthy Renaissance Florentines, such as the Rucellai, Via della Vigna Nuova has a number of fashionable clothes shops. Nearly all the major Italian designers can be found here, as well as several smaller shops selling quality silks, cashmeres and lingerie.

Along Via della Vigna Nuova, you'll find understated elegance at BP Studio (No. 15r) and shoes and leather at Sutor Mantellassi (No. 62r) and Beltrami (No. 70r).

Pucci window display, Via de' Tornabuoni

❹ Via de' Tornabuoni

Map 1 C5 (5 C2). Ferragamo Museum: **Tel** 055 336 04 56. **Open** 10am–7:30pm daily. 📷 for groups of 10 or more. 🐾

This is the most elegant shopping street in Florence, lined with boutiques such as Salvatore Ferragamo (No. 14r), Pucci (No. 20r), Roberto Cavalli (No. 83r), Gucci (No. 73r), Prada for men (No. 67r), Prada for women (No. 53r), Armani (No. 48/50r), Bulgari (No. 56) and Cartier (No. 36). The Ferragamo Museum (No. 2) focuses on the firm's efforts in shoe-making. The medieval tower at the end of the street, now a hotel, used to be a private club for local aristocrats.

The Biggest Palazzo In Florence

The Strozzi family were exiled from Florence in 1434 for their opposition to the Medici, but in 1466, the banker Filippo Strozzi, having built up a fortune in Naples, returned to the city, determined to outdo his great rivals. He became a man obsessed. For years he bought up and demolished other palaces around his home. At last, he acquired enough land to achieve his ambition: to build the biggest palace ever seen in Florence.

Having spent so much money to get this far, nothing was left to chance. Astrologers were brought in to choose the most favourable day on which to lay the foundation stone, and the walls of the monumental palace began to rise in 1489. Two years later, Filippo Strozzi was dead, and, though his heirs struggled on with the building, the cost of pursuing Filippo's grandiose vision finally left them penniless and bankrupt.

Filippo Strozzi (1428–91)

❺ Palazzo Strozzi

Piazza degli Strozzi. **Map** 3 C1 (5 C3). **Tel** 055 264 51 55. 🦽 🐾 for exhibitions.

The Strozzi Palace is awesome because of its sheer size: 15 buildings were demolished to make way for it, and although it is only three storeys high, each floor is as tall as a normal palazzo. The palace was commissioned by the wealthy banker Filippo Strozzi, but he died in 1491, only two years after the foundation stone was laid.

The building was not completed until 1536, and three major architects had a hand in its design – Giuliano da Sangallo, Benedetto da Maiano and Simone del Pollaiuolo (also known as Cronaca). The exterior, built of huge rusticated masonry blocks, remains unspoiled. Look out for the original Renaissance torch-holders, lamps and rings for tethering horses, which adorn the corners and façades.

The elegance of the courtyard itself has been destroyed by a huge iron fire escape, constructed when the building was converted to a major exhibition venue. In recent years, it has hosted world-class exhibitions of art and antiquities. During major exhibitions, visitors can also access "La Strozzina" free of charge. This is a vaulted gallery space at basement level with changing displays. When there are no exhibitions, visitors may access only the central courtyard.

The palace also houses various learned institutes and an excellent library, the Gabinetto Vieusseux, named after the 19th-century Swiss scholar Gian Pietro Vieusseux. He founded a scientific and literary association in 1818, which was attended by, among others, the French author Stendhal.

Exterior of Palazzo Strozzi, with masonry block rustication

⑨ Ponte Vecchio

The Ponte Vecchio, or Old Bridge – indeed, the oldest bridge in Florence – was built in 1345. It was the only bridge in the city to escape being blown up during World War II. There have always been workshops on the bridge, but the butchers, tanners and blacksmiths who were here originally (and who used the river as a convenient rubbish tip) were evicted by Duke Ferdinando I in 1593 because of the noise and stench they created. The workshops were rebuilt and let to the more decorous goldsmiths, and the shops lining and overhanging the bridge continue to specialize in new and antique jewellery to this day.

Private Corridor
The aerial corridor built by Vasari along the eastern side of the bridge is hung with the self-portraits of many great artists, including Rembrandt, Rubens and Hogarth.

Medieval Workshops
Some of the oldest workshops have rear extensions overhanging the river, supported by timber brackets called *sporti*.

The Vasari Corridor

The Corridoio Vasariano was built in 1565 by Giorgio Vasari and links the Palazzo Vecchio to the Palazzo Pitti, via the Uffizi. This private elevated walkway, also known as *Percorso del Principe* ("Prince's Route"), allowed members of the Medici family to move between their residences without having to step into the street below and mix with the crowds. The Corridor is open daily (except Mondays) from May to September; www.florencetown.com.

Palazzo Vecchio
The Uffizi
Ponte Vecchio
Arno
Palazzo Pitti

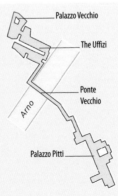

Bust of Cellini
A bust of Benvenuto Cellini (1500–71), the most famous of all Florentine goldsmiths, was placed in the middle of the bridge in 1900.

★ Bridge at Sunset
The Ponte Vecchio is especially attractive when viewed in the setting sun from Ponte Santa Trinità, or from one of the river embankments.

★ Jewellers' Shops
The shops sell everything from affordable modern earrings to precious antique rings.

Mannelli Tower
This medieval tower was built to defend the bridge. The Mannelli family stubbornly refused to demolish it to make way for the Vasari Corridor.

Viewpoint
There are few better places for enjoying the river views; buskers, portrait painters and street traders congregate on the bridge, adding to the colour and bustle.

KEY

① **The three-arched medieval bridge** rests on two stout piers with boat-shaped cutwaters.

② **The Vasari Corridor**, supported on brackets, circumvents the Mannelli tower.

③ **Circular windows**, called *oculi* (eyes), light the corridor.

Piazza di Santa Trinità

❻ Piazza di Santa Trinità

Map 3C1 (5C3).

Noble Palazzi line this busy square. To the south is the Palazzo Spini-Ferroni, originally built in 1290, but much rebuilt in the 19th century; today, the ground floor houses the famous boutique of Salvatore Ferragamo *(see p276)*, specializing in shoes and leather goods. To the north, on the corner with Via

delle Terme, is the Palazzo Bartolini-Salimbeni. Built during 1520–29, it is one of the city's best examples of High Renaissance architecture. In between the two palazzi is a column of oriental granite, originally from the Baths of Caracalla in Rome and given to Cosimo I by Pope Pius IV in 1560. The figure of Justice on top was made in 1581.

Just south of the square is the Ponte Santa Trinità, considered the most beautiful bridge in Florence. It affords fine views of the surrounding hills and especially of the Ponte Vecchio *(see pp110–11)*. It was originally built in wood in 1252, and then rebuilt by Ammannati in 1567 as a monument to Cosimo I's defeat of Siena. Michelangelo is credited with the elegant design, based on an intriguing elliptical curve echoing those on the famous Medici tombs *(see p95)*. The statues of the Four Seasons at each end were added in 1608 for Cosimo II's marriage to Maria of Austria.

The bridge was restored after it was blown up by the Germans in 1944, and the statues were dredged up from the river bed.

Look west from here to the spectacular golden-yellow Palazzo Corsini (1648–56), with statues on the roof balustrade. It is one of the finest examples of Baroque architecture in Florence.

The nave of Santa Trinità

❼ Santa Trinità

Piazza di Santa Trinità. **Map** 3 C1 (5 C3). **Tel** 055 21 69 12. **Open** 7am–noon, 4–7pm daily. ♿

The original church, built in the second half of the 11th century by the Vallombrosan monastic order, was very plain – a reflection of the austerity of an order that was founded in Florence in 1092 to restore the simplicity of monastic rule. Gradually, the building became more ornate, with a Baroque façade added in 1593. Inside, the east wall shows traces of its Romanesque predecessor.

Ghirlandaio's frescoes in the Sassetti Chapel (right of the High Altar) show what the church looked like in 1483–6. In one scene, St Francis of Assisi performs a miracle in the Piazza di Santa Trinità, with the church and the Palazzo Spini-Ferroni in the background. The donors of the chapel, Francesco Sassetti and his wife Nera Corsi, are portrayed on either side of the altar. In another scene, St Francis is receiving the Rule of the Franciscan order from Pope Honorius III in the Piazza della Signoria. Sassetti, who

Ponte Santa Trinità

was general manager of the Medici bank, is shown with his son, Teodoro, and with Lorenzo de'Medici to his right, along with Antonio Pucci. Lorenzo's sons are climbing up steps with their tutors, led by the Humanist scholar Agnolo Poliziano, or Politian. The altar painting, *The Adoration of the Shepherds* (1485), is also by Ghirlandaio; he is the first, dark-haired shepherd. The black sarcophagi of Sassetti and his wife are by Giuliano da Sangallo.

❽ Santi Apostoli

Piazza del Limbo. **Map** 3 C1 (5 C4). **Tel** 055 29 06 42. **Open** 10am–noon, 4–7pm daily.

The little church of the Holy Apostles is, along with the Baptistry, among the oldest surviving churches in Florence. Florentines like to think that the church was founded in AD 800 by the first Holy Roman Emperor, Charlemagne, but it more likely dates to 1059–1100. The church has a simple Romanesque façade and the basilican plan typical of early, Christian churches, but with 16th-century side aisles.

Santi Apostoli fronts Piazza del Limbo, so called because there was a cemetery here for infants who died before they were baptized. Hence, according to medieval theology, their souls dwelt in limbo – halfway between heaven and hell.

Della Robbia glazed terracotta tabernacle in Santi Apostoli

❾ Ponte Vecchio

See pp110–11.

Fresco in a bedroom in the Palazzo Davanzati

❿ Palazzo Davanzati

Via Porta Rossa 13. **Map** 3 C1 (5 C3). **Tel** 055 238 86 10. **Open** 8:15am–1:50pm daily; second and third floors closed. **Closed** 1st, 3rd & 5th Mon and 2nd & 4th Sun of the month; 1 Jan, 1 May, 25 Dec.

Also known as the Museo dell'Antica Casa Fiorentina, the Palazzo Davanzati is preserved as a typical house of wealthy Florentines of the 14th century. The entrance courtyard was designed to trap unwanted visitors; holes in the vaulted ceiling were used for dropping missiles. In the more peaceful inner courtyard, a staircase links all the floors. In one corner is a well and a pulley system, so buckets of water could be raised to each floor – this ingenious mechanism was quite a luxury since most households had to fetch all their water from a public fountain.

The main living room on the first floor looks plain, but hooks beneath the ceiling show that the walls would have been hung with tapestries. Many rooms have bathrooms attached, and are decorated with frescoes of scenes from a French romance.

The restored Salone Madornale, where large gatherings would have been held, and the Sala dei Pappagalli (Parrots Room), with its frescoes and rich tapestries, are impressive. Restoration in two rooms dedicated to lace is ongoing.

⓫ Palazzo di Parte Guelfa

Piazza di Parte Guelfa. **Map** 3 C1 (6 D3). **Closed** to the public.

This characterful building served as the headquarters of the Guelph party and the residence of its captains from around 1266, after the Guelphs began to emerge as the stronger of the two medieval factions struggling for control over Florence. In the complex politics of the period, the Guelphs supported the Pope and the Ghibellines took the

Emblem of the Guelphs

side of the Holy Roman Emperor in the dispute over who should rule northern Italy (*see p50*).

The lower part of the building dates to the 13th century, but the upper part was added by Brunelleschi in 1431. There are *stemmae* (coats of arms) under the crenellations. The elegant open staircase, added in 1589, is by Vasari.

⑱ Santa Maria Novella

The Gothic church of Santa Maria Novella contains some of the most important works of art in Florence. The church was built by the Dominicans from 1279 to 1357. Beside the church is a cemetery walled in with *avelli* (grave niches), which continue along the façade and the wall beyond. The cloisters form a museum. Here, the frescoes in the Spanish Chapel show the Dominicans as whippets – *domini canes*, or hounds of God – rounding up the "stray sheep".

Green Cloister
The name comes from the green tinge to Uccello's *Noah and the Flood* frescoes, unfortunately damaged by the 1966 floods.

★ Spanish Chapel
The chapel used by the Spanish courtiers of Eleonora of Toledo, the wife of Cosimo I (*see p55*), has dramatic frescoes on the theme of salvation and damnation.

★ The Trinity
Masaccio's pioneering work is a masterpiece of perspective and portraiture (*see p30*).

Entrance to museum

Entrance (via courtyard)

Strozzi Chapel
The 14th-century frescoes by Nardo di Cione and his brother, Andrea Orcagna, were inspired by Dante's epic poem, *The Divine Comedy*. Dante himself is portrayed in the *Paradise* fresco on the left, along with members of the Strozzi family.

VISITORS' CHECKLIST

Practical Information
Piazza di Santa Maria Novella.
Map 1 B5 (5 B1).
Tel 055 28 21 87.
Open 9am–5:30pm Mon–Fri, 9am–5pm Sat, noon–5pm Sun.
✝ 7:30am, 6pm Mon–Sat; 8:30am, 10:30am, noon, 6pm Sun & religious hols. **Closed** 8 Dec, 25 Dec. 🚻 ♿ ♿

Transport
🚌 A, 6, 11, 36, 37.

★ Tornabuoni Chapel
Ghirlandaio's famous fresco cycle, *The Life of John the Baptist* (1485), portrays Florentine aristocrats and contemporary costumes and furnishings. Opposite is his other masterpiece, *The Life of the Virgin*.

★ Filippo Strozzi Chapel
Filippino Lippi's dramatic frescoes show St John raising Drusiana from the dead and St Philip slaying a dragon. Boccaccio set the beginning of *The Decameron* in this chapel.

KEY

① **Main door**

② **The billowing sail** emblem of the Rucellai *(see p108)* appears on the façade because they paid for its completion in 1470.

③ **Alberti added the volutes** in 1458–70 to hide the roofs over the side chapels.

④ **Monastic buildings**

⑤ **The arcade arches** are emphasized by grey and white banding.

⑥ **The walls** of the old cemetery are decorated with the emblems and badges of wealthy Florentines.

Interior
The nave piers are spaced closer at the east end to create the illusion of an exceptionally long church.

⑫ Mercato Nuovo

Map 3 C1 (6 D3). **Open** Apr–Oct: 9am–7pm daily; Nov–Mar: 9am–7pm Tue–Sat.

The Mercato Nuovo (New Market) is sometimes called the "Straw Market" because goods woven out of straw, such as hats and baskets, were sold here from the end of the 19th century until the 1960s. In fact, it was originally built in 1547–51 as a central market for silk and other luxury goods. Today's stallholders sell leather goods and souvenirs, and on summer evenings, buskers gather to entertain visitors.

To the south of the market is a little fountain called Il Porcellino. This is a 17th-century copy in bronze of the Roman marble statue of a wild boar that can be seen in the Uffizi. Its snout gleams like gold, thanks to the superstition that any visitor who rubs it will return to Florence some day. Coins dropped in the water basin below are collected and distributed to the city's charities.

Bronze boar in Mercato Nuovo

⑬ Piazza della Repubblica

Map 1 C5 (6 D3).

Until 1890, when the present square was laid out, this had been the site of the Mercato Vecchio (Old Market) and before that of the ancient Roman forum. A single column from the old market still stands on the square, topped by an 18th-century statue of Abundance.

Dominating the western side of the square is a triumphal arch, built in 1895 to celebrate the

One of the many pavement cafés in Piazza della Repubblica

fact that Florence was then the capital of Italy. The demolition of the Old Market was intended as the first step in a wholesale remodelling of Florence, but leading members of the English community led an international campaign opposing this grand scheme, which would have led to the destruction of almost every historic building in the city centre. Fortunately, the campaign was successful and the demolition halted.

The square, popular with both tourists and locals, is lined with pavement cafés, such as the very smart Gilli (No. 39r) or the Giubbe Rosse (No. 13–14r), so called because of the red jackets of the waiters. In the early part of this century, the Giubbe Rosse was the haunt of writers and artists, including those of Italy's avant-garde Futurist movement. Rinascente, one of Florence's department stores (*see p279*), is on the eastern side of the square.

⑭ Palazzo Antinori

Piazza Antinori 3. **Map** 1 C5 (5 C2). **Closed** to the public. Cantinetta Antinori: **Tel** 055 29 22 34. **Open** 12:30–2:30pm, 7–10:30pm Mon–Fri (also open 12 Saturdays a year at the manager's discretion). 🌀

The Palazzo Antinori, originally the Palazzo Boni e Martelli, was built in 1461–6 and, with its elegant courtyard, is considered one of the finest small Renaissance *palazzi* of Florence.

It was acquired by the Antinori family in 1506 and has remained with them since.

The family owns large and productive estates all over Tuscany and in the neighbouring region of Umbria, producing a range of well-regarded wines, olive oils and liqueurs. You can sample these in the frescoed wine bar to the right of the courtyard, the Cantinetta Antinori.

The wine bar also specializes in typical Tuscan cuisine, with dishes such as *crostini alla toscana*, together with traditional cheeses and a range of other produce from the Antinori estates.

Shop in Via dei Fossi selling reproduction statuary

⑮ Via dei Fossi

Map 1 B5 (5 B3).

Via dei Fossi and the nearby streets contain some of the most absorbing shops in Florence, many of them specializing in antiques and works of art and statuary, and in classic Florentine products. Giotti Ceramiche (Borgo Ognissanti 15r) sells ceramic patio furniture and pieces for the garden. Seek out Antichità dei Bardi (Via dei Fossi 11) for antiques and Antonio Frilli (Via dei Fossi 26r) for marble sculpture – original Art Nouveau works and copies of famous Renaissance pieces. Galleria d'Arte Pietro Bazzanti e Figlio (Lungarno Corsini 46) is a fascinating gallery dealing exclusively in ancient and Neo-Classical sculpture. Art & Libri (Via dei Fossi 32) sells antiquarian books. Attached to the convent of the same name, the frescoed Farmacia di Santa Maria Novella (Via della Scala 16r) dates to the 16th century and sells toiletries and liqueurs made by Dominican monks.

⑯ Museo Nazionale Alinari della Fotografia

Piazza Santa Maria Novella 14a. **Map** 1 B5 (5 B2). **Tel** 055 21 63 10. **Open** 10am–7pm Thu–Tue.
w alinari.it

The Alinari brothers began taking pictures of Florence in the 1840s, soon after the invention of photography. The firm they set up in 1852 specialized in supplying top-quality prints, postcards and art books to foreigners who flocked to the city during the 1800s. Today, this archive provides a fascinating insight into the social history of Florence over the last 150 years. The museum also houses a collection of cameras, documents and objects that illustrate the history of photography. There are around six temporary exhibitions a year held here.

⑰ Ognissanti

Borgo Ognissanti 42. **Map** 1 B5 (5 A2). **Tel** 055 239 87 00. **Open** 7:45am–noon, 4:45–6:30pm Mon–Sat. **Closed** Fri morning and first and last Mon of month. Cenacolo del Ghirlandaio: **Open** 9am–noon Mon, Tue & Sat (call 055 239 68 02 to book appointments for other times).

The church of All Saints, or Ognissanti, was the parish church of the merchant family of the Vespucci, one of whose members, the 15th-century navigator Amerigo, gave his name to the New World. Amerigo is depicted in Ghirlandaio's fresco of the *Madonna della Misericordia* (1472), in the second chapel on the right. Amerigo Vespucci

The cloister of Ognissanti, decorated with 17th-century frescoes

was the first to realize that the land discovered by Columbus was a new continent, not the eastern shore of the Indies. He made two voyages following Columbus's route and, because his letters enabled cartographers to draw the first maps (*see p79*) of the new land, it was given his name.

Ognissanti is also the burial place of Sandro Botticelli. His fresco of *St Augustine* (1480) can be seen on the south wall. It is complemented by Ghirlandaio's *St Jerome* (1480) on the opposite wall.

Alongside the church is a cloister and refectory containing Ghirlandaio's fresco The *Last Supper* (1480), with its background of birds and trees.

⑱ Santa Maria Novella

See pp114–15.

⑲ Stazione di Santa Maria Novella

Map 1 B4 (5 B1). **Closed** 1:30–4:15am daily. Train information: **Open** 7am– 9pm daily. Ticket office: **Open** 6am–9pm daily. Bag deposit: **Open** 6am–11pm daily. Assistance: **Open** 7am–9pm daily. **Tel** 055 235 61 20. Disabled passengers assistance: **Open** 7am–9pm daily. **Tel** 055 235 22 75. ℹ **Open** 8:30am–5:30pm Mon–Sat. Chemist: **Open** 24 hrs.

A fine example of modern architecture in Italy, the central railway station was designed in 1935 by a group of Tuscan "Functionalist" artists, including Piero Berardi and Giovanni Michelucci. They believed that a building's form should reflect its purpose. The exterior was designed to compliment the Gothic architecture of the city centre, while the interior uses metal and glass to create a feeling of space and light.

Ghirlandaio's *Madonna della Misericordia* (1472) in Ognissanti, with the boy Amerigo Vespucci

OLTRARNO

Oltrarno means "across the Arno", and living on the south bank of the river was once considered inferior. Here lived people who did not have sufficient wealth to build a palazzo within the city centre. That stigma did not change until the household of the Medici Grand Dukes moved to Oltrarno in 1550.

Medici Power Base

The Palazzo Pitti became the base from which Tuscany was ruled for the next 300 years. Eleonora di Toledo, the Spanish wife of Cosimo I, purchased the Palazzo Pitti in 1549. Suffering from a wasting disease, perhaps malaria or tuberculosis, Eleonora persuaded Cosimo that her health might well improve if they lived in the relatively rural setting of Oltrarno. Over the years, the Palazzo Pitti

increased almost threefold in size in comparison with the original plans, and the Boboli Gardens were laid out on the land around it. A few Florentine aristocrats followed the Medici lead and moved across the river to make their homes here. In the late 16th and 17th centuries, many palazzi were built in the area surrounding Via Maggio and Piazza di Santo Spirito. Today, this is primarily a quiet area full of artisan workshops and antique shops, contrasting with the elegant palazzi and the unfinished austere façade of Santo Spirito. The local merchants' association organizes guided tours, events and fairs to expose visitors to the artisan treasures on the south bank. It is a fascinating area to wander around and a great place to discover the true character of Florence.

Sights at a Glance

Churches
1 Santo Spirito
5 Santa Felicita
10 Brancacci Chapel *pp130–31*
11 San Frediano in Cestello

Museums and Galleries
2 Cenacolo di Santo Spirito
6 Palazzo Pitti *pp124–7*
8 Museo Bardini
9 Museo "La Specola"

Gardens
7 Boboli Gardens *pp128–9*

Streets and Piazzas
3 Piazza di Santo Spirito
4 Via Maggio

🔲 Restaurants *pp267–8*
1 Al Tranvai
2 Antica Porta
3 Borgo San Jacopo
4 La Casalinga
5 Fuori Porta
6 Hemingway
7 io Osteria Personale
8 Il Magazzino
9 O'Caffe
10 O Munaciello

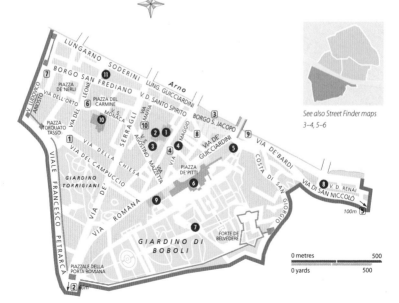

See also Street Finder maps 3–4, 5–6

Street-by-Street: Oltrarno

For the most part, the Oltrarno area consists of relatively small houses and shops selling antiques, bric-à-brac and foodstuffs. The Via Maggio breaks this pattern, with its numerous imposing 16th-century palazzi close to the Medici's Palazzo Pitti. As it is one of the main routes into the city, the road is busy and there is constant traffic noise. Step into the side streets, however, and you escape the noise and bustle to discover traditional Florence; restaurants are authentic and reasonably priced, and the area is full of workshops restoring antique furniture.

② Cenacolo di Santo Spirito
The old refectory is used to display medieval and Renaissance sculpture.

① Santo Spirito
Simplicity is the keynote of Brunelleschi's last church. It was completed after his death in 1446.

Palazzo Guadagni (1500) was the first in the city to be built with a rooftop loggia, setting a trend among the aristocracy.

Key

— Suggested route

0 metres   100
0 yards   100

Palazzo di Bianca Cappello (1579) is covered in ornate *sgraffito* work and was the home of the mistress of Grand Duke Francesco I *(see pp54–5)*.

Casa Guidi was the home of the poets Robert Browning and Elizabeth Barrett Browning from 1846–61, after their secret wedding.

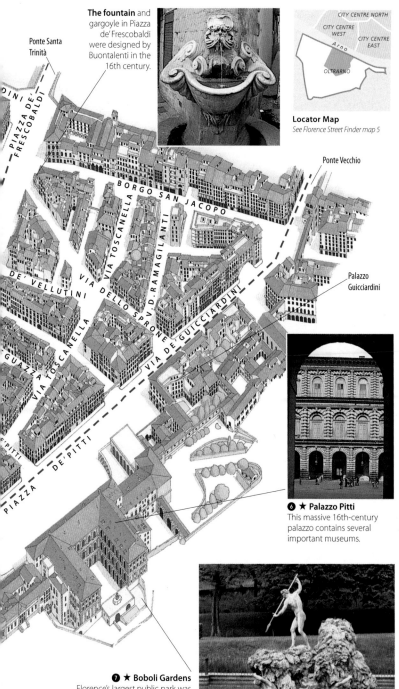

The fountain and gargoyle in Piazza de' Frescobaldi were designed by Buontalenti in the 16th century.

Locator Map
See Florence Street Finder map 5

Ponte Santa Trinità

Ponte Vecchio

PIAZZA DE' FRESCOBALDI

BORGO SAN JACOPO

VIA TOSCANELLA

VIA DELLO SPRONE

V. D. RAMAGLIANTI

DE' VELLUTINI

VIA DE' GUICCIARDINI

GUAZZA

VIA TOSCANELLA

PIAZZA DE' PITTI

DE' PITTI

Palazzo Guicciardini

❻ ★ Palazzo Pitti
This massive 16th-century palazzo contains several important museums.

❼ ★ Boboli Gardens
Florence's largest public park was built as the private garden to the Palazzo Pitti. It contains Classical sculptures such as Stoldo Lorenzi's *Neptune* (1588) spearing fish.

❶ Santo Spirito

Piazza di Santo Spirito. **Map** 3 B2
(5 B4). 🚌 D. **Tel** 055 21 00 30.
Open 9:30am–12:30pm, 3–5:30pm
Thu–Sat & Mon–Tue, 3–5:30pm Sun.
Closed Wed. 📷

The Augustinian foundation of
this church dates from 1250.
The present building has an
unfinished 18th-century façade,
which dominates the northern
end of Piazza di Santo Spirito.
Brunelleschi designed the
church in 1435, but it was not
completed until the late 1400s,
well after his death.

Inside, the harmony of the
proportions has been somewhat spoiled by the elaborate
Baroque baldacchino and the
High Altar, which was finished
in 1607 by Giovanni Caccini.
The church has 38 side altars,
decorated with 15th- and
16th-century Renaissance
paintings and sculpture, among
them works by Cosimo Rosselli,
Domenico Ghirlandaio and
Filippino Lippi. The latter
painted a *Madonna and Child*
(1466) for the Nerli Chapel in
the south transept.

In the north aisle, a door
beneath the organ leads to

a vestibule with an ornate
coffered ceiling. It was designed
by Simone del Pollaiuolo, more
commonly known as Cronaca,
in 1491. The sacristy adjoining
the vestibule was designed by
Giuliano da Sangallo in 1489.

❷ Cenacolo di Santo Spirito

Piazza di Santo Spirito 29. **Map** 3 B1
(5 B4). **Tel** 055 28 70 43. **Open** 10am–
4pm Sat–Mon. **Closed** 1 Jan, Easter
Sun, 1 May, 15 Aug, 25 Dec.
📷 📹 📷

All that survives of the
monastery that stood next to
Santo Spirito is the refectory
(cenacolo), now a small
museum. Inside is a fresco,
The Crucifixion (1360–65),
attributed to the followers
of Andrea Orcagna and his
brother Nardo di Cione.
In a city that has a wealth of
Renaissance art, this is a rare
and beautiful example of
High Gothic religious work.

The Fondazione Salvatore
Romano, a collection of
11th-century Romanesque
sculpture, is displayed in
the refectory.

The façade of Palazzo Guadagni

❸ Piazza di Santo Spirito

Map 3 B2 (5 B5). 🚌 D. 🏛 2nd
(Antiques) & 3rd (Organic) Sun of month.

This part of Florence is best
appreciated by wandering
around the square and its
market, looking at the many
furniture restorers' workshops
and medieval palazzi. The
biggest house in the square is
the Palazzo Guadagni at No. 10,
on the corner with Via Mazzetta.
It was built around 1505,
probably to the designs of
Cronaca. The windows have
distinctive stone surrounds with
tear-drop-shaped keystones. The
top floor forms an open loggia,
the first of its kind to be built in
the city. The loggia set a fashion
among 16th-century Florentine
aristocrats, who incorporated the
design into their own palazzi.

❹ Via Maggio

Map 3 B2 (5 B5).

Opened in the mid-13th
century, this road became a
fashionable residential area
after the Medici Grand Dukes
moved to the Palazzo Pitti in
1550 *(see pp124–5)*. It is lined
with 15th- and 16th-century
palazzi, such as the Palazzo
Ricasoli at No. 7, and antique
shops. Via Maggio runs into
Piazza di San Felice, where a
plaque marks the Casa Guidi.
The English poets Elizabeth
and Robert Browning rented
an apartment here after
eloping in 1847. Inspired by
Tuscan art and landscape, this
is where they wrote much of
their best poetry.

Colonnaded aisle in Santo Spirito

The Virgin from *The Annunciation* (1528), by Pontormo

❺ Santa Felicita

Piazza di Santa Felicita. **Map** 3 C2 (5 C5). **Tel** 055 21 30 18. **Open** 9am–noon, 3:30–6:30pm Mon–Sat.

A church has stood on this site since the 4th century AD, but the current building dates from the 11th century. It was extensively remodelled by Ferdinando Ruggieri in 1736–9, but some original Gothic features and the porch added by Vasari in 1564 were retained.

The Capponi family chapel to the right of the entrance houses two works by Mannerist artist Jacopo da Pontormo: a panel depicting *The Deposition* and an *Annunciation* fresco. Painted in 1525–8, they make use of vivid colours, such as salmon pink, light green, apricot and gold. The roundels at the base of the ceiling vault depict the Four Evangelists, also painted by Pontormo, with help from his pupil Agnolo Bronzino.

❻ Palazzo Pitti

See pp124–7.

❼ Boboli Gardens

See pp128–9.

❽ Museo Bardini

Via dei Renai 37. **Map** 4 D2 (6 E5). **Tel** 055 234 24 27. **Open** 11am–5pm Fri–Mon. **Closed** 1 Jan, Easter Sun, 1 May, 15 Aug, 25 Dec.

Stefano Bardini was a 19th-century antiquarian and avid collector of architectural materials – mostly salvaged from the churches and palazzi demolished when the Piazza della Repubblica was built in the 1860s *(see p116)*. In 1883, he built his palazzo in Piazza de'Mozzi almost entirely from recycled medieval and Renaissance masonry, including carved doorways, chimney pieces and staircases, as well as painted and coffered ceilings. The rooms are full of sculpture, statues, paintings, armour, musical instruments, ceramics and antique furnishings. In 1922, this collection of antiquities was bequeathed to the people of Florence.

Museo Bardini, Piazza de' Mozzi

❾ Museo "La Specola"

Via Romana 17. **Map** 3 B2 (5 B5). **Tel** 055 205 59 30. **Open** 9:30am–4:30pm Tue–Sun. **Closed** public hols. in English, on request. **W** msn.unifi.it

This unusual museum is in the Palazzo Rottigiani, built in 1775 and now used by the natural-science faculty of Florence University. The name "la Specola" refers to the observatory built on the roof of the building by Grand Duke Pietro Leopoldo in the late 18th century. It now contains the museum, which has a zoological section exhibiting vast numbers of preserved animals, insects and fish, and an anatomical section with some very realistic 18th-century wax models showing grotesque aspects of human physiology and disease. Not for the faint-hearted!

❿ Brancacci Chapel

See pp130–31.

⓫ San Frediano in Cestello

Piazza di Cestello. **Map** 3 B1 (5 A3). D, 6. **Tel** 055 21 58 16. **Open** 10–11:30am, 4:30–6pm Mon–Sat; 5–6:30pm Sun.

The San Frediano area, with its small, low houses, has long been associated with the wool and leather industries. The parish church of San Frediano in Cestello stands beside the Arno, looking across the river. It has a bare-stone exterior with a large dome that is a local landmark. It was rebuilt on the site of an older church in 1680–89 by Antonio Maria Ferri: the fresco and stuccowork inside are typical of the late 17th and early 18th centuries. Nearby is a well-preserved stretch of the 14th-century city walls. The Porta San Frediano, built in 1324, has a tower overlooking the road to Pisa. Its wooden doors have retained their original 14th-century locks and detailed ironwork.

The dome and plain façade of San Frediano in Cestello

❻ Palazzo Pitti

The Palazzo Pitti, begun in 1457, was originally built for the banker Luca Pitti. Its huge scale was the work of the Medici, who bought the palazzo a century later when building costs bankrupted Pitti's heirs. The family enlarged the palace and developed it into its current shape. It became the main Medici residence and subsequently all Florentine rulers lived here. Today, the richly decorated rooms exhibit treasures from the Medici collections *(see pp126–7)* and the Habsburg-Lorraine court.

Inner Courtyard
Ammannati designed the courtyard in 1560–70. The Artichoke Fountain by Francesco Susini (1641) was topped by a bronze artichoke, since lost.

★ Palatine Gallery
The gallery contains many masterpieces, among which is the highest concentration of Raphael's paintings.

Entrance to museums and galleries

★ Museo degli Argenti
As well as silverware, the museum displays gold, stone and glassware. This view of Piazza della Signoria *(see pp80–81)* is made of precious stones.

KEY

① **Brunelleschi** is thought to have designed the façade of the palazzo, which was later extended to three times its original length.

② **The side wings** were added in 1828 by the Dukes of Lorraine, who ruled the city after the Medici.

③ **Frescoes** by Pietro da Cortona

(1641–5) cover the ceilings in the Palatine Gallery.

④ **The Boboli Gardens** *(see pp128–9)* were laid out where stone had been quarried to build the Palazzo Pitti.

⑤ **The Carriage Museum** offers another glimpse of the sumptuous, opulent life of the dukes.

Galleria d'Arte Moderna
The gallery, on the second floor of the palazzo, spans the years from 1784 to 1924. *The Tuscan Maremma* (c.1850), by Giovanni Fattori, is a highlight of the collection.

Galleria del Costume
The clothes reflect changing fashion at the court of the Grand Dukes during the 18th and 19th centuries.

VISITORS' CHECKLIST

Practical Information
Piazza Pitti.
Map 3 C2 (5 B5).
Tel 055 29 48 83 (booking & information). Palatine Gallery & Royal Apartments, Galleria d'Arte Moderna, Galleria del Costume: **Open** 8:15am–6:50pm Tue–Sun. **Closed** 1 Jan, 1 May, 25 Dec. ♿ Museo degli Argenti & Museo delle Porcellane: (enter via Boboli Gardens, see p129). **Open** Mar: 8:15am–5:30pm daily; Apr–May & Sep–Oct: 8:15am–6:30pm; Jun–Aug: 8:15am–7:30pm. **Closed** 2nd & 4th Sun and 1st & 5th Mon of the month & public hols. ♿
📷 Ticket offices close 45 mins before the museums: 📷 for each museum. Palatine Gallery: ticket admits to Royal Apartments. Galleria d'Arte Moderna: ticket admits to Galleria del Costume: Occasional temporary exhibitions – call for details.
W **polomuseale.firenze.it**

Transport
🚌 D, 11, 36, 37.

⑤

Massive Windows
The windows of the Palazzo Pitti were built to be larger than the main door of the Palazzo Medici Riccardi.

Royal Apartments
The south wing was used for ceremonial occasions and receiving ambassadors.

Exploring the Palazzo Pitti

The Palatine gallery was realized by the Medici family and the Habsburg-Lorraine duchies in the 1600s and 1700s. The frescoed halls were hung with works from their private collections and the gallery was opened to the public in 1833. Other attractions include the royal apartments, the Medici collection of jewellery and treasures, the gallery of modern art and an exhibition of Italian clothing from the 18th, 19th and 20th centuries.

The Palatine Gallery

The gallery contains a superb collection of works dating from the Renaissance and Baroque. They are hung as the 17th- and 18th-century Grand Dukes wished, placed purely for their effect, regardless of subject or chronology. The decoration of the rooms in the gallery reflects the tastes and preoccupations of the time. Rooms 4 to 8 are painted with Baroque ceiling frescoes begun by Pietro da Cortona between 1641 and 1647, and finished by his pupil Ciro Ferri in 1666. They allegorize the education of a prince by the gods. In Room 1, the prince is torn from the love of Venus by Minerva (knowledge) and in the following rooms he is taught science from Apollo, war from Mars and leadership from Jupiter. Finally, Saturn welcomes him to Mount Olympus, home of the gods in Roman mythology.

The Palatine Gallery

The gallery is on the first floor of the Palazzo Pitti.

Madonna of the Chair, by Raphael (c.1516)

The other rooms in the gallery were private apartments and range from the opulence of the formal drawing rooms to the severity of Napoleon's bathroom (Room 27) *(see p59)*, in a suite of rooms designed by Giuseppe Cacialli

Mary Magdalene, by Titian (c.1535)

for the emperor in 1813 following his conquest of northern Italy.

Although some of the Medici collection has been transferred to the Uffizi over the years, the Palatine Gallery is still packed with masterpieces by artists such as Botticelli, Perugino, Titian, Andrea del Sarto, Pontormo, Tintoretto, Veronese, Caravaggio, Rubens and Van Dyck, among others. There are approximately 1,000 paintings here, providing a vast survey of 16th- and 17th-century European painting.

The Sala di Venere (Venus) is dominated by the statue of *Venus Italica*, by Antonio Canova, commissioned by Napoleon in 1810 as a replacement for *The Medici Venus* in the Uffizi Gallery, which was to be taken to Paris. Napoleon was not normally so generous, as his agents were renowned for stealing a large number of fine works of art from Italy during the Napoleonic Wars.

Several of Titian's works in the following rooms were commissioned by the Duke of Urbino. *La Bella* (1536) is a portrait of a lovely but unknown woman, whom he also used as a model in other paintings. His portrait *Mary Magdalene*, in the Sala di Apollo, was painted in 1530–35 in an overtly sensual manner, bathed in soft light.

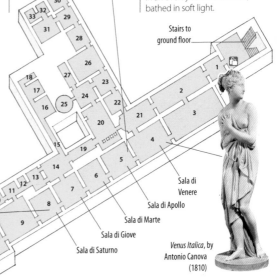

Stairs to ground floor

Sala di Venere

Sala di Apollo

Sala di Marte

Sala di Giove

Sala di Saturno

East stairs

Venus Italica, by Antonio Canova (1810)

Some of Raphael's best High Renaissance work is in the Palatine, including *Portrait of a Woman* (c.1516) and *Madonna of the Chair* (c.1510) in the *tondo* (roundel) form, which became very popular during the Renaissance.

The Consequences of War, by Peter Paul Rubens (1638), is an allegorical painting of the Thirty Years' War (1618–48) showing Venus preventing Mars from unleashing his fury on the cowering, beleaguered figure of Europe, who is depicted completely robed in black mourning.

The Throne Room, in the Royal Apartments

Royal Apartments

The Royal Apartments on the first floor of the south wing of the palazzo were built in the 17th century. They are decorated with frescoes by various Florentine artists and a series of portraits of the Medici by the Flemish painter Justus Sustermans, who worked at the court between 1619 and 1681. In the late 18th and early 19th centuries, the apartments were completely revamped in Neo-Classical style by the Dukes of Lorraine when they succeeded the Medici dynasty as the rulers of Florence *(see pp58–9)*.

The apartments are lavishly appointed with ornate gold and white stuccowork ceilings and rich decoration, as on the walls of the Parrot Room, which are covered with an opulent crimson fabric detailed with a bird design. The apartments'

varied ownership is revealed in their design, which embraces three distinct artistic periods.

Museo degli Argenti

This museum is on the ground and mezzanine floors, below the Palatine Gallery, in the rooms used by the Medici as their summer apartments. It displays the massive private wealth of the Medici dynasty: the collection encompasses rare and beautiful examples of ancient Roman glassware, ivory, carpets, crystal and amber, and fine works by Florentine and German goldsmiths. The pride of the collection are 16 *pietre dure* vases, displayed in the Sala Buia. These belonged to Lorenzo the Magnificent and are from the ancient Roman and Byzantine periods.

14th-century gold and jasper vase

The family's lavish tastes are reflected in the museum's polished ebony furniture inlaid with semi-precious marbles and stones. Portraits of the Medici hang throughout the rooms, including a series of the Grand Duchesses, and Cosimo I and his family carved in an onyx cameo.

Galleria d'Arte Moderna

Here, the paintings span the period from 1784 to 1924; many of them were collected by the Dukes of Lorraine to decorate

the Palazzo Pitti. The present museum has combined this collection with pictures donated by the state and various private collectors.

The museum contains Neo-Classical, Romantic and religious works, but probably the most important collection is of the group of late 19th-century artists known as the Macchiaioli (spot-makers), similar to French Impressionists. The Macchiaioli used bright splashes of colour to represent the sun-dappled Tuscan landscape. This collection was given to the city of Florence in 1897 by the art critic Diego Martelli, and includes paintings by Giovanni Fattori *(see p125)* and Giovanni Boldini. Two works by Camille Pissarro hang in the same room.

Galleria del Costume

Opened in 1983, the gallery is on the ground floor of the Palazzo Meridiana. This was designed in 1776 by Gaspare Maria Paoletti for the Royal Family; they lived until the abolition of the monarchy *(see p56)*. The exhibits reflect the changing tastes in the courtly fashion of the late 18th century up to the 1920s. Some rooms have been restored to correspond to a 1911 inventory, while the rest of the gallery has been renovated.

The Italian Camp after the Battle of Magenta (c.1855), by Giovanni Fattori

❼ Boboli Gardens

The Boboli Gardens were laid out for the Medici in 1550, one year after they bought the Palazzo Pitti. A perfect example of stylized Renaissance gardening, they were opened to the public in 1766. The more formal parts of the garden, nearest the palazzo, consist of box hedges clipped into symmetrical geometric patterns. These lead to wild groves of ilex and cypress trees, planted to create a contrast between artifice and nature. Statues of varying styles and periods are dotted around, and the vistas were planned to give views over Florence.

★ **Amphitheatre**
Stone for the Palazzo Pitti was quarried here, and the hollow was turned into a stage for the first-ever opera performances.

★ **La Grotta Grande**
The casts of Michelangelo's *Quattro Prigioni (see p98)* are built into the walls of this Mannerist folly (1583–93), which also houses Vincenzo de'Rossi's *Paris with Helen of Troy* (1560) and *Venus Bathing* (1565), by Giambologna.

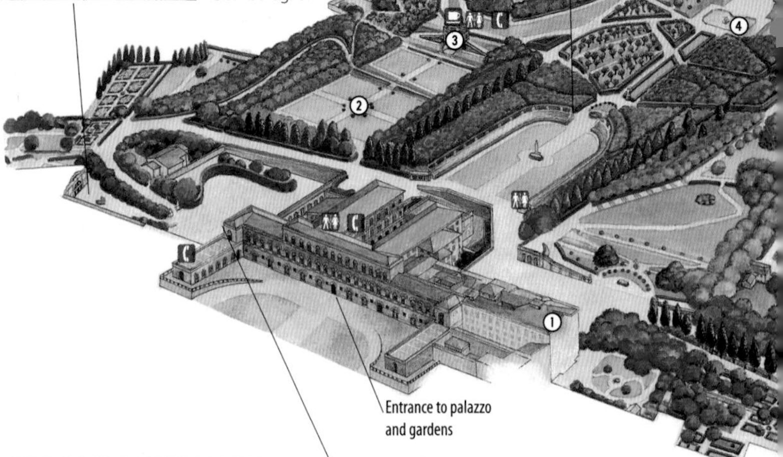

Entrance to palazzo and gardens

KEY

① **Galleria del Costume**

② **Ganymede Fountain**

③ **The Rococo-style pavilion**, housing the *kaffeehaus*, was built in 1774. The café is open during the summer and offers beautiful views over the city.

④ **The Neptune Fountain** was built in 1565–8 by Stoldo Lorenzi.

⑤ **Forte di Belvedere**

⑥ **The Porcelain Museum** is accessed via the Rose Garden.

⑦ **Hemicycle (semicircular lawn)**

Bacchus Fountain (1560)
A copy of the original by Valerio Cioli, the statue shows Pietro Barbino – Cosimo I's court dwarf – as Bacchus, the Roman god of wine, astride a turtle.

Lunette of Boboli Gardens
The Flemish artist Giusto Utens painted this picture of the Palazzo Pitti and Boboli Gardens in 1599.

VISITORS' CHECKLIST

Practical Information
Piazza de' Pitti.
Map 3 B2 (5 B5).
Boboli Gardens: **Tel** 055 29 48 83.
Open Mar: 8:15am–5:30pm daily; Apr, May, Sep & Oct: 8:15am–6:30pm daily; Jun–Aug: 8:15am–7:30pm daily; Nov–Feb: 8:15am–4:30pm daily.
Closed 1st & 4th Mon of month; 1 Jan, 1 May, 25 Dec.
🅿 ♿ Museo degli Argenti & Museo delle Porcellane:
Tel *see p125.* **Open** as for Boboli Gardens, above. 🅿
ⓦ **uffizi.com**

Transport
🚌 D, 11, 36, 37.

Viottolone
The avenue of cypress trees, planted in 1612, is lined with Classical statues.

★ **L'Isolotto** (Little Island)
The centrepiece of the moated garden is Giambologna's *Oceanus Fountain* (1576). The original statue of Oceanus has been moved to the Bargello *(see pp72–3).*

Entrance

Orangery
Zanobi del Rosso's Orangery (1777–8) was built to protect rare, tender plants from frost.

⑩ Brancacci Chapel

The church of Santa Maria del Carmine is famous for *The Life of St Peter* frescoes in the Brancacci Chapel, commissioned by the Florentine merchant Felice Brancacci, in around 1424. Masolino began the work in 1425, but many of the scenes are by his pupil, Masaccio, who died before completing the cycle. Filippino Lippi finished the work 50 years later, in 1480. Masaccio's use of perspective in *The Tribute Money* and the tragic realism of his figures in *The Expulsion of Adam and Eve* placed him at the vanguard of Renaissance painting. Many great artists, including Michelangelo, later visited the chapel to study his pioneering work.

St Peter Heals the Sick
Masaccio's realistic portrayal of cripples and beggars was revolutionary in his time.

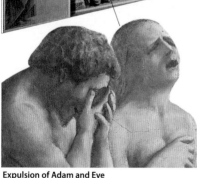

Expulsion of Adam and Eve
Masaccio's ability to express emotion is well illustrated by his harrowing portrait of Adam and Eve being driven out of the Garden of Eden, their faces wracked by misery, shame and the burden of self-knowledge.

KEY

① **Masaccio's simple style** allows us to focus on the figures that are central to the frescoes, without distracting detail.

② **The grouping** of stylized figures in Masaccio's frescoes reflects his interest in the sculpture of his contemporary Donatello *(see p73)*.

③ **In every scene**, St Peter is distinguished from the crowds as the figure in the orange cloak.

④ **St Peter** is depicted against a background of Florentine buildings.

⑤ **Masolino's** *Temptation of Adam and Eve* is gentle and decorous, in contrast with the emotional force of Masaccio's painting on the opposite wall.

Key to the Frescoes : Artists and Subjects

☐ Masolino
☐ Masaccio
☐ Lippi

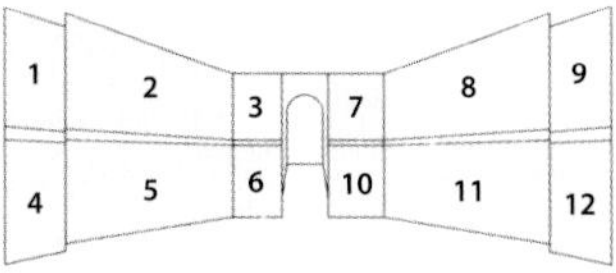

1 Expulsion of Adam and Eve
2 The Tribute Money
3 St Peter Preaching
4 St Peter Visited by St Paul
5 Raising the Emperor's Son; St Peter Enthroned
6 St Peter Healing the Sick
7 St Peter Baptizing the Converts
8 St Peter Healing the Cripple; Raising Tabitha
9 Temptation of Adam and Eve
10 St Peter and St John Giving Alms
11 Crucifixion; Before the Proconsul
12 The Release of St Peter

VISITORS' CHECKLIST

Practical Information
Piazza del Carmine. **Map** 3 A1
(5 A4). **Tel** 055 238 21 95.
Open 10am–5pm Mon, Wed–Sat;
1–5pm Sun (reservations recommended – call 055 276 85 58).
Closed Tue, public hols.

Transport
D.

Woman in a Turban
The freshness of Masaccio's original colours is seen in this rediscovered roundel, hidden behind the altar for 500 years.

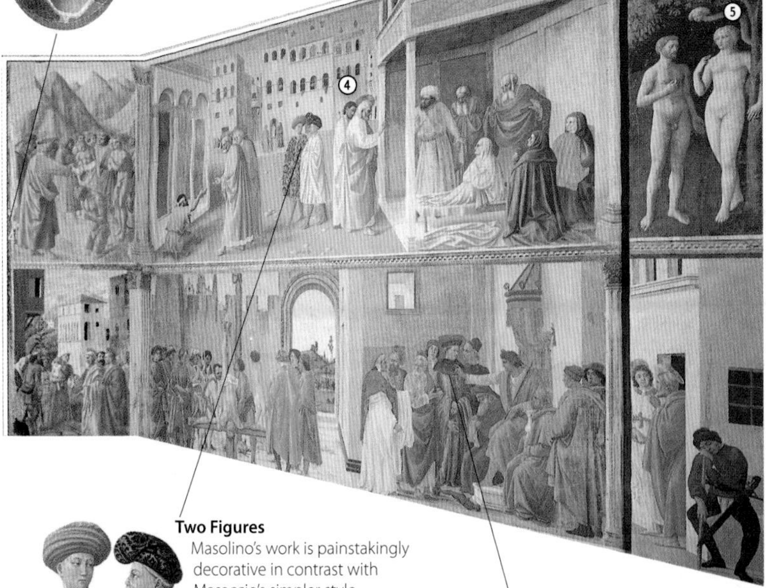

Two Figures
Masolino's work is painstakingly decorative in contrast with Masaccio's simpler style.

Before the Proconsul
Filippino Lippi was called in to complete the unfinished cycle of frescoes in 1480. He added this emotional scene showing the Proconsul sentencing St Peter to death.

FOUR GUIDED WALKS

In Florence, the countryside is never very far away – you can be walking down quiet, rural lanes within just a few minutes of leaving the Ponte Vecchio *(see pp110–11)*, in the bustling heart of the city. The first walk is popular with Florentines who like to stroll on a Sunday beneath the city walls and take in the panoramic views that can be enjoyed from San Miniato al Monte and the Piazzale Michelangelo. Fiesole, the setting for the second walk,

is 8 km (5 miles) north of Florence. It was once a powerful Etruscan city, but was later eclipsed by the rise of Florence, so that it is now merely a village. There are archaeological remains to provide a hint of its previous glory. The third walk shows Renaissance Florence at its best, taking in Brunelleschi's cupola and many of the grand palazzi. The last walk ends in the serene Piazza Santo Spirito after exploring the Florentine backstreets.

Roman ruins in Fiesole
(see Fiesole walk, pp136–7)

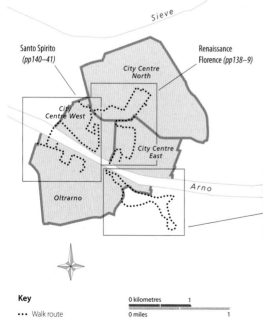

Santo Spirito
(pp140–41)

City Centre
North

Renaissance
Florence (pp138–9)

Sieve

City
Centre West

City Centre
East

Arno

Oltrarno

View over Florence from
Piazzale Michelangelo
(see San Miniato walk, pp134–5)

Key

••• Walk route

0 kilometres   1

0 miles   1

◀ Basilica di Santa Maria Novella, overlooking the *piazza*, on the Santo Spirito walk

A Two-Hour Walk to San Miniato al Monte

This walk takes you from the centre of Florence to the exquisitely decorated church of San Miniato al Monte, high on a hill in the south of the city. The route follows quiet lanes along the city walls, and then takes in the bustling Piazzale Michelangelo, packed with souvenir stalls, before returning to the town centre.

③ No. 19 Costa di San Giorgio

From the Ponte Vecchio ① walk south down Via de'Guicciardini and take the second turning on the left into the square fronting Santa Felicita ②. On the left of the church, take the steep road to the right, Costa di San Giorgio. No. 19 ③ was once the home of Galileo. The Porta San Giorgio (St George's Gate) ④ is straight ahead at the end of the lane.

Built in 1260, this is the oldest city gate to survive in Florence. The weathered fresco within the arch is *The Virgin with St George and St Leonard*, by Bicci di Lorenzo (1460). On the outer face of the arch is a carving of St George fighting the dragon, a copy of the original 1284 work, which has been removed and is being preserved in the Palazzo Vecchio.

The Forte di Belvedere ⑤ is to the right through the gate, and was designed by Bernardo Buontalenti in 1590. Originally, the fortress was built to guard the city against attack from its political rivals, but it soon became a private refuge for the Medici Grand Dukes. From here, there are extensive views over the Boboli Gardens ⑥ below, and across to the olive groves and cypress trees in the countryside south of the city. Head downhill along Via di Belvedere, which

runs along a stretch of city walls (to the left) dating from 1258. Porta San Miniato ⑦, a small arch in the wall, is situated at the bottom of the hill.

San Miniato al Monte

Turn right into Via del Monte alle Croci and walk uphill for 500 m (550 yds) to the Viale Galileo Galilei. Bear right and cross the road to the vast stone steps leading to the terrace in front of San Miniato al Monte ⑧. Catch your breath and admire the view of the Forte di Belvedere.

San Miniato al Monte is one of the most unspoiled of all the Romanesque churches in Tuscany. It was built in 1018 over the shrine of the early Christian martyr, San Miniato (St Minias). He was a rich Armenian merchant beheaded for his beliefs by Emperor Decius in the 3rd century. The façade was begun around 1090 and has geometric patterning in green-grey and white marble, typical of the Romanesque style. The statue on the gable shows an eagle carrying a bale of cloth,

⑧ The façade of San Miniato al Monte

⑤ View across to San Miniato al Monte from Forte di Belvedere

the symbol of the powerful Arte di Calimala (guild of wool importers), who financed the church in the Middle Ages. The restored 13th-century mosaic below the gable shows Christ, the Virgin and St Minias. Inside the church, the High Altar is raised above the nave and there is a Byzantine-style mosaic in the apse, again of St Minias with Christ and the Virgin. Below this is the crypt, built using columns salvaged from ancient Roman buildings. The floor of the nave is covered with seven marble mosaic panels of lions, doves and the signs of the Zodiac (1207); similar intarsia

13th-century mosaic on San Miniato's façade

work panels can be seen on the raised marble choir and pulpit. In the north wall is the funeral chapel of the 25-year-old Cardinal of Portugal, Iacopo di Lusitania, who died in Florence in 1439. Antonio Rossellino carved the figure of the cardinal guarded by angels on the elaborate marble tomb (1466). The terracotta roundels on the ceiling, showing the Holy Spirit and Virtues, were sculpted by Luca della Robbia (1461). Outside, the massive bell tower

was begun in 1523 by Baccio d'Agnolo, but was never finished. Cannons were installed here to shoot at the Medici troops during the Siege of Florence (see pp56–7). The cemetery ⑨ surrounding the church opened in 1854 and this contains tombs the size of miniature houses, built to show off family wealth.

⑩ San Salvatore al Monte

Leave San Miniato by an arch in the buildings to the west and follow the path that threads down to the church of San Salvatore al Monte ⑩. Here, steps lead down to the Viale Galileo Galilei; take a right turn to reach Piazzale Michelangelo ⑪. The piazzale was laid out in the 1860s by Giuseppe Poggi, and is dotted with copies of Michelangelo's famous statues. It is lined with souvenir stalls and has far-reaching views over the rooftops of central Florence.

Either take the No. 13 bus back to the city centre, or the stone steps on the west side of the piazza down to Porta San Niccolò ⑫, a 14th-century gateway in the city wall. Go left along Via di San Niccolò and Via de' Bardi, lined with medieval buildings. This includes the 13th-century Palazzo de' Mozzi ⑬ on Via de' Bardi; the Museo Bardini ⑭ (see p123) is opposite. From here, you can return along the Arno to the Ponte Vecchio ①.

⑪ David in Piazzale Michelangelo

Tips for Walkers

Starting point: Ponte Vecchio.
Length: 3 km (2 miles).
San Miniato al Monte: Open Apr–Oct: 8am–7pm daily; Nov–Mar: 8am–1pm, 3:30–6pm daily.
Stopping-off points: There are several cafés along the route.

Key

••• Walk route

0 metres   500
0 yards   500

For key to symbols see back flap

A Two-Hour Walk Through Fiesole

The village of Fiesole stands in the foothills of the Mugello region, 8 km (5 miles) north of Florence, and has substantial Roman and Etruscan remains. The area has been a popular summer retreat since the 15th century, thanks to its fresh breezes and hilltop position.

② The bell tower of the Duomo

Piazza Mino da Fiesole

The No. 7 bus arrives at its last stop, in Fiesole's main square ①, after a 30-minute journey from Florence through countryside dotted with villas. Settled in the 7th century BC, Fiesole was a powerful force in central Italy by the 5th century BC. It began to decline after the Romans founded Florence in the 1st century BC, but kept its independence until 1125, when Florentine troops razed most of the city. The Duomo of San Romolo ②, in the piazza, was begun in 1028 and has a massive bell tower. The bare Romanesque interior has columns that are

topped with reused Roman capitals. From here, walk up the square to the front of the 14th-century Palazzo Comunale ③. Here, there is a bronze statue of King Vittorio Emanuele II and Garibaldi, called *Incontro di Teano* (Meeting at Teano) ④. Returning to the church, take the first turning right, down Via Dupre, to the Roman theatre ⑤ and into the archaeological park.

After its defeat by Florence in 1125, Fiesole went into a decline, and many Etruscan and Roman

④ The bronze statue *Incontro di Teano*

remains went undisturbed until excavation in the 1870s. The Teatro, built in the 1st century BC, is used for the annual Estate Fiesolana festival *(see p39)*. Its tiers of stone seats can hold 3,000 spectators. Next to the theatre is the Museo Faesulanum ⑥, built in 1912–14. Inside are finds from the Bronze Age onwards: coins, jewellery, ceramics, bronzes and marble sculpture. The building is a copy of a 1st-century Roman temple, whose remains are in the northern part of the complex. It is built on Etruscan foundations, and part of the Roman frieze dating from the 1st century BC is still intact. There are some partly restored Roman baths close by ⑦, and, at the northern edge of the park,

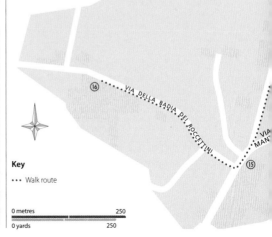

⑤ Roman theatre complex

Tips for Walkers

Starting point: Piazza Mino da Fiesole.
Length: 1.5 km (1 mile). Allow 2–3 hours for the walk to include time to visit the various museums. Note that Via di San Francesco is steep.
Badia Fiesolana: Open Sunday morning for services.
Getting there: No. 7 bus from Piazza di San Marco in Florence.
Stopping-off points: There are several cafés around Piazza Mino da Fiesole. The tiny ice-cream parlour Il Tucano (Via Gramsci 8) is also worth a stop.

Key

••• Walk route

0 metres	250
0 yards	250

VIA DELLA BADIA DEI ROCCETTINI

⑯

⑮

4th-century BC Etruscan walls ⑧. From the theatre, turn into Via Dupre to Museo Bandini ⑨ to the right, with a collection of medieval religious paintings built up by local aristocrat Angelo Bandini in the 19th century.

Back in Piazza Mino da Fiesole, turn right down Via di San Francesco, to the left of the Palazzo Vescovile ⑩. There are views over Florence and back to Fiesole ⑪ on the road up to Sant'Alessandro church ⑫, which has a Neo-Classical façade combined with a 9th-century Romanesque interior. Original Roman columns used in

Fiesole from Via di San Francesco

the nave are made out of *cipollino* (onion ring) marble. From here, carry on up to San Francesco ⑬, a Franciscan friary founded in 1399 and restored in 1907. It has a pretty cloister and a museum of artifacts collected by the monks.

From Fiesole to San Domenico

Retrace your steps or walk through the park back to the town centre. Continue down Via Vecchia Fiesolana. On the left is the Villa Medici ⑭, built in 1461 by Michelozzo for Cosimo de' Medici. Walk down Via Bandini and Via Vecchia Fiesolana to San Domenico. In this little hamlet is the 15th-century church of San Domenico ⑮, with two good works by Fra Angelico,

⑬ The 15th-century church of San Francesco

⑯ Façade of Badia Fiesolana

Dominican prior of the monastery here until 1437. *Madonna with Angels* and *The Crucifixion* are in the chapter house and were both painted around 1430.

Opposite, Via della Badia dei Roccettini leads to the Badia Fiesolana ⑯, a pretty church with a Romanesque façade of inlaid marble. The interior is decorated with local grey sandstone, *pietra serena*. The No. 7 bus back to Florence can be caught from the village square in San Domenico.

For key to symbols *see back flap*

A 90-Minute Walk Around Renaissance Florence

This walk takes in the Renaissance heart of the city and passes some of its great landmarks. Ideally, it should be done early on in your visit to get a real feel for the place, and if you incorporate a climb up Giotto's Campanile, you will get a bird's-eye view of the narrow streets, the characteristic red-tiled rooftops and the many towers that are not so easy to see from ground level.

rising above the surrounding rooftops, is the Badia Fiorentina ⑥, one of the city's oldest churches. Across the street is the forbidding ex-prison building that now houses the Bargello museum ⑦ *(see pp72–3)* and its superb collection of sculpture. Continue north up Via Proconsolo. At no. 10 stands Palazzo Pazzi-Quaratesi, once the home of the Pazzi family of bankers, protagonists in the famous Pazzi conspiracy

① View of Ponte Vecchio and the Vasari Corridor

Ponte Vecchio to Piazza di San Firenze

The walk begins in the centre of the Ponte Vecchio ① *(see pp110–11)*, where butcher's and grocery shops were first built in the 13th century, then replaced by goldsmiths at the end of the 16th century. The bust here is of Benvenuto Cellini, the most famous goldsmith of them all. Note the Vasari Corridor, with its round windows running over the shops on the eastern side of the bridge. Walk north up Via Por Santa Maria. A short way along on the right is Vicolo Santo Stefano and the ancient, deconsecrated church of Santo Stefano al Ponte ②, which was badly damaged in 1993 when a car bomb exploded in nearby Via Lambertesca. Further up Via Por Santa Maria is the Mercato Nuovo ③ *(see p116)*, a site on which there has been a market for centuries. The famous bronze *"porcellino"* (wild boar) is on the southern side; he is a copy of a copy of a sculpture by Tacca. It is said that if you rub his snout you will return to Florence one day. Turn right into Piazza della Signoria, past the open-air sculpture gallery of the Loggia dei Lanzi ④ and turn right to walk the length of the Uffizi

gallery portico *(see pp84–5)* and back along the opposite side. Turn right and take Via della Ninna out of the square; turn left at the end into Piazza di San Firenze ⑤. On the corner of Via dei Gondi stands Sangallo's late 15th-century Palazzo Gondi, which has a very graceful courtyard. The huge Baroque building opposite (1772–5) houses the law courts; to its left is the 17th-century church of San Filippo Neri, which has a painted ceiling.

Via del Proconsolo to Via dei Servi

At the north end of the square on the left, its tall, slim tower

④ Neptune Fountain in Piazza della Signoria

against the Medici of 1478. At no. 12 is Buontalenti's Palazzo Nonfinito *(see p74)*, begun in 1593 and "unfinished", which today houses the Anthropological Museum and its wonderfully old-fashioned collection of curios. Via Proconsolo emerges at the east end of the Duomo ⑧ *(see pp68–9)*. Skirt around the south side of this massive building, past the stone plaque known as *"Il Sasso di Dante"* ⑨, where the poet would sit and contemplate the construction of the cathedral; it's on the left just before Via dello Studio.

Enter Piazza di San Giovanni, with its extraordinary religious buildings, crowds of visitors, and postcard sellers. Just south of the Baptistery at the top of

Via de'Calzaiuoli is the 14th-century Loggia del Bigallo ⑩. Piazza di San Giovanni is the heart of religious Florence and if you have the time and energy to climb the 400-odd steps of Giotto's Campanile, you will be rewarded by a close-up of the great dome by Brunelleschi *(see pp68–9)*, and a view of the city

⑭ Façade of San Marco from Piazza San Marco

below. Afterwards, walk round the north side of the Duomo and turn left up Via dei Servi. At no. 10 is Palazzo Niccolini, with its typical mid-16th century façade ⑪. If the main door is open, you can see into the courtyard and small garden beyond, with its double loggia. A little further up, take a right turn into Via degli Alfani, where Brunelleschi's octagonal Rotonda di Santa Maria degli Angeli ⑫ sits on the right.

Piazza Santissima Annunziata to Santa Maria Novella

Go back to Via dei Servi and right to Piazza Santissima Annunziata ⑬ *(see p102)*, flanked on the right side by Brunelleschi's loggia and the Spedale degli Innocenti *(see p99)*. Turn left out of the square on Via Cesare Battisti and enter the Piazza San Marco ⑭. The portico immediately left dates from 1384 and was once part of a hospital. Today, it is home to the Accademia di Belle Arti, an art school founded in 1784. Also in the piazza is the convent of San Marco *(see pp100–1)*, where Fra Angelico's sublime frescoes are housed. Walk south down Via Cavour to Palazzo Medici-Riccardi ⑮ *(see p93)*, where the Cappella dei Magi is painted with Benozzo Gozzoli's delight-fully vivid fresco. Turn right along Via de'Gori to the church of San Lorenzo and the Medici Chapels ⑯ *(see pp94–5)*.

Walk past the chapels and bear right down Via del Melarancio. Cross Piazza dell'Unita Italiana and Via Panzani to make your way into Piazza di Santa Maria Novella, where the walk finishes at the Santa Maria Novella church, under Alberti's façade ⑰ *(see pp114–15)*. To return to the Duomo, catch the no. 1 bus from the Piazza.

Tips for Walkers

Starting point: The Ponte Vecchio
Length: 3 km (2 miles)
Getting there: The bridge is an easy walk from the city centre.
Stopping-off points: There are plenty of bars and cafés along the way.

⑧ Florence's cathedral, Santa Maria del Fiore, with its distinctive marble cladding

0 metres 300
0 yards 300

Key

••• Suggested route

A 90-Minute Walk to Piazza Santo Spirito

This walk begins under the clock at the Santa Maria Novella train station, which is one of the city's few significant modern buildings. It takes you to one of Florence's greatest churches, leads along one of the city's most fashionable shopping streets and visits Piazza Santa Trinità, with its elegant medieval palaces. You cross the river Arno into the western limits of the Oltrarno area, filled with fascinating artisan workshops, taking in Piazza del Carmine and finishing in the heart of the Bohemian district at Piazza Santo Spirito.

③ View across Piazza di Santa Maria Novella to the parish church

Stazione di Santa Maria Novella

Begin under the digital clock on the south side of Florence's main train station ① *(see p117)*. Designed in 1935, this is one of the few important "modern" buildings in a city dominated by Medieval and Renaissance architecture. The Italians invented the digital clock and the one here is an early version. Cross over Piazza della Stazione and bear left towards the back of the great parish church of Santa Maria Novella *(see pp114–15)* ②. Follow the arched recesses along one side of the church, which were once the family vaults of Florentine nobles, and you will emerge in the Piazza Santa Maria Novella ③, a once scruffy square that has undergone renovation. At the southern end is the

Loggia di San Paolo, a copy of Brunelleschi's famous Loggia degli Innocenti, dating from 1489. In the 17th century, the piazza was used for carriage races and the two obelisks sitting on turtles marked the turning points. Exit the square on the south side along Via dei Fossi and turn left into Via della Spada, a busy local shopping street. On the right is the former church of San Pancrazio ④, one of the oldest in Florence and, today, home to the Museo Marino Marini *(see p108)*. Turning left into Via delle Belle Donne, right into Via del Trebbio and right again will bring you out in Via de'Tornabuoni, with its impressive mansions and designer shops *(see p109)*. On the corner is Palazzo Antinori ⑤ *(see p116)*, built by Giuliano da Maiano from 1461–69; you can walk into the splendid courtyard. Note the 17th-century church of San Gaetano across the road, with its fine Baroque façade.

A designer shop in chic Via de'Tornabuoni

Piazza Santa Trinità

Walk past Palazzo Strozzi *(see p109)* and down to Piazza di Santa Trinità ⑥ *(see p112)*, which marks the meeting of three ancient Roman roads and is lined with noble palaces. Walk towards the river and turn right along Lungarno Corsini. At no. 2 is Palazzo Masetti ⑦, today occupied by the British Consulate but once the home of Bonnie Prince Charlie's widow, the Countess of Albany, who later married the dramatist Vittorio Alfieri.

The huge building a little further down on the right is Palazzo Corsini ⑧; it houses the Corsini

family's private art collection (entrance on Via del Parione), which includes works by artists such as Botticelli.

At Piazza Carlo Goldoni (named after the playwright whose statue is on the far side), continue west along Borgo Ognissanti, which opens onto the Arno at Piazza Ognissanti ⑨. Palazzo Lenzi, on the right, was built in the mid-15th century and has a façade

[Map showing suggested route through the area, with labels including: OGNIS, VIA MONTEBEL, Ponte Amerigo Vespucci, LUNGARNO DI SANTA ROSA, VIA LUNGO LE MURA DI SANTA ROSA, VIA L. BARTOLINI, VIA SANT'ONOFRIO, LUNGAR, VIA DEL PIAGGIONE, PIA, BORGO SAN FREDIANO, ⑩, PIAZZA DE'NERLI, VIA DELL'ORTO, V.D. DRAGO D'ORO, LEONE, PIAZZ, CAR, VIA DEL]

0 metres 300
0 yards 300

Key

••• Suggested route

decorated with *sgraffiti*; today it is home to the French Consulate. Overlooking the square is the church of Ognissanti *(see p117)*, which contains Botticelli's tomb and frescoes by Ghirlandaio. The latter's famous *The Last Supper* is housed in the convent

One of the artisan workshops in the Oltrano area

church of San Frediano in Cestello *(see p123)* faces the river. Return to Borgo San Frediano, turning right into Piazza del Carmine ⑫. The church of Santa Maria del Carmine is famous for its Brancacci Chapel *(see pp130–31)*, which is decorated with frescoes begun by Masolino and Masaccio, and finished by Filippino Lippi.

Leave the square at the southernmost corner along Via Santa Monaca and turn left into Via dei Serragli, where there is a pretty tabernacle. Walk towards the river and turn right into Via di Santo Spirito. Note the Medici Crest at no. 58r. The 13th–14th-century Torre de' Lanfredini stands at no. 40r and Palazzo Frescobaldi (home of the wine-growing Frescobaldi family) is at nos. 5–13. Turn into Via de' Coverelli and walk to Piazza di Santo Spirito ⑬, the heart of this Bohemian district and the walk's end. To return to the city centre, catch bus no. 11 to the Duomo.

refectory next door, reached through a frescoed cloister.

Across the river Arno

Cross the Ponte Amerigo Vespucci and walk on to Borgo San Frediano, a delightful area that's filled with artisan workshops and characteristic houses set on narrow streets. To the right is Porta San Frediano ⑩, built in 1324, whose massive wooden doors are still intact. The adjoining stretch of city wall is particularly well preserved.

Double back along Borgo San Frediano and turn left down Via Cestello into Piazza del Cestello ⑪, where the entrance to the

Tips for Walkers

Starting point: Santa Maria Novella Train Station.
Length: 3.5 km (2 miles)
Getting there: You can walk to the station from the city centre.
Stopping-off points: There are plenty of bars and cafés along the way.

⑬ A pavement café in Piazza di Santo Spirito

FLORENCE STREET FINDER

Map references given for sights, restaurants, hotels and shops in Florence refer to the maps in the *Florence Street Finder* only *(see How the Map References Work, opposite)*.

Where two map references are provided, the second (in brackets) relates to the large-scale maps, 5 and 6.

A complete index of street names is on pages 150–51. The key map below shows the area of Florence covered by each of the six maps in the *Florence Street Finder*. The maps encompass the four city-centre areas (colour-coded pink), which include all the sights. *(See also Florence City Centre, pp20–21.)*

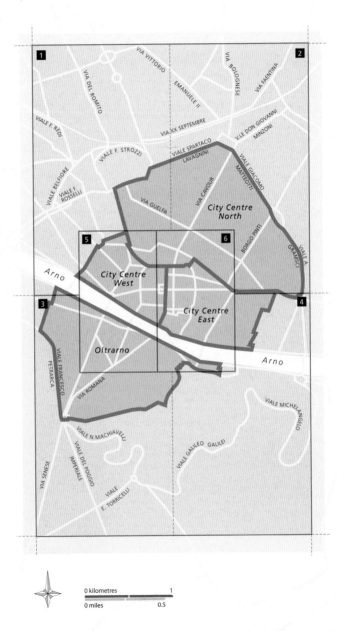

How the Map References Work

The first figure tells you which Street Finder map to turn to.

⑰ Ognissanti

Borgo Ognissanti 42. **Map** 1 B5 (5 A2) **Tel** 055 239 87 00. **Open** 8am–noon, 4–7pm.

The letter and number form a grid reference. You will find the letters at the top and bottom of the map and the numbers at the sides.

The second reference refers to the large-scale maps of Florence (5 & 6). This is read in exactly the same way as the first.

The map continues on map 3 of the Street Finder.

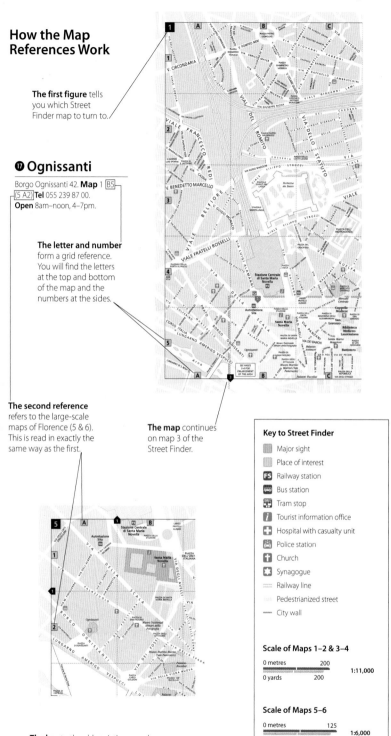

The key to the abbreviations used in the Street Finder is on page 150.

Key to Street Finder

- Major sight
- Place of interest
- **FS** Railway station
- Bus station
- Tram stop
- *i* Tourist information office
- Hospital with casualty unit
- Police station
- Church
- Synagogue
- Railway line
- Pedestrianized street
- City wall

Scale of Maps 1–2 & 3–4

0 metres	200	
0 yards	200	1:11,000

Scale of Maps 5–6

0 metres	125	
0 yards	125	1:6,000

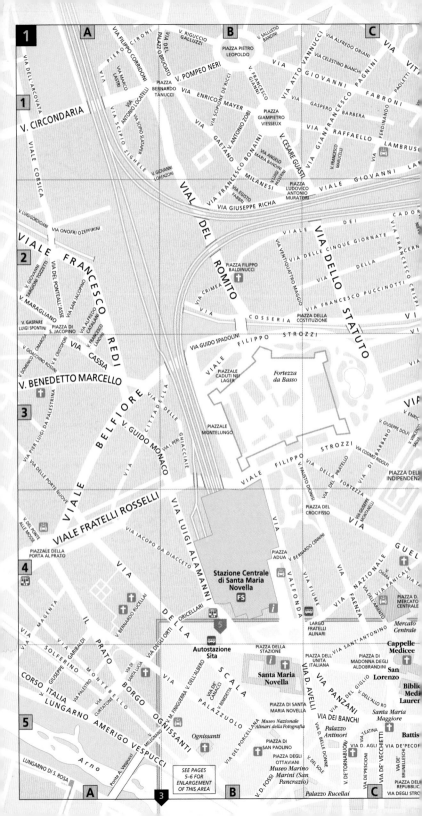

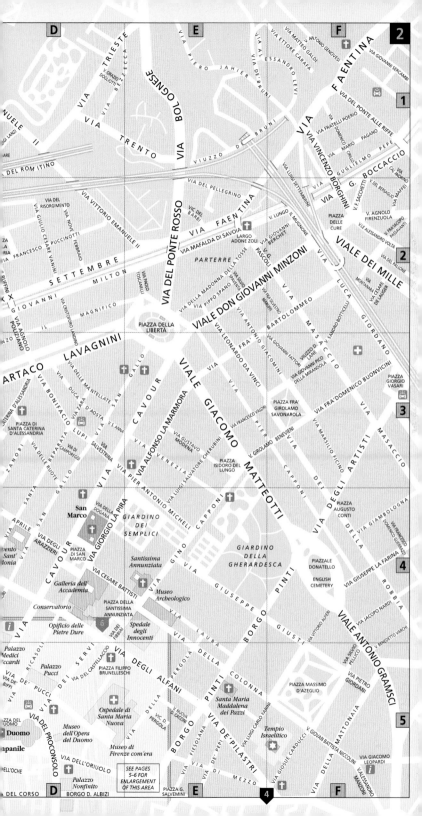

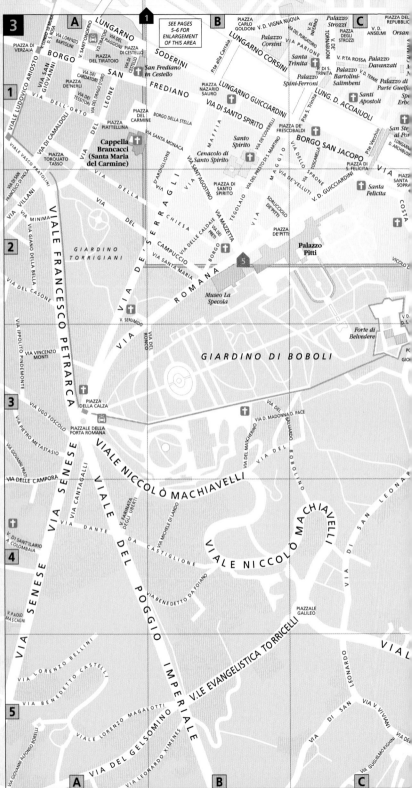

SEE PAGES 5–6 FOR ENLARGEMENT OF THIS AREA

A   **B**   **C**

PIAZZA DEL REPUBBLIC

LUNGARNO

BORGO

PIAZZA CARLO GOLDONI

V. D. VIGNA NUOVA

Palazzo Strozzi

V. D.

PIAZZA DEGLI STROZZI

V. D. ANSELMI   Orsan

PIAZZA DI VERZAIA

SODERINI

Palazzo Corsini

VIA PARIONE

V. P.TA ROSSA

Palazzo Davanzati

M

V. SANT'ONOFRIO

VIA SAN GIOVANNI

V. DI CAMALDOLI

LUNGARNO CORSINI

Santa Trinita

T. DI S. TRINITA

Palazzo Bartolini-Salimbeni

Palazzo di Parte Guelfa

1

VIA LUDOVICO ARIOSTO

VIA DEI CARDATORI

SAN

Santa Felicità

Santi Apostoli

Spe

LUNGARNO GUICCIARDINI

Palazzo Spini-Ferroni

Santi Apostoli

San Ste al Po

Erbc

VIA DELL'ORTO

FREDIANO

PIAZZA NAZARIO SAURO

VIA DI SANTO SPIRITO

LUNGARN D'ARCHIBUSE

San Frediano in Cestello

BORGO DELLA STELLA

PIAZZA DEL CARMINE

PIAZZA DI FRESCOBALDI

BORGO SAN JACOPO

Pte Vecchio

VIA

PIAZZA PIATTELLINA

VIA SANTA MONACA

MAFFIA

VIA DE' COVERELLI

VIA DELLO SPRONE

PIAZZA DI S. FELICITA

PIAZ SANTA SOPRA

Cappella Brancacci (Santa Maria del Carmine)

Cenacolo di Santo Spirito

Santo Spirito

VIA DEL PRESTO DI S. MARTINO

VIA DE' VELLUTI

Santa Felicità

COSTA

PIAZZA TORQUATO TASSO

VIA DELLA

VIA SANT'AGOSTINO

PIAZZA DI SANTO SPIRITO

VIA DEL SANTO SPIRITO

M A G G I O

V. D. GUICCIARDINI

VIA SAN FRANCESCO DI PAOLA

VILLANI

D'ARDIGLIONE

CHIESA

SERRAGLI

VIA MAZZETTA

TEGOLAIO

SDRUCCIOLO DE'PITTI

PIAZZA SANTA SOPRA

VIA GIANO DELLA BELLA

VIA MINIMA

DEL

VIA DELLE CALDAIE

BORGO

PIAZZA DE'PITTI

PIAZZ Z

2

GIARDINO TORRIGIANI

VIA DEL CAMPUCCIO

VIA SANTA MARIA

R O M A N A

Palazzo Pitti

VIA DEL CASONE

DEI

Museo La Specola

VICOLO Z

VIA IPPOLITO PINDEMONTE

VIA VINCENZO MONTI

VIALE FRANCESCO PETRARCA

VIA DEL RONCO

V. SERUMIDO

GIARDINO DI BOBOLI

Forte di Belvedere

PO GIO

3

VIA UGO FOSCOLO

PIAZZA DELLA CALZA

PIAZZALE DELLA PORTA ROMANA

VIA DEL BELVEDERE

VIA D. MADONNA D. PACE

VIA DEL BOBOLINO

VIA PIETRO METASTASIO

VIA GIOVANNI PRATI

VIA DELLE CAMPORA

VIALE NICCOLÒ MACHIAVELLI

VIA MASCHERINO

VIA DANTE DA CASTIGLIONE

VIA CANTAGALLI

V. DI SANT'ILARIO A COLOMBAIA

4

VIA

SENESE

VIA BARNATA DEGLI UBERTI

VIA MICHELE DI LANDO

VIALE NICCOLÒ MACHIAVELLI

VIA DI SAN LEONAR

V. PAOLO MASCAGNI

VIA DEL POGGIO IMPERIALE

VIA BENEDETTO DA FOIANO

PIAZZALE GALILEO

VIA LORENZO BELLINI

VIA BENEDETTO CASTELLI

V.LE EVANGELISTA TORRICELLI

VIA LEONARDO

VIA

5

VIA GIOVANNI ALFONSO BORELLI

VIALE LORENZO MAGALOTTI

VIA DEL GELSOMINO

VIA LEONARDO XIMENES

VIA DI SAN

VIA V. VIVIANI

VIA DE

VIA GUGLIELMO RIGHINI

A   **B**   **C**

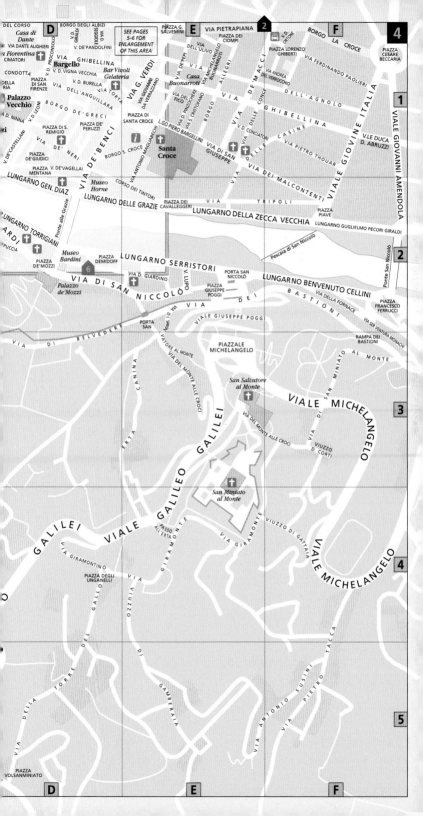

SEE PAGES 5–6 FOR ENLARGEMENT OF THIS AREA

4

D BORGO DEGLI ALBIZI

E PIAZZA G. SALVEMINI

VIA PIETRAPIANA

2

BORGO LA CROCE

F

PIAZZA CESARE BECCARIA

DEL CORSO
Casa di
Dante
a Fiorentina
CIMATORI
CONDOTTA
DELLA
RIA

VIA
Bargello
V. D. VIGNA VECCHIA
PIAZZA
DI SAN
FIRENZE

GHIBELLINA
Bar Vivoli
Gelateria

V.D. GIRALDI
V. DE'PANDOLFINI
V.D. SEGGIOLE

PIAZZA DEI CIOMPI

V.D. ORTONE

PIAZZA LORENZO GHIBERTI

VIA ANDREA DEL VERROCCHIO

VIA FERDINANDO PAOLIERI

Palazzo
Vecchio
D. NINNA
V.D.LEONI

Casa
Buonarroti

VIA DELL'ULIVO
VIA DE'PEPI
VIA MICHELANGELO BUONARROTI
BORGO ALLEGRI

DELL'AGNOLO

V.LE DUCA D. ABRUZZI

VIALE GIOVINE ITALIA

zi

BORGO DE'GRECI

VIA
DELL'ANGUILLARA
VIA
TORTA

VIA GIOVANNI DA VERRAZZANO
VIA DEL FICO
V.D. PINZOCHERE
VIA S. CRISTOFANO

VIA DELLE CASINE
V.D. CONCE

GHIBELLINA

V.LE DUCA

VIALE GIOVANNI AMENDOLA

1

PIAZZA DI S. REMIGIO
V. DE'CASTELLANI
V.DI
PIAZZA DE'GIUDICI

PIAZZA DE'PERUZZI

BORGO S. CROCE

PIAZZA DI SANTA CROCE

Santa Croce

VIA DI SAN GIUSEPPE

V.D. CONCIATORI

VIA PIETRO THOUAR

VIA DEI MALCONTENTI

PIAZZA MENTANA
V. DE'VAGELLAI

VIA DE' BENCI

CORSO DEI TINTORI

VIA ANTONIO MAGLIABECHI

PIAZZA DEI CAVALLEGGERI

VIA

TRIPOLI

PIAZZA PIAVE

LUNGARNO GEN. DIAZ

Museo
Horne

LUNGARNO DELLE GRAZIE

LUNGARNO DELLA ZECCA VECCHIA

LUNGARNO GUGLIELMO PECORI GIRALDI

UNGARNO TORRIGIANI
ARDI
PUCCIA

Ponte alle Grazie

Museo
Bardini

PIAZZA DEMIDOFF

LUNGARNO SERRISTORI

Pescaia di San Niccolò

Ponte San Niccolò

2

PIAZZA DE'MOZZI

Palazzo de'Mozzi

V.D. GIARDINO

VIA DI SAN NICCOLÒ

V. LUPO

PORTA SAN NICCOLÒ

LUNGARNO BENVENUTO CELLINI

VIA DELLA FORNACE

PIAZZA FRANCESCO FERRUCCI

VIA

DEI

BASTIONI

VIA SER VENTURA MONACHI

PORTA SAN

VIA DI

BELVEDERE

VIA DI MO

VIALE GIUSEPPE POGG

PIAZZA GIUSEPPE POGGI

PIAZZALE MICHELANGELO

RAMPA DEI BASTIONI

VIA

DI

SAN

MINIATO

AL

MONTE

3

VIA

CANINA

SALVATORE AL MONTE
VIA DEL MONTE ALLE CROCI

San Salvatore al Monte

VIALE MICHELANGELO

ERTA

VIA DEL MONTE ALLE CROCI

VIA DI

VIUZZO D. CORTI

GALILEO

GALILEI

San Miniato al Monte

PASSO ALL'ERTA MONTE

GIRAMONTE

VIUZZO DI GATTAIA

VIALE MICHELANGELO

4

VIALE

GALILEI

O

VIA GIRAMONTINO

PIAZZA DEGLI UNGANELLI

VIA

VIUZZO

DI

GAMBERAIA

VIA GIRAMONTE

VIA

GALILEI

VIA DELLA TORRE DEL GALLO

VIA ANTONIO SUSINI

VIA PIETRO TACCA

5

PIAZZA VOLSANMINIATO

D

E

F

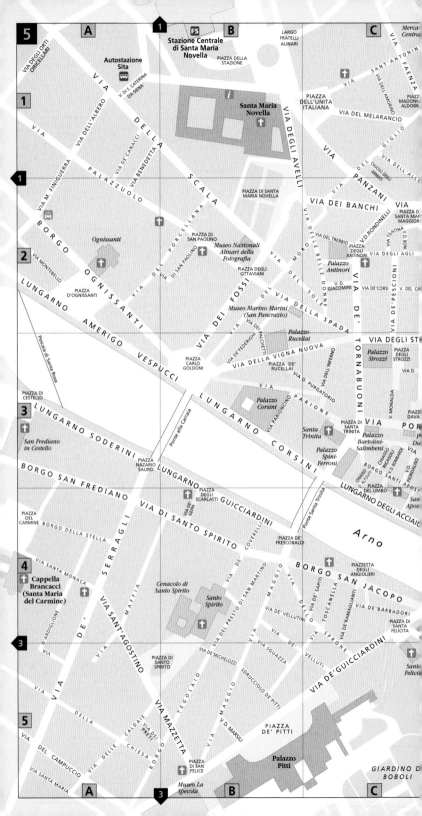

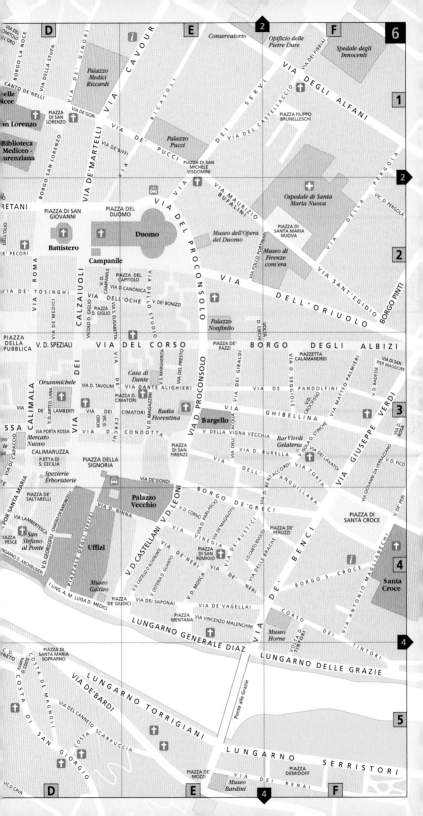

Street Finder Index

Key to Abbreviations Used in the Street Finder

d.	di, del, dell', dello, della, dei, de', delle, degli	**S.**	San, Sant', Santa,
		Santo	
Lung.	Lungarno	**SS.**	Santi, Santissima
P.	Piazza	**V.**	Via
P.ta	Porta	**Vic.**	Vicolo
P.te	Ponte	**V.le**	Viale

Map references in parentheses refer to the larger scale map.

TUSCANY AREA BY AREA

Tuscany at a Glance

Tuscany is rich in culture and has some truly stunning scenery. Out of Florence, most visitors' first port of call is Pisa, in Western Tuscany, with its Leaning Tower. Northern Tuscany has mountains and beaches, and Eastern Tuscany the lush forests of the Mugello. Siena and San Gimignano, in Central Tuscany, draw their own visitors, while Southern Tuscany, with its sparse vegetation and unspoiled beaches, is more off the beaten track.

Sights in Tuscany are grouped within their own sections in this book, corresponding with the colour-coded map below.

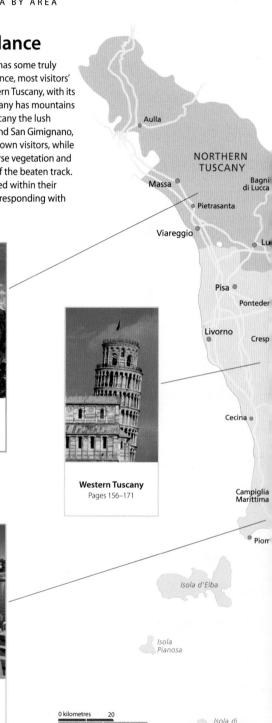

Aulla

NORTHERN TUSCANY

Massa

Bagni di Lucca

Pietrasanta

Viareggio

Lu

Pisa

Ponteder

Livorno

Cresp

Cecina

Campiglia Marittima

Piom

Isola d'Elba

Isola Pianosa

Isola di Montecristo

Northern Tuscany
Pages 172–193

Western Tuscany
Pages 156–171

Southern Tuscany
Pages 234–245

0 kilometres 20
0 miles 20

◀ View of Pienza across rolling hills scattered with poppies

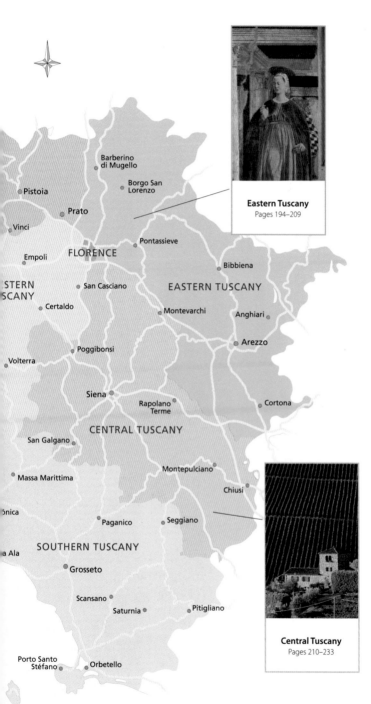

Eastern Tuscany
Pages 194–209

Central Tuscany
Pages 210–233

Barberino
di Mugello

Borgo San
Lorenzo

Pistoia

Prato

Vinci

Pontassieve

FLORENCE

Empoli

Bibbiena

STERN
SCANY

San Casciano

EASTERN TUSCANY

Certaldo

Montevarchi

Anghiari

Poggibonsi

Arezzo

Volterra

Siena

Rapolano
Terme

Cortona

CENTRAL TUSCANY

San Galgano

Montepulciano

Massa Marittima

Chiusi

ónica

Paganico

Seggiano

SOUTHERN TUSCANY

a Ala

Grosseto

Scansano

Saturnia

Pitigliano

Porto Santo
Stéfano

Orbetello

ísola del
Giglio

WESTERN TUSCANY

Tuscany's hard-working economic engine, this area is characterized by its factories and ports, particularly Livorno. There are also some extraordinary sights, most famously the Leaning Tower of Pisa. To the south, the windswept ancient Etruscan town of Volterra, standing high on a barren plateau, has some of the finest museums and medieval architecture in Italy.

From the 11th to the 13th century, when at the height of its powers, Pisa dominated the Western Mediterranean. Its strong navy opened up extensive trading links with North Africa, and brought to Italy the benefits of Arabic scientific and artistic achievement.

These new ideas had a profound effect on 12th- and 13th-century architects working in western Tuscany. Many of the era's splendid buildings – for instance, Pisa's Duomo, Baptistry and Campanile – are decorated with complex geometric patterns made from beautiful inlaid marble, alternating with bizarre arabesques.

During the 16th century, the Arno estuary began to silt up, ending Pisan supremacy. In 1571, work began to establish Livorno as the region's main port. This proved so successful that it remains Italy's second-busiest port. Pisa, meanwhile, is the gateway to Tuscany following the extensive development of Galileo Galilei airport. The Arno valley is mainly an industrial area, with huge factories producing glass, furniture, motorcycles, leather and textiles. Even so, there are some rewarding sights lurking within the urban sprawl, such as the Romanesque church of San Piero a Grado and the entertaining museum in Vinci, which contains models of many of Leonardo da Vinci's brilliant inventions. Though not as famous as the upscale resorts of Northern Tuscany, the long stretches of sandy beach on the Arno estuary are home to some delightful seaside towns, such as Marina di Pisa.

South of the Arno valley, the landscape is pleasant but unremarkable, consisting of rolling hills and expanses of agricultural land. But the imposing ancient town of Volterra, with its unmatched collection of Etruscan artifacts, demands a visit.

Landscape of rolling hills near Volterra

◀ The Leaning Tower of Pisa's distinctive angle, and the adjacent Duomo

Exploring Western Tuscany

Pisa, with its world-famous leaning tower, and Volterra, with its wealth of ancient Etruscan remains, are the highlights of the region. There is, however, much more to see, especially in the gentle hilly countryside that rises on either side of the Arno valley. It was here that Renaissance architects pioneered new styles of villa building; their work can be admired at Poggio a Caiano and Artimino. San Miniato is gloriously sited on a hilltop commanding extensive views; the museum in Vinci, on the other side of the valley, celebrates the inventive genius of Leonardo da Vinci.

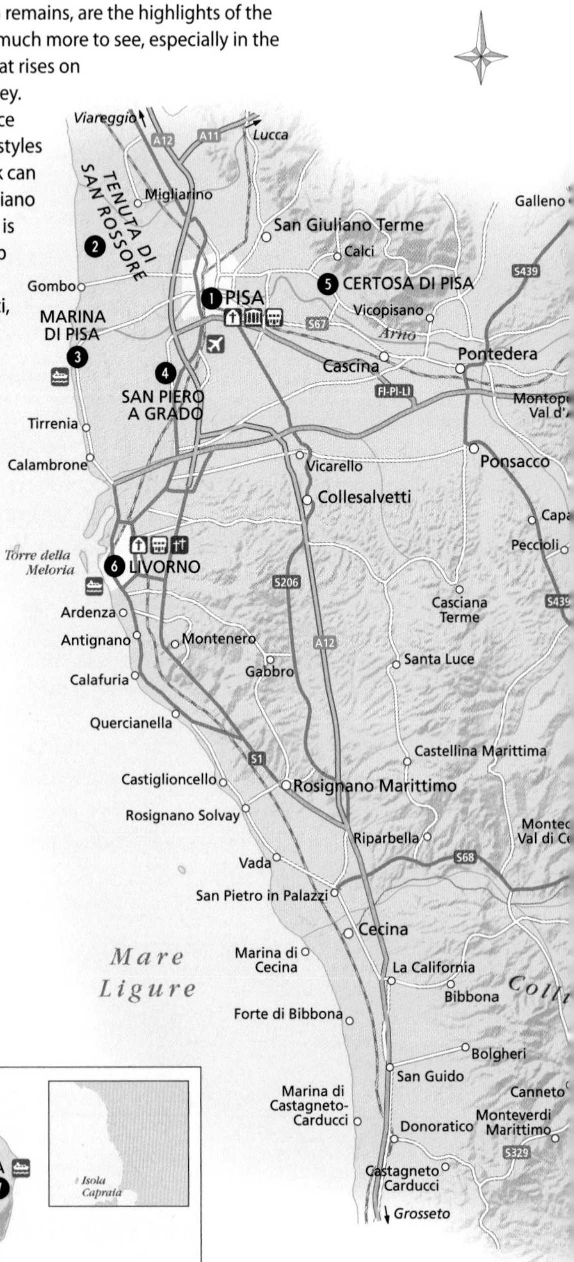

Sights at a Glance

1. Pisa
2. Tenuta di San Rossore
3. Marina di Pisa
4. San Piero a Grado
5. Certosa di Pisa
6. Livorno
7. Capraia
8. San Miniato
9. Empoli
10. Vinci
11. Artimino
12. Poggio a Caiano
13. Certosa di Firenze
14. Volterra

For hotels and restaurants see pp252–7 and pp264–75

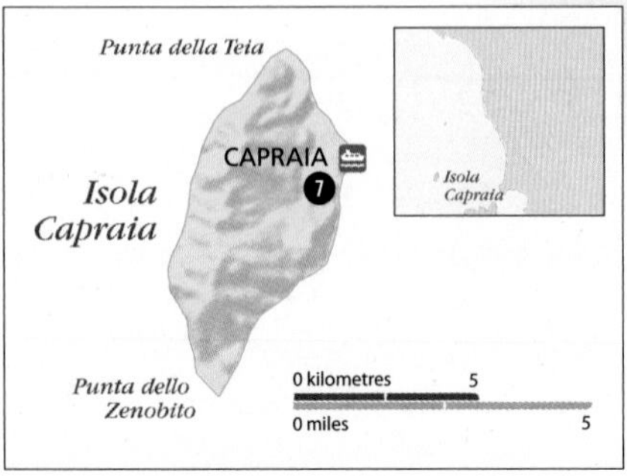

Pistoia

Campi
Bisenzio

Florence

POGGIO
A CAIANO **12**

Monte Albano
627m

Carmignano

Signa

VINCI **10**

ARTIMINO **11**

Montelupo Fiorentino

Lastra
a Signa

Florence

Fucecchio

S67

Arno

CERTOSA DI FIRENZE **13**

EMPOLI **9**

A1

a Croce
Arno

FI-PI-LI

Ponte a Elsa

Cerbaia

Pesa

SAN
MINIATO **8**

Elsa

San Casciano
in Val di Pesa

RA3

Montespertoli

Castelfiorentino

Tavernelle
Val di Pesa

S429

S2

Gambassi

Certaldo

Barberino
Val d'Elsa

San Gimignano

Poggibonsi

Siena

VOLTERRA **14**

S68

line di
lterra

Cecina

S439

marance

tallifere

Larderello

azzano

Castelnuovo di
Val di Cecina

Terme di
Bagnolo

Le Cornate
1060m

Monterotondo
Marittimo

0 kilometres   10

0 miles   10

Moored boats lining the canals of Venezia
Nuova in Livorno

Getting Around

Western Tuscany has a number of busy roads. An express route, the Fi–Pi–Li motorway, links Pisa with Florence, but travellers may find the old S67 more convenient for reaching the sights lining the Arno valley. The S1 coastal road skirts Livorno on its way to Rome.

The region is well served by buses and trains. A regular rail service runs between Florence and Pisa, stopping at the major Arno valley towns.

It can be difficult to reach Volterra, as there is no train service, but several buses depart each day from Florence, Pisa and Livorno.

Key

━━━ Motorway

━━━ Major road

━━━ Secondary road

┄┄┄ Minor road

╍╍╍ Main railway

┅┅┅ Minor railway

△ Summit

The S68 road to Volterra

For keys to symbols *see back flap*

❶ Pisa

From the 11th to the 13th century, Pisa's powerful navy ensured the city's dominance in the Western Mediterranean. Trading links with Spain and North Africa led to a cultural revolution *(see p50)*, reflected in the splendid buildings of the era: the Duomo, Baptistry and Campanile. Pisa's decline was assured when the Arno began to silt up. Salt marsh, partly a nature reserve, now divides the city from the sea.

Campo dei Miracoli

🏛 Campo dei Miracoli
See pp162–3.

▥ Museo delle Sinopie
Piazza del Duomo. **Tel** 050 387 22 10.
Open 10am–5pm daily.
This fascinating museum displays sketches from the fresco cycle that once covered the walls of Campo Santo cemetery *(see p162)*. The frescoes disintegrated when the cemetery was bombed in 1944, but the underlying sketches survived. They were removed from the walls for conservation before being rehoused in the museum. There are also displays showing how fresco artists went about their work.

▥ Museo dell'Opera del Duomo
Piazza Duomo. **Tel** 050 387 22 10.
Open Mar: 9am–6pm daily; Apr–Sep: 8am–8pm daily; Oct: 9am–7pm daily; Nov–Feb: 10am–5pm daily.

Housed in the cathedral's 13th-century former Chapter House, the museum was opened in 1986. All the exhibits were formerly in the Duomo and Baptistry. Exhibits, such as the intricately inlaid marble arabesque panels and fine Corinthian capitals, reveal the twin influences of Rome and Islam on Pisan architects in the 12th and 13th centuries. Be sure to see the imposing 10th-century hippogriff (half horse, half gryphon); this statue, cast in bronze by Islamic craftsmen, was looted by Pisan adventurers during the wars against the Saracens.

The museum also contains 13th-century statues and sculptures by Nicola and Giovanni Pisano, including Giovanni's ivory *Virgin and Child* (1300), carved for the Duomo's High Altar. There are paintings from the 15th to the 18th century, a fine Roman and Etruscan archaeological collection, and ecclesiastical treasures and vestments dating from the 12th century.

The museum cloister offers a wonderful view of the Leaning Tower *(see p164)*.

▥ Piazza dei Cavalieri
The Piazza dei Cavalieri stands at the heart of Pisa's student quarter. The huge building on the north side of the square, covered in exuberant black-and-white *sgraffito* decoration (designs scratched into wet plaster), is the Palazzo dei Cavalieri and houses one of Italy's most prestigious university colleges: the Scuola Normale Superiore. The site was originally occupied by Pisa's medieval town hall, but Cosimo I ordered its destruction when the city fell under Florentine rule. The council chamber, however, was spared and is now a lecture hall. The present flamboyant building was designed in 1562 by Vasari as the headquarters of the Cavalieri di San Stefano, an order of knights created by Cosimo in 1561. An equestrian statue of Cosimo by Pietro Francavilla (1596) stands outside.

10th-century bronze hippogriff

Virgin and Child polyptych (1321), by Simone Martini

VISITORS' CHECKLIST

Practical Information
Road Map B2.
98,929. Piazza Duomo
(050 56 04 64). Piazza Vittorio
Emanuele 16 (050 422 91).
Airport (050 50 37 00). Wed,
Sat. Shops: **Closed** Mon am.
Gioco del Ponte *(see p42)*.
pisaunicaterra.it

Transport
Galileo Galilei. FS
Centrale, Viale Gramsci.

Santo Stefano dei Cavalieri (1565–9), the knights' church, stands next to the Palazzo dei Cavalieri. Also designed by Vasari, it has a splendid gilded and coffered ceiling. The walls are hung with figureheads and battle standards. There is also a splendid organ (look out for notices of recitals).

On the other side of the Palazzo dei Cavalieri is the Palazzo dell'Orologio, incorporating the medieval town jail. The building, which now houses a library, was the scene of a most shameful and gruesome historical episode. In 1288 Count Ugolino, mayor of Pisa, was accused of treachery and imprisoned with his sons and grandsons. The keys were thrown in the Arno and the prisoners left to starve.

🏛 Museo Nazionale di San Matteo

Piazzetta San Matteo in Soarta. **Tel** 050 54 18 65. **Open** 9am–7pm Tue–Fri, 9am–2pm Sat & Sun. **Closed** 1 Jan, 1 May, 15 Aug, 25 Dec.

The medieval convent of San Matteo, with its elegant Gothic façade, is located alongside the river Arno. Many exhibits in the museum inside are poorly labelled and the rooms leading off the cloister are unnumbered. Nevertheless, the museum presents a unique opportunity to examine the complete sweep of Pisan and Florentine art from the 12th to the 17th century.

Grand Duke Cosimo I

Most of the earliest works portray the Virgin and Child. These include Simone Martini's fine polyptych (1321) and a 14th-century statue, the *Madonna del Latte*, attributed to Nino Pisano, another member of the talented family of sculptors. The half-length statue, in gilded marble, shows Christ feeding at his mother's breast. A number of early Renaissance pieces are of interest, particularly Masaccio's *St Paul* (1426), Gentile da Fabriano's radiant 15th-century *Madonna and Child*, and Donatello's reliquary bust of *San Rossore* (1424–7).

Pisa Town Centre

① *Campo dei Miracoli (pp162–3)*
② Museo delle Sinopie
③ Museo dell'Opera del Duomo
④ Piazza dei Cavalieri
⑤ Museo Nazionale di San Matteo
⑥ Santa Maria della Spina
⑦ San Paolo a Ripa d'Arno

0 metres 500
0 yards 500

For key to symbols *see back flap*

Campo dei Miracoli

Pisa's world-famous Leaning Tower is just one of the splendid religious buildings that rise from the emerald-green lawns of the "Field of Miracles". Lying to the northwest of the city centre, it is partnered by the Duomo, begun in 1063, the Baptistry of 1152–1284 and the Campo Santo cemetery, begun in 1278. These buildings combine definite Moorish elements, such as inlaid marble in geometric patterns (arabesques), with delicate Romanesque colonnading and spiky Gothic niches and pinnacles.

Campo Santo
The cemetery contains earth from the Holy Land and carved Roman sarcophagi.

The Triumph of Death
These late 14th-century frescoes depict various allegorical scenes, such as this of a knight and lady overwhelmed by the stench of an open grave.

★ Baptistry Pulpit
Nicola Pisano's great marble pulpit, completed in 1260, is carved with lively scenes from *The Life of Christ*.

KEY

① **Upper Gallery**

② **The domed** Cappella del Pozzo was added to Campo Santo in 1594.

③ **Frescoes** were added to the dome's interior after a fire in 1595.

④ **The Leaning Tower** *(see p164)* was completed in 1350, when its seven bells were hung.

⑤ **A frieze** shows that work began on the tower in 1173.

⑥ **Fragments** of the 11th-century marble floor survive beneath the Duomo's dome.

⑦ **Gleaming white** Carrara marble decorates the walls of the Duomo.

⑧ **This 12th-century wall tomb** is for Buscheto, the Duomo's original architect.

Practical Information
Piazza dei Miracoli. **Tel** 050 387
22 10. Duomo: **Open** daily. Mar:
10am–6pm; Apr–Sep: 10am–8pm;
Oct: 10am–7pm; Nov–Feb: 10am–
12:45pm, 2–5pm. ✠ 8am, 9:30am
daily; also 11am, 12:10pm, 6pm
Sun (5pm in winter). Baptistry
& Campo Santo: **Open** daily. Mar:
9am–6pm; Apr–Sep: 8am–8pm;
Oct: 9am–7pm; Nov–Feb: 10am–
5pm. Tower: **Open** daily. Jan &
Dec: 10am–5pm; Feb & Nov:
9:40am–5:40pm; Mar & Oct:
9am– 7pm; Apr–Sep: 9am–8pm
(30 people every 30 mins).
W opapisa.it

Transport
🚌 3, 11.

★ **Portale di San Ranieri**
Bonanno Pisano's bronze
panels for the south
transept doors depict
The Life of Christ. Palm trees
and Moorish buildings
show Arabic influence.

Cathedral Pulpit
The carved supports
for Giovanni Pisano's
pulpit (1302–11)
symbolize the Arts
and Virtues.

★ **Duomo Façade**
Coloured sandstone, glass and
majolica plates decorate the
lombard-style 12th-century façade.
Its patterned surface includes knots,
flowers and animals in inlaid marble.

The Leaning Tower of Pisa

All the buildings of the Campo dei Miracoli lean because of their shallow foundations and the sandy silt subsoil, but none tilts so famously as the Torre Pendente – the Leaning Tower. Begun in 1173, the tower began to tip sideways before the third storey was completed. Even so, construction continued until its completion in 1350. More than ten years of engineering interventions succeeded in stabilizing the tower in 2008. It should remain stable for at least 200 years.

Belfry
The bell chamber at the top of the tower is smaller in diameter than the other seven storeys. Its addition in 1350 brought the total height to 54.5 m (179 ft).

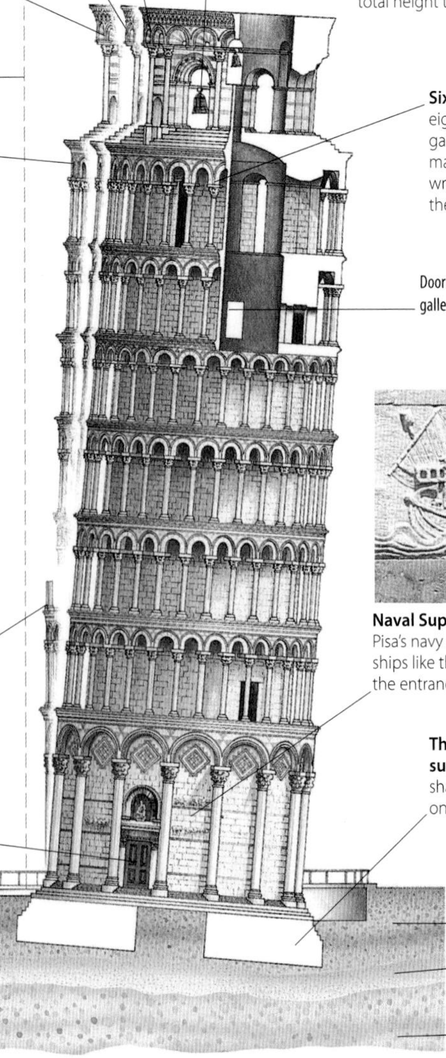

1993: 5.4 m (17.5 ft) from vertical

1817: 3.8 m (12.6 ft) from vertical

1350: tower leaning 1.4 m (4.5 ft) from vertical

The bells add to the pressure on the tower.

True vertical axis

1301: tower completed as far as belfry

Six of the tower's eight storeys consist of galleries with delicate marble arcading wrapped around the central core.

Marble columns

Staircase

Empty core

Doorway linking staircases to galleries

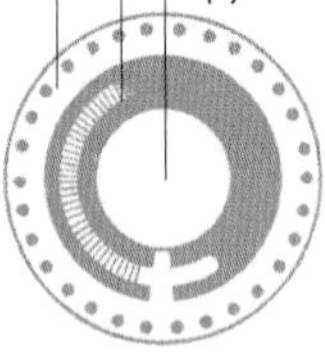

Central Staircase
This cross-section of the third level shows how the staircase rises around the tower's empty core.

Naval Supremacy
Pisa's navy consisted of small ships like the one carved by the entrance to the tower.

1274: third storey added; tower starts to lean

The tower is supported on a shallow stone raft only 3 m (10 ft) deep.

Entrance

Sandy and clay soil with stone and rubble

Grey-blue clay

Sand composed of a variety of minerals

Santa Maria della Spina, by the river Arno in Pisa

🏛 Santa Maria della Spina

Lungarno Gambacorti. **Tel** 055 321
54 46. **Open** Mar–Oct: 10am–1:30pm,
2:30–6pm Tue–Fri, 10am–7pm Sat &
Sun; Nov–Feb: 10am–2pm Tue–Fri,
10am–1:30pm, 2:30–6pm Sat & Sun.

The roofline of Santa Maria della
Spina bristles with spiky Gothic
pinnacles, miniature spires and
niches sheltering statues of
apostles and saints. The church
was built to house an unusual
relic: a thorn from the Crown of
Thorns forced on to Christ's head
during the cruel mock coronation
that preceded His crucifixion.

🏛 San Paolo a Ripa d'Arno

Piazza San Paolo a Ripa d'Arno.
Tel 050 415 15. ♿

This church with an impressive
12th-century façade is closed
indefinitely due to structural
instability. It was built in the
same Pisan-Romanesque style
as the Duomo (see pp162–3).

The Romanesque chapel
(see p48) at the east end is
dedicated to St Agatha. It is
built entirely from brick, with
a cone-shaped roof; Islamic
influence is said to account for
its unusual octagonal shape.

❷ Tenuta di San Rossore

Road map: B2. 🚌 Pisa. **Tel** 050 52 55
00 (050 53 01 01 or 53 37 55 for tours).
Open 8am–5:30pm Sat, Sun & pub
hols (Apr–Sep: to 7:30). 📷 8am–2pm
Mon–Fri (in English by appt).
🌐 parcosanrossore.it

North of the Arno, this area is
part of the Parco Naturale di
San Rossore nature reserve.

Wild boar and deer roam among
the pine forests and salt marsh.
Gombo, to the west, is where
the drowned body of the poet
Percy Shelley was found in 1822.

Moorings at Marina di Pisa, at the mouth
of the river Arno

❸ Marina di Pisa

Road map: B2. 🚹 3,000. 🚌
🛈 Sun in summer, Tue in winter.

Much of the salt marsh to the
west of Pisa has now been
drained and reclaimed, and a
large US Air Force base (Camp
Darby) now occupies the area
south of the Arno. There are
extensive sandy beaches on the
Arno estuary, and here lies
Marina di Pisa, a seaside resort
with some pretty Art Nouveau
houses, backed by pine woods.

On the drive there you may
catch sight of grazing camels –
these are the descendants of a
large herd established under
Duke Ferdinand II in the mid-
17th century. The village of
Tirrenia, with its sandy beaches,
lies 5 km (3 miles) south of
Marina di Pisa.

❹ San Piero a Grado

Road map: B2. **Tel** 050 96 00 65.
Open Apr–Oct: 9am–6:30pm daily;
Nov–Mar: 9am–5pm daily. ♿

San Piero is a handsome 11th-
century church built on the
spot where St Peter is believed
to have first set foot on Italian
soil in AD 42. According to the
New Testament Book of Acts, he
arrived at a set of landing steps
by the Arno. Archaeologists
have discovered the foundations of Roman port buildings
underneath the present church,
which stands at the point where
the Arno once flowed into the
sea. Silt deposits mean that the
church now stands some 6 km
(3.5 miles) from the shore.

An unusual feature of the
church is the lack of any façade.
Instead, it has semi-circular
apses at both the east and west
ends. The exterior is decorated
with blind arcading and with
Moorish-style ceramic plates set
into the masonry around the
eaves – an unusual feature that
it shares with the Duomo in San
Miniato (see p167).

The present church was built
during the reign of Pope John
XVIII (1004–9) and the varied
capitals of the nave come from
ancient Roman buildings.
High up on the nave walls
there are frescoes by Deodato
Orlandi, painted around 1300,
on The Life of St Peter. These are
interspersed with portraits of
all the popes from St Peter to
John XVII.

Interior of San Piero a Grado, with frescoes
by Deodato Orlandi

The 18th-century Certosa di Pisa

❺ Certosa di Pisa

Road map: C2 (località Calci). 🚍 from Pisa. **Tel** 050 93 84 30. **Open** 8:30am–6:30pm Tue–Sat; 8:30am–12:30pm Sun (adm half past the hour; last adm: 1 hour before closing). 🅿️

This Carthusian monastery was founded in 1366 and rebuilt during the 18th century. The splendid church is lavishly decorated, and some buildings form the University of Pisa's **Museo di Storia Naturale**. Exhibits include 16th-century anatomical wax models.

Nearby is the **Pieve di Calci**, a fine 11th-century Romanesque church. The unfinished campanile is alongside.

🏛️ Museo di Storia Naturale

Certosa di Pisa. **Tel** 050 221 29 70. **Open** Mar–May & Sep: 9am–4:45pm Mon–Fri, 10am–6:45pm Sat & Sun; Jun–Aug: 10am–7:45pm daily; Oct–Feb: 9am–3:45pm Mon–Fri, 10am–6:45pm Sat & Sun. **Closed** public hols. 🅿️ 🔱 partial.

🏛️ Pieve di Calci

Piazza della Propositura, Calci. **Open** daily. 🔱

❻ Livorno

Road map: B3. 🅰️ 168,370. 🚇 🚍 🚢 ℹ️ Piazza Cavour 6. (0586 20 46 11). 🚢

The fact that Livorno is now a bustling city (it is Italy's second-busiest container port) is thanks to Cosimo I. In 1571, he chose Livorno, then a tiny fishing village, as the site for Tuscany's new port after Pisa's harbour silted up. From 1607 to 1621 the English marine engineer Sir Robert Dudley built the great sea wall that protects the harbour.

In 1608, Livorno was declared a free port, open to all traders, regardless of religion or race. People fleeing wars or religious persecution, including Jews, Protestants and Greeks, settled here and contributed greatly to the city's success.

🏛️ Piazza Grande

When the architect Buontalenti planned the new city of Livorno in 1576, he envisaged the huge Piazza Grande at the heart of a network of wide avenues.

The square's original appearance has, however, been lost. This is partly due to controversial post-war rebuilding, which cut the square into two halves: the present Piazza Grande, to the south, and the Largo Municipio, to the north.

🏛️ Duomo

Piazza Grande. **Open** daily.
A prominent victim of Livorno's wartime bombing was the late 16th-century cathedral by Pieroni and Cantagallina. It was rebuilt in 1959, retaining the original entrance portico, with its Doric arcades.

The original building was designed by Inigo Jones, who served his apprenticeship under the architect Buontalenti. Jones later used an almost identical design for the arcades of his Covent Garden piazza in London.

🏛️ Piazza Micheli

The piazza, with its views of the 16th-century Fortezza Vecchia, contains Livorno's best-known monument: the *Monumento dei Quattro Mori*.

Bandini's bronze figure of Duke Ferdinand I dates from 1595; but Pietro Tacca's four Moorish slaves, also cast in bronze, were not added until 1626. Naked and manacled, the dejected slaves are a stark reminder that Livorno once had a thriving slave market.

Venezia Nuova canals

🏛️ Venezia Nuova

Originally laid out in the middle of the 17th century, this area, which includes the 18th-century octagonal church of Santa Caterina, is spread between a handful of canals, reminiscent of Venetian waterways. Although it only covers a few blocks, Venezia Nuova is one of the city's most scenic areas. The Fortezza Nuova,

Monumento dei Quattro Mori, by Bandini and Tacca, in Piazza Micheli

Fortezza Vecchia, Livorno harbour

surrounded by a moat, dates to 1590. Its interior has been converted to a public park.

Piazza XX Settembre

Lying south of the Fortezza Nuova, the piazza is renowned for its bustling "American Market". The market's name derives from the large amounts of American army surplus sold here after World War II.

A US army base, Camp Darby, still operates to the north of Livorno.

English Cemetery

Via Giuseppe Verdi 63. **Tel** 0586 83 97 72. **Open** by appt.

The 19th-century memorials to British and American *emigrés*, long untended, are considerably overgrown. Among them is the grave of Tobias Smollett (1721–71), the misanthropic Scottish novelist. He claimed to live in Italy for health reasons, and, predictably, constantly complained about the place.

Museo Civico

Via San Jacopo Acquaviva. **Tel** 0586 80 80 01. **Open** 10am–1pm, 4–7pm Tue–Sun. **Closed** Easter, 1 May.

The Museo Civico houses temporary exhibitions and several paintings by Giovanni Fattori (1825–1908), an artist of the Macchiaioli school *(see p127)*, whose work was similar to that of the French Impressionists.

❼ Capraia

from Livorno. 300.
Pro Loco, The Port (0586 90 51 38).

This tiny mountainous island appeals mainly to keen bird watchers and divers who go to explore the rocky coastline.

Nearby Gorgona, a penal colony, can also be visited by booking in advance. Contact the tourist information office in Livorno.

❽ San Miniato

Road map: C2. 3,852.
Piazza del Popolo 1 (0571 427 45).
Tue, 1st & 2nd Sun of each month.

San Miniato suffers from its proximity to the vast industrial conurbation of the Arno valley. Straddling the crest of one of the region's highest hills, it manages, however, to remain somewhat aloof. There are a number of fine historic buildings, including the 13th-century Rocca (castle) built for Frederick II (1194–1250), the German Holy Roman Emperor.

The town played a major part in Frederick's Italian military campaigns. He dreamed of rebuilding the ancient Roman empire that lay divided between papal and imperial authority. To this end, he conquered large areas of Italy. His battles fuelled fierce local struggles between the imperial Ghibellines and the papal Guelphs *(see p50)*.

Local people still refer to the town as San Miniato *al Tedesco* (of the German).

Façade of the Duomo in San Miniato

Duomo

Piazza del Duomo. **Open** daily.
Only the red-brick façade survives from the original 12th-century building. The majolica plates set within it show evidence of trade with Spain or North Africa. They seem to represent the North Star and the constellations of Ursus Major and Minor: key reference points for early navigators.

The campanile, the Torre di Matilda, is named in honour of the great Countess Matilda *(see p49)*, who was born in Livorno in 1046.

🎴 Piazza della Repubblica

The Piazza della Repubblica (also known as the Piazza del Seminario) occupies a long, narrow space dominated by the decorated façade of the 17th-century seminary. The frescoes and *sgraffito* (scenes scratched out of plaster) on the façade show allegories of the Virtues painted below quotations from key religious texts, for instance, the writings of Pope Gregory (540–604).

To the right of the seminary are several well-restored 15th-century shops. Buildings like these can be seen in many medieval frescoes, such as Lorenzetti's 14th-century *Good Government* (pp222–3).

Façade of the seminary in Piazza della Repubblica

🏛 Museo Diocesano d'Arte Sacra

Piazza Duomo. **Tel** 0571 41 82 71.
Open 9am–1pm Mon–Fri & 4:30–7pm Tue & Thu. 🎴

Next to the Duomo, the Museo Diocesano d'Arte Sacra contains a number of important 15th-century works from local churches, including a *Crucifixion* by Filippo Lippi and a bust of Christ attributed to Verrocchio.

🏰 Rocca

Open 9:30am–12:30pm, 3–5pm Tue–Sun. Book at the port authority; tourist office or private guide required.

A staircase behind the Museo Diocesano leads towards Frederick II's 13th-century Rocca (castle). While the remains are run down, the site offers extraordinary views along the entire Arno valley, from Fiesole to Pisa.

Piazza Farinata degli Uberti in Empoli

❾ Empoli

Road map: C2. 🔼 43,500. 🚉 🚌
ℹ️ Via Giuseppe del Papa 98 (0571 76 115). 🛒 Thu.

An industrial town, specializing in textiles and glass manufacturing, Empoli is worth visiting for the excellent Museo della Collegiata.

🎴 Piazza Farinata degli Uberti

Empoli's arcaded main square is surrounded by a number of 12th-century buildings, notably the church of Sant'Andrea, with its black-and-white marble façade. The large fountain dating back to 1827, with water nymphs and lions, is by Luigi Pampaloni.

🏛 Museo della Collegiata di Sant'Andrea

Piazza della Propositura 3.
Tel 0571 762 84.
Open 9am–noon, 4–7pm Tue–Sun. **Closed** public & relig hols. 🎴

The museum contains a collection of Renaissance paintings and sculpture. Of particular interest are Masolino's *Pietà* fresco (1425) and a marble font by Rossellino, dating from 1447.

🏰 Santo Stefano

Via dei Neri. **Open** for concerts & exhibitions.

Visitors to Santo Stefano can see fresco fragments by Masolino, dating from 1424, and two 15th-century Annunciation statues by Rossellino. Bicci di Lorenzo's painting, *St Nicholas*

Pietà, by Masolino, in Museo della Collegiata

of Tolentino (1445), in the second chapel on the north side, shows Empoli as it was in the mid-15th century.

❿ Vinci

Road map: C2. 🔼 2,000. 🚌 🛒 Wed.
🌐 terredelrinascimento.it

This hilltop town is the birthplace of Leonardo da Vinci (1452–1519). To celebrate his extraordinary genius, the 13th-century castle in the centre of the town was restored in 1952 to create the **Museo Leonardiano**. Among the displays are wooden models of Leonardo's machines and inventions, based on the drawings from his notebooks, copies of which are shown alongside. These range from his conception of a car, to an armoured tank and even a machine-gun. A pair of skis, designed for walking on water, show that he could occasionally miss the mark. The museum is best avoided on Sundays, when it can be extremely crowded.

Close to the museum is Santo Stefano church and the font in which Leonardo was baptized. His actual birthplace, the **Casa di Leonardo**, is 2 km (1.25 miles) from the town centre at Anchiano. This simple farmhouse is worth visiting if you feel like a pleasant, undemanding walk through superb poppy fields; but don't expect to be overawed by the exhibits, which mostly consist of a few reproduction drawings.

Museo Leonardiano
Castello dei Conti Guidi.
Tel 0571 560 55. **Open** Mar–Oct: 9:30am–7pm daily; Nov–Feb: 9:30am–6pm daily.

Casa di Leonardo
Anchiano. **Tel** 0571 560 55.
Open Mar–Oct: 9:30am–7pm daily; Nov–Feb: 9:30am–6pm daily.

Model bicycle based on drawings by Leonardo, Museo Leonardiano

⓫ Artimino

Road map: C2.

Artimino is a fine example of a *borgo*, a small fortified hamlet, and is remarkable for the unspoiled Romanesque church of San Leonardo. The **Archaeology Museum**, located in an old wine cellar, exhibits Etruscan artifacts.

Outside the walls and up the hill lies the **Villa di Artimino**, designed by Buontalenti in 1594 for Grand Duke Ferdinando I. It is often referred to as the "Villa of a Hundred Chimneys", because of the numerous and highly ornate chimney pots crowding the roofline. The building is now a conference and wedding centre.

The church of **San Michele** in Carmignano, only 5 km (3 miles) north of Artimino, contains Pontormo's (1494–1557) great masterpiece, *The Visitation* (1530).

Archaeology Museum
Piazza San Carlo 3. **Tel** 055 871 81 24.
Open Feb–Oct: 9:30am–1:30pm Thu–Tue & 3–6pm Sat, Sun & hols; Nov–Jan: 9:30am–1:30pm, 2–4pm Sat, Sun & hols.

Villa di Artimino
Via Papa Giovanni XXIII.
Tel 055 875 14 27. **W** artimino.com

San Michele
Pza. SS Francesco e Michele, Carmignano. **Tel** 055 871 20 46.
Open daily.

⓬ Poggio a Caiano

Road map: C2. **Tel** 055 87 70 12.
Open daily (except 2nd and 3rd Mon of each month).

The Villa di Poggio a Caiano, built by Giuliano da Sangallo for Lorenzo de'Medici (*see p54*) in 1480, was the first Italian villa to be designed in the Renaissance style. Its original severity is now softened by the graceful, curved staircase (added in 1802–7) leading up to the terrace, with its views of the park beyond.

The villa's barrel-vaulted *salone* contains 16th-century frescoes by Andrea del Sarto and Franciabigio. They were commissioned by the future Leo X, the Medici pope, to portray his family as great

Villa di Artimino

statesmen in the manner of ancient Roman figures.

The *salone* also contains Pontormo's colourful *Conette* fresco (1521). It portrays the Roman garden deities, Vertumnus and Pomona – a perfect evocation of a Tuscan summer afternoon.

⓭ Certosa di Firenze

Road map: D2. Via Buca di Certosa 2.
Tel 055 204 92 26. **Open** daily.
compulsory.

The Charterhouse of Florence lies in the suburb of Galluzzo, where the rivers Ema and Greve meet. The high, fortress-like walls have sheltered a small community of monks since 1341, when the monastery was founded here.

The cloister and Palazzo degli Studi within contain several artworks, including a damaged but still beautiful series of 16th-century frescoes by Pontormo depicting scenes from the Passion of Christ.

Villa di Poggio a Caiano, from the set of lunettes by Giusto Utens (*see p129*)

⑭ Volterra

Situated, like many Etruscan cities, on a high plateau, Volterra offers uninterrupted views over the surrounding hills. In many places, the ancient Etruscan walls still stand. Volterra's famous Museo Guarnacci contains one of the best collections of Etruscan artifacts in Italy. Many of the exhibits were gathered from numerous local tombs. After its museums and medieval buildings, the city is famous for its craftsmen, who carve beautiful white statues from locally mined alabaster.

🏛 Museo Etrusco Guarnacci

Via Don Minzoni 15. **Tel** 0588 863 47.
Open 9am–7pm daily (Nov–mid-Mar: 8:30am–1:30pm). **Closed** 1 Jan, 25 Dec. 🎟 (also allows entry at the Pinacoteca e Museo Civico and the Museo d'Arte Sacra). ♿

The pride of the Guarnacci Museum is its collection of 600 Etruscan funerary urns. Adorned with detailed carving, they offer a unique insight into Etruscan customs and beliefs (see pp46–7). The museum's two main exhibits are on the first floor. Room 20 contains the terracotta "Married Couple" urn. The elderly couple on the lid are portrayed realistically, with haggard, careworn faces.

Room 22 contains the elongated bronze known as the *Ombra della Sera* (Shadow of the Evening). This name was bestowed by the poet Gabriele d'Annunzio, who said that the bronze reminded him of the

Ombra della Sera

shadow thrown by a human figure in the dying light of the evening sun. It is probably a votive figure dating from the 3rd century BC, but it is difficult to speak of it with any certainty; unusually, it was cast with no clothes or jewellery to indicate rank, status or date. It is only by chance that this remarkable figure survived. Ploughed up by a farmer in 1879, it was used as a fire poker until someone recognized it as a masterpiece of Etruscan art.

Detail from *The Deposition* (1521), by Rosso Fiorentino

🏛 Pinacoteca e Museo Civico

Via dei Sarti 1. **Tel** 0588 875 80.
Open mid-Mar–Oct: 9am–7pm daily; Nov–mid-Mar: 10am–4:30pm daily. **Closed** 1 Jan, 25 Dec. 🎟 (also allows entry at the Museo Etrusco Guarnacci and the Museo d'Arte Sacra). ♿

Volterra's excellent art gallery is situated in the 15th-century Palazzo Minucci-Solaini. The best works are by Florentine artists. In Ghirlandaio's *Christ in Majesty* (1492), Christ hovers above an idealized Tuscan landscape. It was meant for the San Giusto monastery, which

was abandoned after a landslip like the one shown in the middle distance of the work and beyond. Luca Signorelli's *Madonna and Child with Saints* (1491) shows his debt to Roman art through the reliefs on the base of the Virgin's throne. His *Annunciation* (1491) is another beautiful composition.

The museum's main exhibit is Rosso Fiorentino's Mannerist work (see p31) *The Deposition* (1521). Attention is focused on the grief-stricken figures in the foreground and the pallid, empty shell of Christ's body, its dead weight symbolizing that His spirit is elsewhere.

🏛 Duomo

Piazza San Giovanni. **Open** daily.
Work on Volterra's cathedral began in the 1200s and continued intermittently over the next two centuries.

To the right of the High Altar stands a Romanesque wood-carving of *The Deposition* (1228). The Altar itself is flanked by graceful marble angels carved by Mino da Fiesole in 1471; they face the same artist's elegant tabernacle, carved with figures of Faith, Hope and Charity.

The nave, remodelled in 1581, has an unusual coffered ceiling with stucco figures of bishops and saints painted in rich blue and gold. The pulpit, in the middle of the nave, dates 1584, but was created using sculptural reliefs from the late 12th and early 13th centuries. The *Last Supper*

View from Volterra over the surrounding landscape

Detail from one of the panels decorating the Duomo pulpit

panel, facing into the nave and thought to be the work of the Pisan artist Guglielmo Pisano, has a number of humorous details including a monster snapping at the heels of Judas. Nearby, in the north aisle, Fra Bartolomeo's *The Annunciation* (1497) hangs above an altar in one of the side chapels.

More sculptures are housed in the oratory off the north aisle, near the main entrance. The best is a tableau of the Epiphany, preserved behind glass. The remarkably humane painted terracotta figures of the Virgin and Child in the foreground are believed to be by Zaccaria da Volterra (1473–1544), a local sculptor.

🏛 Museo d'Arte Sacra

Via Roma 13. **Tel** 0588 862 90. **Open** 9am–1pm, 3–6pm daily (Nov–mid-Mar: 9am–1pm only). **Closed** 1 Jan, 1 May, 25 Dec. ◪ (also allows entry at the Museo Etrusco Guarnacci and the Pinacoteca e Museo Civico). ♿

This museum, in the Palazzo Arcivescovile, contains sculpture and architectural fragments from the Duomo and a few local churches. The main exhibit is a 15th-century della Robbia terracotta of St Linus, Volterra's patron saint.

The collection also has a range of church bells, from the 11th to the 15th century, some church silver and several illuminated manuscripts.

🏛 Teatro Romano

Viale Ferrucci. **Open** mid-Mar–Oct: 10:30am–5:30pm daily; Nov–mid-Mar: 10:30am–4:30pm Sat & Sun (not when raining). **Closed** 1 Jan, 25 Dec. ◪

Just outside the city walls, the ancient Roman theatre, dating to the first century BC, is one of the best-preserved in Italy. Enough of the original structure has survived to enable an almost complete reconstruction.

VISITORS' CHECKLIST

Practical Information
Road Map C3.
🏔 12,200. 🛈 Via G Turazza 2 (0588 861 50). ▣ Sat. Astiludio (1st Sun in Sep).
🌐 volterratur.it

🏛 Piazza dei Priori

This fine square is dominated by the Palazzo dei Priori, dating from 1208. A sober building, it is said to have been the model for the Palazzo Vecchio in Florence (*see pp82–3*).

The 13th-century Porcellino tower, on the other side of the square, is named after the small pig, now almost worn away, carved at its base.

Plaque outside the Palazzo dei Priori

🏛 Arco Etrusco

One of Volterra's more unusual sights, the Etruscan arch is in fact part Roman. Only the columns and the severely weathered basalt heads, representing Etruscan gods, date to the 6th-century BC original. The features of each head are now barely visible.

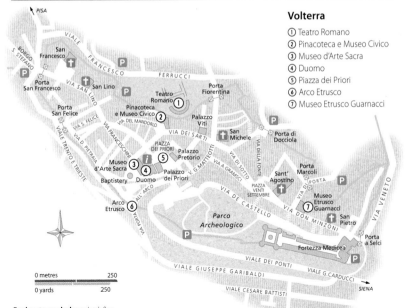

Volterra

① Teatro Romano
② Pinacoteca e Museo Civico
③ Museo d'Arte Sacra
④ Duomo
⑤ Piazza dei Priori
⑥ Arco Etrusco
⑦ Museo Etrusco Guarnacci

0 metres 250
0 yards 250

For key to symbols *see back flap*

NORTHERN TUSCANY

Of all the regions of Tuscany, this one offers something for everyone. The historic towns are known for their art, architecture and music festivals, while many sporting activities can be enjoyed along the coast or in the mountains. The landscape, too, is marked by a vast range of features, from marble quarries to market gardens, and from mountain ranges and nature reserves to beaches.

The heavily populated Lucchese plain between Florence and Lucca is dominated by industry: the textile factories of Prato produce three out of every four woollen garments exported from Italy. But, in spite of their large suburbs, cities such as Prato, Pistoia and, above all, Lucca have rewarding churches, museums and galleries within their historic city centres.

The land between the cities is fertile and is therefore intensively cultivated. Asparagus and cut flowers are two of the most important crops, and the wholesale flower market at Pescia is one of the biggest in Italy. East of Lucca, towards Pescia, are garden centres and nurseries where huge quantities of young trees and shrubs are grown in long, neat rows.

North of the Lucchese plain, the scenery is very different again. A series of foothills is covered in olive groves that produce some of the finest oil in Italy. Then, the land rises to the wild and mountainous areas of the Garfagnana, the Alpi Apuane (Apuan Alps) and the Lunigiana, with its fortified towns and castles built by the Dukes of Malaspina. Here, you will find some of Tuscany's highest peaks, rising to 2,000 m (6,550 ft) or more. Vast areas of the mountains are designated as nature parks and the wild scenery attracts ramblers, trekkers and riders, as well as hang-gliding enthusiasts.

Finally, the coastal area known as the Versilia includes some of Italy's most elegant and popular beach resorts. It stretches from the famous marble-quarrying town of Carrara in the north down to the area's main town, Viareggio, and to Torre del Lago Puccini, the lakeside home of Giacomo Puccini, where he wrote nearly all of his operas.

Lucca's Piazza del Mercato, echoing the shape of the original Roman amphitheatre

◄ The hillside village of Fontia, near Carrara, with the Alpi Apuane rising behind

Exploring Northern Tuscany

The beautiful town of Lucca is a favourite base for exploring. Northwards, industrial suburbs give way to the olive groves, chestnut woods and bare mountains of the Alpi Apuane and the Garfagnana region, a popular area for outdoor sports, from trekking and canoeing to skiing. Castles dot the rugged Lunigiana, while beaches line the Versilia. Due east are large towns with historic centres: Pistoia and Prato.

Orrido di Botri, near Bagni di Lucca

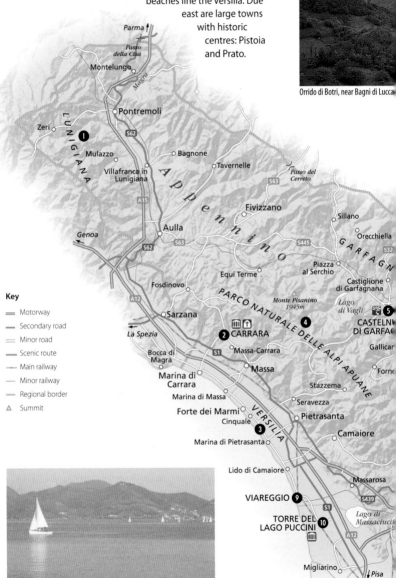

Parma
Passo
della Cisa
Montelungo
Magra
Pontremoli
Zeri
LUNIGIANA
1
S62
Mulazzo
Bagnone
Villafranca in
Lunigiana
Tavernelle
Passo del
Cerreto
S63
A15
APPENNINO
Fivizzano
Sillano
Genoa
Aulla
Orecchiella
S62
S63
S445
GARFAGN
Piazza
al Serchio
S32
Fosdinovo
Equi Terme
Castiglione
di Garfagnana
A12
PARCO NATURALE
Monte Pisanino
1945m
Lago
di Vagli
5
Sarzana
CASTELN
DI GARFA
La Spezia
2 CARRARA
DELLE
4
Bocca di
Magra
S1
Massa-Carrara
Gallicar
Marina di
Carrara
Massa
ALPI APUANE
Forno
Marina di Massa
Stazzema
Forte dei Marmi
Seravezza
Cinquale
VERSILIA
Pietrasanta
3
Marina di Pietrasanta
Camaiore
Lido di Camaiore
Massarosa
VIAREGGIO **9**
S439
S1
Lago di
Massaciucc
TORRE DEL
LAGO PUCCINI **10**
A12
Migliarino
Pisa

Key

═══ Motorway
─── Secondary road
┈┈┈ Minor road
─── Scenic route
╍╍╍ Main railway
─── Minor railway
═══ Regional border
△ Summit

Lago di Massaciuccoli, at Torre del Lago Puccini

For hotels and restaurants see pp252–7 and pp264–75

Getting Around

Lucca, Montecatini Terme, Prato and Pistoia are all on the A11 autostrada and are easy to reach by car from Pisa, Florence and major cities outside Tuscany, such as Bologna. There are several trains a day between Pisa and Florence via Lucca, Montecatini Terme, Prato and Pistoia, and along the coast between Pisa and Carrara. From Lucca you can also travel by train up the Serchio valley to Castelnuovo di Garfagnana. But, since this is a mountainous region, much of it is only accessible by car.

Sights at a Glance

1 The Lunigiana
2 Carrara
3 The Versilia
4 Parco Naturale delle
    Alpi Apuane
5 Castelnuovo di Garfagnana
6 Barga
7 The Garfagnana
8 Bagni di Lucca
9 Viareggio
10 Torre del Lago Puccini
11 Lucca
12 Collodi
13 Pescia
14 Montecatini Terme
15 Pistoia
16 Prato

The hamlet of Montefegatesi in the
Alpi Apuane

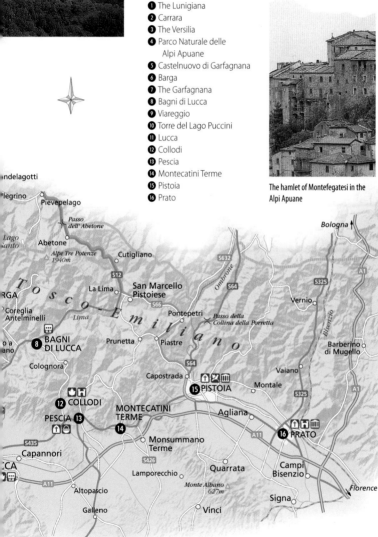

Watercraft and parasols at Lido di Camaiore, one of the popular beach resorts along the Versilia

❶ The Lunigiana

Road map: A1. 🚆 🚌 Aulla. 🛈 Via Salucci 5, Aulla (0187 42 14 39).

The Lunigiana (Land of the Moon) area is named after the port of Luni – so called because of the moon-like luminescence of the marble shipped from here in Roman times. From the 16th century onwards, the Dukes of Malaspina fortified villages against banditry and built castles at Massa, Fosdinovo, Aulla, Fivizzano and Verrucola.

At Pontremoli, the 14th-century Castello del Piagnaro houses the **Museo delle Statue-Stele Lunigianesi**, which shows prehistoric carved-stone figures from the region.

🏛 Museo delle Statue-Stele Lunigianesi
Castello del Piagnaro, Pontremoli. **Tel** 0187 83 14 39. **Closed** for renovation; reopening late 2014. 🅿️ **W** statuestele.org

❷ Carrara

Road map: B1. 🚶 70,000. 🚆 🚌 🛈 Piazza Cesare Battisti 1 (0585 64 14 22). 🗓 Mon.

Carrara is world famous for its white marble. The 300 or so quarries near the town date to Roman times, making this the oldest industrial site in

continuous use in the world. In Carrara itself, there are myriad showrooms and workshops where the marble is sawn into sheets or sculpted into statues and ornaments. Many of the workshops welcome visitors. You can also discover more about the techniques of crafting marble at the **Museo Civico del Marmo**.

Carrara's **Duomo** uses the local marble to good effect in its Pisan-Romanesque façade, featuring a rose window. In the same square is the house where Michelangelo used to stay on his visits to buy marble for his sculptures. The façade is marked by a plaque and by carvings of the sculptor's tools.

Tour buses from Carrara regularly visit the quarries at Colonnata and at Fantiscritti, where a museum displays

marble-quarrying techniques. You can also drive there, following the numerous signs that say "Cave di Marmo".

🏛 Museo Civico del Marmo
Viale XX Settembre. **Tel** 0585 84 57 46. **Open** May–Sep: 9:30am–1pm, 3–6pm Mon–Sat; Oct–Apr: 9am–12:30pm, 2:30–5pm Mon–Sat. 🅿️

🏛 Duomo
Piazza del Duomo. **Open** daily.

❸ The Versilia

Road map: B2. 🚆 🚌 Viareggio. 🛈 Viale Carducci 10, Viareggio (0584 96 22 33). **W** aptversilia.it

The Versilia, sometimes called the Tuscan Riviera because of the many beach resorts that line this 30-km (18-mile) strip, stretches from Marina di Carrara in the

A quarry in the marble-bearing hills around Carrara

north down to Marina di Torre del Lago Puccini. In the 1820s, towns such as Massa, Pietra Santa and Camaiore developed marinas and lidos along the part of the coast they controlled. These inland towns are linked by roads to their coastal twins. Here, villas and hotels with fine walled gardens line the streets, with the mountains of the Alpi Apuane as a backdrop.

The beaches are divided into numerous bathing establishments run by hotels or private operators, who charge for use of the beach and its facilities. Forte dei Marmi is perhaps the most beautiful of these resorts, much favoured by wealthy Florentines and Milanese.

Poster for the Versilia

❹ Parco Naturale delle Alpi Apuane

Road map: B1. 🚆 🚌 Castelnuovo di Garfagnana. 🛈 Piazza Delle Erbe 1, Castelnuovo di Garfagnana (0583 64 42 42).

The Parco Naturale delle Alpi Apuane, northwest of Castelnuovo di Garfagnana, was designated a nature reserve in 1985. Monte Pisanino is the highest peak in the area, at 1,945 m (6,320 ft). It towers above Lago di Vagli, an artificial lake covering the drowned village of Fabbrica. Nearby are Vagli di Sotto and Vagli di Sopra, ancient villages with rugged stone houses.

To the south, in the valley of the Turrite Secca, a spectacular mountain road leads to

The Turrite Secca valley, in the Parco Naturale delle Alpi Apuane

Seravezza, passing through a white-walled tunnel called the Galleria del Cipollaio. Northwest, at Arni, are the Marmitte dei Giganti (Giants' Cooking Pots), great hollows left by the glaciers of the Ice Age.

Southeast, at Calomini, is a 12th-century rock-cut hermitage, home to a Capuchin monk; at Fornovolasco is the Grotta del Vento (Cave of the Wind). To the east, past Barga, at Coreglia Antelminelli, is the

The 13th-century Rocca at Castelnuovo di Garfagnana

Museo della Figurina di Gesso, devoted to the history of locally made plaster figurines, once sold all over Europe.

🏛 **Museo della Figurina di Gesso**
Via del Mangano 17, Coreglia Antelminelli. **Tel** 0583 780 82. **Open** 9am–1pm Mon–Fri, 10am–1pm Sat & Sun. 🚫

❺ Castelnuovo di Garfagnana

Road map: B1. 🔼 6,300. 🚆 🚌
🛈 Via Cavalieri di Vittorio Veneto (0583 64 10 07). 🕑 Thu.

Visitors to the Garfagnana use the town as a base for sporting activities. For details, head to the information office or the **Garfagnana Ambiente e Sviluppo**. The 13th-century Rocca (castle) houses the town hall. Ludovico Ariosto, author of the epic poem *Orlando Furioso* (1516), was town governor in 1522–25.

🏕 **Garfagnana Ambiente e Sviluppo**
Piazza delle Erbe 1. **Tel** 0583 651 69. **Open** Jun–Sep: 9am–1pm, 3–7pm daily; Oct–May: 9am–1pm, 3:30–5:30pm daily.

❻ Barga

Road map: C1. 11,000. FS
Sat.

Barga is the most attractive of
the towns that line the Serchio
valley, leading northwards from
Lucca, and it makes an excellent
base for touring the Garfagnana
area. The little walled town, with
its steep streets paved with
stone, is the setting for a highly
regarded opera festival held in
July and August in the 18th-
century Teatro dell'Accademia
dei Differenti. The festival is
always well attended.

View over Barga rooftops

🏛 Duomo
Propositura. **Open** daily.
Barga's Duomo stands on a
grassy terrace at the highest
point in the town. There are
glorious views from here of
the gleaming whitemarble
and limestone peaks of the
Alpi Apuane.

The 11th-century Duomo is
dedicated to San Cristoforo
(St Christopher). The exterior
is decorated with interesting
Romanesque carvings of
interlaced knots, wild beasts
and knights in armour. Over the
north portal, a frieze thought to
be a scene from a folk tale
depicts a banquet.

Inside, a huge wooden statue
of St Christopher dates to the
12th century, and there is a
gilded tabernacle guarded by
two charming terracotta angels
by Luca della Robbia.

Most impressive of all is the
massive marble pulpit, standing
fully 5 m (16.5 ft) tall, supported
by pillars that, in turn, rest on
the back of man-eating lions.
The pulpit is the work of Guido
Bigarelli of Como and dates from
the early 13th century. The lively
sculptures on the upper part

depict the Evangelists, the Three
Magi, the Annunciation, the
Nativity and the Baptism of Christ.

❼ The Garfagnana

Road map: C1. FS Castelnuovo di
Garfagnana. ℹ Via Cavalieri di Vittorio
Veneto, Castelnuovo di Garfagnana
(0583 64 10 07).

This mountainous region
can be explored from
Barga, Seravezza, or
Castelnuovo di
Garfagnana (see p177).
Here, too, is the Parco
Naturale delle Alpi
Apuane (see p177).
From Castelnuovo, a
scenic drive takes you
to the Alpe Tre Potenze.
You can return via San
Pellegrino in Alpe, with
its **Museo Etnografico**,
and also visit the nature
park **Parco dell'
Orecchiella** and the
**Orto Botanico Pánia di
Corfino**, with its
collection of local
Alpine plants.

Romanesque sculpture
in Pieve di Brancoli

🏛 Museo Etnografico
Via del Voltone 15, San
Pellegrino in Alpe. **Tel** 0583 64 90 72.
Open Sep–Jun: Tue–Sun; Jul & Aug:
daily.

❁ Parco dell'Orecchiella
Centro Visitatori, Orecchiella. **Tel** 0583
61 90 02. **Open** Jun & Sep: Sat & Sun;
Jul–15 Sep: daily; Apr–Nov: Sun.

❁ Orto Botanico
Pánia di Corfino
Parco dell'Orecchiella. **Open** Jul–Aug:
daily; May–Jun & Sep: Sun.

❽ Bagni di Lucca

Road map: C2. 7,402.
ℹ Via del Casino (0583 80 57 45).
Wed & Sat.

Visitors come to Bagni di Lucca
for its lime-sulphate springs.
In the 19th century, it was one
of Europe's most fashionable
spa towns (see p189): the
Casino, built in 1837, was
the first to be licensed in
Europe. Also from that
time are the Neo-Gothic
English Church, the
elegant **Palazzo del
Circolo dei Forestieri**
restaurant and the **Cimitero
Anglicano** (Protestant
Cemetery). Bagni di
Lucca makes a good
base for exploring the
surrounding hills, cloaked
in chestnut woods. You
can walk to Montefegatesi,
a hamlet surrounded by
the peaks of the Alpi
Apuane, and then
continue to Orrido di
Botri, a dramatic gorge.
To the south of Bagni is
San Giorgio, or **Pieve di
Brancoli**, one of many
Romanesque churches
in the area founded
during the reign of Countess
Matilda (1046–1115) (see p49).

The Ponte della Maddalena is
a hump-backed bridge across
the river Serchio, just north of
the village of Borgo a Mozzano.
It is called Ponte del Diavolo
(Devil's Bridge) because,
according to local legend, the
Devil offered to build the bridge
in return for possession of the

Ponte della Maddalena, or "Devil's Bridge", near Bagni di Lucca

A seaside café in the popular beach resort of Viareggio

first soul to cross it; the canny villagers agreed and, when it was finished, sent a dog across.

🏠 **English Church**
Via Crawford. **Tel** 0583 80 84 62.
Open by appt.

🏛 **Palazzo del Circolo dei Forestieri**
Piazza Varraud 10. **Tel** 0583 860 38.
Open Fri–Sun. &

🏛 **Cimitero Anglicano**
Via Letizia. **Tel** 0583 80 84 62.
Open by appt.

🏠 **Pieve di Brancoli**
Vinchiana. **Tel** 0583 96 52 81.
Open by appt.

🟠 Viareggio

Road map: B2. 🚹 60,000. FS 🚌
🛈 Viale Carducci 10 (0584 96 22 33).
🦪 Thu.

Viareggio is famous for its elegant "Liberty" style (Art Nouveau) villas and hotels, built in the 1920s after the original boardwalk and timber chalets of the resort went up in flames in 1917. One example is the Gran Caffè Margherita, designed by Galileo Chini (see p198). The harbour has an interesting mix of boatyards, luxury yachts and fishing boats, and offers fine views of the Versilia coastline. Viareggio's carnival, held on Sundays from February to Lent and on Shrove Tuesday, is famous throughout Italy (see p42).

🔟 Torre del Lago Puccini

Road map: B2. 🚹 11,500. FS 🚌
🛈 Viale Kennedy 2 (0584 35 98 93).
🦪 Fri (Jul & Aug; also Sun). Teatro
Opera Puccini: **Tel** 0584 35 93 22.

The composer Giacomo Puccini (1858–1924) (see p183) lived here, beside Lago di Massaciuccoli, to indulge his passion for shooting waterfowl. He and his wife are buried in the **Museo Villa Puccini,** in the mausoleum between the piano room and the gun room where he kept his rifle ("my second favourite instrument"). The operas are performed in the open-air theatre in summer (see p39). The reed-fringed lake is now a nature reserve.

🏛 **Museo Villa Puccini**
Piazzale Belvedere Puccini 266.
Tel 0584 34 14 45. **Open** Tue–Sun. Jan
& Dec: 10am–12:40pm, 2–5:20pm; Feb
& Mar: 10am–12:40pm, 2:30–5:50pm;
Apr–Oct: 10am–12:40pm, 3–6:20pm.
Closed Nov, 25 Dec. 🎦 &
🌐 **giacomopuccini.it**

Near Puccini's lakeside home at Torre del Lago Puccini

⓫ Street-by-Street: Lucca

Lucca became a colony of ancient Rome in 180 BC, and the town's Roman legacy is still evident in the regular grid pattern of its streets. The remarkable elliptical shape of the Piazza del Mercato *(see p173)* is a survival of the amphitheatre. The name of the church of San Michele in Foro indicates that it stands beside the Roman forum, laid out as the city's main square in ancient times and still serving that function to this day. San Michele is just one of Lucca's many churches built in the 12th and 13th centuries in the elaborate Pisan-Romanesque style.

Most of the Renaissance palazzi of Piazza San Michele are now offices.

Casa di Puccini
This plaque marks the birthplace of Giacomo Puccini (1858–1924), composer of some of the world's most popular operas.

★ San Michele in Foro
The Madonna on the southwest corner of the church is a copy of the original inside, carved by Matteo Civitali (1436–1501).

The Palazzo Ducale, once home to Lucca's rulers, has a Mannerist colonnade by Ammannati (1578).

San Giovanni (1187)

Piazza Napoleone
The square is named after Napoleon, whose sister, Elisa Baciocchi, was ruler of Lucca (1805–15). The statue is of her successor, Marie Louise de Bourbon.

Key

— Suggested route

For hotels and restaurants see pp252–7 and pp264–75

Via Fillungo
Several shop fronts in Lucca's main shopping street are decorated with Art Nouveau details.

To San Frediano

To Anfiteatro Romano

VIA SANT' ANDREA

VIA DEL CARMINE

VIA SAN GREGORIO

V. D CHIAVI D'ORO

VIA SANT' ANASTASIO

A SANTA CROCE

PIAZZA BERNADINI

VIA GUINIGI

VIA SANTA CROCE

PIAZZA DEI SERVI

To Villa Bottoni and Museo Nazionale di Palazzo Mansi

STERO

VIA A. VALLISNERI

PIAZZA ...INELLI

To Giardino Botanico

VIA DELL' ARCIVESCOVADO

0 metres 100
0 yards 100

Torre dei Guinigi
This medieval tower, with holm-oak trees growing at the top, is a familiar landmark of Lucca.

Museo dell'Opera della Cattedrale
This museum features the treasures of San Martino, including church vestments and illuminated manuscripts.

★ **San Martino**
Lucca's cathedral dates from the 11th century. Its marble façade is asymmetrical to accommodate the adjoining belfry. With its columns, arcades and rich decoration, the façade is an outstanding example of the exuberant Pisan-Romanesque style.

Exploring Lucca

Lucca is enclosed by massive red-brick walls that help to give the city its special character by shutting out traffic and the modern world. Built in 1504–1645, the walls are among the best-preserved Renaissance defences in Europe. Within these walls, Lucca is a peaceful city of narrow lanes, preserving intact its original ancient Roman street plan. Unlike several of Tuscany's hilltop cities, Lucca is flat: many locals use bicycles, which lends the city added charm.

Lucca, viewed from the top of the Guinigi Tower

⬆ San Martino
See pp184–5.

🏛 Anfiteatro Romano
Piazza del Mercato.
Almost none of the ancient Roman amphitheatre survives: the stone was gradually stolen for use elsewhere, leaving the atmospheric arena-shaped Piazza del Mercato of today *(see p173)*. The piazza is enclosed by medieval houses that were built up against the walls of the amphitheatre. Its shape, perfectly preserved, is a striking reminder that Lucca was founded by the Romans around 180 BC. Low archways in the north, south, east and west mark the gates through which

beasts and gladiators would once have entered the arena.

🏛 Palazzo dei Guinigi
Via Sant'Andrea 41. **Tel** 0583 31 68 46.
Tower Open daily. Apr–May: 9am–6:30pm; Jun–Sep: 9:30am–7:30pm; Mar & Oct: 9:30am–5:30pm; Nov–Feb: 9:30am–4:30pm. **Closed** 25 Dec. 🗙

This house was once owned by the Guinigi family, rulers of the city in the 15th century. They kept Florence at bay, so Lucca was never conquered by the Medici, remaining independent until the late 1700s. The red-brick palazzo, built in the late 14th century,

has late-Gothic windows. The striking 41-m (133-ft) defensive tower alongside, the Torre del Guinigi, has a small roof garden, hence the ilex (holm-oak) trees sprouting incongruously at the top. This roof garden also has the best view of the city.

🌿 Giardino Botanico
Via dell'Orto Botanico 14. **Tel** 0583 44 21 60. **Open** 10am–5pm daily (to 6pm May & Jun; to 7pm Jul–Sep). **Closed** Sun (Nov–Mar). 🗙 ♿

Lucca's delightful botanical garden, tucked into an angle of the city walls, was laid out in 1820. It displays a wide range of Tuscan plants.

🏛 Museo della Cattedrale
Piazza Antelminelli 5. **Tel** 0583 49 05 30. **Open** mid-Mar–Oct: 10am–6pm daily; Nov–mid-Mar: 10am–2pm Mon–Fri, 10am–6pm Sat & Sun. **Closed** 1 Jan, Easter, 25 Dec. 🗙 ♿

Housed in the 14th-century former Archbishop's Palace, the museum displays the treasures of the Duomo, San Martino. These include the 11th-century carved stone head of a king from the original façade. There is also a rare 12th-century Limoges enamel casket, which possibly held a relic of St Thomas à Becket. The Croce di Pisani made by Vincenzo di Michele in 1411 is a masterpiece showing Christ hanging from the Tree of Redemption.

🏛 Museo Nazionale Villa Guinigi
Via della Quarquonia. **Tel** 0583 49 60 33. **Open** 8:30am–7pm Tue–Sat (to 1pm Sun). **Closed** 1 Jan, 1 May, 25 Dec. 🗙 (a cumulative ticket also allows entry at the Museo Nazionale di Palazzo Mansi).

Romanesque lion at Museo Nazionale Guinigi

This Renaissance villa was built for Paolo Guinigi, who ruled Lucca from 1400 until 1430. The ground floor holds sculpture from Lucca and surrounds, including fine Romanesque reliefs from Lucca's churches. The gallery on the floor above displays paintings and choir

The beautiful galleried staircase at Palazzo Pfanner

stalls from Lucca's cathedral, inlaid with marquetry views of the city in 1529.

🏛 Palazzo Pfanner

Via degli Asili 33. **Tel** 058 395 40 29. **Open** Apr–Nov: 10am–6pm daily; Dec–Mar: by appt.

The imposing Palazzo Pfanner, built in 1667, has a delightful formal garden to the rear, which can also be viewed from the ramparts. Laid out in the 18th century, the garden's central avenue is lined with Baroque statues of ancient Roman gods and goddesses, alternating with lemon trees in huge terracotta pots.

The house itself contains a collection of furniture, antiques and medical instruments.

🏛 Piazza Napoleone and Piazza del Giglio

Piazza Napoleone was laid out in 1806 when Lucca was under the imposed rule of Elisa Baciocchi, Napoleon's sister. The statue in the square is of her successor, Marie Louise de Bourbon. She faces the massive Palazzo Ducale, with its elegant colonnade, built by Ammannati in 1578. Behind her is the Piazza del Giglio, with the Teatro del Giglio (1817) on the south side of the square. The theatre is famous for its productions of operas by Puccini, who was born in Lucca.

🏛 Casa di Puccini

Corte San Lorenzo 8 (Via di Poggio). **Tel** 0583 35 91 54. **Open** Apr–Oct: 10am–6pm Wed–Mon; Nov–Mar: 11am–5pm Wed–Mon.

The 15th-century house in which Giacomo Puccini (1858–1924) was born contains many interesting arti-facts, including portraits of the great composer, costume designs for his operas and the piano he used when composing his last opera, *Turandot*. Left unfinished at his death, the com-position was completed by Franco Alfano and first performed two years later at La Scala, Milan.

The composer Giacomo Puccini

🏛 Museo Nazionale di Palazzo Mansi

Via Galli Tassi 43. **Tel** 0583 555 70. **Open** 8:30am–7pm Tue–Sat. (a cumulative ticket also allows entry at the Museo Nazionale Guinigi).

Lucca's picture gallery is in the impressive 17th-century Palazzo Mansi, with paintings and furnishings of the same period, typical of the time when Mannerism was being superseded by Baroque and Rococo art. There are also works by Bronzino, Pontormo, Sodoma, Andrea del Sarto, Tintoretto and Salvatore Rosa.

🏛 Ramparts

Complete circuit: 4.2 km (2.5 miles). A promenade runs along the top of the city walls, built in 1504–1645. Marie Louise de Bourbon made the ramparts into a public park in the early 19th century, with a double avenue of trees. It makes for a delightful walk, with fine views of Lucca. There are occasional guided tours of the chambers and passages inside one of the bastions. For more information on the tours, which should be booked in advance, contact Compagnia Balestrieri Lucca on 338 237 1277.

The Porta San Donato, along the tree-lined ramparts walk

San Martino

Lucca's extraordinary cathedral, with its façade abutting incongruously on to the campanile, is dedicated to St Martin. He is the Roman soldier depicted on the façade dividing his cloak with a sword to share with a needy beggar. This and other scenes from the life of the saint form part of the complex decorations covering the 13th-century façade. There are also reliefs depicting *The Labours of the Months* and intricate panels of inlaid pink, green and white marble showing hunting scenes, peacocks and flowers.

★ **Tomb of Ilaria del Carretto**
The Sacristy houses Jacopo della Quercia's beautiful portrait in marble (1405–6) of Paolo Guinigi's bride.

KEY

① **Matteo Civitali's marble Tempietto** (1484)

② **Romanesque blank arcades and carved capitals**

③ **Domed chapels encircling the apse**

④ **The altar painting** in the Sacristy, *The Madonna and Saints* (1449–94), is by Ghirlandaio.

⑤ **The campanile** was built in 1060 as a defensive tower. The upper two tiers were added in 1261, when the tower was joined to the cathedral.

⑥ **Circular clerestory windows**, in the nave and above the aisle roof, light the unusually tall nave of the cross-shaped church.

⑦ **Nicola Pisano** (1200–78) carved *The Journey of the Magi* and *The Deposition*, around the left doorway.

★ **Volto Santo**
This revered 13th-century wooden effigy was believed by medieval pilgrims to have been carved by Christ's follower, Nicodemus, at the time of the Crucifixion.

★ Façade
The gabled façade has three tiers of ornate colonnading (1204). Every one of the carved columns is different, and there are lively hunting scenes above them.

St Martin
This sculpture of the saint dividing his cloak to share is a copy. The 13th-century original is now just inside the cathedral entrance.

Inlaid Marble
Scenes from daily life, myths and poems cover the façade. Look out for the maze pattern on the right pier of the porch.

Doorway Sculptures
This 13th-century relief depicts the beheading of St Regulus. *The Labours of the Months* around the central door show the tasks appropriate to each season.

Apostles from the mosaic on the façade of San Frediano in Lucca

🏛 San Frediano

Piazza San Frediano. **Open** daily.

The striking façade of Lucca's San Frediano church features a colourful 13th-century mosaic, *The Ascension,* by the school of Berlinghieri. Inside, to the right, is a splendid Romanesque font that could easily be mistaken for a fountain, because it is so big and impressive. The sides are carved with scenes from *The Life of Christ* and the story of Moses. One dramatic scene shows Moses and his followers dressed in 12th-century armour, looking like Crusaders, as they pass through the divided Red Sea with an entourage of camels.

Amico Aspertini's frescoes (1508–9) in the second chapel in the north aisle tell the story of Lucca's precious relic, the Volto Santo *(see p184),* and give a good idea of what the city looked like in the early 16th century.

Also in the church is a coloured wooden statue of the Virgin, carved by Matteo Civitali, and an altarpiece carved from a single block of marble by Jacopo della Quercia in the Cappella Trenta. It is carved in the shape of a polyptych, with five Gothic-spired niches.

🏛 San Michele in Foro

Piazza San Michele. **Open** daily.

As its name suggests, this church stands on the site of the ancient Roman forum. It has a wonderfully rich Pisan-Romanesque façade that competes in splendour with that of San Martino *(see pp184–5).* John Ruskin, the English artist and art historian whose work did so much to revive interest in Italian art during the 19th century *(see p59),* spent many hours here sketching the rich mixture of twisted marble columns and Cosmati work (inlaid marble). The façade is almost barbaric in its exuberance, and the inlaid marble scenes depict wild beasts

Detail from façade of San Michele in Foro

and huntsmen on horseback, rather than Christian subjects. Only the huge winged figure of St Michael, standing on the pediment and flanked by two angels, marks this out as a church. The splendour of the façade, built over a long period from the 11th to the 14th century, is matched by the arcading of the bell tower.

The interior has little of interest except for Filippino Lippi's beautiful *Saints Helena, Jerome, Sebastian and Roch.*

🏛 Lu.C.C.A.

Via della Fratta 36. **Tel** 0583 57 17 12. **Open** 10am–7pm Tue–Sun. **Closed** Mon, 1 Jan, 24, 25 & 31 Dec. 🅦 **luccamuseum.com**

The exhibitions are always interesting at this innovative contemporary gallery, and many include interactive displays that make it popular for family visits. There is a bookshop and café on site.

🏛 Via Fillungo

Lucca's principal shopping street winds its way through the heart of the city towards the Anfiteatro Romano *(see p182).* The upper end, towards San Frediano church, has several shops with Art Nouveau ironwork, while San Cristoforo, the 13th-century church halfway down the street, holds exhibitions of work by local artists.

🏛 Villa Bottini

Via Elisa. **Tel** 0583 49 14 49. Garden: **Open** 9am–6pm daily.

The pretty walled garden of this late 16th-century building is open to the public. It is also used occasionally in summer for outdoor concerts.

Villa Bottini and garden

A Day Out Around Lucca

This motoring tour takes you by a scenic route to the best of the villas around Lucca. After leaving Lucca, the first stop is the Romanesque church of San Giorgio in Pieve di Brancoli; then comes the ancient hump-backed Ponte della Maddalena, also known as Devil's Bridge *(see p178)*. In the spa town of Bagni di Lucca, the pretty suspension bridge across the Lima dates from 1840. On reaching Collodi, explore the village on foot, as the streets are too steep and narrow for cars. The Villa Garzoni, with its splendid gardens, lies below the town, and the Pinocchio Park is on the other side of the road. Continue to the Villa Torrigiani, which is set in a fine park and contains 13th–18th-century porcelain and furnishings. The tour ends at the 17th-century Villa Mansi, with its Baroque façade and a garden enlivened by statues of Diana and other pagan deities.

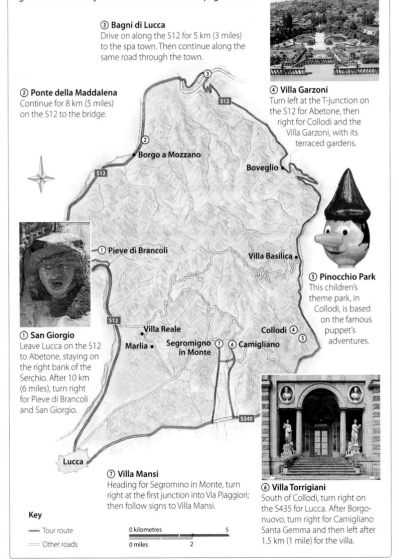

③ **Bagni di Lucca**
Drive on along the S12 for 5 km (3 miles) to the spa town. Then continue along the same road through the town.

② **Ponte della Maddalena**
Continue for 8 km (5 miles) on the S12 to the bridge.

④ **Villa Garzoni**
Turn left at the T-junction on the S12 for Abetone, then right for Collodi and the Villa Garzoni, with its terraced gardens.

Borgo a Mozzano

Boveglio

① **Pieve di Brancoli**

Villa Basilica

⑤ **Pinocchio Park**
This children's theme park, in Collodi, is based on the famous puppet's adventures.

① **San Giorgio**
Leave Lucca on the S12 to Abetone, staying on the right bank of the Serchio. After 10 km (6 miles), turn right for Pieve di Brancoli and San Giorgio.

Villa Reale

Marlia

Segromigno in Monte ⑦ ⑥ **Camigliano**

Collodi ④
⑤

Lucca

⑦ **Villa Mansi**
Heading for Segromino in Monte, turn right at the first junction into Via Piaggiori; then follow signs to Villa Mansi.

⑥ **Villa Torrigiani**
South of Collodi, turn right on the S435 for Lucca. After Borgo-nuovo, turn right for Camigliano Santa Gemma and then left after 1.5 km (1 mile) for the villa.

Key

— Tour route

==== Other roads

0 kilometres   5

0 miles   2

Terme Tettuccio, Montecatini's oldest and most famous spa, rebuilt in 1925–8

⑫ Collodi

Road map: C2. 🗺 3,000.
ℹ Piazza Collodi (0572 42 96 60).

There are two main sights in this town: the **Villa Garzoni**, with its theatrical terraced gardens tumbling down the hillside and, for children, the **Pinocchio Park** *(see p187)*.

The author of *The Adventures of Pinocchio* (1881), Carlo Lorenzini, was born in Florence, but his uncle was custodian of the Villa Garzoni and Lorenzini frequently stayed here as a child. Fond memories led him to use Collodi as his pen name, and, in 1956, the town decided to repay the compliment by setting up the theme park.

The park consists of gardens featuring mosaics and sculptural tableaux based on the adventures of the puppet, plus a maze, playground, exhibition centre and children's restaurant.

🏠 Villa Garzoni
Tel 0572 42 95 90. Villa: **Closed** for restoration. Garden: **Open** 9am–5pm daily. 🍴

🎡 Pinocchio Park
Tel 0572 42 93 42. **Open** 8:30am–sunset daily. 🍴 ♿ partial.
w pinocchio.it

⑬ Pescia

Road map: C2. 🗺 18,000. 🚌
ℹ Via Fratelli Rosselli 2 (0572 49 09 19).
🍴 Sat.

Pescia's wholesale flower market is one of Italy's biggest, and there are some interesting sights to visit in the city.

In the church of **San Francesco** are frescoes on *The Life of St Francis* (1235), by Bonaventura Berlinghieri (1215–74). The artist knew St Francis *(see p51)* and it is claimed that the frescoes are an accurate portrait of the saint. The **Duomo**, remodelled in

Baroque style by Antonio Ferri in 1693, has a massive campanile that was originally built as a tower within the city walls. It was given its onion-dome "cap" in 1771.

There is a small collection of religious paintings and illuminated manuscripts in the **Museo Civico**, and the **Museo Archeologico della Valdinievole** displays material excavated from nearby Valdinievole, the pretty "Vale of Mist".

🏠 San Francesco
Piazza San Francesco. **Open** daily.

🏠 Duomo
Piazza del Duomo. **Open** daily.

🏛 Museo Civico
Palazzo Galeotti, Piazza Santo Stefano 1.
Tel 0572 47 79 44. **Closed** for restoration.

🏛 Museo Archeologico della Valdinievole
Piazza Leonardo da Vinci 1. **Tel** 0572 47 75 33. **Open** 8:30am–1pm Mon–Fri, 3–5:30pm Tue & Thu.

⑭ Montecatini Terme

Road map: C2. 🗺 22,500. 🚌 ℹ Viale Verdi 66 (0572 77 22 44). 🍴 Thu.

Of all Tuscany's many spa towns, Montecatini Terme is the most interesting. It has beautiful formal gardens and the architecture of its spas is particularly distinguished. Terme Leopoldine (1926),

The river Pescia, running through a fertile, cultivated landscape

Theatre building in Montecatini Alto's main square

built in the style of a Classical temple, is named after Grand Duke Leopoldo I, who first encouraged the development of Montecatini Terme in the 18th century.

The most splendid is the Neo-Classical Terme Tettuccio (1925–8), with its circular, marble-lined pools, fountains and Art Nouveau tiles depicting languorous nymphs.

Terme Torretta, named after its mock-medieval tower, is noted for its tea-time concerts, while Terme Tamerici has beautifully tended gardens.

Visitors can obtain day tickets to the spas to drink the waters and relax in the reading, writing and music rooms. More information is available from the Direzione delle Terme, at Viale Verdi 41.

A popular excursion from Montecatini Terme is to take the funicular railway up to the ancient fortified village of Montecatini Alto. In its quiet main piazza, there are antique shops and well-regarded restaurants with outdoor tables. From the Rocca (castle), you can take in sweeping views over the mountainous countryside.

Nearby, at Ponte Buggianese, in **San Michele** church, you can see modern frescoes by the Florentine artist Pietro Annigoni (1910–88) on the theme of Christ's Passion.

At Monsummano Terme, another of Tuscany's well-known spa towns, the **Grotta Giusti** spa prescribes the inhalation of vapours from hot sulphurous springs found in the nearby caves.

Above Monsummano Terme is the fortified hilltop village of Monsummano Alto, with its ruined castle. Today, few people live in the sleepy village, with its pretty 12th-century church and crumbling houses, but there are some fine views from here.

⬆ San Michele
Ponte Buggianese.
Open by appointment.

🏛 Grotta Giusti
Monsummano Terme. **Tel** 0572 907 71. **Open** 9am–7pm daily. 🅿
W grottagiustispa.com

The Terme Tamerici, built in Neo-Gothic style in the early 20th century

Taking the Waters in Tuscany

The therapeutic value of bathing was first recognized by the ancient Romans. They were also the first to exploit the hot springs of volcanic origin that they found all over Tuscany. Here, they built bath complexes where the army veterans who settled in towns such as Florence and Siena could relax. Some of these spas, as at Saturnia (see p242), are still called by their original Roman names.

Other spas came into prominence during the Middle Ages and Renaissance: St Catherine of Siena (1347–80) (see p223), who suffered from scrofula, a form of tuberculosis, and Lorenzo de' Medici (1449–92), who was arthritic, both bathed in the sulphurous hot springs at Bagno Vignoni (see p230) to relieve their ailments. Tuscan spas really came into their own in the early

1920s spa poster

19th century when Bagni di Lucca was one of the most fashionable spa centres in Europe, frequented by emperors, kings and aristocrats (see p178). However, spa culture in the 19th century had more to do with social life: flirtation and gambling took precedence over health cures.

Today, treatments such as inhaling sulphur-laden steam, drinking the mineral-rich waters, hydro massage, bathing and application of mud packs are prescribed for disorders ranging from liver complaints to skin conditions and asthma. Many visitors still continue the tradition of coming to fashionable spas, such as Montecatini Terme or Monsummano Terme, not just for the benefits of therapeutic treatment, but also for relaxation and in search of companionship.

⑮ Pistoia

The citizens of Pistoia acquired a reputation for viciousness and intrigue in the 13th century and the taint has never quite disappeared. The cause was a feud between two of the city's rival factions, the Neri and Bianchi (Blacks and Whites), that spread to involve other cities. Assassination in Pistoia's narrow alleyways was commonplace. The favoured weapon was a tiny but deadly dagger called the *pistole*, made by the city's ironworkers, who also specialized in surgical instruments. The city still thrives on metalworking: everything from buses to mattress springs is made here. Its historic centre has several fine buildings.

Baptistry opposite the Cattedrale

🏛 Cattedrale di San Zeno
Piazza del Duomo. **Tel** 0573 250 95.
Open 8am–12:30pm, 3:30–7pm daily.
♿ 🚻 side entrance. Cappella di San Jacobo: **Open** daily.

Piazza del Duomo, the city's main square, is dominated by the Cattedrale di San Zeno and its bulky campanile, which was originally built in the 12th century as a defensive watchtower in the city walls.

The interior is rich in funerary monuments, including the tomb of poet Cino da Pistoia, in the south aisle. He is depicted in a relief (1337) lecturing to a class of young boys.

Nearby is the Cappella di San Jacobo, with its extraordinary silver altar decorated with more than 600 statues and reliefs. The earliest of these dates from 1287, and the altar was not completed until 1456. During that time, nearly every silversmith of note in Tuscany contributed to the extraordinarily rich design. Among them was Brunelleschi, who began his career working in metal before switching to architecture. Also in Piazza del Duomo, facing the Cattedrale, is the octagonal Baptistry, which was finished in 1359.

🏛 Museo di San Zeno
Palazzo dei Vescovi, Piazza del Duomo. **Tel** 0573 36 92 72.
Open 10–11:30am, 1–3pm, 3:15–5pm Tue, Thu & Fri. ♿
📷 obligatory. 🚻 partial.

In the beautifully restored Palazzo dei Vescovi (Bishop's Palace) is the Museo

della Cattedrale. In the basement, you can see the excavated remains of Roman buildings, and upstairs there are some fine reliquaries, crucifixes and chalices made by local goldsmiths in the 13th–15th century.

🏛 Museo Civico
Palazzo del Comune, Piazza del Duomo. **Tel** 0573 37 12 96. **Open** 10am–6pm Thu–Sun. ♿ 🚻
On the opposite side of the square is the Palazzo del Comune (Town Hall), which has the Museo Civico upstairs. Exhibits here range from medieval altar paintings to the work of 20th-century Pistoian artists, architects and sculptors.

🏛 Centro Marino Marini
Palazzo del Tau, Corso Silvano Fedi 30. **Tel** 0573 302 85. **Open** 10am–5pm Mon–Fri, 9:30am–12:30pm Sat. ♿ 🌐 **fondazione marinomarini.it**

The work of Marino Marini (1901–80), Pistoia's most famous 20th-century artist, is housed in a museum in the Palazzo del Tau. On display are drawings and casts, which trace the development of his style. Marini specialized in sculpting primitive forms in bronze and clay. His subjects included a horse and rider *(see p108)*, and Pomona, the ancient Roman goddess of fertility.

Pomona, by Marino Marini

🏛 Cappella del Tau
Corso Silvano Fedi 70. **Tel** 0573 322 04. **Open** 8:15am–1:30pm Mon–Sat.
This chapel owes its name to the letter T (*tau* in Greek), which appeared on the cloaks of the monks who built it and which symbolized a crutch.

Inside the chapel there are frescoes on *The Creation* and the life of St Anthony Abbot, who founded the order, which is dedicated to tending the sick and crippled.

The Fall, in the Cappella del Tau

🏛 San Giovanni Fuorcivitas
Via Cavour. **Open** daily.
Just north of the Cappella del Tau is the 12th-century church of San Giovanni Fuorcivitas ("St John outside the city", since the church once stood beyond the city walls). Its north flank is strikingly clad in banded marble and there is a Romanesque relief of *The Last Supper* over the portal. Inside is Giovanni Pisano's holywater basin, carved in marble with figures of the Virtues, and an equally masterly

Detail of frieze (1514–25) by Giovanni della Robbia, Ospedale del Ceppo

pulpit by Guglielmo da Pisa, carved in 1270 with New Testament scenes. Both works are among the finest of this period, when artists were reviving the art of carving.

🏠 Sant'Andrea
Via Sant'Andrea 21. **Tel** 0573 219 12. **Open** 8am–12:30pm, 3–6:30pm daily.
This church is reached by walking through Piazza della Sala, the site of Pistoia's lively open-air market. There is a good Romanesque relief of *The Journey of the Magi* over the portal, and inside is Giovanni Pisano's pulpit (completed in 1301). This is considered by some to be his masterpiece, even more accomplished than the pulpit he later made for Pisa cathedral *(see p163)*. It is decorated with reliefs depicting scenes from the life of Christ.

🏠 San Bartolomeo in Pantano
Piazza San Bartolomeo 6. **Open** daily.
The beautiful Romanesque church of San Bartolomeo in Pantano, dating from 760, houses another celebrated pulpit, carved in 1250 by Guido da Como.

🏛 Ospedale del Ceppo
Piazza Giovanni XXIII.
This hospital and orphanage, founded in 1277, was named after the *ceppo*, or hollowed-out tree trunk, that was used in medieval times to collect donations for its work. The striking façade of the main building features coloured terracotta panels (1514–25) by Giovanni della Robbia illustrating the Seven Works of Corporeal Mercy. The portico is by Michelozzo.

Façade of San Bartolomeo

Pistoia City Centre
1. Sant'Andrea
2. Ospedale del Ceppo
3. San Bartolomeo in Pantano
4. Museo Civico
5. Museo della Cattedrale
6. Cattedrale and Baptistry
7. San Giovanni Fuorcivitas
8. Cappella del Tau
9. Centro Marino Marini

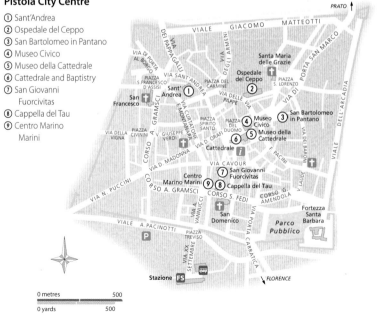

⑯ Prato

Prato has been one of Italy's most important textile-manufacturing cities since the 13th century. One of its most famous citizens was the immensely wealthy Francesco di Marco Datini (1330–1410), who has been immortalized by Iris Origo in *The Merchant of Prato* (1957). Datini left all his money to charity, and the city contains several reminders of him, particularly in his own Palazzo Datini. Prato also attracts pilgrims from all over Italy, who come to see the Virgin's Girdle, a prized relic kept in the Duomo and on view five times a year.

Madonna del Ceppo by Fra Filippo Lippi in the Museo Civico

Duomo façade and pulpit

🏠 Duomo

Piazza del Duomo. **Tel** 0574 26 234.
Open 7am–noon, 3:30–7pm Mon–Sat; 7am–1pm, 3:30–8pm Sun.

The Duomo stands on the main square, with the Pulpit of the Holy Girdle to the right of its façade, its frieze of dancing cherubs designed by Donatello (1438). Inside, the first chapel on the left holds the Virgin's Girdle, which is displayed from the pulpit on religious holidays. Frescoes by Agnolo Gaddi (1392–5) relate how the girdle reached Prato. In 1141, a local merchant married a Palestinian woman who brought it with her after inheriting it from the Apostle Thomas, who had been given it by the Virgin herself. Also in the Duomo is Fra Filippo Lippi's masterpiece, *The Life of John the Baptist* (1452–66).

🏛 Museo dell'Opera del Duomo

Piazza del Duomo 49. **Tel** 0574 293 39.
Open 10am–1pm, 3–6:30pm Mon–Sat.
🖼 (a cumulative ticket allows entry at the Museo Civico and the Castello dell'Imperatore). 🚻 partial.

Donatello's original panels for the Holy Girdle pulpit are on display here. The museum also houses the reliquary (1446), made for the Girdle by Maso di Bartolomeo, and *St Lucy* by Filippino Lippi, the son of Fra Filippo Lippi.

🏛 Piazza del Comune

The streets around the Duomo contain several important buildings. The city's main street, Via Mazzoni, leads west to the Piazza del Comune, with its Bacchus fountain. The original, made in 1659, is in the nearby Palazzo Comunale.

🏛 Museo Civico

Palazzo Pretorio, Piazza del Comune 19.
Tel 0574 183 6302. **Open** 10:30am–1pm, 4–8pm Mon, Wed–Fri, 10am–8pm Sat & Sun. 🖼 (a cumulative ticket allows entry to the Museo dell'Opera del Duomo and Castello dell'Imperatore). 🚻 partial.

The Museo Civico houses the altar painting *The Story of the Holy Girdle*, by Bernardo Daddi (1312–48), and Fra Filippo Lippi's *Madonna del Ceppo* (circa 1452–3), featuring a portrait of Francesco Datini, a patron of the Ceppo charity (*see p191*).

🏛 Palazzo Datini

Via Ser Lapo Mazzei 43.
Tel 0574 213 91. **Open** 9am–12pm, 4–7:30pm Mon–Sat. 🚻
🌐 museocasadatini.it

This house, where Francesco Datini lived, is now a museum. Its archive contains 140,000 business letters and Datini's account books, on which Iris Origo based her biography.

The Story of the Holy Girdle, by Bernardo Daddi, in the Museo Civico

🏠 Santa Maria delle Carceri

Piazza delle Carceri. **Open** 7am–noon, 4–7pm daily.

Prato's most important church stands on the site of a prison *(carceri)* on whose wall an image of the Virgin miraculously appeared in 1484. With its harmoniously proportioned interior, the domed church (1485–1506) is a fine work by Renaissance architect Giuliano da Sangallo. Andrea della Robbia created the blue-and-white glazed terracotta roundels of the Evangelists (1490).

🏠 Castello dell'Imperatore

Piazza delle Carceri. **Open** Wed–Sat, Sun morning & Mon. 🎨 *(see Museo dell'Opera del Duomo).*

This castle (1237) was built by the German Holy Roman Emperor Frederick II during his campaign to conquer Italy.

🏛 Museo del Tessuto

Via Santa Chiara 24. **Tel** 0574 61 15 03. **Open** 10am–3pm Tue–Thu, 10am–7pm Fri & Sat, 3–7pm Sun. ♿ 🌐 **museodeltessuto.it**

The history of Prato's textile industry, the basis of its wealth, is charted in this textile

VISITORS' CHECKLIST

Practical Information

Road Map D2.
🗺 170,000. ℹ Piazza delle Carceri 15 (0574 241 12). **Open** 9am–6:30pm Mon–Sat (daily in the summer). 🚌 Mon.

Transport

🚆 Prato Centrale and Porta al Serraglio. 🚌 Piazzas Ciardi, San Francesco & Stazione.

museum. Located on the city's southern outskirts, it houses historic looms and examples of various types of cloth, such as lush Renaissance embroidery, velvets, lace and damask.

🏛 Centro per l'Arte Contemporanea Luigi Pecci

Viale della Repubblica 277. **Tel** 0574 53 17. **Closed** due to renovation; reopening 2015. 🎨 ♿ 🌐 **centropecci.it**

Near the Prato Est Autostrada exit and housed in an interesting modern building, the Luigi Pecci cultural centre is used for changing displays of contemporary art, concerts and films.

The imposing Castello dell'Imperatore (1237), built by Frederick II

Prato City Centre

① Duomo
② Museo dell'Opera del Duomo
③ Piazza del Comune
④ Museo Civico
⑤ Palazzo Datini
⑥ Santa Maria delle Carceri
⑦ Castello dell'Imperatore

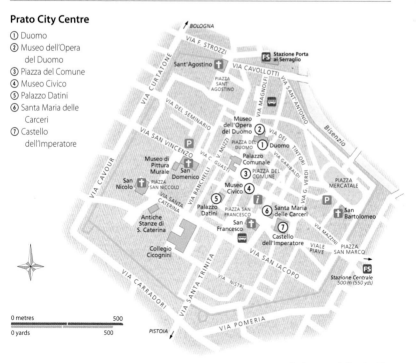

EASTERN TUSCANY

From the forests of the Mugello and the Casentino to the heights of La Verna, this is an area of outstanding natural beauty. Hermits and mystics have long favoured its more remote reaches, where ancient monastic orders continue to flourish. Only this part of Tuscany could have produced an enigmatic artist like Piero della Francesca, whose celebrated frescoes decorate San Francesco in Arezzo.

Eastern Tuscany's main transport route, the A1 Autostrada, channels speeding traffic southwards along the Arno valley towards Arezzo and Rome. Away from this busy artery, Eastern Tuscany is a little-visited region of steep hills cloaked in beech, oak and sweet chestnut trees. It is particularly attractive in autumn, when the huge forests of the Mugello and the Casentino take on fiery shades of red and gold. This is also the season when mushrooms and truffles abound. Driving through the region at this time of year, you'll see them for sale at roadside stalls.

The tiny mountain pastures to the east of the region are grazed both by sheep, whose milk is made into cheese, and by beautiful white cattle, which were once highly prized by the Romans as sacrificial beasts.

This is also a land of saints, hermits and monasteries. The mountain-top sanctuary of La Verna is reputed to be the place where St Francis received the stigmata – marks resembling Christ's wounds. The 11th-century hermitage at Camaldoli was intended as the site for a Benedictine order who wished to live in complete isolation, but proved so popular with religious day-trippers that a visitors' centre soon had to be built nearby. The monastery at Vallombrosa has such glorious woodlands that John Milton was moved to describe them in his epic poem, *Paradise Lost* (1667).

For art-lovers, eastern Tuscany is the region of Piero della Francesca. His frescoes in Arezzo, largely ignored until the late 19th century, form one of the world's greatest fresco cycles.

Pieve di Santi Ippolito e Donato in Pratovecchio, between Poppi and Stia

◄ Detail from Piero della Francesca's fresco cycle *Legend of the True Cross*, from the church of San Francesco, Arezzo

Exploring Eastern Tuscany

The ancient city of Arezzo and the hilltop
town of Cortona, with its steep streets,
narrow, ladder-like alleys and ancient
houses, will amply satisfy visitors in
search of culture, art and architecture.
The region will also appeal to those who
love nature. The woodlands, meadows
and streams are ideal for exploring on
foot. There are plenty of well-marked
paths and picnic areas to encourage
you, especially within the beautiful
ancient forests surrounding the
monasteries at Vallombrosa
and Camaldoli.

Key

▬▬	Motorway
▬▬	Major road
▬	Secondary road
▭▭	Minor road
▭▭	Minor railway
▭▭	Main railway
▬	Regional border
△	Summit

0 kilometres   10

0 miles   10

Cortona, with its steep streets and medieval towers

Getting Around

The region's main highways,
the A1 Autostrada and the S71,
linking Bibbiena, Poppi and
the Casentino, offer swift
access to most of the region.
The remaining roads are
delightfully rural, particularly
the S70, with its fine views near
Vallombrosa, but be prepared
for steep gradients and hairpin
bends. Some roads in the
Casentino are very narrow.
There are passing places, but a
speed limit of 40 km/h (25 mph)
means you should leave plenty
of time for your journey.

    Bus and rail transport is very
limited. An intercity train service
links Florence to Arezzo, from
where there are irregular bus
services to other major towns
in the region.

For hotels and restaurants see pp252–7 and pp264–75

Sights at a Glance

Ancient forest in the Casentino: a rich ecological enclave

Medieval street in Monte San Savino

For keys to symbols *see back flap*

① The Mugello

Road map: D2. Borgo San Lorenzo. **𝑖** Largo La Vacchini (055 845 62 30).

The Mugello is the area to the north and east of Florence. The scenic S65 passes the **Parco Demidoff** at Pratolino, to the south of the region. Here, you can see a giant statue of the mountain god, Appennino, carved by Giambologna in 1580. Just to the north, the **Convento di Montesenario** offers excellent views. Further east lies the wine town of Rufina, with its **Museo della Vita e del Vino della Val di Sieve**.

Parco Demidoff
Via Fiorentina 6, Pratolino. **Tel** 055 40 94 27. **Open** Apr–Oct: 10am–5pm Fri, 10am–7pm Sat & Sun (until 8pm Jun–Aug).

Convento di Montesenario
Via Montesenario 1, Bivigliano. **Tel** 055 40 64 41. Church: **Open** daily. Convent: **Open** by request.

Museo della Vita e del Vino della val di Sieve
Villa di Poggio Reale, Rufina. **Tel** 055 839 79 32.

② Borgo San Lorenzo

Road map: D2. 15,500. **𝑖** Largo La Vacchini (055 845 62 30). Tue.

Substantially rebuilt after an earthquake in 1919, this is the largest town of the Mugello. The parish church, the **Pieve di San Lorenzo**, has an odd

Tabernacle of St Francis, in Borgo San Lorenzo

Romanesque campanile, circular in its lower stages and hexagonal above. In the apse, the wall paintings (1906) are by the Art Nouveau artist Galileo Chini. He also worked on the Tabernacle of St Francis (1926), a shrine outside the church, and the Santuario del Santissimo Crocifisso, a church on the edge of town.

To the west are the **Castello del Trebbio**, with its gardens, and the **Villa di Cafaggiolo**, with its bulging clock tower. Among the first Medici villas, both were built for Cosimo il Vecchio by Michelozzo di Bartolommeo (1396–1472).

Pieve di San Lorenzo
Via Cocchi 4. **Open** Mon–Sat, Sun pm.

Castello del Trebbio
San Piero a Sieve. **Tel** 055 845 87 93 (Mon, Wed, Fri pm). **Open** Nov–Easter: Tue–Fri by appt.

Villa di Cafaggiolo
Cafaggiolo, Barberino del Mugello. **Tel** 055 849 81 03 (Mon, Wed, Fri am). **Closed** indefinitely.

Woodland landscape at Vallombrosa

③ Vallombrosa

Road map: D2. from Florence. **Tel** 055 86 20 03. Church: **Open** from 3:30pm daily. Abbey: **Open** by appt.

Like the monasteries of the Casentino *(see p200)*, the abbey buildings at Vallombrosa are surrounded by woodland. The routes to this sight are all very scenic.

The Vallombrosan order was founded by Saint Giovanni Gualberto Visdomini in 1038. He aimed to persuade like-minded aristocrats to join him in relinquishing their wealth and adopting a life of great austerity. Contrary to these worthy ideals, the order grew wealthy and powerful during the 16th and the 17th century. It was then that today's fortress-like abbey was built. Today, the order comprises some 20 monks.

In 1638, the English poet John Milton (1608–74) visited the abbey. The beautiful scenery of this area inspired a passage in his epic poem, *Paradise Lost*.

Façade of Santa Maria Assunta in Stia

❹ Stia

Road map: D2. 3,017.
Piazza Tanucci 65 (0575 50 41 06) (summer only). Tue.

Stia is a bustling, attractive village on the Arno. In the main piazza is the Romanesque church of **Santa Maria Assunta**, with a rather plain façade. Inside is a 16th-century terracotta *Madonna and Child* by Andrea della Robbia.

There are two medieval Guidi family castles close by: **Castello di Palagio**, with an attractive garden, and the **Castello di Porciano**, which houses an agricultural museum.

Santa Maria Assunta
Piazza Tanucci. **Open** daily.

Castello di Palagio
Via Vittorio Veneto. **Tel** 0575 58 33 88. **Open** Jul–Sep: Sat–Sun, Tue.

Castello di Porciano
Porciano. **Tel** 3290 20 92 58. **Open** by appointment only.

❺ Camaldoli

Road map: E2. from Bibbiena. **Tel** 0575 55 60 12. Monastery: **Open** 9am–1pm, 2:30–7pm daily (to 7:30pm in summer). Hermitage: **Tel** 0575 55 60 21. **Open** 8:30–11:15am, 3–6pm daily. Museo Ornitologico Forestale: **Tel** 0575 55 61 30.
camaldoli.it

The monastery was founded in 1046 and today houses 40 Carthusian monks. Visitors to Camaldoli will want to see not only the monastery, but the original *eremo* (hermitage), 2.5 km (1.5 miles) away. A narrow, winding road leads up from the monastic complex to the hermitage through thick forest. This ancient woodland, some of the most ecologically rich in Europe, was declared a National Park in 1991. The hermitage dates back to 1012 when San Romualdo (St Rumbold) came here with a small group of followers, to cut themselves off completely from the outside world. Today's monks lead a more gregarious life, running a small café in the monastery below. As you descend to the monastery complex you will also pass numerous picnic spots and some of the many local footpaths. The monks still tend the magnificent beech and chestnut woodland that surrounds the ancient monastery, as their predecessors have done for nearly 1,000 years. A pharmacy, dating from1543, now sells soaps, toiletries and liqueurs made by the monks. There is a small, privately owned ornithological museum across the road from the monastery, opposite the car park, which illustrates the area's rich bird life.

❻ Poppi

Road map: E2. 6,700.
Via Cesare Battisti 23 (0575 52 96 82). Tue.

The older part of Poppi is located high above the town's bus and train termini. Its splendid castle, the imposing **Castello di Poppi**, can be seen from as far away as Bibbiena *(see p200)*. Just to the south of the town is the **Zoo Fauna Europa**, which specializes in the conservation of endangered European species, such as the Apennine wolf and the lynx.

Visible from Poppi, a short drive to the northwest up the Arno valley, is the 11th-century **Castello di Romena**, where Dante stayed as a guest of the local rulers in the early 14th century. Romena's *pieve*, dating to 1152, is a typical example of a Romanesque village church.

Castello di Poppi
Tel 0575 52 99 64. **Open** Apr–Oct: daily; Nov–Mar: Thu–Sun. partial.

Zoo Fauna Europa
Poppi. **Tel** 0575 52 90 79. **Open** 9am–sunset daily.

Castello di Romena
Pratovecchio. **Tel** call Tourist Office for info. **Closed** to the public.

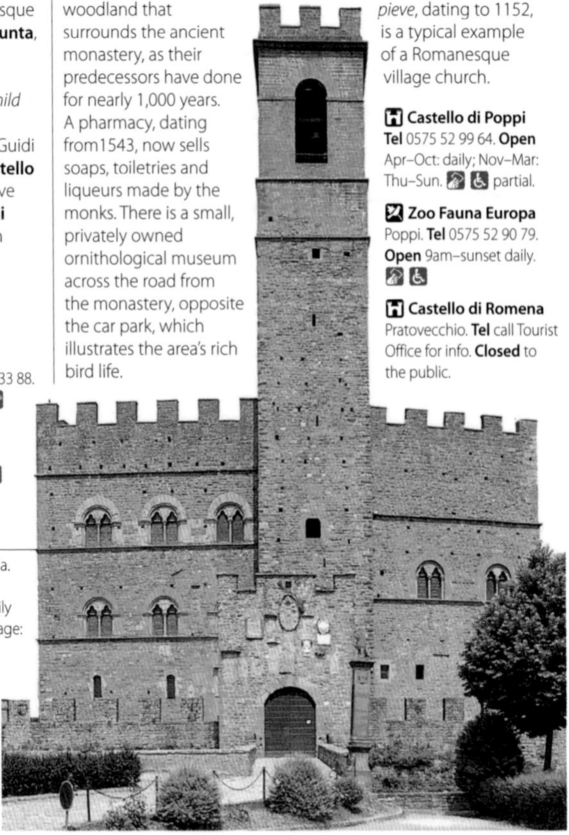

Castello di Poppi, which towers over Poppi and overlooks the entire Casentino

Casentino landscape

❼ Bibbiena

Road map: E2. 🔼 11,000. 🚗 🚌
ℹ️ Bibbiena train station (0575 59
30 98). 🛒 Thu.

One of the oldest towns in the
region, Bibbiena was the subject
of intense territorial feuding
between Arezzo and Florence
in medieval times. It is now the
commercial centre of the
Casentino region, surrounded
by sprawling factories and
industrial buildings.

The town's main attraction
is the **Pieve di Santi Ippolito e
Donato**. Dating from the
12th century, this church
contains some fine Siena school
paintings and an altarpiece by
Bicci di Lorenzo (1373–1452).

Bibbiena's main square, the
Piazza Tarlati, offers excellent
views of Poppi (see p199).

🏛 Pieve di Santi Ippolito
e Donato
Piazza Tarlati. ⏱ 8am–noon, 3–6pm
daily. 🛒

❽ La Verna

Road map: E2. 🚌 from Bibbiena.
Tel 0575 53 41. **Open** 7am–7pm daily.
🛒 partial.

The rocky outcrop on which La
Verna monastery stands – called
La Senna – was split, according
to legend, by an earthquake
when Christ died on the Cross.
The site was given to St Francis
by the local ruler, Count Orlando
Cattani, in 1213, and it was here,
in 1224, that the saint was
miraculously marked with the
stigmata – the wounds of Christ.

Today, the monastery is
both a popular tourist
sight and a charismatic
religious centre. Its
modern buildings are
not particularly
attractive, but they
contain numerous
sculptures by the della
Robbia workshops.
There are several
waymarked paths
through the surrounding
woodland, leading to
some excellent viewpoints.

❾ The Casentino

Road map: E2. 🚉 🚌 from Bibbiena.
ℹ️ Bibbiena.

The vast Casentino region, an
area of tiny villages dotted
among hills covered with ancient
woodland, lies to the north of
Arezzo. The river Arno has its
source here, on the slopes of
Monte Falterona. Countless
streams run down the region's

valleys to join it, creating
stunning waterfalls.

A favourite destination for
walkers, the area is renowned
for its abundant autumn
mushroom crop (see p206).

❿ Caprese
Michelangelo

Road map: E2. 🔼 1,671. 🚌
from Arezzo. ℹ️ Via Capoluogo 1
(0575 79 37 76).

Michelangelo Buonarroti was
born in Caprese on 6 March
1475, while his father served as
the town's *podestà* –
a combination of
magistrate, mayor and
chief of police. His
birthplace is now a
museum, the **Comune
Casa Natale Michel-
angelo**, housing
photos and copies
of the artist's work.
The town walls feature
modern sculptures
and have fine views
over the alpine
landscape. Michelangelo
attributed his keen mind to the
mountain air he breathed here
as a child.

Michelangelo
Buonarroti
(1475–1564)

🏛 Comune Casa Natale
Michelangelo
Casa del Podestà, Via Capoluogo 1. **Tel**
0575 79 37 76. **Open** daily; call ahead
for up-to-date details of opening
hours. **Closed** Tue (Oct–May). 🎫

⓫ Sansepolcro

Road map: E3. 🔼 15,700. 🚌
ℹ️ Via Matteotti 8 (0575 74 05 36).
🛒 Tue, Sat.

Sansepolcro is a busy industrial
town, famous as the birthplace
of the artist Piero della Francesca
(1410–92). The **Museo Civico**,
housed in the 14th-century
Palazzo Comunale, contains a
collection of his work. The most
famous exhibit is Piero's fresco
The Resurrection (1463), in which
a curiously impassive Christ
strides out of His tomb. The
sleeping soldiers at His feet, in
their Renaissance armour, seem
trapped in time, while the Son
of God takes possession of a

The monastery at La Verna, founded by St Francis in 1213

primitive, eternal landscape. Other works by Piero are displayed in the same room, notably the *Madonna della Misericordia* (1462).

Sansepolcro is home to a number of other major works. Chief among these are Luca Signorelli's 15th-century *Crucifixion* (also in the Museo Civico) and Rosso Fiorentino's Mannerist *Deposition*, in **San Lorenzo** church.

🏛 Museo Civico
Via Aggiunti 65. **Tel** 0575 73 22 18. **Open** Oct–May: 9:30am–1pm, 2:30–6pm daily; Jun–Sep: 9am–1:30pm, 2:30–7pm daily. **Closed** 1 Jan, 25 Dec. 🅿 🚻 *(partial).*

🏠 San Lorenzo
Via Santa Croce. **Tel** 0575 74 05 36. **Open** 10am–1pm, 3–6pm daily. 🚻

⑫ Anghiari
Road map: E3. 🚶 5,874. 🚌
🛈 Via Matteotti 103 (0575 74 92 79). 🍴 Wed.

The Battle of Anghiari, between Florence and Milan in 1440, was to have been the subject of a fresco by Leonardo in Florence's Palazzo Vecchio. It was never painted – one of the greatest

Anghiari, a typical medieval walled town

"lost" works of the Renaissance. Today, this historic little town sits peacefully amid fields of tobacco, a traditional crop of the upper valley of the river Tevere (Tiber), which rises nearby on the slopes of Monte Fumaiolo.

🏛 Museo Statale di Palazzo Taglieschi
Piazza Mameli 16. **Tel** 0575 78 80 01. **Open** 9am–6pm Tue–Thu, 10am–7pm Fri–Sun. **Closed** 1 Jan, 1 May, 25 Dec. 🅿

Several major works, such as Jacopo della Quercia's fine wooden *Madonna* (1420), can be seen here. There are also displays of locally made furniture and toys.

🏠 Santa Maria delle Grazie
Propositura. **Open** daily. 🚻
The town's main church, dating to the 18th century, contains a High Altar and tabernacle from the della Robbia workshops. There is also a 15th-century *Madonna and Child* painted by Matteo di Giovanni.

🏛 Museo della Misericordia
Via Francesco Nenci 13. **Tel** 0575 78 95 77. **Open** by appointment.
The Misericordia, a charitable organization, was founded in the 13th century to look after ailing pilgrims on their way to Rome. Today, it operates Tuscany's ambulance service *(see p293)*. This small museum records their work.

⑬ Monterchi
Road map: E3. 🚶 1,910. 🚌
🛈 Arezzo. 🍴 Sun.

The cemetery chapel at Monterchi was the site chosen in 1460 by Piero della Francesca for his *Madonna del Parto* (Pregnant Madonna) *(see p32)*, possibly because his mother may be buried here. The restored fresco is now in the **Museo Madonna del Parto**. A work of haunting ambiguity, it simultaneously captures the Virgin's pride in the impending birth, the weariness of pregnancy and the sorrow borne of knowing that her child will be no ordinary man.

🏛 Museo Madonna del Parto
Via Reglia 1. **Tel** 0575 707 13. **Open** 9am–1pm, 2–7pm daily (to 5pm Nov–Mar). **Closed** 25 Dec. 🅿 🚻 *(partial).*

The Resurrection (1463), by Piero della Francesca, in Sansepolcro

⑭ Arezzo

One of the wealthiest cities in Tuscany, Arezzo produces gold jewellery for shops all over Europe. It is famous for Piero della Francesca's frescoes and for its antiques market. Following World War II, there was much rebuilding – broad avenues have replaced many of the medieval alleys. The Chimera fountain near the station is a reminder of the city's past. It is a copy of an Etruscan bronze *(see p46)* cast here in 380 BC.

Duomo façade, completed as recently as 1914

Chimera fountain

🔲 San Francesco
See pp204–205.

🔲 Pieve di Santa Maria
Corso Italia 7. **Tel** 0575 226 29.
Open 8:30am–12:30pm, 3–6:30pm daily. 🔲 pievesantamaria.it

Arezzo's main shopping street, Corso Italia, leads uphill to the Pieve di Santa Maria, which has a beautifully ornate Romanesque façade. Sadly, the complex filigree of interlaced arches has weathered badly.

The splendid campanile, the "tower of a hundred holes", dates to 1330. Its name derives from the many arches running through it.

🔲 Piazza Grande
The square is famous for its antiques market. On the west side, the façade of the Palazzo della Fraternità dei Laici is decorated with a relief of the Virgin (1434) by Bernardo Rossellino. The lower half of the building dates from 1377. The belfry and clock tower date from 1552.

The north side of the square features a handsome arcade designed by Vasari in 1573.

🔲 Fortezza Medicea e Parco il Prato
Tel 0575 37 76 78. **Open** summer: 7am–8pm; winter: 7:30am–6:30pm.

Antonio da Sangallo the Younger's imposing fortress was built for Cosimo I during the 16th century. It was partly demolished in the 18th century, leaving only the ramparts intact. With its excellent views across the Arno valley, it remains an excellent spot for a picnic.

The same can be said of the city's large public park, the Parco il Prato, with its extensive lawns. It contains a huge statue (1928) of the great poet Petrarch. The house where he was born stands at the entrance to the park.

🔲 Duomo
Piazza del Duomo. **Open** daily.

Begun in 1278, the Duomo remained incomplete until 1510; its façade dates to 1914. A huge building, its Gothic interior is lit through windows containing beautiful 16th-century stained glass by Guillaume de Marcillat, a French artist who settled in Arezzo.

High on the wall to the left of the 15th-century High Altar can be seen the tomb of Guido Tarlati, bishop and ruler of Arezzo from 1312 until his death in 1327. Carved reliefs depict scenes from his unconventional life. Next to the tomb is a small fresco of Mary Magdalene by Piero della Francesca (1410–92).

The Lady Chapel, fronted by an intricate wrought-iron screen (1796), contains a terracotta *Assumption* by Andrea della Robbia (1435–1525).

🔲 Museo del Duomo
Piazzetta behind the Duomo 13.
Tel 0575 239 91. **Open** 10am–noon Thu–Sat. Ask the sacristan to let you in. 🔲

Among the artifacts removed from the cathedral are three wooden crucifixes, dating from the 12th and the 13th century. The oldest of these was painted by Margaritone di Arezzo in 1264.

Also of interest are Bernardo Rossellino's terracotta bas-relief of *The Annunciation* (1434), a number of frescoes by Vasari (1512–74) and an *Annunciation* by Spinello Aretino (1373–1410).

Apse of Pieve di Santa Maria and Palazzo della Fraternità dei Laici in Piazza Grande

🏠 Casa del Vasari

Via XX Settembre 55.
Tel 0575 40 90 40. **Open** 9am–
7pm Mon, Wed–Fri, 9am–1pm
Sat & Sun. 🐾

Vasari (1512–74) built this
house for himself in 1540 and
decorated the ceilings and
walls with portraits of fellow
artists, friends and mentors.
He also painted himself
looking out of one of
the windows. A prolific
painter and architect,
Vasari is most famous
for his book, *Lives of the
Most Excellent Painters, Sculptors
and Architects* (1550). An account
of many great Renaissance
artists, it has, in spite of an often
cavalier attitude to the truth, led
to Vasari being described as the
first art historian.

**Detail of fresco from
Casa del Vasari**

🏛 Museo Statale d'Arte Medioevale e Moderna

Via di San Lorentino 8. **Tel** 0575 40
90 50. **Open** 8:30am–7pm daily.
Closed 1 Jan, 1 May, 25 Dec. 🐾 ♿
The museum is housed in the
graceful 15th-century Palazzo
Bruni. Its courtyard contains
architectural fragments and
sculptures dating from the
10th to the 17th century.

The collection includes one
of the best displays of majolica
pottery in Italy. There are also
several terracottas by Andrea
della Robbia and his followers;
frescoes by Vasari
and Signorelli; and
paintings by 19th- and
20th-century artists,
including members of
the Italian Macchiaioli
school (*see p127*).

🏛 Anfiteatro Romano e Museo Archeologico

Via Margaritone 10. **Tel** 0575 222 59.
Amphitheatre Open 8:30am–6pm
daily (to 8pm in summer).
Museum Open 8:30am–7:30pm daily.
Closed 1 Jan, 1 May, 25 Dec. 🐾 for
the museum. ♿

A ruined Roman amphitheatre
stands near the Museo
Archeologico.
Famous for its
extensive collection
of Roman Aretine
ware, the museum
has a display showing
how this high-quality red-
glazed pottery was produced
and exported throughout
the Roman Empire during
the 1st century BC.

**1st-century BC
Aretine ware**

🏠 Santa Maria delle Grazie

Via di Santa Maria. **Open** 8am–
7pm daily.

Completed in 1449 and set
in its own walled garden, this
church, fronted by Benedetto
da Maiano's pretty loggia
(1482), stands on the south-
eastern outskirts of the town.
The High Altar,
by Andrea
della Robbia
(1435–1525),
encloses Parri
di Spinello's fresco
of the Virgin (1430).
A damaged fresco by
Lorentino d'Arezzo
(1430–1505) is on
the right of the altar.

Arezzo

① Casa del Vasari
② Museo Statale d'Arte
　　Medioevale e Moderna
③ Museo del Duomo
④ Duomo
⑤ San Francesco
⑥ Pieve di Santa Maria
⑦ Piazza Grande
⑧ Fortezza Medicea
　　e Parco il Prato
⑨ Anfiteatro Romano e
　　Museo Archeologico

0 metres　　　　500
0 yards　　　　　500

For key to symbols *see back flap*

San Francesco

The 13th-century church of San Francesco contains Piero
della Francesca's *Legend of the True Cross* (1452–66), one of
Italy's greatest fresco cycles. The frescoes, now visible again
after a long restoration, show how the Cross was found near
Jerusalem by the Empress Helena. Her son, the Emperor
Constantine, adopted it as his battle emblem. In reality,
Constantine granted the Christian faith official recognition
through the Edict of Milan, signed in 313. He is said to have
bequeathed the Empire to the Church in 337, although
this was still hotly disputed when Piero painted the
frescoes. Visitors have a limited time in the chapel
and advance booking is mandatory.

Exaggerated Hats
Piero often depicted historical
figures in Renaissance garb.

Painted Crucifix
The 13th-century Crucifix
forms the focal point of
the fresco cycle. The figure
at the foot of the Cross
represents St Francis.

KEY

① **The Annunciation**, with its
stately figures and aura of serenity,
is typical of Piero's enigmatic style.

② **The Queen of Sheba** recognizes
the wood of the Cross.

③ **The buildings** reflect the newly
fashionable Renaissance style.

④ **The wood** of the Cross is buried.

⑤ **Judas reveals** where the Cross
is hidden.

⑥ **The Empress Helena** watches
the Cross being dug up. The town
in the background, symbolizing
Jerusalem, is 15th-century Arezzo.

⑦ **The Cross** returns to Jerusalem.

⑧ **The prophets** appear to play no
part in the narrative cycle; their
presence may be purely decorative.

⑨ **Constantine dreams** of the
Cross on the eve of battle.

⑩ **Constantine adopts** the Cross as
his battle emblem.

The Defeat of Chosroes
The battle scene shows the chaos of Renaissance warfare.
Piero was influenced by ancient Roman carving, especially
the battle scenes that often decorated sarcophagi.

The Death of Adam

This vivid portrayal of Adam and Eve in old age illustrates Piero's masterly treatment of anatomy. He was one of the first Renaissance artists to paint nude figures.

Solomon's Handshake

The Queen's handshake with Solomon, King of Israel, symbolizes 15th-century hopes for a union between the Orthodox and Western churches.

Mushrooms in Tuscany

The people of Tuscany consider mushrooms a great delicacy. Collecting fungi can be dangerous, unless you are an expert, but you can sample the best varieties in the region's restaurants. The smaller edible varieties are sometimes chopped and combined with mashed garlic to make a pasta sauce. As starters, many menus include *funghi trifolati* (sautéed mushrooms with garlic and parsley), or the region's most popular mushrooms, porcini, served *in gratella* (grilled). The prized truffle is often simply grated over home-made pasta; it has a pronounced flavour and should be used sparingly.

Gathering chanterelles *(right)* and saddle fungus *(left)*

Cauliflower fungus
(*Sparassis crispa*)

Field blewit
(*Lepista personata*)

Chanterelle
(*Cantharellus cibarius*)

Parasol
(*Lepiota procera*)

Cep
(Boletus edulis)

Oyster
(*Pleurotus ostreatus*)

Morel
(*Morchella esculanta*)

Champignon
(*Marasmius oreades*)

The Best Tuscan Mushrooms

Prized species have a rich flavour and a firm texture. They are sold from mid-September to late November at shops and markets throughout the region.

Porcini
This popular mushroom, known in England as the cep, is one of the few wild species available all year, either fresh or dried.

⓯ Monte San Savino

Road map: E3. 7,794.
Piazza Gamurrini 3 (0575 817 71).
Wed.

The town stands on the western edge of the Valdichiana, once a marshy and malaria-ridden plain that was drained by Cosimo I in the 16th century. It is now an area of rich farmland used to rear cattle whose meat is used for *bistecca alla fiorentina*, the famous beefsteaks served in Florentine restaurants (*p261*).

Agriculture has made the town prosperous, and its streets are lined with handsome buildings and churches. Some of these are by the High Renaissance sculptor and architect Andrea Contucci, known as Sansovino (1460–1529), who was born in the town; a number are by Antonio da Sangallo the Elder (1455–1537), his contemporary.

The town's main street, Corso Sangallo, starts at the Porta Fiorentina town gate, built in 1550 to Giorgio Vasari's design. The street leads past the 14th-century Cassero, or Citadel, whose exterior walls are now almost entirely hidden by 17th-century houses. There are good views from the interior, which contains the tourist office and the small **Museo del Cassero**, with its extensive collection of

Locally made vase, Museo di Ceramica

local work. Further up the street is the handsome Classical Loggia dei Mercanti (1518–20), designed by Sansovino, and the Palazzo Comunale, originally built as the Palazzo di Monte by Sangallo for Cardinal Antonio di Monte in 1515. Sansovino's house can be seen in the Piazza di Monte. He laid out the square, built the fine double loggia with Ionic columns that fronts **Sant'Agostino** church and went on to design the cloister standing alongside it. Inside the church is a series of 15th-century frescoes illustrating scenes from *The Life of Christ*, and Vasari's *Assumption* altarpiece (1539). Sansovino's worn tomb slab lies beneath the pulpit.

Ⅲ Museo del Cassero
Piazza Gamurrini. **Tel** 0575 84 30 98. **Open** Apr–Oct: 9am–1pm Tue, 9am–1pm & 4–7pm Wed–Fri, 9am–1pm & 2:30–7:30pm Sat & Sun; Nov–Mar: 9am–1pm Wed–Sun, plus 4–7pm Sat & Sun.

⚑ Sant'Agostino
Piazza di Monte. **Open** daily.

⓰ Lucignano

Road map: E3. 3,349.
Piazza del Tribunale 22 (0575 838 01). Thu.

An attractive medieval town, Lucignano contains many well-preserved 14th-century houses. The street plan is extremely unusual, consisting of a series

Lucignano, with its oval street plan

of four concentric rings encircling the hill upon which the town sits, sheltered by its ancient walls. There are four small piazzas at the centre.

The **Collegiata** is fronted by some attractive steps whose circular shape reflects the town's street plan. Completed by Orazio Porta in 1594, the church contains some fine gilded wooden angels added in 1706.

The 14th-century Palazzo Comunale houses the **Museo Comunale**. Its highlight is a massive gold reliquary, 2.5 m (8 ft) high, to which numerous artists contributed over the period 1350–1471. Because of its shape, it is known as the *Tree of Lucignano*.

Also of note are two 14th-century paintings by Luca Signorelli: a lunette showing St Francis of Assisi miraculously receiving the wounds of Christ to his hands and feet, and a *Madonna and Child*. There are several fine 13th- to 15th-century Siena school paintings and a small painting of the Madonna by Lippo Vanni (1341–75).

The vaulted ceiling of the main chamber, the Sala del Tribunale, has frescoes of famous biblical figures and characters from Classical mythology, painted from 1438–65 by various Siena school artists.

⚑ Collegiata
Costa San Michele. **Tel** 0575 83 61 22.

Ⅲ Museo Comunale
Piazza del Tribunale 22. **Tel** 0575 83 80 01. **Open** 10am–1pm, 3–6pm Tue, Thu–Sun; by appt Wed (winter: open only Sat & Sun).

Corso Sangallo in Monte San Savino

⓱ Cortona

Cortona is one of the oldest cities in Tuscany. It was founded by the Etruscans *(see p46)*, whose work can still be seen in the foundations of the town's massive stone walls. The city was a major seat of power during the medieval period, able to hold its own against larger towns like Siena and Arezzo; its decline followed defeat by Naples in 1409, after which it was sold to Florence and lost its autonomy. The main street, Via Nazionale, is remarkably flat in comparison with the rest of Cortona. The numerous ladder-like alleys leading off it, for instance the Vicolo del Precipizio (Precipice Alley), are far more typical.

Medieval houses in Via Janelli

Palazzo Comunale

🏛 Palazzo Comunale

Closed to the public.
Dating from the 13th century, the building was enlarged at the beginning of the 16th century to incorporate the distinctive tower. Its ancient steps are the ideal place to linger in the early evening.

🏛 Museo dell'Accademia Etrusca

Palazzo Casali, Piazza Signorelli 9.
Tel 0575 63 72 35. **Open** Apr–Oct: 10am–7pm daily; Nov–Mar: 10am–5pm Tue–Sun. **Closed** 1 Jan, 25 Dec. 🅿 ♿ partial.

This is one of the region's most rewarding museums. It contains a number of major Etruscan artifacts, including a unique bronze chandelier *(see p47)* dating from the 4th century BC. There are also a number of Egyptian objects. These include a wooden model funerary boat dating to the second millennium BC.

On the west wall of the main hall is a beautiful fresco of Polymnia, the muse of song. It was once believed to be

Roman and date from the 1st or 2nd century AD, but it is now known to be a brilliant 18th-century fake.

🏛 Duomo

Piazza del Duomo. **Open** daily. ♿
The present Duomo was designed by Giuliano da Sangallo in the 16th century. Remains of an earlier Romanesque building were incorporated into the west façade. The entrance is through an attractive doorway (1550) by Cristofanello.

🏛 Museo Diocesano

Piazza del Duomo 1. **Tel** 0575 628 30.
Open Apr–Oct: 10am–7pm daily; Nov–Mar: 10am–5pm Tue–Sun.
🅿 ♿
Housed in the 16th-century church of Gesù, the museum contains several masterpieces. Chief among these are Fra Angelico's *Annunciation* (1428–30), a *Crucifixion* by Pietro Lorenzetti (c.1280–1348) and a *Deposition* by Luca

Signorelli (1441–1523). There is also a Roman sarcophagus featuring Lapiths and Centaurs, which was much admired by Donatello and Brunelleschi.

🏛 Via Janelli

The medieval houses in this short street are some of the oldest to survive in Italy. A striking feature is their over-hanging upper floors, built out on massive timbers.

🏛 San Francesco

Via Maffei. **Closed** to the public.
The church was built in 1245 by Brother Elias, a native of Cortona, who succeeded St Francis as leader of the Franciscan order. He and the Painter Luca Signorelli (1441–1523), also born locally, are buried here.

🏛 Piazza Garibaldi

Located on the eastern edge of town, this square is a favourite haunt of American students, who come to Cortona each

The Annunciation (1428–30), by Fra Angelico, in the Museo Diocesano

summer. It offers superb views of the handsome Renaissance church of Santa Maria delle Grazie al Calcinaio.

🔼 Via Crucis and Santa Margherita

The Via Crucis, a long uphill lane with gardens on either side, leading to the 19th-century church of Santa Margherita, was laid out as a war memorial in 1947. It is decorated with Futurist mosaics depicting episodes in Christ's Passion by Gino Severini (1883–1966).

The church, rebuilt from 1856 to 1897 in the Romanesque-Gothic style, has excellent views over the surrounding country-side. Inside, to the right of the altar, lie a number of Turkish battle standards and lanterns captured during 18th-century naval battles. A single rose window remains from the original church.

🔼 Santa Maria delle Grazie

Calcinaio. **Open** daily.
A 15-minute stroll from the centre of town, this remarkable

Santa Maria delle Grazie

Renaissance church (1485) is one of the few surviving works by Francesco di Giorgio Martini (1439–1502). The building is opened on request – ask at the caretaker's house, beyond a garden to the right of the main entrance.

The attractive High Altar (1519), built by Bernardino Covatti, contains a 15th-century image of the Madonna del Calcinaio. The stained glass is by Guillaume de Marcillat (*see p202*).

🔼 Tanella di Pitagora

Maestà del Sasso, on the road to Sodo. **Tel** 0575 63 04 15. **Open** daily. Book one day in advance at the Museo dell'Accademia Etrusca.

VISITORS' CHECKLIST

Practical Information
Road Map E3.
🏛 22,620. 🛈 Via Nazionale 42 (0575 63 03 52). 🗓 Sat. 🎭 Sagra della Bistecca (14–15 Aug). Shops: **Closed** Mon am.

Transport
🚆 Camucia, 5 km (3 miles) SE. 🚌 Piazza Garibaldi.

"Pythagoras's tomb" draws its name from a mix-up between Cortona and Pythagoras's birthplace, Crotone. Two Etruscan tombs nearby are called "melons", because of the grassy mounds around them.

Tanella di Pitagora, a Hellenic-style tomb on the plain below Cortona

---

Cortona

① Via Janelli
② Museo Diocesano
③ Duomo
④ Museo dell'Accademia Etrusca
⑤ Palazzo Comunale
⑥ San Francesco
⑦ Piazza Garibaldi
⑧ Santa Margherita

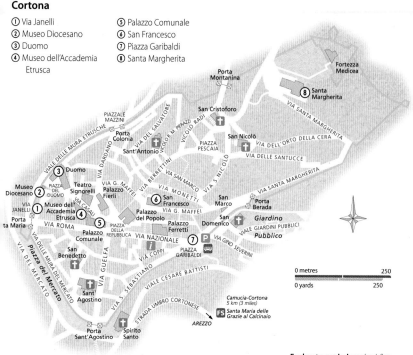

CENTRAL TUSCANY

With Siena at its heart, central Tuscany is an agricultural area of great scenic beauty, noted for its historic walled towns, such as San Gimignano and Pienza. To the north of Siena is the Chianti Classico region, where some of Italy's best wines are produced; to the south is the Crete, with landscapes characterized by round clay hillocks, eroded of topsoil by heavy rain over the centuries.

The vine-clad hills to the north of Siena are dotted with farmhouses, villas and baronial castles. Many are now turned into luxury hotels or rental apartments, offering various leisure facilities, such as tennis courts, swimming pools and riding stables: this is now one of the most popular areas for family holidays in the Tuscan countryside.

To the south of Siena, in the Crete, shepherds tend sheep whose milk is used to produce the Pecorino cheese that is popular throughout Tuscany. Cypress trees, planted to provide windbreaks along roads and around isolated farms, are an important sculptural feature in this empty and primeval landscape.

Linking the two regions is the S2 highway, an ancient road along which pilgrims made their way in the Middle Ages, followed by travellers on the Grand Tour *(see p59)* in the 18th and 19th centuries. Romanesque churches line the roads, and the valleys and passes are defended by castles and garrison towns, most of which have hardly changed over the years.

Constant Conflict

The history of the region is of a long feud between the two city states of Florence and Siena. Siena's finest hour was its victory in the Battle of Montaperti in 1260, but when the city finally succumbed to the Black Death, and subsequently to a crushing defeat by Florence in the siege of 1554–5, it went into decline.

As several other central Tuscan cities experienced the same fate, this lovely region became a forgotten backwater, frozen in time. But after centuries of neglect, the graceful late-medieval buildings in many of the towns are now being well restored, making this the most architecturally rewarding part of Tuscany to explore.

The beautifully preserved fortified town of Monteriggioni

◄ Chianti vineyards and farmhouse near Panzano

Exploring Central Tuscany

The beautiful city of Siena, with its narrow streets and medieval buildings of rose-coloured brick, is the natural starting place for exploring the heart of Tuscany. From here, it is only a short drive to the castle-dotted landscapes of Chianti to the north, or to historic towns, such as San Gimignano and Montepulciano. Although these towns are full of visitors during the day, at night they revert to their timeless Tuscan character and many have first-class restaurants serving local fare. The landscape is of cypresses, olive groves, vineyards, simple churches and stone farmhouses.

Wicker-covered *damigiane* (demijohns) transporting local Chianti wine

Getting Around

The S2 is the main road south through Siena. The S222 links Florence with Siena and is known as the *Chiantigiana* (Chianti Way), as it passes through the Chianti wine-growing area. Both routes are well served by bus services, and tour operators in both cities offer tours of the main sites. Train services are limited to one line between Florence and Siena. A car is a great advantage, especially for visiting the Chianti wine estates.

View over Siena from the surrounding hills

For hotels and restaurants see pp252–7 and pp264–75

Key

═══ Motorway

═══ Major road

━━━ Secondary road

╌╌╌ Minor road

----- Minor railway

⋯⋯ Main railway

━━━ Scenic route

═══ Regional border

△ Summit

Landscape with cypresses typical of the Crete area

Sights at a Glance

1 San Gimignano
2 Colle di Val d'Elsa
3 Monteriggioni
4 Siena
5 Asciano
6 Monte Oliveto Maggiore
7 San Galgano
8 Montalcino
9 San Quirico d'Orcia
10 Bagno Vignoni
11 Pienza
12 Montepulciano
13 Chiusi
14 Sant'Antimo

● Street-by-Street: San Gimignano

The distinctive skyline of San Gimignano must have been a welcome sight to the faithful in medieval times, for the town lay on the main pilgrim route from northern Europe to Rome. This gave rise to its great prosperity at that time, when its population was twice what it is today. The plague of 1348, and later the diversion of the pilgrim route, led to its economic decline. Following World War II, there was a rapid recovery thanks to tourism and local wine production. For a small town, San Gimignano is rich in works of art, and boasts good shops and restaurants.

Sant'Agostino
Here, Bartolo di Fredi painted *Christ, Man of Sorrows*.

To Sant'Agostino

Via San Matteo, in contrast with the more commercial Via San Giovanni, caters mainly for the local residents, selling food and wine, clothes and other typical Tuscan products.

Rocca (1353)

La Buca, Via San Giovanni, selling local wine and wild-boar ham

★ Collegiata
This 11th-century church is covered in delightful frescoes, including *The Creation* (1367), by Bartolo di Fredi.

Museo Ornitologico

Museo d'Arte Sacra
The museum contains religious paintings, sculpture and liturgical objects from the Collegiata.

Key

— Suggested route

0 metres	250
0 yards	250

★ **Piazza del Duomo**
Among the historic buildings located here is the Palazzo Vecchio del Podestà (1239), whose tower is probably the town's oldest.

There are spectacular views from the top of the Torre Grossa.

VISITORS' CHECKLIST

Practical Information
Road Map: C3.
7,041. Piazza del Duomo 1 (0577 94 00 08).
Thu. Shops: **Closed** Mon am (summer); souvenir shops stay open. Patron Saints' Festivals: 31 Jan, 12 Mar; Ferie delle Messi: 3rd weekend of June; Fiera di Santa Fina: 1st wk of Aug; Fiera di Sant'Agostino: 29 Aug; Festa della Madonna di Pancole: 8 Sep.
W sangimignano.com

Transport
Porta San Giovanni.

★ **Palazzo del Popolo**
The impressive town hall (1288–1323) has a huge *Maestà* by Lippo Memmi in the council chamber.

Piazza della Cisterna
is named after the well at its centre.

Museo Civico
This gallery, found on the upper floors of the Palazzo del Popolo, houses *The Madonna with Saints Gregory and Benedict* (1511), which was one of the last works to be painted by Pinturicchio.

Via San Giovanni
is lined with shops selling local goods.

Exploring San Gimignano

The "city of beautiful towers" is one of the best-preserved medieval towns in Tuscany. Its stunning skyline bristles with tall towers dating from the 13th century: 14 of the original 76 have survived. These windowless towers were built to serve both as private fortresses and symbols of their owners' wealth. In the Piazza della Cisterna, ringed by a jumble of unspoilt 13th- and 14th-century palazzi, is a wellhead built in 1237. Shops, galleries and jewellers line the two main streets, Via San Matteo and Via San Giovanni, which still retain their medieval feel.

![San Gimignano's skyline, almost unchanged since the Middle Ages]

San Gimignano's skyline, almost unchanged since the Middle Ages

🏛 Palazzo Vecchio del Podestà

Piazza del Duomo.
Closed to the public.
The Palazzo Vecchio del Podestà (the old mayor's palace) is in a group of public buildings clustered around the central Piazza del Duomo. It has a vaulted loggia and the 51-m (166-ft) Torre della Rognosa, one of the oldest towers in San Gimignano. A law was passed in 1255 forbidding any citizen to build a higher tower, but the rule was often broken by rival families.

🏛 Museo Civico

Palazzo del Popolo, Piazza del Duomo.
Tel 0577 99 03 12. **Museum & Tower Open** Apr–Sep: 9:30am–7pm daily; Oct–Mar: 11am–5:30pm daily.
Closed 31 Jan. 🗞
The museum is on the south side of the Piazza del Duomo, in the Palazzo del Popolo (town hall). Its tower, finished in 1311, is the tallest in the city, at 54 m (175 ft). This is open to the public and the views from the top are quite

stunning. Worn frescoes in the courtyard feature the coats of arms of city mayors and magistrates, as well as a 14th-century *Virgin and Child* by Taddeo di Bartolo. The first public room is the Sala di Dante, where an inscription records the poet's plea to the city council in 1300 to support the Guelph (pro-pope) alliance, led by Florence. The walls are covered with hunting scenes and a huge *Virgin Enthroned* by Lippo Memmi (1317).

12th-century well and medieval palazzi in the triangular Piazza della Cisterna

The floor above has a small art collection, which includes Pinturicchio's *Madonna with Saints Gregory and Benedict* (1511), painted against a landscape of blues and greens. The painting of *San Gimignano and his Miracles*, by Taddeo di Bartolo, shows the saint holding the town – recognizably the same city we see today. The *Wedding Scene* frescoes, by Memmo di Filippucci (early 14th-century), show a couple sharing a bath and going to bed – an unusual record of life in a wealthy household in 14th-century Tuscany.

🏛 Museo d'Arte Sacra

Piazza Pecori. **Tel** 0577 94 03 16.
Open Apr–Oct: 10am–7:10pm Mon–Fri, 10am–5:10pm Sat, 12:30–7:10pm Sun; Nov–Mar: 10am–4:40pm Mon–Sat, 12:30–4:40pm Sun).
Closed 2 weeks in Nov & Jan. 🗞

The museum is entered from Piazza Pecori, where buskers play in summer. A chapel on the ground floor contains elaborate tomb slabs. The first floor houses paintings, sculpture and liturgical objects from the Collegiata. A marble bust (1493), by Benedetto da Maiano, commemorates the scholar Onofrio di Pietro.

🏛 Collegiata

Piazza del Duomo. **Tel** 0577 94 03 16.
Open as Museo d'Arte Sacra, above.
Closed 21 Jan–28 Feb. 🗞
The plain façade of this 12th-century Romanesque church belies its exotic interior; it is one of the most frescoed churches in Italy. The arches bordering the central aisle are painted in striking blue and white stripes, and the deep blue paint of the vaulted roof is speckled with gold stars. The aisle walls are extensively covered with dramatic fresco cycles of scenes from the Bible. In the north aisle, the frescoes are on three levels and comprise 26 episodes from the Old Testament, including *The Creation of Adam and Eve*, *Noah and his Ark*, *Moses Crossing the Red Sea* and *The Afflictions of Job*,

The ceiling of the Collegiata, painted with gold stars

finished by Bartolo di Fredi in 1367. On the opposite walls are scenes from the life of Christ, dated 1333–41, now attributed to Lippo Memmi, a pupil of Simone Martini. At the back of the church, on the nave walls, are scenes from *The Last Judgment*, painted by Taddeo di Bartolo (1393–6). They depict the souls of the damned being tortured in hell by devils relishing their task.

The tiny Santa Fina chapel, off the south aisle, is covered with a cycle of frescoes by Ghirlandaio (1475) telling the life story of St Fina; legend has it that she spent most of

her short life in prayer. The towers of San Gimignano feature in the background of the funeral scene.

Under an arch to the left of the Collegiata is a courtyard containing the loggia to the Baptistry, frescoed with an *Annunciation* that was painted in 1482 by Ghirlandaio.

🏰 Rocca

Piazza Propositura. **Open** daily.
The Rocca, or fortress, was built in 1353. It now has only one surviving tower following its dismantling by Cosimo I de' Medici in the 16th century. It encloses a public garden filled with fig and olive trees, and commands superb views over the vineyards where wine has been produced for hundreds of years.

🏰 Sant'Agostino

Piazza Sant'Agostino. **Tel** 0577 90 70 12. **Open** 7am–noon, 3–7pm Tue–Sun (from 10am Dec–Mar). ♿

This church was consecrated in 1298 and has a simple façade that contrasts markedly with the heavily decorated Rococo interior (c.1740) by Vanvitelli, architect to the kings of Naples. Above the main altar is the *Coronation of the Virgin*, by Piero del Pollaiuolo, dated 1483, and the choir is entirely covered in

a cycle of frescoes of *The Life of St Augustine* (1465), by the Florentine artist Benozzo Gozzoli and his assistants.

In the Cappella di San Bartolo, on the right of the main entrance, is an elaborate marble altar completed by Benedetto da Maiano in 1495. The bas-relief carvings show the miracles performed by St Bartholomew, all topped by flying angels and a roundel of the Madonna and Child.

Detail from *The Life of St Augustine*

🏛 Museo Ornitologico

Via Quercecchio. **Tel** 0577 94 13 88.
Open Apr–Sep: 11am–5:30pm daily. 🎟

The museum is in an elaborate 18th-century Baroque church. This is in total contrast to the sturdy cases of stuffed birds that form the collection, put together by a local dignitary.

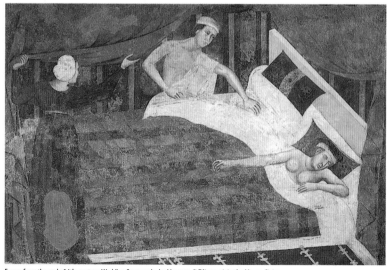

Fresco from the early 14th-century *Wedding Scene* cycle, by Memmo di Filippucci, in the Museo Civico

Palazzo Campana, the gateway to Colle Alta, in Colle di Val d'Elsa

❶ San Gimignano

See pp214–17.

❷ Colle di Val d'Elsa

Road map: C3. ⛰ 17,200.
FS 🚌 🛈 Via Campana 43
(0577 92 27 91). 🛒 Fri.

Colle di Val d'Elsa has a lower and an upper town. Colle Alta, the upper town, is of great medieval architectural interest. Arnolfo di Cambio, who built the Palazzo Vecchio in Florence *(see pp82–3)*, was born here in 1232. In the modern lower town, shops sell locally made crystal glass.

🏛 Palazzo Campana
Closed to the public.
This Mannerist palazzo was built on a viaduct in 1539 by Baccio d'Agnolo, forming a gateway to Colle Alta.

↟ Duomo
Piazza del Duomo. **Open** 4–5pm
Mon–Fri, Sun morning (for Mass only).
The Duomo has a marble Renaissance pulpit carved with bas-reliefs of the Madonna (1465), attributed to Giuliano da Maiano. The façade was rebuilt in 1603.

🏛 Museo Archeologico
Palazzo Pretorio, Piazza del Duomo.
Tel 0577 92 04 90. **Open** Oct–Apr: 3:30–
5:30pm Tue–Fri, 10:30am–12:30pm,
3–6:30pm Sat & Sun; May–Sep:
10:30am–12:30pm, 4:30–7:30pm
Tue–Sun (from 3pm Sat & Sun). 🈂
The museum houses many Etruscan funerary urns. The building was once a jail: Communist slogans written on the walls survive from the 1920s.

🏛 Museo d'Arte Sacra
Via del Castello 31. **Tel** 0577 92 38 88.
Open see Museo Civico.
Part of the Museo Civico, this museum features 14th-century frescoes of hunting scenes by Bartolo di Fredi, Sienese paintings and a collection of Etruscan pottery.

Sgraffito cherub, Museo Civico

🏛 Museo Civico
Via del Castello 31. **Tel** 0577 92 38 88.
Open May–Sep: 10:30am–12:30pm,
4:30–7:30pm Tue–Sun; Oct–Apr: 3:30–
5:30pm Tue–Fri, 10:30am–12:30pm,
3:30–6:30pm Sat & Sun. 🈂
The museum is housed in the ancient Palazzo dei Priori, whose façade is decorated with *sgraffito* work scratched in the plaster, incorporating cherubs and Medici

coats of arms. There is a collection of Siena school paintings and some fine examples of Etruscan pottery. The chapel next to the main room has a portico decorated with frescoes by Simone Ferri in 1581.

↟ Santa Maria in Canonica
Via del Castello. **Open** sporadically.
The Romanesque church has a simple bell tower and a stone façade decorated with brickwork. The interior was altered in the 17th century. A tabernacle by Pier Francesco Fiorentino shows scenes from the lives of the Madonna and Child.

🛡 Porta Nova
Via Gracco del Secco. **Open** daily.
This large Renaissance fortress was designed by Giuliano da Sangallo in the 15th century to guard against attack from the Volterra road. Two heavily fortified cylindrical towers are on the outside of the building.

❸ Monteriggioni

Road map: D3. ⛰ 720. 🚌
🛈 Piazza Roma 23 (0577 30 48 10).

Monteriggioni is a gem of a medieval hilltop town. It was built in 1203 and ten years later became a garrison town. It is encircled by high walls with 14 heavily fortified towers, built to guard the northern borders of Siena's territory against invasion by Florentine armies.

Dante used the town as a simile for the abyss at the heart of his *Inferno*, which compares

Craft shop in the main piazza of Monteriggioni

Monteriggioni's "ring-shaped citadel … crowned with towers" to giants standing in a moat.

The walls, which are still perfectly preserved, are best viewed from the direction of the Colle di Val d'Elsa road. Within the walls, the sleepy village consists of a large piazza, a pretty Romanesque church, a few houses, a couple of craft shops, restaurants, and shops selling many of the excellent local Castello di Monteriggioni wines.

❹ Siena

See pp220–27.

❺ Asciano

Road map: D3. 🅰 6,250. 🚉 🚌
ℹ️ Corso Matteotti 78 (0577 71 88 11).
🗓️ Sat.

The road from Siena to Asciano passes through the strange Crete landscape, which is almost bare of vegetation and full of clay hillocks resembling massive anthills. Asciano itself is medieval, and retains much of its fortified wall, built in 1351. The main street, Corso Matteotti, is lined with smart shops and Classical *palazzi*. At the top of the street, in Piazza della Basilica, there is a large fountain built in 1472. Facing it is the late 13th-century Romanesque **Basilica di Sant'Agata**.

The **Museo Civico Archeologico e d'Arte Sacra** in the Palazzo Corboli unites two

Temptation of St Benedict (1508), by Sodoma, in Monte Oliveto Maggiore

previously separate museums under one roof. Included in the collection are late Siena school masterpieces – Duccio's *Madonna and Child* and Ambrogio Lorenzetti's unusual *St Michael the Archangel*. Also on display are local Etruscan finds from the **Necropoli di Poggio Pinci**, 5 km (3 miles) east of the village. The artifacts come from tombs built between the 7th and 4th century BC. On Via Mameli, the **Museo Amos Cassioli** has a display of portraits by Cassioli, who lived here from 1832 to 1891, and other modern works by local artists.

🏛 Basilica di Sant'Agata
Piazza della Basilica. **Open** daily.

🏛 Museo Civico Archeologico e d'Arte Sacra
Corso Matteotti 122. **Tel** 0577 71 95 24. **Open** Mar–Oct: 10:30am–1pm, 3–6:30pm Tue–Sun; Nov–Feb: 10:30am–1pm, 3–5:30pm Thu–Sun. 🏛

🏛 Necropoli di Poggio Pinci
Poggio Pinci. **Open** call tourist office for opening times.

🏛 Museo Amos Cassioli
Via Mameli. **Tel** 0577 71 72 33. **Open** Sat & Sun. 🏛 ♿

❻ Monte Oliveto Maggiore

Road map: D3. 🚉 Asciano MOM **Tel** 0577 70 70 18. **Open** 9:15am–noon, 3:15–5pm daily (to 6pm in summer).

The approach to this abbey is through thick cypresses, with stunning views of eroded cliffs and sheer drops to the valley floor. It was founded in 1313 by the Olivetan order, who were dedicated to restoring the simplicity of Benedictine monastic rule. The 15th-century rose-pink abbey church is a Baroque building with outstanding choir stalls of inlaid wood.

Alongside is the Great Cloister (1427–74), whose walls are covered with a cycle of frescoes on the life of St Benedict, begun by Luca Signorelli, a pupil of Piero della Francesca, in 1495. He completed nine panels; the remaining 27 were finished by Sodoma in 1508. The cycle, which begins on the east wall with Benedict's early life, is considered a masterpiece of fresco painting for its combination of architectural and naturalistic detail.

The Romanesque Basilica di Sant'Agata in Asciano

❹ Street-by-Street: Siena

The principal sights of Siena are found in the network of narrow streets and alleys around the fan-shaped Piazza del Campo. Scarcely any street is level, as Siena, like Rome, is built on seven hills. This adds to the pleasure of exploring: one minute the city is laid out to view before you and the next you are in a warren of medieval houses. Packed into Siena are the 17 *contrade* (parishes) whose animal symbols are everywhere on carvings, plaques and car stickers.

Aerial bridges and corridors linking buildings on opposite sides of the street are characteristic of Siena.

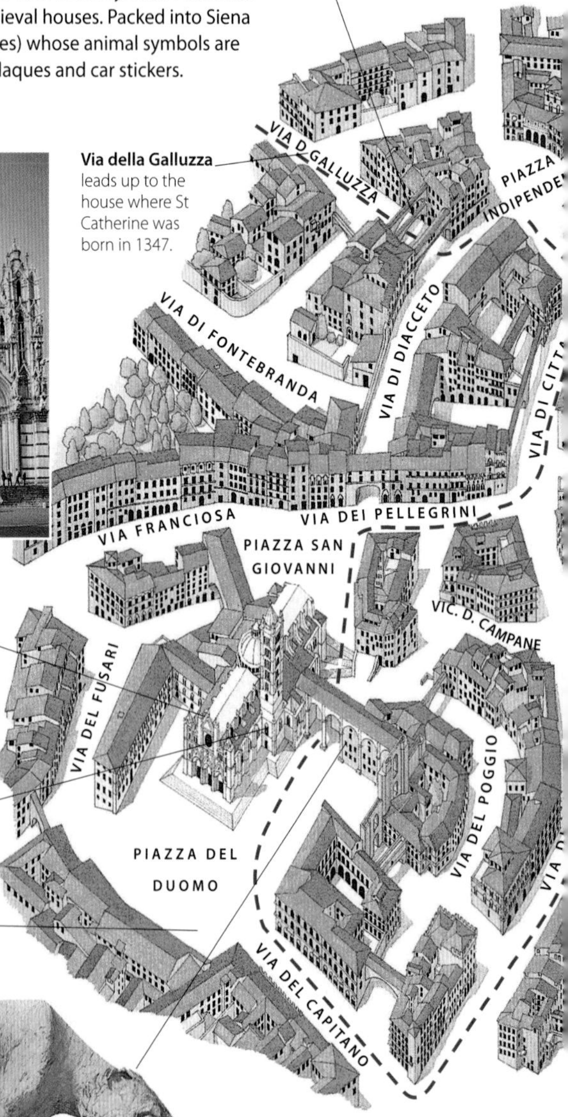

Via della Galluzza leads up to the house where St Catherine was born in 1347.

★ Duomo
Statues of prophets carved by Giovanni Pisano in the 1290s fill the Gothic niches of the marble façade *(see pp224–5)*.

Each tier of the Duomo's bell tower has one window fewer than the floor above.

Antique shops line the streets near the Duomo square.

PIAZZA SAN GIOVANNI

PIAZZA DEL DUOMO

VIA D GALLUZZA

VIA DI FONTEBRANDA

VIA DI DIACCETO

VIA DI CITTÀ

PIAZZA INDIPENDE

VIA FRANCIOSA

VIA DEI PELLEGRINI

VIC. D. CAMPANE

VIA DEL FUSARI

VIA DEL POGGIO

VIA DEL CAPITANO

Museo dell'Opera Metropolitana
The cathedral museum includes works like this statue of Remus *(left)*, whose son is said to have founded Siena.

0 metres — 300
0 yards — 300

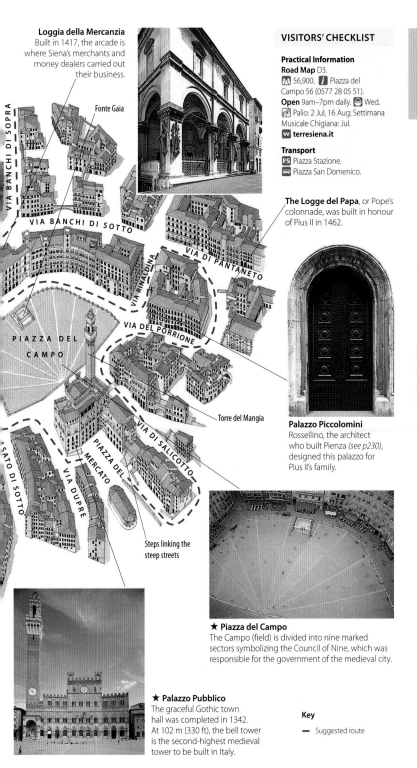

Loggia della Mercanzia
Built in 1417, the arcade is where Siena's merchants and money dealers carried out their business.

Fonte Gaia

VIA BANCHI DI SOPRA

VIA BANCHI DI SOTTO

VIA RINALDINA

VIA DI PANTANETO

VIA DEL PORRIONE

PIAZZA DEL CAMPO

Torre del Mangia

VIA DI SALICOTTO

PIAZZA DEL MERCATO

VIA DUPRE

...SATO DI SOTTO

Steps linking the steep streets

VISITORS' CHECKLIST

Practical Information
Road Map D3.
56,900. Piazza del Campo 56 (0577 28 05 51).
Open 9am–7pm daily. Wed.
Palio: 2 Jul, 16 Aug; Settimana Musicale Chigiana: Jul.
terresiena.it

Transport
FS Piazza Stazione.
Piazza San Domenico.

The Logge del Papa, or Pope's colonnade, was built in honour of Pius II in 1462.

Palazzo Piccolomini
Rossellino, the architect who built Pienza (see p230), designed this palazzo for Pius II's family.

★ **Piazza del Campo**
The Campo (field) is divided into nine marked sectors symbolizing the Council of Nine, which was responsible for the government of the medieval city.

★ **Palazzo Pubblico**
The graceful Gothic town hall was completed in 1342. At 102 m (330 ft), the bell tower is the second-highest medieval tower to be built in Italy.

Key
— Suggested route

Exploring Siena

Siena is a city of steep medieval alleys surrounding the Piazza del Campo. The buildings around the square symbolize the golden age of the city, between 1260 and 1348, when wealthy citizens contributed to a major programme of civic building. Siena's decline began in 1348 when the Black Death hit the city, killing a third of the population; 200 years later many more died in an 18-month siege led by the Florentines, which ended in defeat. The victors repressed all further development and building in Siena, and the town largely remains frozen in time, crammed with many renovated medieval buildings.

Aerial view of Siena's Piazza del Campo and surrounding palazzi

🏛 Piazza del Campo

The shell-shaped, 12th-century Piazza del Campo is bordered by elegant palazzi. It has an elaborate fountain as its focal point, the Fonte Gaia – a rectangular marble basin decorated by statues. The fountain now seen in the square is a 19th-century copy of the original, which was carved by Jacopo della Quercia in 1409–19. This was removed to preserve it from the ravages of the weather.

The reliefs on the fountain depict Adam and Eve, the Madonna and Child, and the Virtues. Water is fed into it by a 25-km (15-mile) aqueduct, which has brought fresh water into the city from the hills since the 14th century.

🏛 Torre del Mangia

Piazza del Campo. **Tel** 055 29 23 42.
Open 10am–7pm (mid-Oct–Feb: to 4pm). **Closed** 25 Dec. 🎫

The bell tower to the left of the Palazzo Pubblico is the second-highest in Italy, at 102 m (330 ft). Built by the brothers Muccio and Francesco di Rinaldo between 1338 and 1348, it is

named after the first bell-ringer, who was nicknamed *Mangiaguadagni* (literally "eat the profits") because of his great idleness. (It was the bell-ringer's responsibility to warn the citizens of impending danger.) There are 505 steps to the top of the tower, which has views across Tuscany.

🏛 Palazzo Pubblico

Piazza del Campo 1. **Tel** 055 29 26 14.
Museo Civico Open Daily. Nov–mid-Mar: 10am–6pm; mid-Mar–Oct: 10am–7pm. **Closed** 2 Jul, 16 Aug, 25 Dec. 🎫

The Palazzo Pubblico serves as the town hall, but the state rooms are open to the public. The main council chamber is called the Sala del Mappamondo, after a map of the world painted by Ambrogio Lorenzetti in the early 1300s. One wall is covered by Simone Martini's *Maestà* (Virgin in Majesty). Painted in 1315, it depicts the Virgin Mary as the Queen of Heaven, attended by the Apostles, saints and angels. Opposite is Martini's fresco of the mercenary Guidoriccio da Fogliano (1330).

The walls of the adjacent chapel are covered with frescoes of the *Life of the Virgin* (1407) by Taddeo di Bartolo, and the choir stalls (1428) feature wooden panels inlaid with biblical scenes.

The Sala della Pace contains the famous *Allegory of Good and Bad Government*, a pair of frescoes by Ambrogio Lorenzetti, finished in 1338. In *The Good Government (see pp50–51)* civic life flourishes, while *The Bad Government* reveals ruins and rubbish-strewn streets. The Sala del Risorgimento is covered with late 19th-century frescoes

Fonte Gaia, in Piazza del Campo

Guidoriccio da Fogliano, by Simone Martini (1330), in the Palazzo Pubblico

illustrating events leading up to the unification of Italy under King Vittorio Emanuele II (*see pp58–9*).

🏛 Palazzo Piccolomini

Via Banchi di Sotto 52. **Tel** 0577 405 63. **Open** entrances at 9:30am, 10:30am & 11:30am Mon–Sat, by appt only. **Closed** 1st two weeks in Aug & public hols. ♿

This imposing palazzo was built in the 1460s by Rossellino for the very wealthy Piccolomini family. It houses the state archives, including the *Tavolette di Biccherna* – municipal ledgers from the 13th century, with covers by Sano di Pietro, Ambrogio Lorenzetti, Domenico Beccafumi and others.

🏛 Pinacoteca Nazionale

Via San Pietro 29. **Tel** 0577 28 11 61. **Open** 8:15am–7:15pm Tue–Sat, 9am–1pm Sun & Mon. **Closed** 1 Jan, 1 May, 25 Dec. ♿

Pisano's *Simone* (c.1300) in the Museo dell'Opera del Duomo

Housed in the 14th-century Palazzo Buonsignori, this gallery contains important works by the Siena school. Lorenzetti's *Two Views*, painted in the 14th century, are early examples of landscape painting, and Pietro da Domenico's *Adoration of the Shepherds* (1510) shows how the art of the Siena school remained stylized long after

Renaissance naturalism had influenced the rest of Europe. There is also a striking *Deposition* (1502) by Sodoma.

⬆ Duomo

See pp224–5.

🏛 Museo dell'Opera Metropolitana

Piazza del Duomo 8. **Tel** 0577 28 30 48. **Open** mid-Mar–Oct: 9:30am–7pm daily (to 8pm Jun–Aug); Nov–mid-Mar: 10am–5pm daily. **Closed** 1 Jan, 25 Dec. ♿

This museum is built into the unfinished side aisle of the Duomo (*see pp224–5*). Part of it houses sculptures from the exterior of the Duomo that had become eroded. Duccio's double-sided *Maestà*, one of the best Siena school works, has a room to itself. Painted in 1308–11, it depicts the Madonna and Child on one side and scenes from *The Life of Christ* on the other. A loggia on the top floor offers views of the town and countryside.

🏛 Santa Maria della Scala

Piazza del Duomo. **Tel** 0577 29 26 15. **Open** 10:30am–6:30pm daily. ♿ 📷

This former hospital is now a museum housing a collection of paintings and sculpture. In the Sala del Pellegrino, frescoes by

Domenico di Bartolo depict hospital scenes from the 1440s, including monks attending to the sick.

Cloister of Casa di Santa Caterina

🏛 Santuario e Casa di Santa Caterina

Costa di Sant'Antonio 6. **Tel** 0577 28 81 75. **Open** 9:15am–1pm, 3–7:30pm daily.

Siena's patron saint, Catherine Benincasa (1347–80), was the daughter of a tradesman. She took the veil aged eight, and experienced many visions of God, from whom she also received the stigmata. Her eloquence persuaded Gregory XI to return the seat of the papacy to Rome in 1376, after 67 years of exile in Avignon. She died in Rome and was canonized in 1461. Today, her house is surrounded by chapels and cloisters. It is decorated with paintings of events from her life by artists such as Pietro Sorri and Francesco Vanni, both her contemporaries.

Siena Duomo

Siena Duomo (1136–1382) is one of the most spectacular in Italy, and one of the few to have been built south of the Alps in full Gothic style. Many ordinary citizens helped to cart the black and white stone used in its construction from quarries on the outskirts of the city. In 1339, the Sienese decided to build a new nave to the south, with the aim of making it the biggest church in Christendom. This plan came to nothing when the plague hit the city soon afterwards, killing off much of the population. The uncompleted nave now contains a museum of Gothic sculpture.

★ **Pulpit Panels**
Carved by Nicola Pisano in 1265–8, the panels on the octagonal pulpit depict scenes from *The Life of Christ.*

★ **Inlaid Marble Floor**
The Massacre of the Innocents is one of a series of scenes in the inlaid marble floor. The marble is usually uncovered each year, in September and October.

Nave
Black-and-white marble pillars support the vault.

KEY

① **Chapel of St John the Baptist**

② **Archway leading to the Baptistry**

③ **The side aisle** of the unfinished nave was roofed over and turned into the Museo dell'Opera del Duomo.

④ **Column base in unfinished nave**

⑤ **The façade** was built in two parts: the doors in 1284–97, the rest in 1382–90.

★ **Piccolomini Library**
Pinturicchio's frescoes (1509) portray the life of Pope Pius II *(see p230)*. Here, he presides at the betrothal of Frederick III to Eleonora of Portugal.

Unfinished Nave

If completed, the nave would have measured 50 m (162 ft) in length and 30 m (97 ft) in breadth.

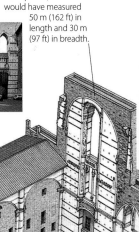

VISITORS' CHECKLIST

Practical Information
Piazza del Duomo. **Tel** 0577 28 30 48. **Open** Mar–mid-Aug: 10:30am–7pm Mon–Fri, 1:30–6pm Sat & Sun; mid-Aug–Oct (inlaid floor on show): 10:30am–7:30pm Mon–Sat, 9:30am–6pm Sun; Nov–Feb: 10:30am–5:30pm Mon–Fri, 1:30–5:30pm Sat & Sun. ✝ 8, 9, 11am Mon–Sat; 8, 11am, 12:15, 6:30pm (5:30pm Sep–Mar) Sun. 🚻 ♿ 📷 W **operaduomo.siena.it**

Transport
🚌 Pollicino.

Façade Statues
Many statues on the façade have been replaced by copies; the originals are in the Museo dell'Opera del Duomo.

Sun Symbol
Hoping to end bloodshed and rivalry, St Bernardino of Siena (1380–1444) wanted the feuding Sienese to give up all loyalty to their *contrada* emblems and unite under this symbol of the risen Christ.

Entrance to Duomo

The Sienese Palio

The Palio is Tuscany's most celebrated festival and takes place on 2 July and 16 August each year in the Campo *(see p222)*. It is a bareback horse race and was first recorded in 1283, but may have had its origins in Roman military training. The jockeys represent the 17 *contrade*, or districts; the horses are chosen by the drawing of straws and are then blessed at the local *contrada* churches. The races are preceded by heavy betting and pageantry, but only last about 90 seconds each. The winner is awarded a *palio* (banner).

Ringside View
Huge sums are paid for a view of the races.

Flag-Throwing
The Sienese display their flag-throwing skills in the procession and pageantry before the race.

Medieval Knight
The traditional outfits worn in the processions are all hand-made.

Traditional drummer taking part in pre-race pageant

Racing Crowds
Thousands of people cram into the piazza to watch the race, and rivalry is intense between competitors.

Galloping towards the finish

View across the Campo during a race

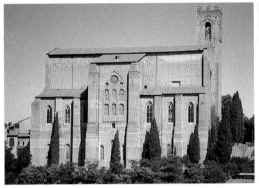

The façade of San Domenico

🏛 San Domenico

Piazza San Domenico. **Open** daily.

This barn-like Gothic church was begun in 1226 and its bell tower was added in 1340. Inside is an exquisite chapel dedicated to St Catherine *(see p223)*. It was built in 1460 to store her preserved head, which is now kept in a gilded marble tabernacle on the altar. This is surrounded by frescoes showing Catherine in a state of religious fervour, painted by Sodoma in 1526. The marble pavement is attributed to Giovanni di Stefano.

Catherine experienced many of her visions and received her stigmata in the Cappella delle Volte, at the west end of the church. Here, there is an authenticated portrait of her by contemporary Andrea Vanni, dated around 1380.

🏛 Fortezza Medicea

Viale Maccari. Fortezza: **Open** daily. Theatre: **Open** Nov–Apr: performances only. **Closed** May–Oct.

This huge red-brick fortress was built for Cosimo I by Baldassarre Lanci in 1560, following Siena's defeat by the Florentines in the 1554–5 war. The fortress now houses an open-air theatre, and from the entrance bastions there are fine views of the countryside.

🏛 Accademia Musicale Chigiana

Palazzo Chigi Saracini, Via di Città 89. **Tel** 0577 220 91. **Open** for concerts and exhibitions – call or check website for details. **W** chigiana.it

Founded by Count Guido Chigi Saracini in 1932, the Accademia holds master classes for the principal musical instruments. Housed in one of the finest buildings in Siena, there is also a fine-art collection, a museum of musical instruments and a library containing original manuscripts. Concerts and occasional exhibitions are also held here.

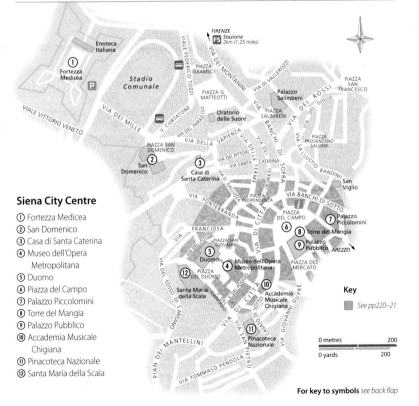

Siena City Centre

① Fortezza Medicea
② San Domenico
③ Casa di Santa Caterina
④ Museo dell'Opera Metropolitana
⑤ Duomo
⑥ Piazza del Campo
⑦ Palazzo Piccolomini
⑧ Torre del Mangia
⑨ Palazzo Pubblico
⑩ Accademia Musicale Chigiana
⑪ Pinacoteca Nazionale
⑫ Santa Maria della Scala

Key

See pp220–21

0 metres 200
0 yards 200

For key to symbols *see back flap*

The ruined abbey at San Galgano, surrounded by dense woodland

❼ San Galgano

Road map: D4 (località Chiusdino).
🚌 from Siena. Abbey and oratory:
Open daily.

The ruined Cistercian abbey is in a superb setting, surrounded by woodland. It is very remote but well worth the effort of getting there for the beauty of the surroundings and the majesty of the roofless building. Begun in 1218, the abbey is Gothic in style; unusual in Tuscany, this reflects the French origins of the Cistercian monks who designed and built it.

The monks avoided contact with civilization and divided their lives between prayer and labour, clearing the hills of vegetation to graze their sheep. Despite the Cistercian emphasis on poverty, the monks became wealthy from the sale of wool; by the middle of the 14th century, the abbey was corruptly administered and gradually fell into decline.

In the late 14th century, the English mercenary Sir John Hawkwood sacked the abbey, and by 1397, the abbot was the sole occupant. Numbers recovered for a time, but the abbey was eventually dissolved in 1652. Empty for many years, the cloister and other monastic buildings alongside the church are now being restored for the Olivetan order of nuns. On a hill

above the abbey is the beehive-shaped chapel of Montesiepi, built on the site of St Galgano's hermitage around 1185, a few years after his death in 1181.

St Galgano's sword stands embedded in a stone just inside the door of the circular oratory. The 14th-century stone walls of the side chapel are covered with frescoes showing scenes from Galgano's life by Ambrogio Lorenzetti (1344); some are now in a poor state of repair.

The shop alongside the chapel sells locally made herbs, wines, olive oils and toiletries, along with books on the history of the region.

❽ Montalcino

Road map: D4. 🚐 5,100. 🚌
🛈 Costa del Municipio 8 (0577 84 93 31). **Closed** Mon. 🛒 Fri.

Montalcino's foremost activity is wine-producing, as is evident from the number of shops where you can both sample and buy the excellent local Brunello wines *(see p262)*.

The town, situated on the top of a hill, has a timeless character and the streets are narrow, winding and steep. The highest point is the 14th-century **Fortezza** and its impressive ramparts, built by Cosimo I in 1571. Spectacular views over

The Legend of St Galgano

Galgano was born in 1148, the son of noble parents, and grew into a brave but dissolute young knight. He saw his life as futile and turned to God, renouncing the material world. When he tried to break his sword against a rock as a symbol of his rejection of war, it was swallowed by the stone. This he interpreted as a sign of God's approval. He built a hut on the site of today's chapel at Montesiepi, and died a hermit in 1181. In 1185, Pope Urban III declared him a saint and an example to all Christian knights.

Montalcino's 14th-century Fortezza

Collegiata in San Quirico

the surrounding countryside are available from the walkway on the ramparts.

There is an *enoteca* (wine shop) in the grounds of the Fortezza, where the Brunello red wines are on sale.

Inside the fortress there is an ancient Sienese battle standard, a reminder that the town gave refuge to a band of rebels after Florence conquered Siena in 1555. In remembrance of this, flag-bearers from the village of Montalcino are given the honour of leading the parade before the Palio in Siena every year *(see p226)*. As you walk down into the town from the Fortezza, the monastery of Sant'Agostino and its 14th-century church, with an attractive rose window, are on the right. Just beyond is the **Palazzo Vescovile**, formerly the bishop's palace. The **Palazzo Comunale** stands on the Piazza del Popolo. Constructed in the 13th and the 14th century, its tall, slim tower rises above the town.

The Duomo, San Salvatore, was designed in 1818–32 by Agostino Fantastici, and replaced the original Romanesque church building.

🏠 **Fortezza**
Piazzale della Fortezza. **Tel** 0577 84 92 11. Enoteca: **Open** Nov–Mar: 9am–6pm daily; Apr–Oct: 9am–8pm daily. 🏛 for ramparts.

🏛 **Palazzo Vescovile**
Via Spagni 4. **Tel** 0577 84 81 68. **Closed** to the public.

🏛 **Palazzo Comunale**
Costa del Municipio 1. **Tel** 0577 84 93 31. **Closed** to the public.

❾ San Quirico d'Orcia

Road map: E4. 🚗 2,390. 🚌
🛈 Piazza Chigi 2 (0577 89 97 24).
📅 2nd & 4th Tue of month.

Standing just inside the city walls, San Quirico d'Orcia's pride is the **Collegiata**, featuring three ornately carved Romanesque portals built onto an 8th-century structure. Begun in 1080, the capitals and lintels of the portals are carved with details of dragons, mermaids and other mythical beasts.

The church commemorates the 3rd-century martyr St Quiricus, who was killed at the age of five by the Romans for the simple act of declaring himself a Christian. Quiricus is depicted in the elaborate altar piece by Sano di Pietro, along with the Virgin and Child and other saints.

Next to the church is the 17th-century **Palazzo Chigi**, whose frescoed interior has been restored. The **Horti Leonini** nearby is a 16th-century garden of box hedges nestling within the town walls. It was intended as a refuge for pilgrims, and is now used as a public sculpture garden during the summer months.

🏠 **Collegiata**
Via Dante Alighieri. **Tel** 0577 89 72 36. **Open** 8am–5pm daily.

🏛 **Palazzo Chigi**
Piazza Chigi. **Open** 10am–1pm, 4–7pm (Oct–Mar: 3:30–6:30pm) Tue–Sun.

🌳 **Horti Leonini**
Piazza Libertà. **Tel** 0577 89 72 11. **Open** sunrise–sunset daily. ♿ partial.

Flower-covered house in the pretty town of Montalcino

The Terme di Bagno Vignoni

⑩ Bagno Vignoni

Road map: D4. 🔼 32. 🚌 from Siena.
🅸 0577 88 73 65.

This is a tiny medieval spa village that consists of a handful of houses built around a huge piazza containing an arcaded, stone-lined pool. Constructed by the Medici, the pool is full of hot sulphurous water that bubbles up to the surface from the volcanic rocks deep underground. The healing quality of the water has been known since Roman times and, according to legend, famous people who have sought a cure in Bagno Vignoni include St Catherine of Siena (see p223) and Lorenzo the Magnificent (to relieve his arthritis). The pool is no longer open for bathing, but is still well worth a visit to admire the architecture. Sulphur pools in the grounds of the Posta Marcucci hotel are open for swimming.

⑪ Pienza

Road map: E4. 🔼 1,300. 🚌 🅸 Corso il Rossellino 59 (0578 74 90 71). 🛒 Fri.

The centre of Pienza was completely redesigned in Renaissance times by Pope Pius II (see p53). Born here in 1405, when it was called Corsignano, Aeneas Sylvius Piccolomini became known as a leading Humanist scholar and philosopher. He was elected pope in 1458 and in the following year decided to commission a new centre in

Corsignano and rename it Pienza in his own honour. He planned to transform his birthplace into a model Renaissance town, but the grand scheme never progressed beyond the handful of buildings around the Piazza Pio II. The architect Bernardo Rossellino was commissioned to build a Duomo, papal palace and town hall here, which were finished in three years. Subsequently, Rossellino was caught embezzling papal funds, but Pius II forgave him because he was so delighted with his new buildings.

The isolated monastery of Sant'Anna in Camprena, with its wonderful frescoes painted by Sodoma, is nearby. The original monastery dates from the 13th century, however, the present building is 16th century.

⛪ Duomo

Piazza Pio II. **Open** daily.
The Duomo was built by the architect Rossellino in 1459, and is now suffering from subsidence at its eastern end. There are cracks in the walls and floor of the nave, but this does not detract at all from the splendid Classical proportions of this Renaissance church. It is flooded with light from the vast stained-glass windows requested by Pius II; he wanted a *domus vitrea* (literally "a house of glass"), which would symbolize the spirit of intellectual enlightenment of the Humanist age.

Coat of arms of
Pope Pius II

🏛 Palazzo Piccolomini

Piazza Pio II. **Tel** 0578 74 85 03.
Open 10am–1pm, 2–6:30pm Tue–Sun (guided tours only). **Closed** mid-Nov– early Dec & mid-Feb–early Mar. 🈲

The palazzo is next door to the Duomo and was home to Pius II's descendants until 1968. Rossellino's design for the building was influenced by Leon Battista Alberti's Palazzo Rucellai in Florence (see p108). The apartments open to the public include Pius II's bedroom and library, which are full of his belongings. At the rear of the palazzo there is an arcaded courtyard and a triple-tiered loggia. The spectacular view looks across the garden and takes in the wooded slopes of Monte Amiata.

Courtyard in Palazzo Piccolomini

⛪ Pieve di Corsignano

Via delle Fonti. **Tel** 0578 74 82 03.
Open by appt or through tourist office.
Pope Pius II was baptized in this 11th-century Romanesque parish church on the outskirts of Pienza. It has an unusual round tower and a doorway decorated with flower motifs.

Pienza's piazza and the town hall, viewed from the steps of the Duomo

The church of Madonna di San Biagio, on the outskirts of Montepulciano

⑫ Montepulciano

Road map: E4. 🗺 14,000. 🚌
ℹ Piazza Don Minzoni 1 (0578 75 73 41). 🛒 Thu.

Montepulciano is built along a narrow limestone ridge and, at 605 m (1,950 ft) above sea level, is one of the highest of Tuscany's hilltop towns. The town is encircled by walls and fortifications designed by Antonio da Sangallo the Elder in 1511 for Cosimo I. Inside the walls, the streets are crammed with Renaissance-style palazzi and churches, but the town is chiefly known for its good local Vino Nobile wines (see p262). A long winding street called the Corso climbs up into the main square, which crowns the summit of the hill.

On the Corso is the Art Deco Caffè Poliziano, which has an art gallery in the basement. In July, the café hosts a jazz festival and the town fills with musicians who perform at the Cantiere Internazionale d'Arte (see p39), an arts festival directed by the German composer Hans Werner Henze.

In August, there are two festivals: the Bruscello takes place on the 14th, 15th and 16th, when scenes from the town's turbulent history are re-enacted. For the Bravio delle Botti, on the last Sunday in August, there is a parade through the streets followed by a barrel race and a banquet.

🔼 Madonna di San Biagio
Via di San Biagio 14.
Open 8:30am–7pm daily. 🚻
This beautiful church, with a restored façade, is perched on a platform below the city walls, on the outskirts of Montepulciano. Built of honey- and cream-coloured travertine, it is Sangallo's masterpiece, a Renaissance gem begun in 1518. The project occupied him until his death in 1534.

🏛 Palazzo Bucelli
Via di Gracciano del Corso 73.
Closed to the public.
The lower façade of the palazzo (1648) is studded with ancient Etruscan reliefs and funerary urns, collected by its 18th-century antiquarian owner, Pietro Bucelli.

🔼 Sant'Agostino
Piazza Michelozzo. **Open** daily.
Michelozzo built the church in 1427 with an elaborate carved portal featuring the Virgin and Child flanked by St John and St Augustine.

🏛 Palazzo Comunale
Piazza Grande 1. **Tel** 0578 71 73 00.
Tower Open Apr–Oct: 10am–1pm, 2–6pm daily. 🏛 Museum: **Open** 10am–1pm, 3–6pm Tue–Sun (Jun & Jul: to 7pm; Aug: 10am–7pm). 🏛
In the 15th century, Michelozzo added a tower and façade on to the Gothic town hall. The building is now a smaller version of the Palazzo Vecchio (see pp82–3).

🏛 Palazzo Tarugi
Piazza Grande. **Closed** to the public.
This imposing 16th-century palazzo is located next to the town hall.

🔼 Duomo
Piazza Grande. **Open** 8:30am–1pm, 3–7pm daily.
The Duomo was designed between 1592 and 1630 by Ippolito Scalza. The façade is unfinished and plain, but the interior is Classical in proportions. It is the setting for an earlier masterpiece from the Siena school, the *Assumption of the Virgin* triptych painted by Taddeo di Bartolo in 1401. Placed over the High Altar, it is rich in bright, jewel-like colours and heavily embossed with gold leaf.

Taddeo di Bartolo's triptych (1401)

🔼 Santa Maria dei Servi
Via del Poliziano. **Open** by appt. 🚻
The Corso continues from the Piazza up to the Gothic church of Santa Maria dei Servi. The wine bar alongside sells Vino Nobile from medieval storage cellars cut out of the limestone cliffs below the town.

Etruscan frieze in the Museo Archeologico Nazionale in Chiusi

🔞 Chiusi

Road map: E4. 🚗 10,000. 🚆 🚌
ℹ️ Piazza Duomo 1 (0578 22 76 67).
🏛️ Mon, Tue.

Chiusi was one of the most powerful cities in the Etruscan league, reaching the height of its influence in the 7th and the 6th century BC *(see pp46–7)*. There are many Etruscan tombs in the surrounding countryside.

🏛️ Museo Archeologico Nazionale
Via Porsenna 93. **Tel** 0578 201 77.
Open 9am–8pm daily. 🚹 ♿
The museum, founded in 1871, is packed with cremation urns, vases decorated with black figures and Bucchero ware, burnished to resemble bronze. Most of these were excavated from local tombs, which can be visited by arrangement with the museum.

🏛️ Duomo
Piazza del Duomo. **Open** daily.
The Romanesque cathedral is built from recycled Roman pillars and capitals. The decorations on the nave walls seem to be mosaics, but in fact were painted by Arturo Viligiardi in 1887. There is a Roman mosaic under the High Altar.

🏛️ Museo della Cattedrale
Piazza del Duomo. **Tel** 0578 22 64 90.
Open Jun–mid-Oct: 9:30am–12:45pm, 4–7pm daily; mid-Oct–May: 9:30am–12:45pm Mon–Sat, 3:30–6:30pm Sun (Jan–Mar: open only Tue, Thu, Sat). 🚹 ♿ partial.

The museum has an interesting display of Roman, Lombardic and medieval sculpture. Visits can be arranged here to the

underground galleries beneath the city, which were dug by the Etruscans and used as Christian catacombs in the 3rd to the 5th century.

🔞 Sant'Antimo

Road map: D4. Custodian: 0577 83 56 59. **Open** 10:30am–12:30pm, 3–6:30pm Mon–Sat, 9:15–10:45am, 3–6pm Sun. ♿

This beautiful abbey church *(see pp48–9)* has inspired many poets and painters, and enchants everyone who comes here.

The creamy travertine church is set against a background of tree-clad hills in the Starcia valley. The very earliest surviving church on the site dates back to the 9th century, but locals prefer to think the church was founded by the Holy Roman Emperor Charlemagne in 781. The main part of the church was built in 1118 in the French Romanesque style, and the exterior is decorated with interlaced blank arcades carved with the symbols of the Four Evangelists.

The soft, honey-coloured alabaster interior has an odd luminous quality that is seen to change according to the time of day and season. The capitals in the nave are carved with geometric designs, leaf motifs and biblical scenes. Recorded plainsong echoes around the walls, adding to the eerie atmosphere.

The Augustinian monks who tend the church sing Gregorian chants at mass every Sunday, and there are organ concerts in the church during July and August.

The beautiful abbey church of Sant'Antimo

A Day Out in Chianti

This tour takes in the main villages of the Chianti Classico wine region. Castles and wine estates line the route, and vineyards offer tastings and sell direct to the public. Look for signs along the way saying "vendita diretta".

The first stop on leaving Siena is the Castello di Brolio, which has been owned by the Ricasoli family since 1167. From Brolio, drive to Gaiole, diverting to see the 13th-century castle at Meleto. Gaiole is a very quiet agricultural town with a stream running down the main street; wine can be sampled here at the local cooperative. In Badia a Coltibuono, there is a Romanesque church, and Radda in Chianti offers extensive views over the Parco Naturale della Viriglia. At Castellina in Chianti, there is a 15th-century underground passage built for defence purposes, and the Enoteca Vini Gallo Nero (Via della Rocca 13), which is a showcase for the region's wines *(see pp262–3).*

④ Badia a Coltibuono
At the crossroads in Gaiole, follow the signs to Montevarchi and divert to the left off the main road before heading right towards the village of Badia.

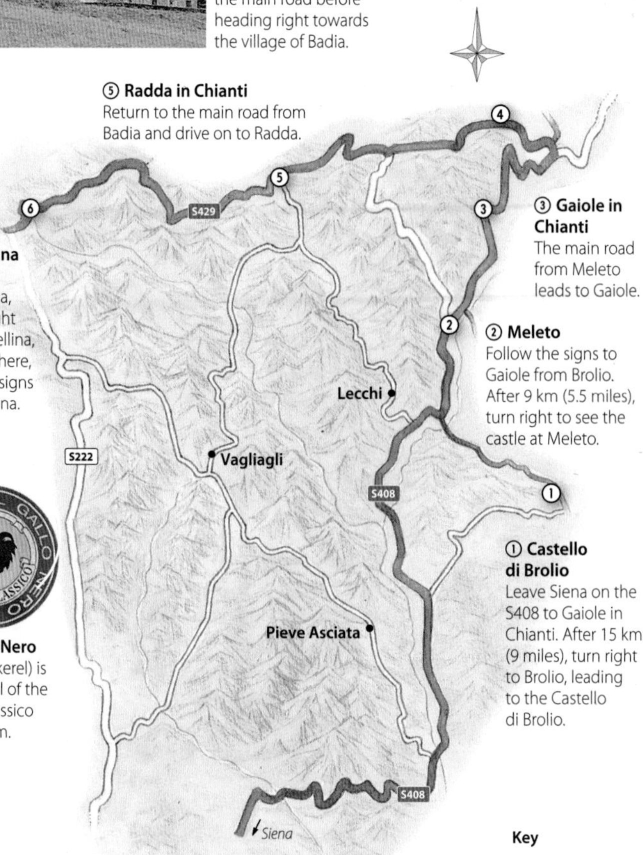

0 kilometres   2
0 miles   2

⑤ Radda in Chianti
Return to the main road from Badia and drive on to Radda.

S429

⑥ Castellina in Chianti
From Radda, drive straight on to Castellina, and from there, follow the signs back to Siena.

③ Gaiole in Chianti
The main road from Meleto leads to Gaiole.

② Meleto
Follow the signs to Gaiole from Brolio. After 9 km (5.5 miles), turn right to see the castle at Meleto.

S222

Lecchi

Vagliagli

S408

The Gallo Nero (black cockerel) is the symbol of the Chianti Classico Consortium.

① Castello di Brolio
Leave Siena on the S408 to Gaiole in Chianti. After 15 km (9 miles), turn right to Brolio, leading to the Castello di Brolio.

Pieve Asciata

↙ Siena

S408

Key

▬▬ Tour route
══ Other road

SOUTHERN TUSCANY

The southernmost part of Tuscany and the island of Elba have a very different feel to any other Tuscan region. Thanks to the hotter, drier and sunnier climate, the hills are cloaked in aromatic Mediterranean scrub, known as *macchia*. Palm trees grow in towns and also edge the sandy beaches, and strands of prickly pear cactus are traditionally used to mark field boundaries in the countryside.

The coastline, lined with fishing villages and beaches, is very popular in the summer, with numerous holiday villages and caravan sites. Resorts such as Monte Argentario have a much more exclusive image, and are favoured by wealthy, yacht-owning Italians from Rome and Milan. Inland, the region's wild and unspoiled hills are popular with sportsmen, who come to hunt for wild boar and deer.

The transformation of the marshy coastal strip known as the Maremma into a holiday playground is a recent development. The ancient Etruscans, followed by the Romans (*see p46*), drained its swamps to create richly fertile farming land. After the collapse of the Roman Empire, the drainage channels became choked, turning the Maremma into an inhospitable wilderness of marshland and stagnant pools plagued by malaria-carrying mosquitoes. Re-draining of the land began again in the late 18th century and, with the help of insecticides, the malaria-mosquito was finally eliminated in the 1950s.

Little Development

The region slumbered from Roman times and for long periods was virtually uninhabited, except for farmers and fishermen. Consequently, there are few cities or major architectural and artistic monuments. On the other hand, archaeological remains have survived because there were few people here to salvage the stone for new buildings. The relative lack of intensive farming means the region is still rich in wildlife, from butterflies and orchids to tortoises and porcupines.

Detail of Romanesque *tympanum* on the Duomo at Massa Marittima

◀ Idyllic harbour of Porto Ercole, at exclusive Monte Argentario

Exploring Southern Tuscany

Away from the coastal resorts, this region remains relatively undiscovered; quiet roads and a lack of tourists only add to the pleasure of exploring rock-cut tombs in Sovana, bathing in hot sulphurous springs at Saturnia or wandering through the Maremma spotting the wildlife. For a busier atmosphere, visit the resorts of Orbetello and Monte Argentario, which have plenty of choice for shopping, restaurants and nightlife.

Statue above gateway, Orbetello

Key

═══ Major road
─── Secondary road
═══ Minor road
∼∼∼ Main railway
─── Minor railway
▬▬▬ Scenic route
▬▬▬ Regional border
△ Summit

Getting Around

The S1 coastal route cannot cope with the traffic in summer and is best avoided. A busy railway line runs alongside; most trains stop at Grosseto and Orbetello, and buses from Grosseto serve most towns in the area. Vehicle and passenger ferries depart from Piombino to Elba every 30 minutes during the day in summer. Bus services from Portoferraio cover all parts of the island.

View across the rooftops of Massa Marittima to the hills beyond

For hotels and restaurants see pp252–7 and pp264–75

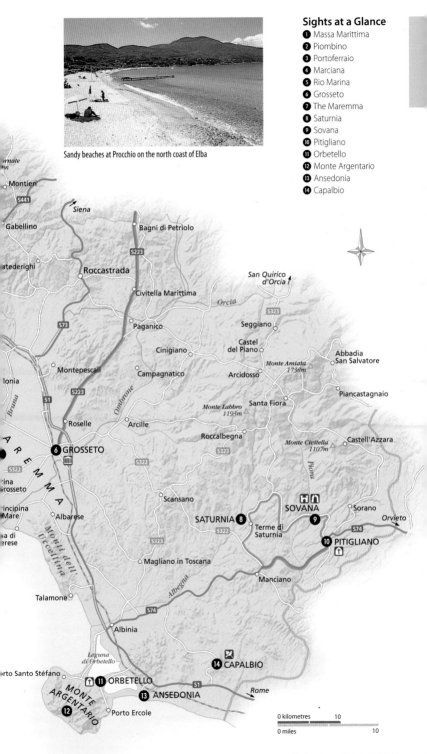

Sandy beaches at Procchio on the north coast of Elba

Sights at a Glance

1. Massa Marittima
2. Piombino
3. Portoferraio
4. Marciana
5. Rio Marina
6. Grosseto
7. The Maremma
8. Saturnia
9. Sovana
10. Pitigliano
11. Orbetello
12. Monte Argentario
13. Ansedonia
14. Capalbio

For keys to symbols *see back flap*

● Massa Marittima

Road map: C4. 🏔 9,469. 🚌
ℹ️ Amatur, Via Todini 3–5 (0566
90 27 56). 🗓 Wed.

Set in the Colline Metallifere
(metal-bearing hills), from which
lead, copper and silver ores
were mined, Massa Marittima
is far from being a grimy
industrial town. Its history is
closely associated with
mining and there are some
excellent examples of
Romanesque architecture.

↑ Duomo
The Romanesque cathedral
is dedicated to St Cerbone,
a 6th-century saint whose
story is told in stone above
the door.

The skyline of Massa Marittima

🏛 Museo Archeologico
Palazzo del Podestà, Piazza Garibaldi.
Tel 0566 90 22 89. **Open** Tue–Sun. 🅿️
An archaeological museum
with material from Paleolithic
to Roman times.

🏛 Museo d'Arte Sacra
Convento di San Pietro all'Orto,
Corso Diaz 36. **Tel** 0566 90 22 89.
Open daily. 🅿️
Art from local churches and
basilicas can be admired here.

🏛 Museo della Miniera
Via Corridoni. **Tel** 0566 90 22 89.
Open Tue–Sun. 📷 compulsory. 🅿️
Parts of this museum of mining
are located within a former
mine shaft.

● Piombino

Road map: C4. 🏔 36,774. FS 🚌 🚢
ℹ️ Via Ferruccio 1 (0565 22 56 39).
🗓 Wed.

Piombino is a busy town
dominated by iron and steel
works. It is at the end of the

A Day Out on Elba

Elba's most famous resident was Napoleon, who
spent nine months here after the fall of Paris in
1814. Today, the island is mainly populated by
holiday-makers, who come by ferry from Piombino,
10 km (6 miles) away on the mainland. The main
town is Portoferraio, which has an old port and a
modern seafront with smart hotels. The landscape
of the island is varied: on the west coast there
are sandy beaches, suitable for all water sports;
inland, olive groves and vineyards line hillsides
and vegetation covers
the mountains. The east
coast is more rugged,
with high cliffs and
stony beaches.

③ **Marciana Marina**
Return to the main road and
follow the coast round past
Procchio, with its long sandy
bays. From here, it is 7.5 km
(4.5 miles) to the marina.

Key

▬▬ Tour route

══ Other road

0 kilometres   2

0 miles   2

④ **Marciana Alta**
From the marina, take the
main road into the hills to this
old medieval town. After 8 km
(5 miles), turn left on to a minor
road leading to the cable car up
to the top of Monte Capanne.

⑤ **Marina di Campo** Stay on the
coast road around the west end of
the island until Marina di Campo.

Massoncello peninsula and was originally an island. It is the main port for ferries to Elba, which run every half hour in summer and at frequent intervals in winter. Nearby are the extensive ruins of Etruscan Populonia and the **Museo Etrusco Gasparri**, which contains a collection of bronze and terracotta works found in the surrounding necropolises.

🏛 **Museo Etrusco Gasparri**
Tel 0565 296 66 **Open** 9am–12:30pm, 2–7pm daily. 🖼 ♿

❸ Portoferraio

Road map: B4. 🗺 11,500. 🚌 🚢 **i**
Calata Italia 43 (0565 29 46 71). 🚢 Fri.

The ferry from mainland Piombino arrives here. The town has a pretty harbour, but the main sights are Napoleon's two houses. In the centre of Portoferraio is the **Palazzina Napoleonica** (also known as the Villetta dei Mulini), a modest house built around two windmills. **Villa San Martino**, his country residence, had a Classical façade imposed on it by the Russian *emigré*, Prince Demidoff in 1851. Egyptian-style frescoes in the house, painted in 1814, are a reminder of Napoleon's Nile campaigns of 1798–9.

🏛 **Palazzina Napoleonica**
Villa Napoleonica dei Mulini. **Tel** 0565 91 58 46. **Open** 9am–7pm Wed–Mon in summer; 9am–4pm in winter (to 1pm Sun & public hols). 🖼 ♿

🏛 **Villa San Martino**
San Martino. **Tel** 0565 91 46 88. **Open** 9am–7pm Tue–Sun (to 1pm Sun) in summer, 9am–4pm in winter. 🖼

❹ Marciana

Road map: B4. 🗺 3,000. 🚌
i Municipio, Marciana Alta (0565 90 12 15).

On Elba's northwest coast is Marciana Marina, while further inland is the well-preserved medieval town of Marciana Alta.

Shady beaches and inlets at Marciana Marina on Elba

The **Museo Civico Archeologico** houses exhibits from Etruscan ships wrecked off Elba. From here, take the cable car up Monte Capanne, Elba's highest peak, at 1,018 m (3,300 ft).

🏛 **Museo Civico Archeologico**
Via del Pretorio, Marciana Alta. **Tel** 0565 90 12 15. **Open** Apr–Sep: daily. 🖼

---

② **Villa San Martino**
Divert left off the main road to San Martino, and on to Napoleon's country residence.

① **Portoferraio** Take the main coast road towards Marciana Marina.

②

①

⑨ **Cavo** Drive for 7.5 km (4.5 miles) to Cavo, along the east coast, to see the scenic northern tip of Elba.

⑨

⑧

⑧ **Rio Marina**
This mining town, 12 km (7.5 miles) to the north, has an excellent museum of mineralogy.

⑦

⑥

⑦ **Porto Azzurro**
Return to the main road and carry on for 2 km (1.25 miles) to Elba's second-largest port – a fashionable resort overlooking a lovely bay dominated by a 17th-century fortress.

⑥ **Capoliveri** Follow the road round the south of the island and divert to the right, just before Porto Azzurro, to visit this charming old mining village.

❼ The Maremma

The ancient Romans were the first to cultivate the marshes of the Maremma, but after the collapse of their empire the area went virtually uninhabited until the 18th century. The land has since been reclaimed, the irrigation canals unblocked and farming developed on the fertile soil. The Parco Naturale dell'Uccellina was set up in 1975 to protect the abundant local flora and fauna and prevent more development taking place.

Wildlife
The undergrowth and marshes are home to wild boar and other wildlife.

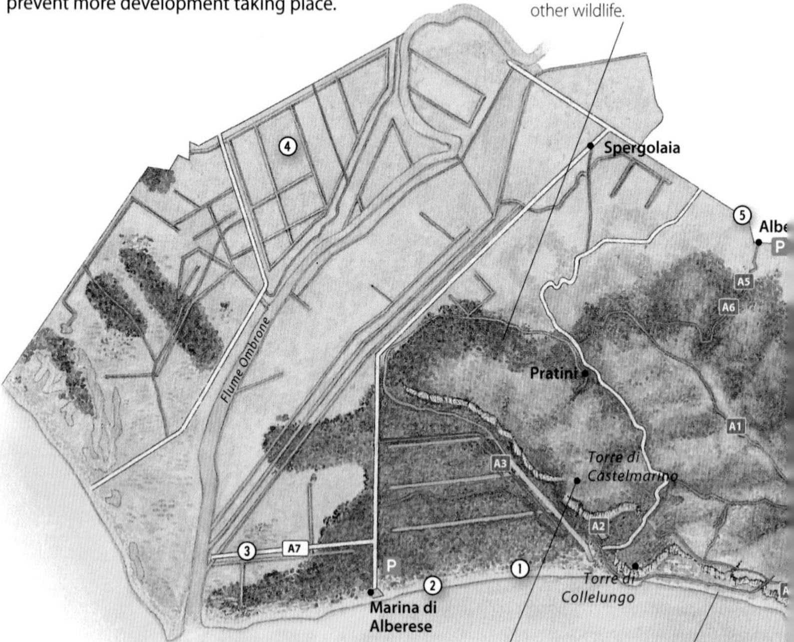

Spergolaia

⑤ Albe
P

A5

A6

Pratini

A1

Fiume Ombrone

A3

Torre di Castelmarino

A2

③ A7

P

②

①

Torre di Collelungo

Marina di Alberese

KEY

① **Sea lilies and hollies** grow along the sandy shoreline, backed by groves of parasol pines, mastic trees and juniper.

② **There are picnic tables** on the beach in the shade of pine trees.

③ **Canoes** can be hired to explore the irrigation canals.

④ **This salt marsh,** cut by irrigation canals, is home to herons, storks and other wading birds.

⑤ **Entry permits** are sold at Alberese.

⑥ **The hills** running parallel to the coast are cloaked in scrub called *macchia*, consisting of rosemary, broom, rock rose, sea lavender and rowan trees.

⑦ **Birds of prey** hunt in remote parts of the parkland.

⑧ **Talamone** is a fishing village.

Torre di Castelmarino
The cliffs are crowned by 16th-century watchtowers, part of a defence system built by the Medici to protect the coastal region from attack.

Beaches
The shoreline south of Marina di Alberese has wide, sandy beaches sheltered by steep cliffs.

★ Abbazia di San Rabano
The ruined Cistercian abbey, built in the
12th century, stands close to the park's highest
peak, Poggio Lecci. The tower and fortifications
date back to the 14th century, the time of the
fierce battles between Pisa and Siena.

★ Waymarked Paths
Footpaths give access to areas
where you can see butterflies,
lizards and poisonous snakes,
including vipers.

FS
• **Alberese
Scalo**

San Rabano
• *Torre dell'Uccellina*

⑥

⑦

T3

FS
• **Fonteblanda**

T2

T1

Rocca di Talamone •

⑧ P
Talamone

Long-horned Cattle
The docile white Maremma cattle
are raised by cowboys (*butteri*)
who also stage rodeos.

VISITORS' CHECKLIST

Practical Information
Centro Visite di Alberese.
Road map D5.
Tel 0564 40 70 98. Marginal areas:
Open 9am–1 hr before sunset
daily (mid-Jun–Sep: 7:30–10am,
4–6pm daily). Entrances: Alberese,
Marina di Alberese, Talamone.
Itineraries: A/5:, A/6: nature trails
5 km (3 miles), 2 hrs; A/7: Ombrone
estuary, 4 km (2.5 miles), 2 hrs;
T/1:, T/2: short trails (Oct–mid-
Jun). 🎫 adv booking (in spring).
Inner park areas: **Open** 9am–1 hr
before sunset Wed, Sat, Sun and
pub hols. **Closed** 1 May, 25 Dec.
Entrance: Alberese. Tour transport
departs from Pratini, 9 km
(5.5 miles). Itineraries: A/1: Abbazia
di San Rabano, 6 km (3.75 miles),
5 hrs; A/2: Le Torri, 5 km (3 miles),
3 hrs; A/3: Le Grotte, 8 km
(5 miles), 4 hrs; A/4: Cala di Forno,
12 km (7.5 miles), 6 hrs. Note: A/3
and A/4 are closed mid-June–
Sep. 🚫 🎫 mid-Jun–Sep:
compulsory for A/1: (7am) and
A/2: (4pm). Park regulations: Dress
adequately & bring drinking
water. Some walks are strenuous.
🌐 parco-maremma.it

Key

═══ Roads
━━━ Paths
═══ Canals and rivers

0 kilometres   1

0 miles   1

❺ Rio Marina

Road map: B4. 🚗 2,038. 🚌
ℹ️ Lungomare G Marconi 2, Gli
Spiazzi (0565 96 20 04). 🗓️ Mon.

Around Rio Marina there are still
open-cast mines that extract
the ores that attracted the
Etruscans to Elba. The **Museo dei
Minerali** explains the geology
of the island. Shops in the town
centre sell jewellery made of
local semiprecious stones.

🏛 Museo dei Minerali
Palazzo Comunale. **Tel** 0565 96 20 88.
Open Apr–mid-Oct: daily; mid- Oct–
Mar: by appt. 🎟️

❻ Grosseto

Road map: D4. 🚗 71,472. 🚆 🚌
ℹ️ Via Monterosa 206 (0564 46 26 11).
🗓️ Thu.

Grosseto is the largest town in
southern Tuscany. World War II
destroyed many of its buildings,
but the 16th-century walls still
stand and several of the
bastions are now parks.

🏛 Museo Civico
Archeologico e d'Arte
della Maremma
Piazza Baccarini 3. **Tel** 0564 48 87 53.
Open Nov–Feb: 9am–1pm Tue–Sun
(also 4:30–7pm Sat); Mar–Apr:
9:30am–1pm, 4:30–7pm Tue–Sun;
May–Oct: 10am–1pm, 5–8pm Tue–
Sun. **Closed** 1 Jan, 1 May, 25 Dec.

The museum has Etruscan and
Roman artifacts from Roselle
and Vetulonia. There is also a
collection of coins, intaglios
(carved stones) and pottery.

Grosseto, a busy town full of narrow streets
and shops

Cascate del Gorello, free for all to enjoy, at Saturnia

❼ The Maremma

See pp240–41.

❽ Saturnia

Road map: D5. 🚗 550. 🚌
ℹ️ Via Mazzini 4 (0564 60 12 80).

Holiday-makers come to Saturnia
to enjoy the good Maremma
food or seek a health cure in the
modern spa of Terme di Saturnia.
Others prefer to bathe for free in
the hot sulphurated waters of the
waterfall at Cascate del Gorello on
the Montemerano road. This is a
pretty spot, with its pools and
rocks stained coppery green.

❾ Sovana

Road map: E5. 🚗 100.

Sovana sits on a ridge high
above the Lente valley.
Its main street is lined with
cafés, restaurants and shops.
The 13th-century Romanesque
Rocca Aldobrandesca, named
after the Teutonic family that
ruled in the area until 1608,
is now in ruins.

The frescoes of the late
15th-century Siena school
in the medieval church of
Santa Maria were discovered
under the whitewashed walls.
The main altar is sheltered by
a 9th-century canopy that was
originally in the Romanesque
Duomo. This 12th-century
building incorporates sculpture
from earlier churches built on
the same site.

The Etruscans dug tombs
nearby in the soft limestone
cliffs bordering the river Lente.
The most complete set of
Necropoli Etrusca can be
found in a valley just to the
west of Sovana.

🏰 Rocca Aldobrandesca
Via del Pretorio.
Closed to the public.

⛪ Santa Maria
Piazza del Pretorio. **Open** daily.

⛪ Duomo
Piazza del Pretorio. **Open** daily in
summer; Sat, Sun only in winter.

🏛 Necropoli Etrusca
Poggio di Sopra Ripa. **Tel** 0564 61 40
74. **Open** Feb–Nov: 10am–7pm daily;
Dec–Jan: 9am–5pm Sat & Sun.

Cafés and shops in Sovana's medieval piazza

⑩ Pitigliano

Road map: E5. ⚏ 4,361. 🚌 ℹ
Piazza Garibaldi 51 (0564 61 71 11).
🛒 Wed.

Pitigliano looks spectacular perched on a plateau, high above cliffs carved out by the river Lente. The houses seem to grow out of the cliffs, which are riddled with caves cut out of soft limestone. The caves have been used for many years to store wines and olive oils.

A maze of tiny medieval streets passes through the Jewish ghetto, formed when Jews fleeing from Catholic persecution took refuge here in the 17th century. The Palazzo Orsini, in the town centre, has its water supply brought in by an aqueduct, built in 1545, that overhangs Via Cavour. The **Museo Palazzo Orsini**, in the palazzo, has a small exhibition of work by the artist Francesco Zuccarelli (1702–88). He also painted two of the altarpieces in the medieval **Duomo**, whose huge bell tower supports a bell that weighs 3 tonnes.

The **Museo Civico Archeologico** contains a range of finds from ancient local settlements.

🏛 Museo Palazzo Orsini
Piazza della Fortezza Orsini.
Tel 0564 61 60 74. **Open** 10am–1pm, 3–7pm (until 5pm in winter) Tue–Fri (daily in Aug). 📷

🏛 Duomo
Piazza San Gregorio.
Open daily. ♿

🏛 Museo Civico Archeologico
Piazza della Fortezza Orsini 59. **Tel** 0564 61 40 67. **Open** call to check times.

⑪ Orbetello

Road map: D5. ⚏ 15,455.
FS 🚌 ℹ Piazza della Repubblica 1 (0564 86 04 47). 🛒 Sat.

Orbetello is a crowded resort bordered by two tidal lagoons. Part of the northernmost lagoon is managed by the Worldwide Fund for Nature as a wildlife park. The town was the capital of a tiny Spanish state, called the Presidio, from 1557 until 1808, when it was absorbed into the Grand Duchy of Tuscany. The Porta del Soccorso bears the coat of arms of the king of Spain. Inside the gates is the **Polveriera Guzman**,

Coat of arms on the Porta del Soccorso

which was originally used as an arsenal. The Duomo, **Santa Maria Assunta**, also has Spanish-style decoration, but the altar in the Cappella di San Biagio is typically Romanesque in design. The Fontone di Talamone, in Piazza della Repubblica, is a terracotta plinth from the Roman-Etruscan era.

🏛 Polveriera Guzman
Viale Mura di Levante. **Open** call Tourist Information for details.

🏛 Santa Maria Assunta
Piazza del Duomo. **Open** daily.

View over Pitigliano showing soft limestone cliffs and caves bordering the river Lente

Porto Ercole, on Monte Argentario

Panoramica there are views over rocky coves, cliffs and bays. Ferries from Porto Santo Stéfano go to the island of Giglio, popular with Italian tourists for its sandy beaches and rich wildlife.

In the summer, the Porto Santo Stéfano ferry also calls at Giannutri, a privately owned island where visitors are not allowed to stay overnight.

⓫ Ansedonia

Road map: D5. 300.

Ansedonia is a prosperous village of luxurious villas and gardens, high on a hill above the coast. The ruins of the city of Cosa, founded by the Romans in 173 BC, are on the summit of the hill looking over Ansedonia. The **Museo di Cosa**, containing relics from the ancient settlement, is close by. East of Ansedonia is a long stretch of sandy beach and the remains of the Etruscan Canal. The date

⓬ Monte Argentario

Road map: D5. 14,000.
Piazzale Sant'Andrea, Porto Santo Stéfano (0564 81 42 08). Tue.

Monte Argentario was an island until the early 18th century, when the shallow waters separating it from the mainland began to silt up, creating two sandy spits of land, known as *tomboli*, that enclose the Orbetello lagoon. Orbetello itself was linked to the island in 1842, when a dyke was constructed linking the mainland to Terrarossa.

The two harbour towns of Porto Ercole and Porto Santo Stéfano are both favoured by wealthy yacht owners. There are good fish restaurants in both towns (*see p275*), and from the Strada

An Etruscan Tour

The Etruscans gained much of their wealth from Tuscany's vast mineral resources, and their monied classes were cultured and worldly. Both their elaborate burial sites and the artifacts found in their tombs give us an insight into their lives (*see pp46–7*). Etruscan burial sites were carved into soft rock or built of huge stone slabs with rock-cut roads leading down to the tombs.

① Grosseto
The Museo Civico Archeologico has a collection of Etruscan artifacts found in local tombs.

Also Worth Seeing

Museo Archeologico, Florence (*see p103*).

Museo Etrusco, Volterra (*see p170*).

Vulci and **Tarquinia** These excavated sites, just over the Tuscany border in Lazio, have impressive Etruscan ruins, painted tombs and art collections.

⑦ Talamone
Follow the S74 to the S1. Turn right and after 8 km (5 miles) fork off to the left, into the Maremma, for the Etruscan temple, Roman villa and baths.

Maglia

This Etruscan bone brooch, called a *fibula*, was found near Grosseto and is now in the Museo Archeologico in Florence.

The Etruscan Canal at Ansedonia

and purpose of the canal are debatable, but it may have been dug in Roman times to keep the harbour free of silt. Alternatively, it may have been part of a canal leading to the Lago di Burano, 5 km (3 miles) down the coast. This lagoon is 4 km (2.5 miles) long and has been turned into a wildlife refuge (rifugio faunistico) by the Worldwide Fund for Nature. It is a very important habitat for wading birds.

▥ Museo di Cosa

Via delle Ginestre 35, Ansedonia. **Tel** 0564 88 14 21. **Open** 9am–7pm daily. **Closed** 1 Jan, 25 Dec. ▨

⑭ Capalbio

Road map: D5. ▨ 4,049.
▤ ▨ Wed.

Capalbio is another village that is popular with wealthy Italians. The hilltop town has several restaurants and hotels, and is busy all year round. Summer tourists come for the beaches, and winter visitors flock to hunt deer and wild boar in the surrounding woodland, which is now managed as a game reserve. A game festival is held in September each year.

View across the rooftops of Capalbio

◪ Giardino dei Tarocchi

Garavicchio, Pescia Fiorentina. **Tel** 0564 89 51 22. **Open** Apr–mid-Oct: 2:30–7:30pm daily; mid-Oct–Mar: group reservations only. ▨

At Pescia Fiorentina, southeast of Capalbio, is a modern sculpture garden created by the late French artist Niki de Saint-Phalle in 1982. It was inspired by the figures of the Tarot and was over ten years in the making. The bigger pieces each represent one card from the Tarot pack. Among the sculptures is *The Tower*, a glittering three-storey edifice made out of broken mirrors.

② **Roselle** Head north on the S223 to the most important excavated Etruscan and Roman remains in Tuscany.

③ **Saturnia** Continue east for 54 km (34 miles) for the rock-cut tombs below this tiny village of Etruscan origin.

④ **Sovana** From Saturnia, drive towards Sovana to the famous Ildebranda Tomb in a valley to the west.

Scansano

⑥ **Marsiliana** Head west on the S74, through Manciano to the vast necropolises on the outskirts of Marsiliana.

⑤ **Pitigliano** The town, on the junction with the S74, is built on tufa cliffs riddled with Etruscan tombs and tunnels, now used for storing produce.

Manciano

Key

━━ Tour route

╍╍╍ Other road

0 kilometres 5

0 miles 5

TRAVELLERS' NEEDS

WHERE TO STAY

Tuscany has some of the most charming places to stay in all of Italy. Inland, these range from decadent country villas to elegant town houses. Smaller, family-run places may also offer exceptional cuisine and often occupy historic properties filled with antiques. The major cities also offer some outstanding B&B accommodation. Hotels on the riviera tend to be less distinctive, but the popularity of coastal resorts in summer means that standards are high. Many visitors opt for self-catering holidays. Often the accommodation is a small hotel or rustic farmhouse, and the prices can prove very reasonable. Other options include hostels and, for walking enthusiasts, there are mountain huts throughout the region. The hotel listings *(see pp252–7)* are arranged by area and cater to a variety of different budgets.

Views of the Duomo from the penthouse terrace at Gallery Hotel Art, Florence *(see p252)*

Where to Look

Florence has a wide range of hotels, apartments and B&Bs, but prices can be high. The most attractive locations are along the north bank of the Arno, the historic centre and in nearby Fiesole. Parking is a problem in the city centre, so if you have a car it is best to choose a hotel with parking facilities.

Hotels in central Pisa are generally substandard. Opt for a good-quality B&B, or take a short drive outside of the city and stay in one of the excellent villas in the surrounding countryside.

There are some lovely hotels in Northern Tuscany. The area just around Lucca is home to some particularly good places to stay. These offer a great base for exploring the rugged countryside typical of the area.

Though large, Arezzo has relatively few hotels and those in the centre are mostly geared towards business people. Stay in the countryside outside the town or in nearby Cortona instead.

The hill towns of central Tuscany offer a number of quality villas, manor houses and even former palaces. San Gimignano and Montepulciano, in particular, are home to some fantastic hotels. The Chianti region is rich in Agriturismo accommodation, with excellent regional restaurants, particularly around Castellina and Gaiole. Siena has some great B&Bs and boutique hotels in the centre, but the really luxurious options are mainly outside the city walls.

Hotel Prices

Outside of Florence and Siena, prices are cheaper and often negotiable during the low season (November to March), although many smaller establishments close in winter. Florence is less busy than other parts of Tuscany in July and August, but this is the peak holiday season on the coast. In certain weeks of January and July, fashion shows fill the top hotels in Florence, raising prices, so make sure you compare a few dates before you book.

Single-room rates are higher than individual rates for two people sharing a double room. Prices include tax and service, although you are usually expected to tip porters and room-service staff. Bear in mind that hotels in Florence and Siena are generally more expensive than elsewhere in the region.

Hidden Extras

Before making a reservation, establish whether breakfast is included in the price. Hotels usually add hefty surcharges for international phone calls, and may charge for Wi-Fi, air-conditioning, laundry and garage parking. Check the rates carefully before using any of these services. The cost of drinks in minibars can also be exorbitant. Some hotels may expect you to take full- or half-board during the high season.

Stunning hilltop views from Castello di Vicarello, Cinigiano *(see p257)*

Spectacular grounds at Villa San Michele, on the outskirts of Florence *(see p254)*

Hotel Gradings and Facilities

Hotels in Italy are classified by a star-rating system, from one to five stars. However, each area sets its own levels for grading; consequently, standards may vary from one city to another. Some hotels don't have a restaurant, but those that do usually welcome nonresidents.

Some of the converted castles and ancient villas are not air-conditioned, but the thick stone walls provide insulation and protection from the summer heat.

Children are welcome, but the smaller hotels generally have limited facilities. Often, more up-market hotels will arrange a baby-sitting service.

What to Expect

In Florence, street numbers can be confusing *(see p297)*, so refer to the map references given in the listings on pages 252–4.

Hotel proprietors are obliged by law to register you with the police, so they will ask for your passport when you arrive.

Even the most basic hotel should have a reasonably smart bathroom. Rooms without a bathroom will usually have wash basins and towels.

Hotel decoration across Tuscany tends to be very stylish, both in cities and in rural areas. Expect sleek, minimalist design in boutique hotels and sumptuous period details in historic country villas and town palazzi. In some of the more budget historic hotels, however, you may have to sacrifice smart decor for the charm of an old establishment.

Florence can be very noisy. Top-class hotels usually have some form of soundproofing, but ask for a room facing away from the street if you are easily disturbed by noise.

Checkout time is usually noon in four- and five-star hotels and between 10am and noon in other establishments. If you stay longer, you will be asked to pay for an extra day. However, many hotels will store your baggage if you plan on leaving the city several hours after checkout time. Most hotels offer Internet access and accept credit cards, but be sure to check when booking, if you require these or any other facilities.

Booking and Paying

It is best to book through the hotel website, by phone or email. You should do this at least two months in advance if you want a particular hotel in high season. If a deposit is required, you can usually pay by credit card. Under Italian law, a booking is valid as soon as the deposit is paid and confirmation is received. Many hotels have strict cancellation policies, so you may lose money if you pull out.

When you check out, the hotel will issue you with a receipt *(ricevuta fiscale)* for final payment. You are required by law to keep this until you leave Italy.

Disabled Travellers

In general, only newer hotels in Tuscany have special facilities for disabled travellers. Older hotels will do what they can to accommodate people in wheelchairs, but ramps, handrails and wide doorways are rare. Contact the hotel before booking to check what facilities are available.

Historic Hotels

The Tuscany regional tourist board publishes a leaflet that lists hotels in historic buildings and those of artistic interest. Some of the best are included in the listings here. **Relais & Châteaux** produces a guide that includes a number of fine Tuscan hotels and hotel restaurants of historic interest, all of high quality.

Fresh modern decor at the Continentale, Florence *(see p252)*

14th-century villa at Locanda dell'Amorosa *(see p257)*

Agriturismo

Across Tuscany, hundreds of farms and villas offer accommodation as part of the **Agriturismo** scheme. Options range from former palaces with first-class facilities to simple rooms on a working farm. Some have excellent restaurants serving farm produce; others will arrange outdoor pursuits, such as horseback riding and cycling. Look for the annual *Agriturist* publication in tourist offices and bookshops.

Bed & Breakfast

B&Bs are a popular option for visitors to Florence and Tuscany. These can vary from a couple of rooms in someone's house to a luxurious bijou establishment that is a hotel in all but name. Contact **Bookintoscana** for listings, or visit the **Bed and Breakfast Italy** website.

Self-Catering

Self-catering accommodation is a good alternative and can allow you more freedom. Choices range from luxury villas to small flats with basic facilities. Bookings can be arranged through special agencies, such as **Your Way to Florence**, **Interhome** and **Villas4you**. Make sure you book well in advance as the best places get snapped up quickly. Another option is a *residenza*, or

residential hotel. This offers the services of a hotel with the privacy of self-catering flats. There will usually be cooking facilities and some form of restaurant service. Look for *residenza* in the accommodation lists of the Italian State Tourist Office (**ENIT**).

Budget Accommodation

Dormitory accommodation in hostels can be found throughout Tuscany. Prices start at around €12 per person per night (€15 during peak season). Dorms may be single- or mixed-sex, though many hostels also have private rooms.

A peaceful alternative is to stay in a convent or monastery with guest accommodation. Note that many have strict curfews and will not admit members of the opposite sex even when accompanied by their spouses.

The **AIG (Associazione Italiana Alberghi per la Gioventù)** has lists of youth hostels across Italy. ENIT and individual tourist offices across the region can also provide accommodation lists and offer advice on where to find rooms in religious institutions. The main youth hostel in Florence is **Europa Villa Camerata**.

DIRECTORY

Historic Hotels

Relais & Chateaux
ⓦ relaischateaux.com

Agriturismo

Agriturismo
Corso Vittorio Emanuele II 101, 00186 Rome.
Tel 06 685 23 37.
ⓦ agriturist.it

Bed & Breakfast

Bed and Breakfast Italy
ⓦ bed-and-breakfast-in-italy.com

Bookintoscana
ⓦ turismo.intoscana.it/ bookintoscana

Self-Catering

ENIT
(Italian State Tourist Office)
1 Princes Street, London W1B 2AY.
Tel 020 7408 1254.
ⓦ enit.it
ⓦ italiantouristboard. co.uk

Interhome
Tel UK: 020 8780 6633.
Tel US: 800 882 6864.
ⓦ interhome.com

Villas4you
PO Box 1310, Maidstone ME14 9QH.
Tel 0800 096 3439.
ⓦ villas4you.co.uk

Your Way to Florence
ⓦ yourwaytoflorence. com

Budget Accommodation

AIG (Youth Hostels Association)
Viale Augusto Righi 2–4, 50137 Florence.
Tel 055 60 03 15.
ⓦ aighostels.it

CTS Viaggi
Tel 06 462 04 31.
ⓦ cts.it

Europa Villa Camerata
Viale Augusto Righi 2–4, 50137 Florence.
Tel 055 60 14 51.
ⓦ hihostels.com/ hostels/florence-villa-camerata

Staying in Private Homes

Airbnb
ⓦ airbnb.com

Mountain Refuges and Camp Sites

Club Alpino Italiano
Via E Petrella 19, 20124 Milan.
Tel 02 205 72 31.
ⓦ cai.it

Touring Club Italiano
Corso Italia 10, 20122 Milan.
Tel 02 852 61.
ⓦ touringclub.it

CTS Viaggi (Centro Turistico Studentesco) can help find rooms in university accommodation – a good option during the summer months.

Staying in Private Homes

Rooms or apartments in private homes can be rented through a number of agencies, such as **Airbnb**. Prices start at around €20, but be aware that deposits may be requested and cancellation fees imposed. For stays of several months or more, accommodation agencies for apartments can be found under *Immobiliari* in the *Pagine Gialle* (Yellow Pages).

Mountain Refuges and Camp Sites

Mountain refuges and huts are dotted throughout Tuscany, perfect for walkers and trekkers. The Garfagnana, in the northwest, caters for tourists well and is renowned for its outstanding natural beauty. There are also camp sites on the fringes of most towns. A list of camp sites and mountain refuges is available from ENIT or local tourist offices. **Club Alpino Italiano** owns most of the huts in the mountain districts of Italy. The **Touring Club Italiano** publishes a list of camp sites in *Campeggi e Villaggi Turistici in Italia*. Many of them offer basic accommodation in family-sized cabins, as well as space for tents and caravans.

Wonderful views over Siena from the Campo Regio Relais *(see p257)*

Recommended Hotels

The accommodation options featured in this guide – listed by area and then by price – have been selected across a wide price range for their excellent facilities and unique appeal. They have been divided into a number of categories to help you make the best choices for your trip. Most of the hotels are spread across the main tourist areas.

Tuscany is full of historic places to stay; many former palaces, villas and town houses have now been converted into hotels or B&Bs. These usually feature period details, such as frescoes, vaulted ceilings, tapestries and antique furniture.

Luxury hotels provide five-star service and facilities, most with stunning rooms, panoramic rooftop terraces and award-winning restaurants. You should expect impeccable service at these establishments.

Hotels labelled as contemporary combine up-to-date facilities and amenities with sleek, modern decor.

Country-villa hotels are set in beautiful surroundings in the Tuscan countryside. Rooms are often in historic buildings with lots of character, for example former hunting lodges or Renaissance palazzi.

Though often set in heritage buildings, traditional hotels focus on providing modern comforts rather than historic authenticity. The rooms may not be decked out with period furnishings, but these hotels usually offer great facilities and impeccable service.

Boutique hotels can be found all over Tuscany. These small hotels place an emphasis on chic design. They generally offer the same facilities and services as larger hotels, but in a more intimate setting.

In choosing the very best accommodation for your stay, look out for the entries marked DK Choice in this guide. These establishments have been highlighted because they are outstanding in some way. They may be set in beautiful surroundings or in a historically important building. They might offer exceptional value, excellent service or a romantic ambience. Whatever the reason, the DK Choice label guarantees an especially memorable stay.

Grand Palazzo Magnani Ferone on the south side of the Arno, Florence *(see p254)*

Where to Stay

Florence

City Centre East

Four Rooms €
B&B **Map** 6 D4
Borgo Santi Apostoli 2, 50123
Tel *055 21 26 76, 0328 367 22 52*
Rooms in a great location, a couple of minutes' walk from the Uffizi and Ponte Vecchio. Modern decor with a 1960s feel.

Martin Dago €
B&B **Map** 5 C2
Corso dei Tintori 6, 50122
Tel *0338 522 88 10*
W martindago.com
Stylish place with a welcoming owner in the lively Santa Croce district. Excellent breakfasts.

Novecento €
B&B **Map** 6 E1
Via Ricasoli 10, 50122
Tel *055 21 41 38*
W bbnovecentofirenze.it
Small, pretty rooms in a third-floor attic apartment, with stunning views of the dome of the cathedral from the roof terrace.

Sani Tourist House €
B&B **Map** 6 E3
Piazza dei Giuochi 1, 50122
Tel *0335 822 41 33*
W sanibnb.it
Simple, reasonably priced rooms, tucked behind the Casa di Dante, on the third floor (with lift) of a medieval palazzo. Air-conditioning is extra.

DK Choice

Granduomo €€
Apartments **Map** 6 D2
Piazza Duomo 1–7, 50121
Tel *055 267 00 04*
W granduomo.com
These sumptuous apartments have an enviable location, right opposite the Duomo. Think plush decor in muted tones, huge bathrooms and truly spectacular views. The staff are extremely helpful and there is a fantastic top-floor lounge bar.

Hotel il Balestri €€
Traditional **Map** 6 E4
Piazza Mentana 7, 50122
Tel *055 21 47 13*
W whythebesthotels.com
Established in 1888, this hotel has pretty rooms either facing the Arno or a quiet inner courtyard. Impressive breakfast buffet.

In Piazza della Signoria €€
B&B **Map** 6 E3
Via dei Magazzini 2, 50122
Tel *055 239 95 46*
W inpiazzadellasignoria.com
Exceptional, classically furnished rooms in a 15th-century palazzo with views of the piazza.

Platinhome €€
Apartments **Map** 6 E1
Via Ricasoli 48, 50122
Tel *055 535 98 19*
W platinhome.it
Luxury apartments, many with elegant terraces, in a lovely Neo-Classical palazzo. Spa bathrooms and a catering service.

Residence Hilda €€
Apartments **Map** 6 E2
Via dei Servi 40, 50122
Tel *055 28 80 21*
W residencehilda.com
Bright, stylish apartments near the Duomo, with contemporary furniture and wooden floors.

Le Stanze di Santa Croce €€
Boutique **Map** 4 E1
Via delle Pinzochere 6, 50123
Tel *0347 259 30 10*
W lestanzedisantacroce.com
Bright, cozy rooms and a friendly owner who runs cookery courses. Outstanding breakfasts.

Continentale €€€
Contemporary **Map** 6 D4
Vicolo dell'Oro 6r, 50123
Tel *055 272 62*
W lungarnocollection.com
Achingly hip hotel, with romantic views of Ponte Vecchio from many of its rooms. The fitness centre is in a medieval tower.

Bright white façade of Il Guelfo Bianco, a restored 14th-century palazzo *(see p253)*

Price Guide

Prices are based on one night's stay in high season for a standard double room, inclusive of service charges and taxes.

€	under €150
€€	€150 to 300
€€€	over €300

Gallery Hotel Art €€€
Boutique **Map** 6 D4
Vicolo dell'Oro 5, 50123
Tel *055 272 63*
W lungarnocollection.com
Cutting-edge style over eight storeys. Sleek minimalist decor, with contemporary art showcased in the lobby and lounge.

Palazzo Niccolini al Duomo €€€
Historic **Map** 6 E2
Via dei Servi 2, 50122
Tel *055 28 24 12*
W niccolinidomepalace.com
A 16th-century palazzo, with period paintings, chandeliers and antiques. Right by the Duomo.

Relais Santa Croce €€€
Historic **Map** 4 F1
Via Ghibellina 87, 50122
Tel *055 234 22 30*
W baglionihotels.com
Abundant period splendour and luxurious rooms in an elegant 18th-century palazzo, close to Michelangelo's house.

City Centre North

Casa Rovai €
B&B **Map** 2 E5
Via Fiesolana 1, 50122
Tel *055 200 16 47*
W casarovai.it
Spacious en-suite rooms, some with frescoes, in a beautifully renovated family home. Stunning views across the city from the roof terrace.

Orto de'Medici €
Boutique **Map** 2 D4
Via San Gallo 30, 50129
Tel *055 48 24 27*
W ortodeimedici.it
Flower-filled terrace, historic garden, frescoed public rooms and a stylish assembly of rooms and suites. Very central location.

Palazzo Benci €
Traditional **Map** 5 C1
Piazza Madonna Aldobrandini 3, 50123
Tel *055 21 38 48*
W palazzobenci.com
A 16th-century palazzo with a gorgeous courtyard. Modern decor in the rooms, but with plenty of period features.

Residenza Johanna 2 €
B&B Map 1 C2
Via Cinque Giornate 2, 50129
Tel *055 47 33 77*
w johanna.it
This Liberty (Italian Art Nouveau) villa is one of three neighbourhood B&Bs run by the Johanna group.

Antica Dimora €€
B&B Map 2 D3
Via San Gallo 72, 50129
Tel *055 462 72 96*
w johanna.it
Sumptuous, superior B&B with four-poster beds and a comfortable lounge.

Firenze Number Nine €€
Boutique Map 5 C1
Via dei Conti 9, 50123
Tel *055 29 37 77*
w firenzenumbernine.com
Stylish accommodation with contemporary furnishings and art set against period features.

Boutique split-level penthouse at the modern Continentale *(see p252)*

DK Choice

Il Guelfo Bianco €€
Historic Map 6 E1
Via Cavour 29, 50129
Tel *055 28 83 30*
w ilguelfobianco.it
Rooms in this meticulously restored 14th-century palazzo retain their beamed or vaulted ceilings and are furnished with 18th- and 19th-century pieces. Contemporary art from the owner's collection is on the walls, and there is a courtyard garden.

Hotel Botticelli €€
Historic Map 2 E5
Via Taddea 8, 50123
Tel *055 29 09 05*
w hotelbotticelli.it
Restored 16th-century palazzo with vaulted, frescoed ceilings and views of the cathedral dome.

Loggiato dei Serviti €€
Historic Map 2 D4
Piazza SS Annunziata 3, 50122
Tel *055 28 95 92*
w loggiatodeiservitihotel.it
Lavishly styled bedrooms occupying a 15th-century convent, hidden away on one of the city's most evocative piazzas.

Monna Lisa €€
Boutique Map 2 E5
Borgo Pinti 27, 50121
Tel *055 247 97 51*
w monnalisa.it
With a formal garden and rooms full of aristocratic panache, the Monna Lisa offers an experience akin to staying at a country estate. Witty collection of Mona Lisas.

Four Seasons €€€
Luxury Map 2 F4
Borgo Pinti 99, 50121
Tel *055 262 61*
w fourseasons.com/florence
Sumptuous hotel occupying two beautifully preserved Renaissance palazzi. Gorgeous grounds with a delightful walled garden.

City Centre West

Della Signoria €
Traditional Map 6 D3
Via delle Terme 1, 50123
Tel *055 21 45 30*
w hoteldellasignoria.com
Views of Ponte Vecchio, a roof bar and a range of tasteful, simply decorated rooms.

Hotel Cestelli €
Traditional Map 5 C3
Borgo Santi Apostoli 25, 50123
Tel *055 21 42 13*
w hotelcestelli.com
Charming and affordable small hotel in a 12th-century palazzo.

Beacci Tornabuoni €€
Historic Map 5 C3
Via de'Tornabuoni 3, 50123
Tel *055 21 26 45*
w tornabuonihotels.com
Plush rooms with antiques and tapestries on three floors of a 15th-century palazzo.

Casa Howard €€
B&B Map 5 B1
Via della Scala 18, 50129
Tel *0335 26 60 17, 066 992 45 55*
w casahoward.com
The decor effortlessly fuses old and new. Well-stocked honesty bar and a garden with a Turkish bath.

Davanzati €€
Traditional Map 6 D3
Via Porta Rossa 5, 50123
Tel *055 28 66 66*
w hoteldavanzati.it
Beautifully furnished family-run hotel. Free *aperitivo* each evening.

Golden Tower and Spa €€
Boutique Map 5 C3
Piazza Strozzi 11r, 50123
Tel *055 28 78 60*
w goldentowerhotel.it
A beautifully renovated palace incorporating a medieval tower. Gleaming marble floors.

Grand Hotel Baglioni €€
Historic Map 5 C1
Piazza Unità Italiana 66, 50123
Tel *055 235 80*
w hotelbaglioni.it
Fin de siècle style in abundance, with rich interiors, lush gardens and a stunning rooftop restaurant.

L'O €€
Boutique Map 5 B2
Piazza Santa Maria Novella 24, 50123
Tel *055 27 73 80*
w whythebesthotels.com
Contemporary hotel with stylish, masculine decor inspired by the owner's passion for wristwatches.

Porta Rossa €€
Historic Map 6 D3
Via Porta Rossa 19, 50123
Tel *055 28 75 51*
w hotelportarossa.com
Slick hotel in a 16th-century town house. The breakfast room and bar exude *belle-époque* glamour.

DK Choice

Rosso 23 €€
Boutique Map 5 B2
Piazza S Maria Novella 23, 50123
Tel *055 27 73 00*
w whythebesthotels.com
The bold use of grey and scarlet – ranging from ruby Moroccan lamps to red Perspex busts – gives an exuberant contemporary twist to this period palazzo. The colour scheme continues in the rooms (many with views of Santa Maria Novella) and the courtyard is perfect for a peaceful drink.

For more information on types of hotels *see pp248–51*

Torre Guelfa €€
Historic Map 5 C3
Borgo Santi Apostoli 8, 50123
Tel *055 239 63 38*
W hoteltorreguelfa.com
Incorporating the tallest tower in
the city, this hotel occupies two
floors of a medieval palace.

Hotel Savoy €€€
Luxury Map 6 D3
Piazza della Repubblica 7, 50123
Tel *055 273 51*
W hotelsavoy.it
Lavish interiors, an iconic bar and
a sixth-floor gym with great views
of the Duomo and Campanile.

JK Place €€€
Contemporary Map 5 B2
Piazza Santa Maria Novella 7, 50123
Tel *055 264 51 81*
W jkplace.com
Hip town-house hotel with a very
trendy rooftop bar.

Palazzo Vecchietti €€€
Apartments Map 5 C3
Via degli Strozzi 4, 50123
Tel *055 230 28 02*
W palazzovecchietti.com
Understated luxury in a 15th-
century palace converted into
suites. Butler service.

St Regis €€€
Luxury Map 5 A2
Piazza Ognissanti 1, 50123
Tel *055 28 87 81*
W starwoodhotels.com/stregis
Breathtaking views from the river-
facing rooms up to the Ponte
Vecchio. Glassed-in winter garden.

Westin Excelsior €€€
Luxury Map 5 A2
Piazza Ognissanti 3, 50123
Tel *055 271 51*
W starwoodhotels.com/westin
Bags of old-world charm, plus
liveried staff, opulent public areas
and spacious, sumptuous rooms.

Courtyard at the opulent Palazzo Magnani
Ferone, just south of the Arno

Key to Price Guide *see p252*

Oltrarno

Istituto Gould €
Hostel Map 3 B2
Via dei Serragli 49, 50100
Tel *055 21 25 76*
W istitutogould.it
Charitable institution with rock-
bottom rates for hostel-like rooms.
Sparsely furnished, but spotless.

Palazzo Guadagni €
Historic Map 5 B5
Piazza S Sprito 9, 50125
Tel *055 21 53 08*
W palazzoguadagni.com
Located on an appealing square,
this palazzo has a romantic
loggia where scenes from *Tea
with Mussolini* were filmed.

Relais il Cestello €
Traditional Map 5 A3
Piazza di Cestello 9, 50125
Tel *055 28 06 32*
W relaisilcestello.it
Comfortable, spacious rooms in a
quiet location. Just 10 minutes'
walk from the historic centre.

San Frediano Mansion €
B&B Map 5 A3
Via Borgo San Frediano 8, 50124
Tel *055 21 29 91*
W sanfredianomansion.com
Huge rooms with frescoed ceilings
in a 15th-century palazzo. It's
worth paying extra for a river view.

Floroom 1 €€
B&B Map 5 B4
Via del Pavone 7, 50125
Tel *055 894 90 15*
W floroom.com
Guests have their own keys to
these slick monochrome rooms,
allowing the freedom of an apart-
ment with the service of a B&B.

DK Choice

Grand Hotel Villa Cora €€€
Luxury Map 5 B4
Viale Machiavelli 18, 50125
Tel *055 22 87 90*
W whythebesthotels.com
Impressive 19th-century villa with
the feel of a country house set in
stunning gardens. Lavish public
rooms with lashings of gilt and
stucco, plus frescoes and huge
Venetian chandeliers. Opulent
rooms and a state-of-the-art spa
in the villa's former stable block.

Lungarno €€€
Boutique Map 5 C4
Borgo San Jacopo 14, 50125
Tel *055 272 61*
W lungarnohotels.com
Crisp, cool boutique style. The
best rooms have private terraces
jutting out over the Arno.

Palazzo Magnani Ferone €€€
Historic Map 5 A3
Borgo San Frediano 5, 50124
Tel *055 239 95 44*
W palazzomagniferone.com
Live like an aristocrat in one of
the splendidly appointed suites
in this magnificent palazzo.

Further Afield

Hotel Villa Betania €
Country Villa Map 3 A4
Viale del Poggio Imperiale 23, 50125
Tel *055 22 22 43*
W villabetania.it
Long-established family-run hotel
in a villa with gardens. Ten minutes'
walk from the Porta Romana.

Villa Villoresi €
Country Villa
Via Ciampi 2, Sesto Fiorentino, 50019
Tel *055 44 32 12*
W villavilloresi.it
Atmospheric country villa with
frescoes, murals and antiques.

Pensione Bencista €€
Country Villa
Via Benedetto di Maiano 4, 50014
Tel *055 591 63*
W bencista.com
Welcoming 16th-century villa
with good food and wonderful
views over Florence.

Relais Marignolle €€
Country Villa
*Via di San Quirichino a Marignolle 16,
50124*
Tel *055 228 69 10*
W marignolle.com
Impeccably designed rooms set in
a countryside retreat surrounded
by orchards and olive groves.

Il Salviatino €€€
Country Villa
Via del Salviatino 71, Fiesole, 50137
Tel *055 904 11 11*
W salviatino.com
Palatial 15th-century villa set in a
large garden overlooking Florence.

Villa San Michele €€€
Luxury
Via Doccia 4, 50014
Tel *055 567 82 00*
W belmond.com/villa-san-michele-
florence
Former monastery with exquisite
rooms and stunning views. Great
restaurant in a romantic loggia.

Villa la Vedetta €€€
Country Villa Map 4 F3
Viale Michelangelo 78, 50125
Tel *055 68 16 31*
W villalavedettahotel.com
Luxurious rooms and suites in a
19th-century hilltop villa. Stunning
panoramas from the pool.

Western Tuscany

ARTIMINO: Hotel Paggeria €€
Agriturismo   Map C2
Via Papa Giovanni XXIII, 59015
Tel 055 87 51 41
w artimino.com
Stay in the servant quarters on a wine estate dominated by the Medici villa La Ferdinanda, a UNESCO World Heritage site.

CRESPINA: Poggio al Casone €€
Agriturismo   Map C3
Via Volpaia 16, 56042
Tel 050 64 22 59
w poggioalcasone.com
Sophisticated apartments on a wine estate offering a pool, a small fishing lake and excursions.

DK Choice

MONTAIONE: Fattoria Barbialla Nuova €
Agriturismo   Map C3
Via Casatrada 49, 50050
Tel 0571 67 72 59
w barbiallanuova.it
Idyllic rural retreat on a rambling estate in the hills between Pisa and Florence, where wild boar and deer roam free and Chianina cattle graze. Guests can join a truffle hunt, eat fruit straight off the trees, learn to make bread or pizza and explore the estate's hiking trails. Two country houses, each with its own pool, have been divided into apartments. A third farmhouse caters to groups of eight to ten.

PISA: Campanile €
B&B   Map B2
Piazza Arcivescovado 16, 56126
Tel 050 56 30 40
w ilcampanile.pisa.it
Mini-apartments with cooking facilities and a garden. Right opposite the Leaning Tower.

RIGOLI: Relais Dell'Ussero €€
Country Villa   Map B2
Via Statale Abetone 50, 56010
Tel 050 81 81 93
w corliano.it
Spectacular renaissance villa on a country estate, 7 km (5 miles) from Pisa. Luxurious rooms, frescoed ceilings and a first-rate restaurant.

VOLTERRA: Hotel la Locanda €€
Traditional   Map C3
Via Guarnacci 24–28, 56048
Tel 0588 81547
w hotel-lalocanda.com
Modern hotel with antique furnishings in a former convent near the amphitheatre. Etruscan relics embedded in the façade.

Private balcony with a view of the Ponte Vecchio at boutique hotel Lungarno *(see p254)*

Northern Tuscany

LUCCA: Albergo Villa Marta €
Country Villa   Map C2
Via del Ponte Guasperini 873, San Lorenzo a Vaccoli, 55100
Tel 0583 37 01 01
w albergovillamarta.it
Serene hotel in a former hunting lodge surrounded by gardens.

LUCCA: Palazzo Alexander €
Historic   Map C2
Via Santa Giustina 48, 55100
Tel 0583 58 35 71
w hotelpalazzoalexander.it
Plush rooms featuring plenty of gilding and brocade in a centrally located 12th-century palazzo.

DK Choice

LUCCA: Tenuta San Pietro €€
Agriturismo   Map C2
Via per San Pietro 22–26, San Pietro a Marcigliana, 55012
Tel 0583 92 66 76
w tenuta-san-pietro.com
Scandinavian minimalism adds a contemporary touch to this restored 16th-century farmhouse with exposed stone walls, wooden floors and paintings by the Norwegian owner. The food is superb and the chef offers cookery classes, plus wine and olive-oil tastings. A swimming pool overlooks the terraced olive groves and a courtesy bus shuttles guests to Lucca twice daily.

PIETRASANTA: Palazzo Guiscardo €€
Boutique   Map B2
Via Provinciale 16, 55045
Tel 0584 73 52 98
w palazzoguiscardo.it
Elegant hotel in a small palazzo. Antique furniture, brocades and bathrooms clad in local marble.

VIAREGGIO: Hotel President €€
Traditional   Map B2
Viale Carducci 5, 55049
Tel 0584 96 27 12
w hotelpresident.it
Liberty-style beachfront villa with comfortable modern rooms and a very good restaurant.

Eastern Tuscany

AREZZO: Cento Passi dal Duomo €
B&B   Map E3
Via de Montetini 13, 52100
Tel 0575 25 00 48, 0334 689 54 15
w centopassidalduomo.it
Bright, diversely decorated rooms with IKEA furniture and en-suite bathrooms, close to the Duomo.

CASTIGLION FIORENTINO: Relais San Pietro €€
Traditional   Map E3
Località Polvano 3, 52043
Tel 0575 65 01 00
w polvano.com
Whitewashed rooms with beamed ceilings and terracotta floors in a hilltop 17th-century farmhouse.

CORTONA: Hotel San Michele €
Historic   Map E3
Via Guelfa 15, 52044
Tel 0575 60 43 48
w hotelsanmichele.net
Beautifully restored Renaissance palazzo in the heart of town. Fabulous rooms with exposed brickwork and beamed ceilings.

CORTONA: Relais la Corte dei Papi €€
Country Villa   Map E3
Via la Dogana 12, Località Pergo, 52040
Tel 0575 61 41 09
w lacortedeipapi.com
Luxurious, romantic rooms in an 18th-century country house in the Cortona hills. Perfect summer base, with a spa and restaurant.

For more information on types of hotels see pp248–51

CORTONA: Relais Villa Baldelli €€
Country Villa **Map** E3
San Pietro al Cegliolo 420, 52044
Tel *0575 61 24 06*
W villabaldellicortona.com
Restored 17th-century villa set in parkland. Rooms with beamed ceilings and antique furniture. On-site swimming pool, cookery courses and horse riding.

DK Choice

MONTE SAN SAVINO: Castello di Gargonza €€€
Luxury **Map** E3
Località Monte San Savino, 52048
Tel *0575 84 70 21*
W gargonza.it
Magical. Rooms, apartments and a house in a fairy-tale *borgo*, a diminutive medieval hamlet clustered around a castle, in the hills between Arezzo and Siena. The *borgo* is surrounded by parkland that is crisscrossed with hiking and nature trails. Rooms feature beamed ceilings and simple rustic furniture. Gargonza boasts a great restaurant, plus a pool with wonderful views over the countryside.

PONTICINO: Poggio del Drago €
B&B **Map** E3
Località Poggio del Drago, 52041
Tel *0331 549 87 67*
W poggiodeldrago.it
A country cottage with pleasant grounds. Six modern rooms with white walls and deft splashes of colour, plus a swimming pool.

REGGELLO: I Bonsi €€€
Agriturismo **Map** D2
Via i Bonsi 47, 50066
Tel *055 865 21 18*
W agriturismoibonsi.it
A 15th-century turreted villa converted into luxury apartments and surrounded by parkland.

Central Tuscany

CASTELLINA IN CHIANTI: Fonterutoli €
Agriturismo **Map** D3
Via Ottone III di Sassonia 5, 53011
Tel *0577 74 13 85*
W fonterutoli.com
Refined hotel in a tranquil estate village owned by one of Chianti's foremost wine producers.

CASTIGLIONCELLO DEL TRINORO: Hotel Monteverdi €€€
Boutique **Map** E4
Via di Mezzo, 53047
Tel *0578 26 81 46*
W monteverdituscany.com
Sophisticated Tuscan decor, a pool and an exceptional restaurant at this hotel in a minuscule hamlet.

CHIANCIANO TERME: La Foce €€
Agriturismo **Map** E4
Strada della Vittoria 61, 53042
Tel *0578 69101*
W lafoce.com
Rooms, apartments and rustic houses set in one of Tuscany's loveliest landscaped gardens.

GAIOLE IN CHIANTI: Castello di Tornano €
Agriturismo **Map** D3
Località Tornano, 53013
Tel *0577 74 60 67*
W castelloditornano.it
A choice of simple apartments or sumptuous rooms in a formidable castle on a forested hilltop.

MONCIONI: Villa Sassolino €€
Boutique **Map** D3
Via del Solatio Moncioni 85, 52020 Montevarchi
Tel *055 970 29 42*
W villasassolini.it
Chic hotel in an austere 15th-century country palazzo – limed floorboards, muted earth shades and natural textures. Free minibars.

MONTALCINO: Il Giglio €
B&B **Map** D4
Via Soccorso Saloni 5, 53024
Tel *0577 84 81 67*
W gigliohotel.com
Pretty rooms and apartments in a relaxed hill town. Family-run and long-established. Stunning views.

MONTEPULCIANO: Follonico €€
B&B **Map** E4
Località Casale 2, Torrita di Siena, 53049
Tel *0577 66 97 73*
W follonico.it
A romantic stone farmhouse decorated with vintage finds and reclaimed rustic furniture.

MONTEPULCIANO: Hotelito Lupaia €€
Agriturismo **Map** E4
Località Lupaia 74, Torrita di Siena, 53049
Tel *0577 66 80 28*
W lupaia.com
Fizzing colours, lustrous silks and grand antique beds. Each room has its own garden or terrace.

MURLO: Residence Bosco della Spina €€€
Country Villa **Map** D4
Via della Tinaia 13, 53016
Tel *0577 81 46 05*
W boscodellaspina.com
Apartments and a restaurant within the barns, haylofts and granaries of a medieval farm.

PALAZZETTO: Borgo Santo Pietro €€€
Boutique **Map** D4
Località Palazzetto, Chiusdino, 53012
Tel *0577 75 12 22*
W borgosantopietro.com
Opulence in an isolated 13th-century villa. Modern luxuries include iPods and docks in each room, a spa and a fresh-water infinity pool.

PIENZA: La Bandita Townhouse €€
Boutique **Map** E4
Corso Rossellino 111, 53026
Tel *0578 74 90 05*
W labanditatownhouse.com
A shrine to urban minimalism in an historic village. Freestanding designer tubs, medieval garden and great views from upper suites.

SAN CASCIANO VAL DI PESA: Villa le Corti €€
Agriturismo **Map** D2
San Piero di Sotto, 50026
Tel *055 82 93 01*
W principecorsini.com
Lovely wine estate belonging to the Corsini, one of Italy's oldest aristocratic families. B&B and self-catering options in two houses.

The ancient – and now luxurious – Castello di Vicarello, in Cinigiano *(see p257)*

**SAN GIMIGNANO:
Vecchio Asilo** €
B&B Map C3
Via delle Torri 4, Ulignano 53030
Tel *0577 950 03*
W vecchioasilo.it
A medieval towered house in a
tiny village. Rustic-style rooms.

**SAN GIMIGNANO: Albergo
Leon Bianco** €€
Traditional Map C3
Piazza della Cisterna 13, 53037
Tel *0577 94 12 94*
W leonbianco.com
Modern rooms with beamed
ceilings in an 11th-century palazzo.

**SAN GIMIGNANO: Locanda
dell'Artista** €€
B&B Map C3
Loc. Canonica-Lucignano 43, 53037
Tel *0577 94 60 26*
W locandadellartista.com
A roomy farmhouse with modern
comforts, set amid olive groves.

DK Choice

**SAN GIOVANNI D'ASSO:
Lucignanello Bandini** €€
Agriturismo Map D4
Località Lucignano d'Asso, 53020
Tel *0577 80 30 68*
W borgolucignanello.com
A tiny, preserved estate village
belonging to the Piccolomini family (who count Pope Pius II among
their forebears). There are no cars,
just beautiful cobbled streets.
Five apartments accommodate
between two and six adults, and
a house, with its own pool,
sleeps six. All guests have access
to the hilltop infinity pool.

SIENA: Casa Cecchi €
B&B Map D3
Strada d'Istieto 71, 53100
Tel *0392 798 16 16*
W casacecchisiena.com
Comfortable rooms in a traditional
stone farmhouse with a garden.

**SIENA: Castello delle Quattro
Torra** €
B&B Map D3
Strada di Pieve al Bozzone 36, 53100
Tel *0333 466 32 08*
W quattrotorra.it
Tuscan-style rooms and apart-
ments in an impressive fortified
13th-century building. Great views.

SIENA: Campo Regio Relais €€
Boutique Map D3
Via della Sapienza 25, 53100
Tel *0577 22 20 73*
W camporegio.com
Marvellous views of Duomo-
crowned Siena. Rooms have silk
drapes and antique furniture.

Refined decor at welcoming Campo Regio
Relais, in Siena

**SIENA: Pensione Palazzo
Ravizza** €€
Historic Map D3
Pian dei Mantellini 34, 53100
Tel *0577 28 04 62*
W palazzoravizza.it
Terracotta floors, frescoed ceilings
and antique furnishings in a
Renaissance palazzo with a
fantastic gourmet restaurant.

SIENA: Castello di Casole €€€
Luxury Map D3
Località Querceto, Casole d'Elsa, 53031
Tel *0577 96 15 08*
W castellodicasole.com
Utter luxury in suites or villas on
a large estate. Pool, spa and a
personal chef (should you so wish).

**SIENA: Grand Hotel
Continental** €€€
Luxury Map D3
Via Banchi di Sopra 85, 53100
Tel *0577 560 11*
W royaldemeure.com
Stunning fabrics and frescoed
ceilings in a 16th-century palazzo.
Access to golf and tennis.

**SINALUNGA: Locanda
dell'Amorosa** €€€
Agriturismo Map E3
Località l'Amorosa, 53048
Tel *0577 67 72 11*
W amorosa.it
Graceful rooms in an idyllic
14th-century villa cascading with
flowers. Fantastic restaurant.

Southern Tuscany

CAPALBIO: Locanda Rossa €€
Agriturismo Map D5
*Strada Capalbio Pescia Fiorentina 11b,
58011*
Tel *0564 89 04 62*
W locandarossa.com
Bright, modern rooms in a brick-
red farmhouse. Views stretch
over olive groves to the sea.

**CINIGIANO: Castello di
Vicarello** €€€
Boutique Map D4
*Località Castello di Vicarello, Poggi
del Sasso, 58044*
Tel *0564 99 07 18*
W castellodivicarello.eu
Seductive suites – think a
Balinese-Tuscan fusion – in an
exquisite hilltop castle. Two
ozone-treated pools and a spa.
Fabulous food.

ELBA: Hotel Ilio €€
Boutique Map B4
Via Sant'Andrea 5, 57030
Tel *0565 90 80 18*
W hotelilio.com
Stylish public areas, a lovely
garden and simple rooms, some
with views of Capo Sant'Andrea.

GIGLIO: Albergo il Porticciolo €
Traditional Map C5
*Via della Torre 3, Campese, Isolo del
Giglio, 58012*
Tel *0564 80 42 21*
W albergoilporticciolo.it
Plain rooms in an unpretentious,
modern, family-run hotel in the
little port of Campese.

DK Choice

MANCIANO: Quercia Rossa €
Agriturismo Map D5
*Frazione Montemerano,
Santarello 89, 58014*
Tel *0564 62 95 29*
W querciarossa.net
Tranquil farmhouse overlooking
the rolling hills of the Maremma.
Rooms are furnished with
antiques collected by Victorian
traveller Augusta Belloc: French-
polished Rococo beds, Murano
chandeliers, bronze sconces and
exotic souvenirs. Animal print
throws, cow-hide rugs and stone
basins add a contemporary
twist to the decor. Meals using
local and organic ingredients
are available by arrangement.

**PORTO ERCOLE:
Hotel don Pedro** €
Traditional Map D5
Via Panoramica 7, 58018
Tel *0564 83 39 14*
W hoteldonpedro.it
Simple hotel with private beach
and stunning views over the yacht-
filled port and Fortezza Spagnola.

PORTO ERCOLE: Il Pellicano €€€
Luxury Map D5
Località Sbarcatello, 58018
Tel *0564 85 81 11*
W pellicanohotel.com
Understated elegance, sea views
and bright, modern rooms, many
with their own terrace.

For more information on types of hotels *see pp248–51*

WHERE TO EAT AND DRINK

Food is one of the great Italian passions, and eating out on a balmy summer's evening can be a memorable experience in Florence and Tuscany. Few restaurants serve anything but Italian food, and most focus on the robust fare that typifies the region's cuisine. Most Tuscans take their lunch *(pranzo)* at around 1pm, and have dinner *(cena)* from 8pm. Restaurants may shut for several weeks during the winter and also during the holiday season in August. If in doubt, phone first to check that the restaurant is open. Finding restaurants in Florence can be confusing due to the dual numbering of the streets *(see p297)*, so use the map references in this guide. The restaurants listed on pages 264–75 have been selected from the best the city and region can offer across all price ranges.

Places to Eat

Italian restaurants have a bewildering variety of names, but in practice you'll find that most places serve variations on the same hearty regional food. In general, a *trattoria* and an *osteria* will offer cheaper and more casual food with an emphasis on home cooking, while a *ristorante* will be smarter, offering more expensive upmarket cuisine. Historically, the term *osteria* was used to describe a place serving a range of wines with simple food. The focus has now shifted from wine to food, but an *osteria* tends to be slightly more informal with a less extensive menu than a *trattoria*.

There will probably be times when you do not want a large meal, and Florence and Tuscany offer a huge range of places for more casual eating. One option is a *birrerie*, which offers great value meals, including pizzas, pastas and burgers. An *enoteca* or *vineria* will offer a selection of wines to try, along with a range of light dishes. They also double as a well-stocked wine shop for browsers and connoisseurs. A *pizzeria* is a cheap, informal restaurant with pasta, meat and fish on the menu, as well as pizzas. It is usually open only in the evening, especially if it has wood-fired ovens.

At lunchtime, you could visit a delicatessen or *tavola calda* (snack bar), which will offer a range of hot and cold pasta dishes, vegetables and meats. A *rosticceria* offers spit-roast chicken to take away, often with other fast foods. Most bars sell filled rolls *(panini)* and

Da il Latini, a particularly popular *trattoria* in Florence *(see p267)*

sandwiches *(tramezzini)*, and small pizza bars sell slices of pizza *(pizza taglia)* to eat on the street.

If you fancy a snack, stop into a *pasticceria* for a wide variety of sweet and savoury pastries, cakes and biscuits. Many cafés also serve delicious nibbles all day. Alternatively, visit one of the region's many ice-cream parlours *(gelaterie)*, which usually offer a dazzling array of flavours.

Vegetarian Food

Purely vegetarian restaurants are few and far between in Florence and Tuscany, but you will find dishes suitable for non-meat-eaters wherever you go. Many pasta and risotto dishes do not use meat, and you can ask for a range of vegetable-based side dishes *(contorni)* for your main course. Most menus are adaptable because dishes are prepared to order. Tell your waiter or waitress that you are *vegetariano* (female – *vegetariana)*, and they will advise accordingly.

Paying

Tax and service are usually included in the menu prices, but it is normal to leave a tip of about 10 per cent. Many restaurants include a fixed charge *(coperto)* on the bill *(il conto)*, which covers bread and is charged per person.

Credit cards are not always accepted, particularly in rural areas, so check before you order.

Dining on La Grotta's patio, overlooked by Madonna di San Biagio in Montepulciano *(see p273)*

La Porta, offering alfresco dining with amazing views from a tiny medieval hamlet, just outside Pienza *(see p273)*

Making Reservations

Booking (*prenotazione*) is highly recommended. Sunday lunch and Saturday evening, in particular, get very busy. Most places are closed a couple of days a week, and some are closed for weeks at a time in winter and August, so check opening times if you do not intend to make a reservation.

Smoking

Italians now adhere to strict government regulations that prohibit smoking inside restaurants and cafés. Smoking is generally permitted at outdoor tables, but it is best to use your discretion.

Choice of Wine

House wines will usually be from the Chianti region, Montepulciano or Montalcino. The cheaper establishments often have only house wine, or a small choice of other Tuscan wines. Those in the top price range will have a fuller selection of regional wines, as well as wines from other parts of Italy. In the most exclusive establishments, there should be a wide range of Italian and local wines, and a selection of French and other foreign vintages, with many available by the glass.

Children

Children are usually welcome in restaurants, particularly in family-run places. You can often order a half portion (*mezza porzione*), and some places will supply high chairs (*seggioloni*).

Wheelchair Access

Few restaurants make special provision for wheelchairs, though a word when you are booking should ensure a conveniently situated table and assistance on arrival.

The Menu

A meal in a restaurant will usually start with *antipasti,* or hors d'œuvres (hams, olives, salamis, crostini), followed by *primi* (soups, pasta or rice). Main courses – *secondi* – will be meat or fish, either served alone or accompanied by vegetables (*contorni*) or a salad (*insalata*).

To finish, there will probably be a choice of fruit (*frutta*), cheese (*formaggio*), desserts (*dolci*), or a combination of all three. Coffee – always an espresso, never cappuccino – is ordered at the end of a meal, often with a *digestivo (see p263)*. In cheaper restaurants, the menu may be written on a blackboard and in many establishments the waiter (*cameriere*) will recite the chef's daily specials at your table.

Recommended Restaurants

The restaurants listed in this guide cover a wide range of eateries, from the simple *pizzeria* and delicatessen to the elegant *ristorante*. Each restaurant listed is given a cuisine category. Most of these descriptions are self-explanatory, but the *Places to Eat* section on page 258 provides more information on what you can expect from the menu.

Establishments labelled DK Choice have been selected because they are outstanding in some way. They may offer superb cuisine, a stunning setting, excellent value or a combination of these.

Ristorante Enoteca del Duca, situated in an 18th-century palazzo in Volterra *(see p270)*

The Flavours of Florence and Tuscany

Tuscany is the orchard and vegetable garden of Italy, a vision of rolling, vine-clad hills and silvery-grey olive groves, while the Ligurian sea yields a fabulous bounty of fish and other seafood. The cuisine is rustic and simple, but always uses the finest ingredients. It is said that Tuscany is where Italian cooking was born, thanks to Catherine de'Medici, an accomplished gourmet. Tuscans are known as *mangiafagioli* (bean eaters), because pulses are used so much in soups and robust stews. Juicy steaks from prized Valdichiana cattle, pork and game all feature strongly. Fungi are highly prized; even more so are truffles – "black gold".

Black truffles

Freshly harvested Tuscan olives, for pressing into olive oil

First and Foremost

Tuscan olive oil is simply outstanding in quality. This "liquid gold" has countless uses and is an integral part of *crostini*, slices of toasted bread smeared with olive oil on which are spread different toppings, such as *crostini alla Toscana*, topped with sautéed chickens livers. *Salumi* producers are an important feature of the region and *prosciutto di cinghiale*

(wild-boar ham) is a rich, gamey delicacy. Soups and minestrones are also very popular, often made with beans, especially the white kidney beans known as *cannellini*. The most typical pasta is pappardelle, broad noodles that are often served with a rich hare sauce called *pappardelle alla lepre*.

Earth and Water

The shining star of meat dishes is tender, succulent beef steak, *bistecca alla fiorentina*. The best is from cattle raised in Valdichiana, south of Arezzo, which is delicious marinated with extra-virgin olive oil and herbs, grilled over an open fire and served very rare. Tuscans are passionate hunters and

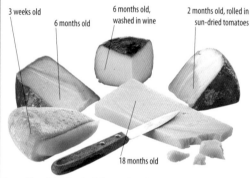

3 weeks old

6 months old

6 months old, washed in wine

2 months old, rolled in sun-dried tomatoes

18 months old

Some of the varieties of ewe's milk Pecorino cheese found in Tuscany

Regional Dishes and Specialities

The olive is the staple ingredient – even the branches of the tree are used for grilling. Soups vary from those enriched with beans – such as *ribollita* ("boiled again"), a rich soup of beans, herbs and vegetables whose second boiling makes it thicker and intensifies the flavour – to the simple, thin vegetable *acquacotta* (literally meaning "cooked water"), to which an egg is added before serving. The vast array of salamis and cold cuts includes *finocchiona*, salami flavoured with wild fennel. Robust stews include *lepre in dolce e forte*. This hare stew is cooked with citrus fruits, cocoa, garlic, rosemary, vegetables and red wine. For the sweet-toothed, Tuscany offers *ricciarelli* (diamond-shaped almond cakes), *cantucci* (above) and *torta di riso* – a golden, rich rice cake that is mouthwateringly delicious.

Cantucci

Minestrone alla fiorentina
This thick vegetable and bean soup may also contain chicken and pork giblets.

A colourful assortment of local produce

everything from the smallest songbird to the largest wild boar features on menus. Hare is a special favourite.

Seafood and fish includes especially good red mullet *(triglie)* from Livorno and *cacciucco* soup, claimed as the ancestor of *bouillabaisse*.

Fungi Forays

From late August to early October, Tuscans are seized by fungi fever. Armies of people with baskets make an annual pilgrimage to the Garfagna, Mugello and Maremma for prize pickings. The most sought after are *porcini* (boletus or cep). Picking tends to be limited by licence and is certainly only advisable to those who know their edible fungi. Out of season, dried wild mushrooms accompany many dishes. But the star and most

highly prized fungi hide underground, waiting to be sniffed out by hunters with their keen-scented dogs – the truffle *(tartufo)*. The location of truffle troves is a closely guarded secret as they are, literally, worth their weight in gold. San Miniato produces

An array of beans on display in a Tuscan market square

about a quarter of Italy's truffle crop, including the prized white truffle.

Sweet Delights

Chestnuts are plentiful and have many uses. With almonds and honey, they are the main ingredients in some favourite and famous recipes. Castelnuovo della Garfagnana produces a superb chestnut cake, called *torta garfagnana*. Panforte, the Christmas cake originating from Siena, is a rich mix of fruits, nuts and spices. For something a little less rich, almond *cantucci* biscuits are sublime dipped into sweet *vin santo* wine.

TUSCAN TREATS

Cacciucco di Livorno Rich tomatoey fish soup served over toasted garlic bread.

Cantucci Sweet, very hard almond biscuits.

Cheeses Ricotta, Mucchino (cow's cheese made near Lucca), Pecorino and Cacciotte (made with ewe, cow and goat milk).

Chestnuts Made into flour, pancakes, soup and sweet cakes like *castagnaccio*, flavoured with rosemary.

Chianti The fine Tuscan red wine, used in many recipes.

Crostini Toasted bread that is smeared with olive oil and rubbed with garlic.

Pappardelle alla Lepre Thick noodles are served with a sauce of hare cooked with herbs and red wine.

Arista alla Fiorentina Pork loin is roasted with rosemary in a recipe dating from the 15th century.

Zuccotto In this Tuscan speciality, sponge cake is filled with almonds, hazelnuts, chocolate and cream.

What to Drink in Florence and Tuscany

Tuscany is a major wine-producing region whose wines make ideal partners for the robust local food. Both reds and whites are made here, ranging from light house wine (*vino della casa*) to the very best that Europe can produce. The most famous reds, notably Brunello di Montalcino, Vino Nobile di Montepulciano and Chianti, are made from the Sangiovese grape and are produced inland, on the hills of Tuscany. A number of estates, particularly in Chianti Classico, also experiment with non-Italian grape varieties with considerable success. Throughout Tuscany, bars and cafés are open all day serving drinks from wine to beer and coffee. See also *A Day Out in Chianti* on page 233.

Il Poggione is an excellent producer of Brunello di Montalcino.

Red Wine

Solaia

Chianti produced by Ruffino

Chianti is made in seven defined zones, but the best wines generally come from the hilly areas of Classico and Rufina. Brunello, from further south, needs ageing and can be expensive, but Rosso di Montalcino, made for younger drinking, often offers better value. Tuscan table wine can be cheap or expensive – the top-priced wines may not fit the traditional Chianti regulations, but are likely to be extremely good. Sassicaia is an example – it's one of the finest and most expensive wines in the country and made from the Cabernet Sauvignon grape. Other fine reds include Fontalloro, Cepparello and Solaia.

Carmignano, a good dry red, is made north of Florence.

Sassicaia is made from Cabernet Sauvignon grapes.

White Wine

Galestro

Tuscany's white wines are less interesting than the reds, although some producers are experimenting with a handful of quality whites from grapes such as Chardonnay and Sauvignon. Most Tuscan white wine is made from the Trebbiano grape, at its lightest in the spritzy style called Galestro, but usually sold as plain dry Bianco della Toscana. Vernaccia di San Gimignano, from the Vernaccia grape, is sometimes good, and Montecarlo, from near Lucca, is a blend of grapes that offers more interesting drinking. Most Tuscan whites need to be drunk young.

Vin Santo

Vin Santo

Vin Santo, or "Holy Wine", is a traditional wine once made on farms throughout the region. It is now seeing a revival of interest from modern producers. The best versions are sweet, though it can be found as a dry wine. It is often offered with *cantucci*, small almond biscuits, in Tuscan restaurants and homes. Vin Santo is made from Trebbiano and Malvasia grapes that are semi-dried, made into wine and then aged in small barrels for a number of years before bottling. The best are very concentrated in flavour. Quality varies, but superb versions are made by Avignonesi and Isole e Olena.

How Chianti is Made

Chianti is made as soon as possible after the October harvest. The quality of the wine can be very high, as wineries have combined the best of traditional and modern techniques.

De-stemmer

Crushing and De-stemming
The Sangiovese grapes are separated from the stalks. The tannin from the skins preserves the wine, but the stalk tannin is too harsh for fine wine.

Fermentation
The juice and grape skins go into a vat, where a pump circulates wine over the floating "cap" of skins to extract colour, tannin and flavour. Fermentation may take up to 15 days or more.

Fermentation vat

Harvest at the Brolio estate in Gaiole in Chianti

Pressing the Residue
Once the new wine has been drained off, the remaining skins and pips are pressed, producing dark and sometimes harsh press wine. Stored separately, this may be used in the final blend.

Press

Wooden cask

The barrels are topped up to prevent air from reaching the wine.

Maturation
A second fermentation, the malolactic, occurs in the spring, softening the wine, which is then run into wooden barrels to mature.

Cinzano, a popular early evening aperitivo

Aperitifs and Digestifs

Pre- and post-meal tipples include Campari, Cinzano and the artichoke-based Cynar, as well as Crodino, the best-known of several non-alcoholic drinks. The herb-flavoured *amaro* or a *grappa* commonly round off a meal; otherwise, try a *limoncello*, a sweet, lemon-based liqueur, the aniseed-scented Sambuca or almond-flavoured Amaretto.

Beer

Beer can be a great thirst-quencher, especially in the summer heat. Draught beer (*birra alla spina*) is less expensive than bottled beer, and is sold by the measure. Good Italian lager-style beers include Peroni and Moretti.

Other Drinks

Fruit juices are sold in small bottles (*succo di frutta*) or freshly squeezed (*spremuta*). In summer, iced tea or coffee can be refreshing. Italian coffee is drunk with frothy milk for breakfast (*cappuccino*) or black after meals (*espresso*). An *espresso* with a spot of milk is called a *macchiato*.

Espresso   Cappuccino

Where to Eat and Drink

Florence

City Centre East

All'Antico Vinaio   €
Vineria   **Map** 6 E4
Via dei Neri 65r–74r, 50100
Tel 055 238 27 23   **Closed** *Sun dinner*
Bustling little wine bar between
Piazza della Signoria and Piazza
Santa Croce. Perch on a stool
outside on the pavement and
order a glass of wine and a
sandwich. Hams, salamis and
cheeses are partnered with a
variety of savoury condiments,
such as olives, sundried tomatoes
and pesto.

Il Bufalo Trippone   €
Vineria   **Map** 6 E3
Via dell'Anguillara 48r, 50122
Tel 055 29 05 18   **Closed** *Sun*
Bustling, extremely popular
vineria with Tuscan wines by
the glass and sandwiches made
to order, filled with locally
sourced produce. The cheese
and charcuterie platter is also
highly recommended.

Caffè Cibrèo   €
Café   **Map** 4 F1
Via Andrea del Verrocchio 5r, 50122
Tel 055 234 58 53   **Closed** *Mon*
A tiny, beautifully crafted old-
fashioned café, with an outdoor
terrace where you can breakfast
on superior coffee and croissants,
sugar-crusted doughnuts or even
a delicate, chilled rice pudding.
There is also a fantastic selection
of bar snacks in the evening. It is
always packed and service can
be slow.

Il Cernacchino   €
Café   **Map** 6 D3
Via della Condotta 38r, 50122
Tel 055 29 41 19
A little family-run place that serves
delicious sandwiches, soups and
paninis, accompanied by a glass
of wine or beer. Everything is
freshly made on the premises.
Order at the counter and take
your food upstairs to eat.

Chiaroscuro   €
Café   **Map** 6 D3
Via del Corso 36r, 50122
Tel 055 21 42 47
Cosmopolitan café owned by
one of the city's coffee-bean
roasters and blenders. Lovely
interior featuring contemporary
chandeliers and a sinuous zinc
bar. Come for breakfast, a quick
lunch or an evening *aperitivo*
with nibbles.

La Divina Pizza   €
Pizzeria   **Map** 4 E1
Via Borgo Allegri 50r, 50122
Tel 055 234 74 98   **Closed** *Sun*
Superior takeaway pizza near
Santa Croce. Ingredients are
bought daily at the Sant'Ambrogio
market. Try the Divin Corbello, a
basket made of pizza bread filled
to order; stuff it with *burrata*
(creamy mozzarella).

I Due Fratellini   €
Vineria   **Map** 6 D3
Via de'Cimatori 38r, 50122
Tel 055 239 60 96   **Closed** *Sun
Jul–Aug*
A local institution lined with
shelves of wine. Every lunchtime,
queues form outside this tiny
alcove. Excellent *crostini* and
custom-made sandwiches are
served across a wooden counter
and eaten on the curb outside.

Edoardo il Gelato Biologico €
Gelateria   **Map** 6 D2
Piazza del Duomo 45r, 50122
Tel 055 28 10 55
Handmade waffle cones, crepes
and organic ice cream right on
Piazza Duomo. There are usually
long queues, but it's worth the
wait. The cinnamon is divine, and
the Chianti sorbet unforgettable.

Grom   €
Gelateria   **Map** 6 D2
Via del Campanile 2, 50122
Tel 055 21 61 58
Branch of an exclusive chain of
gelaterie dedicated to using carefully sourced natural and organic
ingredients. Offers classic choices,
such as Venezuelan chocolate
and Madagascan vanilla.

Local food hero and restaurateur Fabbio
Picchi at Caffè Cibrèo

Price Guide
Prices are based on a three-course meal
for one person, including tax and all
service charges.

€	up to €25
€€	€25–€50
€€€	over €50

Pane e Toscana   €
Delicatessen   **Map** 6 E3
Borgo Albizi 31r, 52100
Tel 0345 173 36 04   **Closed** *Sun*
The thing to eat here is *schiacciata*
(Florentine focaccia) split and
filled with a variety of hams, cured
meat, cheeses, and condiments.
You'll also find a wide variety of
good artisan beers, including the
local brew Lorum Ipsum.

Pizzeria del Caffè Italiano   €
Pizzeria   **Map** 6 F3
Via Isole delle Stinche 11–13r, 50122
Tel 055 28 93 68   **Closed** *lunch;
Mon Nov–Feb*
Genuine Neapolitan pizza – the
slow-risen dough is made from
Neapolitan flour and even the
tomatoes come from Mount
Vesuvius. The focus is on simple,
traditional pizzas made from the
very best ingredients.

La Prosciutteria   €
Delicatessen   **Map** 6 E4
Via dei Neri 54r, 50122
Tel 055 265 44 72   **Closed** *Sun*
Typical Florentine delicatessen,
perfect for a light lunch of hams,
cheeses and salamis cut to order
and accompanied by a glass of
wine. Unlike many other eat-in
delis, this one has tables and
chairs, and is a little more
expensive than its rivals.

Rivoire   €
Café   **Map** 6 D3
Piazza della Signoria 4r, 50123
Tel 055 21 44 12   **Closed** *Mon*
An enviable location – right
opposite the Palazzo Vecchio, with
a commanding view of the Piazza
della Signoria. The quality of the
food is excellent – crisp croissants
at breakfast, light meals at lunch
and deftly mixed cocktails in the
evening. Delicious hot chocolate
and handmade sweets.

Da Rocco   €
Trattoria   **Map** 4 F1
Mecato di Sant'Ambrogio
Closed *dinner & Sun*
Cheap, no-frills market *trattoria*
open for lunch only. A bit rough
around the edges, but it's the
experience of eating alongside
the stallholders, amid the buzz of
the market, that counts.

Il Teatro del Sale €
Buffet restaurant **Map** 4 E1
Via de'Macci 111, 50122
Tel *055 200 14 92* **Closed** *Mon*
Interesting venture by Fabio
Picchi of Cibrèo fame. Set-price
buffet lunches and dinners in
a semi-private theatre club –
there's a small membership
fee. Dinner is followed by a
theatre performance or
concert most evenings.

Venchi €
Gelateria **Map** 6 D3
Vicolo Calimaruzza 18, 50123
Tel *055 28 85 05*
Founded in 1876, Venchi is
one of Italy's most renowned
chocolate-makers. Ice cream is
a newish venture (launched in
2006), but they now have
gelaterie all over the world.
Naturally, the chocolate is
heavenly, but the seasonal
fruit and nut flavours are
exceptional too.

La Via del Tè €
Café **Map** 4 F1
Piazza Ghiberti 22–23r, 50122
Tel *055 21 27 97* **Closed** *Sun*
Elegant English-style tea room at
the heart of the Sant'Ambrogio
food market. Hundreds of
different teas, accompanied by
English cakes, smoked-salmon
sandwiches, bread and jam,
brownies and scones.

Vivoli €
Gelateria **Map** 6 F3
Via Isola delle Stinche 7r, 50122
Tel *055 29 23 34*
Though it now has serious rivals,
the city's most famous *gelateria*,
founded in 1930, continues to
pull in crowds of loyal regulars
and curious tourists for its signature ice creams. The flavours
change with the season.

Antico Fattore €€
Trattoria **Map** 6 D4
Via Lambertesca 1/3r, 50123
Tel *055 28 89 75* **Closed** *Sun*
Founded in 1908, and once the
favoured haunt of the Florentine
literati. Old-fashioned food and
service. Try the pappardelle with
wild boar or baked artichoke
hearts filled with cheese.

Boccadama €€
Vineria **Map** 6 F4
Piazza Santa Croce 25–6r, 50122
Tel *055 24 36 40*
Wine bar with great views of
lively Piazza Santa Croce from its
outside tables. Wine by the glass
and bottle. Nibble on a selection
of cold meats and cheeses, or
opt for a full meal.

The pretty Ristorante, part of the popular Cibrèo family of eateries

Buca dell'Orafo €€
Trattoria **Map** 6 D4
Via di Girolami 28, 50122
Tel *055 21 36 19* **Closed** *Mon*
Cellar restaurant in an alley close
to Ponte Vecchio. Fantastic Tuscan
fare prepared using seasonal
produce – try spaghettini with
fresh local peas.

La Cantinetta del Verrazzano €€
Café **Map** 6 D3
Via dei Tavolini 18–20, 50122
Tel *055 26 85 90*
Bakery-cum-wine bar belonging
to the Verrazzano wine estate.
There are excellent pastries and
biscuits, fresh from the wood-
burning oven. At lunch, there's
focaccia, split and filled with a
choice of hams and cheeses.

DK Choice

Cibrèo Trattoria €€
Trattoria **Map** 4 E1
Via de'Macci 122r, 50122
Closed *Mon*
You can't book ahead, so join
the queue of businessmen and
market folk to eat at communal
marble-topped tables. No pasta,
but many other dishes that
have become Cibrèo classics,
such as yellow pepper soup,
and potato and ricotta soufflé.
To follow, try sausages with
cannellini beans and cavolo
nero, or the splendid *inzimino*,
a juicy spicy stew of squid,
chard and spinach.

Del Fagioli €€
Trattoria **Map** 6 F4
Corso de'Tintori 47r, 50122
Tel *055 24 42 85* **Closed** *Sat, Sun*
Traditional *trattoria* with certain
dishes featuring on specific days
of the week. The kale, white bean
and sausage soup is outstanding,
served with slices of toasted
bread drizzled with oil.

Osteria del Caffè Italiano €€
Contemporary **Map** 6 F3
Via Isola delle Stinche 11–13r, 50122
Tel *055 28 93 68*
Eat any time of the day in this
stylish *osteria*. Full menus at lunch
and dinner, but snacks throughout
the day – excellent charcuterie
and cheeses, and quality wines
by the glass or bottle.

Cibrèo Ristorante €€€
Fine Dining **Map** 4 F1
Via Andrea del Verrocchio 8r, 50122
Tel *055 234 11 00* **Closed** *Mon*
Supreme versions of classic
Tuscan dishes, with an emphasis
on authenticity, not unnecessary
elaboration. The house selection
of *antipasti* is served with a
welcome Prosecco. Great soups –
try the yellow pepper – and
traditional meat dishes ranging
from offal to stuffed pigeon.

Enoteca Pinchiorri €€€
Fine Dining **Map** 4 E1
Via Ghibellina 87, 50122
Tel *055 24 27 57* **Closed** *lunch &
Sun, Mon*
This three-Michelin-starred
restaurant – considered one
of Italy's finest – is run by Annie
Féolde and has one of the most
prestigious wine cellars in
Europe. An experience dedi-
cated wine buffs and foodies
will never forget.

Frescobaldi Wine Bar €€€
Vineria **Map** 6 E3
Via dei Magazzini 2–4r, 50122
Tel *055 28 47 24*
This wine bar and restaurant,
owned by one of Tuscany's
foremost wine producers,
serves creative, elegant food.
Lunch is fairly casual, but
dinner is quite formal, with
white linen and crystal.
If you're after a light bite
and a glass of wine, pop into
Frescobaldini next door.

City Centre North

Casa del Vino €
Vineria   Map 5 C1
Via dell'Ariento 16r, 50123
Tel *055 21 56 09*   **Closed** *Sun*
Old-fashioned wine bar where
you can have a glass of wine
standing at the counter, or,
if you're lucky, at one of the
few tables. There's a choice of
delicious cheeses, hams, salamis
and sandwiches to accompany
your drink.

Dolci e Dolcezze €
Café   Map 4 F1
Piazza Beccaria 8r, 50121
Tel *055 234 54 58*   **Closed** *Sun*
Liberty-style café that is perfect
for afternoon tea or coffee with
a slice of famous flourless
chocolate cake or an exquisitely
decorated fresh-fruit flan.
Fantastic cheesecakes and
an unforgettable raspberry
cake, too.

Sergio Gozzi €
Trattoria   Map 6 D1
Piazza di San Lorenzo 8r, 50129
Tel *055 28 19 41*   **Closed** *Sun*
This popular, family-run *trattoria*
serves up Tuscan *casalinga*
(home-style) cooking at big
tables – you may well end up
sharing. There is always tripe on
Mondays and Thursdays, and fish
on Fridays.

Il Vegetariano €
Vegetarian   Map 2 D3
Via delle Ruote 30r, 50129
Tel *055 47 50 30*   **Closed** *Mon*
Long-established self-service
vegetarian restaurant. Rustic
decor and excellent-value
wholesome food. Choose from
the menu written on the
blackboard, pay at the till and
then take your receipt to the
counter to collect your food.

DK Choice

Il Desco €€
Bistro   Map 6 D1
Via Cavour 27, 50129
Tel *055 28 83 30*   **Closed** *Sun*
dinner
Next door to – and run by the
same family as – the hotel
Guelfo Bianco, this lovely bistro
makes wonderful use of organic
produce from the family farm
in the Reggello hills. Serves
refreshingly light, modern
European food that changes
with the seasons and relies
heavily on garden vegetables
and fruit. Great artisan beers
and a judicious selection of
Tuscan wines.

Trattoria Mario €€
Trattoria   Map 1 C4
Via Rosina 2r, 50123
Tel *055 21 85 50*   **Closed** *Sun*
Lively *trattoria* inevitably packed
with stallholders, city workers and
tourists. A handwritten menu,
posted daily on the wall by the
kitchen, features pasta and a
number of meat dishes.

Trattoria Za Za €€
Trattoria   Map 1 C4
Piazza del Mercato 26r, 50129
Tel *055 21 54 11*
Touristy but pleasant old-style
trattoria famous for its soups –
the hearty *ribollita*, made with
bread and vegetables, is
excellent. The grilled meats are
fantastic, too. Finish with home-
made apple tart.

La Taverna del Bronzino €€€
Fine Dining   Map 2 D3
Via delle Ruote 25–7r, 50129
Tel *055 49 52 20*   **Closed** *Sat lunch,
Sun*
Elegant Tuscan food, a seasonally
changing menu and a refined
atmosphere in a Renaissance
palazzo designed by the artist
Bronzino. Impeccably mannered
staff and a fantastic wine cellar.

City Centre West

DK Choice

Cacio Vino Trallallà €
Vineria   Map 6 D4
Borgo Santi Apostoli 29r, 50123
Tel *055 21 55 58*   **Closed** *Sun*
This innovative contemporary
vineria ascribes to the "zero
kilometre" philosophy, sourcing
produce as locally as possible.
Intelligent selection of wines and
artisan beers, speciality cheeses
and cured meats and sausages
made exclusively from Cinta
Senese pork. Look out for special
tastings designed to showcase
particular wines and produce.
Make sure you try *cioccobirra* –
a cream of beer and white
chocolate, eaten as a dessert
or to accompany cheeses.

Caffè Giocosa Roberto Cavalli €
Café   Map 5 B2
Via della Spada 10r, 50123
Tel *055 277 63 28*
Historic café revitalized by fashion
designer Cavalli, now forming an
annexe to his boutique. Stylish
place for breakfast, lunch (elegant
white-bread sandwiches, salads
and a couple of hot dishes) or an
aperitivo (the Negroni cocktail
was invented here in 1927).

Fine ingredients at the family-run
bistro Il Desco

Florian €
Café   Map 5 C3
Via del Parione 28r, 50123
Tel *055 28 42 91*
A little Florence branch of the
famous Venetian café. Good, old-
fashioned service and novelty
coffees. Nice for breakfast, for a
light lunch of Venetian nibbles or
for a cozy, winter *aperitivo*.

Gilli €
Café   Map 6 D2
Via Roma 1r, 50123
Tel *055 21 38 96*   **Closed** *Tue*
Founded in 1733, this place is
a city institution. Dine in *belle-
époque* style, with wood, marble
and glass glinting in the light of
Murano chandeliers. Particularly
well-known for hot chocolate
and for the spread of finger food
at *aperitivo* hour.

Paskowski €
Café   Map 6 D3
Piazza della Repubblica 8r, 50123
Tel *055 21 02 36*   **Closed** *Mon*
Founded in 1846, Paskowski fast
became a meeting place for
artists, writers and musicians.
These days, it's good for breakfast
or a quick pit stop during a busy
day of sightseeing. Despite the
evocative Art Deco interior, the
café lacks the cachet of the city's
other historic bars.

Procacci €
Bar   Map 5 C2
Via de'Tornabuoni 64r, 50123
Tel *055 21 16 56*   **Closed** *Sun*
Quaint, stand-up bar where
genteel Florentines congregate
before lunch or dinner for a
glass of Prosecco and a truffle
sandwich. You can also purchase
white truffles here when they're
in season.

Cantinetta Antinori €€
Vineria   **Map** 5 C2
Piazza Antinori 3, 50123
Tel *055 29 22 34*   **Closed** *Sat, Sun*
Belonging to one of Tuscany's foremost wine producers, this establishment is more than a wine bar, but not quite a restaurant. The setting, on the ground floor of one of Florence's finest Renaissance palazzos, is magical, and the food and wine are splendid.

Coco Lezzone €€
Trattoria   **Map** 5 B3
Via del Parioncino 26r, 50123
Tel *055 28 71 78*   **Closed** *Tue dinner, Sun*
A rustic *trattoria* serving deliciously textured *crostini di fegatini* (chicken liver on rounds of bread) and classic Tuscan soups. There's pasta too, and a good choice of *secondi*.

Colle Bereto €€
Bar   **Map** 5 C3
Piazza Strozzi 4–6, 50123
Tel *055 28 31 56*
Trendy bar right opposite Palazzo Strozzi. Light meals are served during the day, alongside succulent grilled steaks and gourmet hamburgers. Dinners in the evening are more elaborate.

Da il Latini €€
Trattoria   **Map** 5 B3
Via dei Palchetti 6r, 50123
Tel *055 21 09 16*   **Closed** *Mon*
There is always a queue of people clamouring for a table at this noisy *trattoria*. Food is traditional, and portions are enormous. Bypass the pasta course and head straight for the grilled meats.

Obika €€
Contemporary   **Map** 5 C2
Via de'Tornabuoni 16, 50123
Tel *055 277 35 26*
Stunning setting within the inner courtyard of Palazzo Tornabuoni. Devoted to the glories of buffalo mozzarella, this place offers delicious, unusual salads, tasting plates featuring different kinds of mozzarella and several hot dishes. Perfect for a relaxed lunch.

Oliviero €€€
Fine Dining   **Map** 5 C3
Via delle Terme 51r, 50123
Tel *055 21 24 21*   **Closed** *lunch & Sun*
Elegant restaurant in the centre of town with a retro feel, but up-to-the-minute food. Try seared tuna steak with ginger and white beans or a galantine of rabbit. A welcoming Prosecco is offered on arrival and the staff are friendly and helpful.

Oltrarno

Antica Porta €
Pizzeria   **Map** 3 A3
Via Senese 23, 50124
Tel *055 22 05 27*   **Closed** *Sun*
Local favourite turning out light, crispy pizzas. Some of the best ones are topped with *burrata* (fresh buffalo mozzarella) after they have left the oven. In season, opt for the wild mushroom and truffle topping. Expect to queue, and be prepared to share a table.

La Casalinga €
Trattoria   **Map** 5 B5
Via del Michelozzo 9r, 50125
Tel *055 21 86 24*   **Closed** *Sun*
Founded in 1964, this no-frills *trattoria* has become legendary among tourists, yet manages to retain its family-run charm. Hearty, traditional cooking using seasonal ingredients bought daily from the nearby market.

Fuori Porta €
Vineria   **Map** 4 E3
Via Monte alle Croci 10r, 50125
Tel *055 234 24 83*
The perfect place to stop for a snack after visiting the church San Miniato al Monte, which is just a short walk away *(see p134)*. Enjoy a good glass of wine accompanied by *crostoni* (toasted, open sandwiches). There are more substantial meals as well.

Hemingway €
Café   **Map** 3 A1
Piazza Piattalina 9, 50124
Tel *055 28 47 81*   **Closed** *until 4:30pm*
Chocoholic paradise. Home-made hot chocolate, coffees served with chocolate spoons, handmade chocolates, and a menu marrying different chocolates with the perfect wines. Vintage interior, and a superb selection of teas and tea cocktails.

O'Café €
Café   **Map** 6 D5
Via dei Bardi 54–6r, 50125
Tel *055 21 45 02*
Take in views of the Arno, Uffizi and Ponte Vecchio, and enjoy the contemporary art on show at this café, serving pastries made on the premises. There are superb nibbles at *aperitivo* hour.

Al Tranvai €
Trattoria   **Map** 3 A1
Piazza Torquato Tasso 14r, 50124
Tel *055 22 51 97*   **Closed** *Mon lunch, Sun*
Styled as the interior of an old tram, with long bench seats as well as a cozy back room, this is a popular place with locals. It serves light, crisp fried courgettes and artichokes, and, should you wish to try it, deep-fried brain.

DK Choice

O Munaciello €
Pizzeria   **Map** 5 A5
Via Maffia 31, 50125
Tel *055 28 71 98*
Neapolitan pizzeria in a 17th-century convent. The dough is left to rise over two days to maximize taste and digestibility. Try *Positana*, with cherry tomatoes, buffalo mozzarella, anchovies and olives, or *salsiccia e friarelli*, a Naples speciality, with sausage and turnip greens.

Il Magazzino €€
Trattoria   **Map** 5 C4
Piazza della Passera 2–3r, 50125
Tel *055 21 59 69*
Eat inside or out at this spartan shrine to offal run by a wine salesman and a tripe dealer. Dishes range from tongue *carpaccio* to ravioli with eel and red onion, but there are vegetarian options too, including linguini with a tasty pesto of cavolo nero.

Classy wooden bar at Oliviero

For more information on types of restaurants *see pp258–9*

Borgo San Jacopo €€€
Contemporary Map 5 C4
Borgo San Jacopo 62r, 50125
Tel *055 28 16 61*
Hip restaurant on the bank of
the Arno, where the most
coveted tables are on a tiny
terrace overhanging the water.
The views from this spot are
breathtaking. Unpretentious food
is exquisitely presented. Don't
miss the citrus-crusted sea bass
with sweet bell-pepper sauce.

DK Choice

io Osteria Personale €€€
Contemporary Map 5 A3
Borgo San Frediano 167r, 50124
Tel *055 933 13 41* **Closed** *lunch
& Sun*
Small restaurant with two fixed-
price menus and jazz playing
quietly in the background.
The focus is on inventive and
sophisticated light food. Try the
tempura of courgette flowers
stuffed with mozzarella and
accompanied by tomato sorbet,
capers and fresh oregano.
Modern decor with muted
colours and leather seats.
Fabulous staff.

Further Afield

Badiani €
Gelateria Map 2 F2
Viale dei Mille 20r, 50131
Tel *055 57 86 82* **Closed** *Tue*
Long-established *gelateria*
credited with inventing the
Buontalenti flavour of ice cream
(a creamier version of *crema* –
vanilla cream, with extra cream).
Great pistacchio and *cioccolato
fondente* (dark chocolate), too.
Also serves excellent snacks and
light lunches. A great place to
eat outside in summer.

DK Choice

Bar Gelateria Dario €
Gelateria
*Via Capo di Mondo 40, off Piazza
Beccaria, 50136*
Tel *055 66 05 61* **Closed** *Sun*
Tiny neighbourhood bar off the
tourist track where a husband-
and-wife team have been
making and serving their own
pastries and ice cream since
the 1960s. There's one table
inside and a few on the street.
Try a jam tart or ricotta cake
for breakfast, or come in the
afternoon for ice cream and
sorbets made of fruit from
their garden. The fig ice cream
is amazing.

Dogma €
Vegetarian
Via Filippo Pacini 45–7, 50144
Tel *055 933 65 22*
A great local lunch spot, just
northwest of the centre, serving
tasty vegetarian Sicilian food.
Sample the artichoke hearts
stuffed with creamed lentils,
followed by cannoli with a
sweet ricotta cheese filling.

Pugi €
Pizzeria
Via Giampaolo Orsini 63, 50126
Tel *055 68 97 63* **Closed** *Sun*
Founded in 1925 and still in the
same family, Pugi is famous
throughout the city for its classic
pizza slices. Try the Margherita
or Napoli, or go for a slice of
white pizza bread, split and filled
with ham or mixed vegetables.

Sabatino €
Trattoria
Via Pisana 2r, 50143
Tel *055 22 59 55* **Closed** *Sat, Sun*
The food, decor and ambience
haven't changed much over
the 50 years this modest *trattoria*
has been in business. Serves
Tuscan classics, such as *ribollita*
(bread and vegetable soup),
meatballs and rabbit.

Tre Soldi €
Trattoria
Via d'Annunzio 4r/a, 50135
Tel *055 67 93 66* **Closed** *Fri dinner,
Sat*
This traditional *trattoria* has been
in business since 1952. Daily
changing lunch menu and a
wider à la carte choice at dinner.
Dishes include potato tortelli
with cheese and black pepper,
and buckwheat tagliatelle with
porcini mushrooms.

Austere, minimal design accompanies great
food at io Osteria Personale

Da Burde €€
Trattoria
Via Pistoiese 6r, 50145
Tel *055 31 72 06* **Closed** *Mon–Thu
dinner, Sun*
Soak up the nostalgic atmosphere at this family-run *trattoria*
in the country, 6 km (3.5 miles)
from the city centre. Expect to
find all the Florentine classics,
from *ribollita* to tripe stew.

Da Ruggero €€
Trattoria Map 3 A5
Via Senese 89, 50124
Tel *055 22 05 42* **Closed** *Tue, Wed*
Off the beaten track, this
restaurant has a loyal clientele
who come in search of simple,
yet first-rate, peasant dishes,
such as *spaghetti alla carrettiera*
(with oil, chilli, garlic and parsley).
The menu changes every week.
Great service.

Da Settimo €€
Seafood
Via del Barco 21, 50127
Tel *055 43 34 58* **Closed** *Sun*
A short drive from the city centre,
locals flock to this restaurant for
an excellent selection of fresh
fish. Opt for the catch of the day,
delicately cooked to enhance
the natural flavours. Staff are
friendly and welcoming.

Fuor d'Acqua €€€
Seafood
Via Pisana 37r, 50143
Tel *055 22 22 99* **Closed** *lunch &
Sun*
Exclusive restaurant specializing
in the freshest, finest fish, brought
in daily from the boats at Versilia.
Try the raw fish starter or black
tagliolini (a thicker tagliatelle)
with calamari and sage.

Onice €€€
Fine Dining Map 4 F3
Viale Michelangelo 78, 50125
Tel *055 68 16 31*
Michelin-starred restaurant that
forms part of the Villa La Vedetta
hotel. Fantastic views over the
city, an elegant atmosphere
and superb, unfussy food that
changes with the seasons.

Targa €€€
Bistro
Lungarno Colombo 9, 50136
Tel *055 67 73 77* **Closed** *Sun*
This restaurant is set on the Arno
just outside the centre. The glass
and wood interior is softened by
greenery, with jazz playing in the
background, while the food is
understated and based on
seasonal local produce. Try the
crepes with artichokes and
Taleggio cheese.

Western Tuscany

ARTIMINO: Da Delfina €€€
Fine Dining **Map** C2
Via della Chiesa 1, 59015
Tel *055 871 80 74* **Closed** *Mon*
Serene, romantic restaurant in a farmhouse perched on the lip of a hill, with views of the Medici villa of Artimino. Handmade pasta, locally reared meat, wild vegetables and a wide range of wines from all over Italy.

DK Choice

LIVORNO: Cantina Nardi €
Vineria **Map** B3
Via Leonardo Cambini 6/8, 57100
Tel *0586 80 80 06* **Closed** *dinner & Sun, public hols*
Traditional *vineria* with a huddle of bottle-lined rooms, plus a garden for summer eating. The full lunch menu is made up of fish and seafood dishes that have been cooked by local families for generations. Try spaghetti with *telline* (tiny clams) or *cicale di mare* (small slipper lobsters). To sample the famous Livornese fish stew, *cacciucco*, you will need to book ahead.

LIVORNO: Da Gagarin €
Street Food **Map** B3
Via del Cardinale 24, 57100
Tel *0586 88 40 86* **Closed** *Sun*
Da Gagarin's *cecina* (a kind of yeastless bread-cake made of chickpea flour) is fantastic – crisp on the outside, soft and tasty within – and best eaten inside a freshly baked *schiacciatina* (focaccia).

LIVORNO: L'Ostricaio €
Seafood **Map** B3
Viale Italia 100, 57100
Tel *0586 58 13 45* **Closed** *Mon Nov–Apr*
Eat in or take away at this quaint little seafront place, which has been serving locals oysters with a glass of wine for over 20 years. All manner of other shellfish are available – try sea urchins or *fasolari* (giant clams). Several hot dishes are also on the menu, including *cacciucco* (fish stew).

LIVORNO: Trattoria da Galileo €€€
Seafood **Map** B3
Via della Campana 20, 57122
Tel *0586 88 90 09* **Closed** *Sun dinner, Wed*
Opened in 1959 and still in the same family, this *trattoria* is famous for its *cacciucco*, but good for other hearty seafood dishes, too.

A sophisticated setting for well-presented food – Borgo San Jacopo, in Florence *(see p268)*

PISA: Café Salza €
Café **Map** B2
Borgo Stretto 48, 56127
Tel *050 58 01 44* **Closed** *Mon*
Pisa's best-loved traditional café-bar serves great coffee and a magnificent array of cakes and pastries. A choice of light meals at lunchtime, eaten in a room that remains a 1920s classic.

PISA: Trattoria della Faggiola €
Trattoria **Map** B2
Via Uguccione della Faggiola 1, 56126
Tel *050 55 61 79* **Closed** *Sun*
Perfect place to stop for lunch or dinner after seeing the Leaning Tower. The daily menu is chalked on a blackboard and based on seasonal ingredients. Look out for spaghetti with *friggitelli* (green peppers).

PISA: La Curva €€
Sicilian **Map** B2
Via Livornese 233, 56122
Tel *050 53 24 05* **Closed** *Tue*
Informal Sicilian restaurant serving pizza and dishes such as *busiate* (hollow spaghetti) with Trapanese pesto (basil, almonds, tomatoes).

PISA: Osteria San Paolo €€
Contemporary **Map** B2
Via San Paolo 16, 56100
Tel *050 50 11 94* **Closed** *Sun*
Tasteful ambience, with exposed brick walls, chandeliers and soft lighting. Dishes are artistically presented and ingredients all locally sourced.

PISA: Peperosa Pisa €€
Emilia-Romagnan **Map** B2
Via Renato Fucini 10, 56126
Tel *050 314 41 70* **Closed** *Sun–Thu dinner*
Tucked behind a renowned delicatessen, this tiny restaurant is run by an Emilia-Romagnan family. Specialities include lasagne and homemade *tortelli* (ravioli), with Parma ham and sausage.

PISA: Vero Bistro Pisa €€
Bistro **Map** B2
Viale Gramsci 5, 56125
Tel *050 291 33* **Closed** *Sun*
Relaxed little bistro with a constantly changing seasonal menu. If available, try the black squid-ink tagliatelle with lobster. Also serves lighter dishes and snacks.

PISA: V Beni €€€
Seafood **Map** B2
Piazza Giambacorti Chiara 22, 56125
Tel *050 250 67* **Closed** *Sun, 3 wks in Aug*
Popular place for expertly prepared fish, set on a lively square a 15-minute walk from the Leaning Tower. Tables outside in summer. Booking advised.

SAN MINIATO: Il Convio €€
Trattoria **Map** C2
Via San Maiano 2, 56028
Tel *0571 40 81 14*
Classic local food in a converted 19th-century farmhouse on the edge of town. The chef uses plenty of home-grown vegetables, handmade olive oil and truffles when in season.

SAN MINIATO: Papaveri e Paperi €€
Contemporary **Map** C2
Via Dalmazia 159d, 56028
Tel *0571 40 94 22* **Closed** *lunch (except Sun) & Wed*
Creative cuisine in a small, centrally located restaurant. Look out for duck fillet in a pistachio crust drizzled with raspberry vinegar.

VOLTERRA: La Carabaccia €
Trattoria **Map** C3
Piazza XX Settembre 4–5, 56048
Tel *0588 862 39* **Closed** *Mon Nov–Apr*
Friendly, traditional place right in the historic centre. They offer just two *primi* and two *secondi* every day, chalked on a blackboard. All ingredients are sourced locally.

VOLTERRA: L'Incontro €
Café **Map** C3
Via Matteotti 18, 56048
Tel *0588 805 00* **Closed** *Wed*
Art Nouveau-style café. Serves
great coffee, tasty pastries and
outstanding chocolate. There's
also a little room at the back, with
four marble tables, where you
can have an inexpensive lunch.

VOLTERRA: Da Badò €€
Trattoria **Map** C3
Borgo San Lazzero 9, 56048
Tel *0588 804 02* **Closed** *Wed*
Run by a mother and son, with
a traditional menu and daily
seasonal specials. Try the *zuppa
Volterrana* made with beans and
greens, or a hearty wild-boar stew.

**VOLTERRA: Ristorante Enoteca
del Duca**
Vineria €€
Via del Castello 2, 56048
Tel *0588 815 10*
Small restaurant in a charming
18th-century palazzo, with an
ancient wine cellar and a secret
garden. Try pigeon breast cooked
with locally grown saffron.

Northern Tuscany

**CASTELNUOVO DI
GARFAGNANA: Vecchio Mulino** €
Vineria **Map** B1
Via Vittorio Emanuele 4, 55032
Tel *0583 621 92* **Closed** *Mon*
This traditional wine bar has
changed little since the 1900s
and serves a wide range of wines,
along with some of Italy's rarest
salamis, hams and cheeses.

DK Choice

**FORNOVOLASCO: Rifugio
la Buca** €
Traditional **Map** B2
*Via San Pelegrinetto,
Fornovolasco 55020*
Tel *0583 77 20 13* **Closed** *Thu*
This unpretentious mountain
restaurant looks rather like an
Alpine Chalet and is amazing
value for money, serving good,
honest food and easily drinkable
house wine. Try the home-made
pasta with wild mushrooms.

LUCCA: Antico Caffè di Simo €
Café **Map** C2
Via Fillungo 58, 55100
Tel *0583 49 62 34* **Closed** *Mon*
Composers Puccini and
Leoncavallo used to meet at this
Art Nouveau café. The choice of
sweets is vast – try the Lucchese
rice and chocolate pudding.

LUCCA: Da Felice €
Street Food **Map** C2
Via Buia 12, 55100
Tel *0583 49 49 86* **Closed** *Sun
(except Sep & Dec)*
This eternally popular pizzeria,
close to San Michele, serves a
fantastic range of local specialities
as well as renowned pizzas. Take
away or perch on stools inside.

LUCCA: Il Mecenate €
Trattoria **Map** C2
Via del Fosso 94, 55100
Tel *0583 51 21 67*
Pleasant place in the heart of the
city, with tables outside in summer.
Don't miss the spaghetti with duck
ragù. Fans of salt cod should try
the grilled *baccalà*.

LUCCA: Taddeucci €
Café **Map** C2
Piazza San Michele 34, 55100
Tel *0583 49 49 33*
Perfect for a light lunch, Taddeucci
serves excellent *buccellato* – a
kind of sweet bread typical of
Lucca – and lots of savoury tarts.
Wonderful 1920s wood-and-
mirrors interior.

DK Choice

LUCCA: L'Imbuto €€€
Contemporary **Map** C2
Via della Fratta 36, 55100
Tel *0583 49 12 80* **Closed** *Mon*
This restaurant, inside LuCCA
(Lucca Centre of Contemporary
Art), offers complex, eccentric
dishes, exquisitely presented.
The daily menus of four, six and
nine courses might include Italian
fish and chips (with the fish
encased in tiny crisp envelopes of
potato), or beef served on a slice
of oven-baked pine bark. Diners
will be asked if they have any
intolerances or strong dislikes.

LUCCA: Locanda Vigna Ilaria €€€
Fine Dining **Map** C2
*Via della Pieve Santo Stefano 967c,
Sant'Alessio, 55100*
Tel *0583 33 20 91* **Closed** *lunch*
Creative cuisine in an 18th-
century villa in the hills.
Excellent pasta and risotto, and
perfectly cooked, rigorously
sourced meats. The seafood
salad is superb.

**MONTECATINI: Ristorante
Montaccolle** €€€
Fine Dining **Map** C2
Via Marianese 27, 51016
Tel *0572 724 80* **Closed** *lunch & Mon*
This relaxed place serves top-
notch Tuscan classics and has a
lovely location overlooking the
town and valley below.

Antico Caffè di Simo, in Lucca – the perfect
spot for coffee or an after-dinner drink

**MONTECATINI TERME:
Enoteca Giovanni** €€€
Fine Dining **Map** C2
Via Garibaldi 25–7, 51016
Tel *0572 716 95* **Closed** *Mon*
Innovative cuisine by one of the
region's most renowned chefs.
Service is superb – among the
slickest and most professional in
Tuscany – and the wine cellar is
second to none.

**PIETRASANTA:
Locanda di Bruno** €€
Seafood **Map** B2
Via Solaio 67 C, 55049
Tel *0584 79 08 87*
Fish so fresh it's best eaten raw
with just oil and lemon as a simple
starter. Follow with spaghetti and
roasted prawns, but leave room
for one of the decadent desserts.

PIETRASANTA: Martinatica €€
Seafood **Map** B2
*Località Buabbatoio, Via Martinatica
20, 55049*
Tel *0584 79 25 34* **Closed** *Tue*
In an old olive mill straddling a
fast-running stream, this is a
deliciously cool place to eat in
summer. Dishes include pasta
with clams and oven-baked
turbot with tomatoes and olives.
Lovely home-made desserts.

**PIETRASANTA:
Enoteca Marcucci** €€€
Vineria **Map** B2
Via Garibalci 40, 55049
Tel *0584 79 19 62* **Closed** *Mon;
Nov–Apr lunch (except Sun)*
This famous restaurant regularly
attracts celebrities. Paintings
donated by well-known artists
cover its walls. Fantastic wines
and excellent interpretations of
Tuscan classics.

PISTOIA: La Bottegaia €
Osteria **Map** C2
Via del Lastrone 17, 51100
Tel *0573 36 56 02* **Closed** *Mon*
Well-known restaurant with a
delicatessen next door. Great value
lunches. Sample tasty mushroom
soup in winter and melt-in-the-
mouth gnocchi in summer.

**PISTOIA: Trattoria
dell'Abbondanza** €€
Trattoria **Map** C2
Via dell'Abbondanza 10–14, 52100
Tel *0573 36 80 37* **Closed** *Thu
lunch, Wed*
Family-run place serving classics,
such as *pappa al pomodoro*
(bread and tomato soup), along
with more unusual dishes, such as
spaghetti with veal and orange.

**PRATO: L'Angolo della
Stazione** €€
Osteria **Map** D2
Via de Neroni 4, 59100
Tel *0574 60 35 83* **Closed** *Sun*
Simple place near the train station.
Try the roast pork, deep-fried
artichokes or potato tortelli with
Taleggio cheese and pancetta.

VIAREGGIO: Nitens €€
Seafood **Map** B2
Piazzetta Viani 16, 55049
Tel *0584 37 05 85* **Closed** *dinner
Sat & Sun*
Little place behind the docks.
Start with the *antipasto* of raw
tuna, and follow with spaghetti
with red prawns and pine nuts.

VIAREGGIO: La Darsena €€€
Seafood **Map** B2
Via Virgilio 150, 55409
Tel *0584 38 31 15* **Closed** *Sun in
winter*
Friendly *trattoria* in the lively docks
area. Great *antipasto* platter of
lots of little dishes, based on the
morning's catch.

Eastern Tuscany

ANGHIARI: Da Alighiero €€
Trattoria **Map** E3
Via Garibaldi 8, 52031
Tel *0575 78 80 40* **Closed** *Tue*
Set within the hefty stone walls of
a 15th-century rustic house, this
place serves up delicious home-
made pasta and Tuscan classics.

**ANGHIARI: Locanda al Castello
di Sorci** €€
Trattoria **Map** E3
Località San Lorenzo 25, 52030
Tel *0575 78 90 66* **Closed** *Mon; Aug*
A lively country inn overlooking a
castle, with a set menu of home-
made pasta and grilled meat.

AREZZO: Caffè dei Costanti €
Café **Map** E3
Piazza San Francesco 19, 52100
Tel *0575 182 40 75* **Closed** *Mon*
A scene from Roberto Benigni's
Life is Beautiful was filmed in this
19th-century bar on the main
piazza. Excellent coffee and
pastries, and superbly mixed
martini cocktails.

AREZZO: Menchetti €
Pizzeria **Map** E3
Via Avvocato Croce 11, 52100
Tel *0575 35 06 82*
Scrumptious pizza. Offerings
include the Pizza Rossa, with
cherry tomatoes, mozzarella and
basil, and the Pizza Bianca, to which
Parma ham, rocket and parmesan
are added after it leaves the oven.
Eat in or take away.

AREZZO: La Torre di Gnicche €€
Vineria **Map** E3
Piaggia San Martino 8, 52100
Tel *0575 35 20 35* **Closed** *Wed*
Prime local ingredients to
accompany an overwhelming
choice of wine from a cellar with
over 700 labels. Superb meatballs
and oven-baked onion soup.

AREZZO: I Tre Bicchieri €€
Seafood **Map** E3
Piazzetta Sopra i Ponti 3, 52100
Tel *0575 265 57* **Closed** *Sun*
Refined but unpretentious eatery
run by two brothers. Try ravioli –
one black, one white – stuffed with
lobster and served in an exquisite
flame-coloured tomato reduction.

**BORGO SAN LORENZO:
Ristorante degli Artisti** €€€
Fine Dining **Map** D2
Piazza Romagnoli 1, 50032
Tel *055 845 77 07* **Closed** *Tue, Wed*
Pleasant restaurant in the historic
centre where a glass of Prosecco
greets you. Serves home-made
bread, fresh pasta and tasty
meat stews.

CAMALDOLI: Il Cedro €€
Trattoria **Map** E2
*Via di Camaldoli 20, Località
Moggiona, 52010*
Tel *0575 55 60 80*
Popular restaurant with
spectacular views. It is known for
its game, hunted in the forested
Casentino Mountains.

**CASTELNUOVO BERARDENGA:
La Bottega del 30** €€€
Fine Dining **Map** D3
*Via Santa Caterina 2, Località Villa a
Sesta, 53019*
Tel *0577 35 92 26* **Closed** *Tue*
Serious award-winning restaurant.
Superb home-made spaghetti
with nettle, wild mint and
porcini mushrooms. The duck
breast with wild fennel is also
truly delicious.

CORTONA: Caffè Tuscher Hall €
Café **Map** E3
Via Nazionale 43, 52044
Tel *0575 620 53* **Closed** *Mon*
Quintessential and elegant small-
town café with tables outside.
Excellent coffee, good pastries
and a wide choice of salads, local
cured hams and salamis.

CORTONA: Osteria del Teatro €€
Trattoria **Map** E3
Via Maffei 2, 52044
Tel *0575 63 05 56* **Closed** *Wed*
Traditional place serving
delicious soups. Follow with
home-made pasta parcels stuffed
with radicchio and ricotta. They
also do a very good guinea fowl
with mushrooms.

CORTONA: Il Preludio €€
Fine Dining **Map** E3
Via Guelfa 11, 52044
Tel *0575 63 01 04* **Closed** *Mon*
Welcoming restaurant serving
innovative dishes, such as cheese
soufflé with pear and truffles, and
more traditional dishes like risotto
with mushrooms and truffles.

Wonderful tarts and treats at Taddeucci, in Lucca *(see p270)*

For more information on types of restaurants *see pp258–9*

DK Choice

CORTONA: Taverna Pane e Vino
Trattoria   €€
Map E3
Piazza Signorelli 27, 52044
Tel 0575 63 10 10   **Closed** *Mon*
Eat inside or out at this pleasant restaurant right opposite the archaeological museum. They produce wine and oil, ingredients are locally sourced, and dishes are seasonal and traditional. For *antipasto*, there is a choice of bruschetta or hams, cheese and salami; then there are rustic pasta dishes and soups. The main courses use Chianina beef with memorable results.

CORTONA: Relais il Falconiere
Contemporary   €€€
Map E3
Località San Martino 370, 52044
Tel 0575 61 26 79
Elegant restaurant occupying the *limonaia* (lemon house) of a 17th-century villa in the countryside. Features an inventive menu incorporating seasonal local produce.

LUCIGNANO: Il Goccino
Fine Dining   €€
Map E3
Via Matteotti 88–90, 52046
Tel 0575 83 67 07   **Closed** *Mon*
Fabulous views from the terrace, especially at sunset, best savoured as you sip a Prosecco and peruse the menu. Food is fresh and local, and the cooking is creative.

LUCIGNANO: La Rocca
Osteria   €€
Map E3
Via Matteotti 15–17, 52046
Tel 0575 83 67 75   **Closed** *Tue*
Relaxed atmosphere, excellent service and innovative as well as traditional dishes that change with the season. The salad of fresh pasta with bacon, tomato, ricotta and pear is stunning.

SANSEPOLCRO: Pasticceria Chieli
Café   €
Map E3
Via Fraternita 12, 52037
Tel 0575 74 20 26   **Closed** *Mon*
Outstanding café and *pasticceria*; those with a sweet tooth may feel they've died and gone to heaven. Mouthwatering range of mini-desserts and *choux* pastries.

SANSEPOLCRO: Ristorante da Ventura
Trattoria   €
Map E3
Via Aggiunti 30, 52037
Tel 0575 74 25 60   **Closed** *Mon*
Charming and run by a family, this is the place to come for tender, slow-cooked meats. Be sure to sample the veal in Chianti.

SANSEPOLCRO: Fiorentino
Trattoria   €€
Map E3
Via Luca Pacioli 60, 52037
Tel 0575 74 20 33   **Closed** *Wed*
Opened in 1807, this family-run restaurant occupies a beautifully frescoed Renaissance dining room. Many of the dishes are inspired by Renaissance recipes, such as rabbit cooked with apple and sprinkled with gold dust.

TERRANUOVA BRACCIOLINI: Il Canto del Maggio
Contemporary   €€
Map D3
Località 30D, 52028
Tel 055 970 51 47   **Closed** *Mon*
Modern *osteria* in a tiny flower-filled hamlet. Good locally sourced food – the *antipasto* course is pretty much a gastronomic tour of Tuscan hams, salamis and cheeses. Main courses feature a superb peppery stewed beef.

Central Tuscany

BAGNO VIGNONI: La Bottega di Cacio
Vineria   €
Map D4
Piazza del Moretto 31
Tel 0577 88 74 77   **Closed** *Tue*
Little *vineria* serving light snacks with a glass of good wine. Opt for a platter of charcuterie, cheese and olives served with crusty bread.

BARBERINO VAL D'ELSA: Paese dei Campanelli
Trattoria   €€
Map D3
Località Petrognano Semifonte, 50021
Tel 055 807 53 18   **Closed** *Mon*
Stone walls, linen tablecloths and candlelight in a well-regarded restaurant popular with locals. Tuscan food with a twist.

Stunning views from the terrace of La Porta, just outside Pienza *(see p273)*

CHIUSI: I Salotti
Fine Dining   €€€
Map E4
Il Patriarca Hotel, SS 146, Località Quercia al Pino, 53043
Tel 0578 27 44 07   **Closed** *lunch & Mon, Tue*
At this Michelin-starred restaurant, the chef produces original versions of traditional dishes made with locally sourced ingredients.

COLLE VAL D'ELSA: L'Antica Trattoria
Fine Dining   €€€
Map D3
Piazza Arnolfo 23, 53034
Tel 0577 92 37 47   **Closed** *Tue*
This well-run family restaurant serves Tuscan fish and meat classics, as well as several more inventive dishes. In autumn, try venison cooked in juniper.

COLLE VAL D'ELSA: Arnolfo
Fine Dining   €€€
Map D3
Piazza XX Settembre 50–52A, 53034
Tel 0577 92 05 49   **Closed** *Tue, Wed*
Michelin-starred restaurant where a reverent hush pervades, and the emphasis is on perfect renditions of Tuscan dishes.

GAIOLE IN CHIANTI: Il Carlino d'Oro
Osteria   €
Map D3
Località San Regolo 33, 53013
Tel 0577 74 71 36   **Closed** *dinner & Mon*
Simple, authentic food in a tiny hamlet surrounded by vineyards and olive groves. Try the *bistecca all Fiorentina* (T-bone steak).

GAIOLE IN CHIANTI: Osteria del Castello
Osteria   €€
Map D3
Località Madonna a Brolio, 53013
Tel 0577 73 02 90   **Closed** *dinner*
Lovely setting among the vineyards of Castello di Brolio. The chef works wonders with local produce. Try the handmade pasta.

GAIOLE IN CHIANTI: Il Pievano di Castello Spaltenna
Fine Dining   €€€
Map D3
Località Pievano di Spaltenna, 53013
Tel 0577 74 94 83
Flower-filled hotel restaurant set in a medieval castle. Delicious dishes, such as scampi with asparagus, tomato confit and parmesan salsa.

GREVE IN CHIANTI: Borgo Antico
Trattoria   €€
Map D3
Via delle Convertoie 11A, 50022
Tel 055 85 10 24   **Closed** *Tue*
In the midst of an oak forest just outside Greve, this restaurant serves traditional Tuscan fare, such as bean soups and meaty mains.

DK Choice

GREVE IN CHIANTI:
Mangiando Mangiando €€
Osteria   **Map** D3
Piazza Matteotti 80, 50022
Tel *055 854 63 72*   **Closed** *Thu*
Contemporary restaurant that
staunchly avoids artificial
preservatives and genetically
modified or frozen foods.
The bread comes from the
bakery across the street and the
menu changes with the season.
If it's available, try the superb
risotto with broccoli, ricotta and
crispy pancetta, or the *peposo di
chianina alla fornacina*, a
peppery beef stew. Choose
from a selection of excellent
local wines, many available by
the glass.

GREVE IN CHIANTI: La Cantinetta
di Rignana   €€€
Fine Dining   **Map** D3
Località Rignana, 50022
Tel *055 85 26 01*
Enjoy incredible views from the
large terrace, and splendid, yet
simple, Tuscan food. Try the creamy
pasta with chestnuts, a garden-
fresh salad, or delectable rabbit.

MONTALCINO: Il Pozzo   €
Trattoria   **Map** D4
*Piazza del Pozzo 2, Sant'Angelo in
Colle, 53024*
Tel *0577 84 40 15*   **Closed** *Tue*
Restaurant in a tiny *borgo* (hamlet).
Fresh pasta followed by
exceptional fried rabbit. Home-
made meringues or tarts to finish.

MONTALCINO: Il Boccon
Divino   €€
Trattoria   **Map** D4
Località Colombaio, 53024
Tel *0577 84 82 33*   **Closed** *Tue*
Stunning views and delicious food,
including *carabaccia* (onion soup)
and *pappardelle* with wild boar.

MONTALCINO: Osticcio   €€
Osteria   **Map** D4
Via Matteotti 23, 53024
Tel *0577 8482 71* **Closed** *Thu dinner*
Lovely views over the Val d'Orcia,
and a garden for summer dining.
Try *spaghettone* (thick spaghetti)
with *guanciale* (cured ham).

MONTALCINO: Le Potazzine €€
Vineria   **Map** D4
Piazza Garibaldi 8, 53024
Tel *0577 84 60 54*   **Closed** *Mon
Nov–Apr*
The owners produce their own
Brunello di Montalcino wine,
which can be sampled alongside
simple, well-chosen local dishes,
such as pasta with beans.

Bottle-lined dining room at Le Potazzine, in Montalcino

MONTEFOLLONICO:
La Chiusa   €€€
Fine Dining   **Map** E4
Via della Madonnina 88, 53040
Tel *0577 66 96 68*
This critically acclaimed restau-
rant, filled with wild flowers and
antiques, serves refined versions of
peasant dishes. Local truffles and
mushrooms abound in season.

MONTEPULCIANO: Osteria
dell'Acquacheta   €
Osteria   **Map** E4
Via del Teatro 22, 53045
Tel *0578 71 70 86*   **Closed** *Mon*
Friendly place with wooden
tables serving simple food and
meat roasted in a wood-fired oven.
Try tagliatelle with artichokes,
or *carabaccia* (onion soup).

MONTEPULCIANO: Piccola
Trattoria Guastini   €€
Trattoria   **Map** E4
Via Lauretana Nord 20, Valiano, 53045
Tel *0578 72 40 06*   **Closed** *Wed*
This little restaurant has been
going since the 1930s and serves
home-made bread and pasta,
local olive oil and wine, and
traditional dishes such as ravioli
stuffed with pigeon.

MONTEPULCIANO: La Grotta €€€
Fine Dining   **Map** E4
Località San Biagio, 53045
Tel *0578 75 76 07*   **Closed** *Wed*
Restaurant for discerning diners
opposite Sangallo the Elder's San
Biagio. Specialities include home-
made pasta with duck and saffron,
and Chianina beef with truffles.

MONTERIGGIONI:
Futura   €€
Osteria   **Map** D3
Località Abbadia Isola 7, 53035
Tel *0577 30 12 40*   **Closed** *Tue*
This fabulous place in a tiny medie-
val hamlet serves refreshingly
innovative food that is more
Mediterranean than Tuscan.

MONTERIGGIONI: Il Pozzo   €€
Fine Dining   **Map** D3
Piazza Roma 20, 53035
Tel *0577 30 41 27*   **Closed** *Mon*
Occupying 13th-century stables,
this is the perfect place for an
authentic Tuscan lunch. Try *tortelli
al cartoccio*, in which the pasta is
cooked with truffles in a parcel of
tinfoil to preserve the aromas.

PANZANO IN CHIANTI:
Solociccia   €
Contemporary   **Map** D3
Via Chiantigiana 5, 50022
Tel *055 85 27 27*   **Closed** *Sun
dinner, Mon, Tue, Wed*
Butcher Dario Cecchini's quest to
promote all cuts of meat is the
impetus behind this quirky
restaurant, with its six-course
set meal. Communal tables and
every cut of meat imaginable.

PIENZA: Dopolavoro La Foce €€
Contemporary   **Map** E4
*Località La Foce, Strada della
Vittoria 90, 53026*
Tel *0578 75 40 25*   **Closed** *Mon*
A *trattoria*, bar, café and even a
meditation room, housed in the
former social club for workers on
the La Foce estate. Serves
possibly the best hamburger in
Italy, made with Chianina beef.

PIENZA: La Pergola   €€
Osteria   **Map** E4
Via dell'Acero 2, 53026
Tel *0578 74 80 51*
Unpretentious yet inventive
restaurant. Try the silky vegetable
mousse in a sauce of potato and
leek. Excellent wine list.

PIENZA: La Porta   €€
Osteria   **Map** E4
Via del Piano 1, 53026, Monticchiello
Tel *0578 75 51 63*   **Closed** *Thu*
Fantastic views over the Val d'Orcia.
Traditional Tuscan dishes along
with less-common offerings like
spelt with seasonal vegetables.

POGGIBONSI: Osteria 1126 €€
Osteria   Map D3
Località Cinciano 2, 53036
Tel *0577 93 65 88*   **Closed** *Tue*
Sit outside on a pretty little piazza
in a tiny medieval *borgo* to enjoy
traditional food made with a
touch of imagination.

**SAN CASCIANO VAL DI PESA:
Nello**   €
Trattoria   Map D2
Via 4 Novembre 66, 50026
Tel *055 82 01 63*   **Closed** *Tue lunch,
Mon*
Simple, excellent food in a large
unfussy restaurant, an easy drive
from Florence. Delicious gnocchi
that changes with the season –
look out for pumpkin with ricotta.

**SAN CASCIANO VAL DI PESA:
La Tenda Rossa**   €€€
Fine Dining   Map D2
*Piazza del Monumento 9, Località
Cerbaia in Val di Pesa, 50026*
Tel *055 82 61 32*   **Closed** *Mon lunch,
Sun*
This elegant, old-fashioned
restaurant offers a series of tasting
menus, including a special – and
very ample – Saturday lunch.

**SAN GIMIGNANO: Un Mondo
di Sapori**   €
Vineria   Map C3
Via San Martino 5, 53037
Tel *0577 94 31 23*
This *vineria* and delicatessen
serves cold cuts, cheeses and
more elaborate dishes to accompany a glass or two of wine.

**SAN GIMIGNANO:
Cum Quibus**   €€
Contemporary   Map C3
Via San Martino 17, 53037
Tel *0577 94 31 99*   **Closed** *Tue*
Lively restaurant with marvellous
food. Charismatic staff bring
tasters of this and that from the
kitchen for diners to sample
alongside their main meal. Try
fettuccine with duck breast.

SAN GIMIGNANO: Dorando' €€€
Fine Dining   Map C3
Vicolo dell'Oro 2, 53037
Tel *0577 94 18 62*   **Closed** *Mon*
Many of the dishes at this civilized
restaurant are inspired by Etruscan,
medieval and Renaissance recipes.
An elaborate use of nuts, fruits
and spices.

SARTEANO: Santa Chiara €€
Fine Dining   Map E4
Via Costa S Chiara 30, 53047
Tel *0578 26 54 12*   **Closed** *Tue*
Lovely views across the valley from
a romantic former convent. Look
out for exquisite handmade
ravioli stuffed with borage leaves.

Un Mondo di Sapori, perfect for wine and
nibbles, in San Gimignano

**SIENA: Antica Pizzicheria al
Palazzo della Chigiana**   €
Delicatessen   Map D3
Via di Città 93–5, 53100
Tel *0577 28 91 64*   **Closed** *Sun*
Bread is made on the premises
and served with a huge choice of
hams, salamis and cheeses. Try
salami spiked with wild fennel
seeds, or wild-boar sausage.

SIENA: Enoteca i Terzi €
Vineria   Map D3
Via dei Termini 7, 53100
Tel *0577 443 29*   **Closed** *Sun*
Friendly place to enjoy a good
bottle of wine accompanied by a
plate of charcuterie and cheeses,
or steak tartare. A choice of three
dishes each day.

SIENA: Gino Cacino €
Delicatessen   Map D3
Piazza del Mercato 31, 53100
Tel *0577 22 30 76*   **Closed** *Sun*
Long-established place in the
market selling home-produced
cured meats and cheeses. Take
away for a picnic, or have them
stuffed into a sandwich to eat in.

SIENA: Nannini €
Café   Map D3
Via Banchi di Sopra 24, 53100
Tel *0577 23 60 09*
This big, bustling bar, with inevit-
able displays of *panforte* (fruit
cake), serves good coffee, hot
chocolate and delicious pastries.
Several light-lunch dishes daily.

SIENA: La Sosta di Violante €
Vineria   Map D3
Via di Pantaneto 115, 53100
Tel *0577 437 74*   **Closed** *Sun*
Impressive, underground vaulted
space with a fantastic wine cellar
and interesting food, such as
deep-fried pecorino and *millefeuille*
of aubergine and courgette.

SIENA: La Taverna del Capitano €
Trattoria   Map D3
Via del Capitano 6–8, 53100
Tel *0577 28 80 94*
Quintessentially Sienese restaurant
with vaulted ceilings near the
Duomo. Serves rustic dishes, such
as stewed rabbit and *ribbolita*.

**SIENA: Compagnia dei
Vinattieri**   €€
Vineria   Map D3
Via delle Terme 79, 53100
Tel *0577 23 65 68*
Underground vaulted space with
a great wine cellar and excellent
food. Plenty of wines available by
the glass.

SIENA: Osteria le Logge €€€
Osteria   Map D3
Via del Porrione 33, 53100
Tel *0577 480 13*   **Closed** *Sun*
Siena's prettiest restaurant, with a
dark-wood and marble interior, and
white linen on the tables. Creative
food and Montalcino wines.

South Tuscany

CAPALBIO: Gelateria Gusto €
Gelateria   Map D5
Via Umbria, 58011
Tel *0348 710 82 35*
Excellent ice creams and granitas
made by a Sicilian family. Inventive
as well as classic flavours – try the
caramel and peanut.

CAPALBIO: Da Maria €€
Trattoria   Map D5
Via Nuovo 3, 58011
Tel *0564 89 60 14*
Capalbio's summer population of
Roman politicians and media types
join local residents in this pleasant
trattoria, serving Maremma cuisine.

**CASTIGLIONE DELLA PESCAIA:
Il Cantuccio**   €€
Osteria   Map C4
*Piazza Indipendenza 31, Buriano,
58043*
Tel *0564 94 80 11*   **Closed** *Mon*
A small, modern restaurant in a
pretty medieval hamlet. Creates
just a few dishes daily from local,
carefully sourced ingredients.

**CASTIGLIONE DELLA PESCAIA:
Ristorante Miramare**   €€
Seafood   Map C4
Via Vittorio Veneto 35, 58043
Tel *0564 93 35 24*
Lovely sea views, and excellent
fresh seafood and fish. Begin
with a warm seafood salad with
limoncello sauce, move on to
linguine with clams and mussels,
and for the main course opt for
the catch of the day.

ELBA: Publius €€
Trattoria **Map** B4
Piazza del Castagneto, Località
Poggio Marciana, 57030
Tel *0565 992 08* **Closed** *Nov–Apr*
Food with a view in a historic
restaurant with the best cellar on
the island. Fish is the speciality
here, but plenty of meat dishes
are on offer, too. The lamb
roasted in herbs is delicious.

DK Choice

ELBA: Tamata Wine Bar
and Restaurant €€€
Contemporary **Map** B4
Via Cesare Battisti, 3 Angolo via
Cavallotti, Porto Azzurro, 57036
Tel *0349 358 69 56* **Closed** *Wed*
Contemporary and informal,
Tamata serves beautifully
presented dishes that you won't
find anywhere else in Tuscany.
The menu changes with the
season – look out for scallops
with Thai sauce, red prawns with
frozen sake or spaghetti with
seaweed, wild fennel and a
foam of sea urchin. Mains might
include a delectable pistachio-
crusted tuna. Meat dishes make
imaginative use of duck, wild
boar and Chianina beef.

MAGLIANO IN TOSCANA:
Antica Trattoria Aurora €€
Trattoria **Map** D5
Via Chiasso Lavagnini 12–14, 58051
Tel *0564 59 27 74* **Closed** *Wed*
Delicious food with an inventive
touch – tortellini with duck
cooked in Morellino wine, for
example, or breast of goose with
a sour bilberry sauce. Lovely
hanging gardens in summer.

MAGLIANO IN TOSCANA:
Da Sandra €€
Trattoria **Map** D5
Via Garibaldi 50, 58051
Tel *0564 59 21 96* **Closed** *Mon*
Quietly elegant, Da Sandra
showcases some great local
wines and offers a seasonal
menu – including wild asparagus
in spring. In autumn, game
dominates. Exceptional service.

MARINA DI BIBBONA:
La Pineta €€€
Seafood **Map** C3
Via dei Cavallaggeri Nord, Marina di
Bibbona, 57020
Tel *0586 60 00 16* **Closed** *Mon,*
Tue
Smart, romantic – and expensive –
restaurant right on the sand in
what is essentially a beach hut.
It is run by a former fisherman,
Zazzeri, who gets the catch each
day from the family boats.

MASSA MARITTIMA:
Taverna Vecchio Borgo €€
Trattoria **Map** C4
Via Norma Parenti 12, 58024
Tel *0566 90 39 50* **Closed** *Mon; Sun*
dinner in winter
Ancient barrel-vaulted rooms
and a well-stocked wine cellar.
Try handmade pasta stuffed with
ricotta and scattered with hazelnuts and herbs. The wild boar
cooked with olives is also highly
recommended.

MASSA MARITTIMA:
Da Tronca €€
Trattoria **Map** C4
Vicolo Porte 5, 58024
Tel *0566 90 19 91* **Closed** *Wed*
Rustic place with some dishes you
won't find elsewhere – particularly
those using wild vegetables. Try
the tortellini stuffed with wild kale.
There is always a bewildering
choice of *crostini* and an
excellent chickpea soup.

MASSA MARITTIMA: Bracali €€€
Fine Dining **Map** C4
Via di Perolla 2, Località Ghirlanda,
58020
Tel *0566 90 23 18* **Closed** *Sun, Mon*
This sumptuous restaurant has
been awarded two Michelin stars.
It excels at revitalizing traditional
dishes. Sample the delicate
mixture of flavours on the chef's
tasting menu. Excellent service
and a very extensive wine list.

ORBETELLO: Trattoria del
Pesce Povero €
Seafood **Map** D5
Via delle Saline 7, Località Giannella,
58015
Tel *0564 87 13 00* **Closed** *Mon, Tue,*
Wed; Nov–Apr dinner
Refreshingly simple *trattoria* with
a fixed menu that changes every
day according to the catch. You
might find a warm salad of octopus and potato on the menu, or a
delicious spaghetti with clams.

ORBETELLO: I Pescatori €€
Seafood **Map** D5
Via Leopardi 9, 58015
Tel *0564 86 06 11* **Closed** *Mon*
This no-frills place, run by a local
fishermen's cooperative, serves
fish caught in the adjacent lagoon.
Order and pay as you arrive, then
take a seat and sip a local white
as you wait for your fish to arrive.

PITIGLIANO: Hostaria del
Ceccottino €€
Contemporary **Map** E5
Piazza San Gregorio VII 64, 58017
Tel *0564 61 42 73* **Closed** *Thu*
Lots of organic local produce,
including *bottarga* (salted tuna
roe) from Orbetello. Save room
for the great rare-breed meat
dishes, such as roast pork shank
with potatoes, herby rabbit or a
steak of Maremma beef.

PORTO SANTO STEFANO:
L'Osteria del Porto le Chicche €€
Seafood **Map** D5
Via Scalo Colombo 22, 58019
Tel *0564 81 22 86* **Closed** *Tue*
Little restaurant with a lovely
terrace specializing in fish and
seafood. Light starters, such as
tuna tartare and octopus salad.

SATURNIA: I Due Cippi €€
Fine Dining **Map** D5
Piazza V Veneto 26, 58050 Saturnia
Tel *0564 60 10 74* **Closed** *Tue*
Smart restaurant serving
delicious local food. Try the
aubergine and fennel soufflé or
grilled local steak.

SEGGIANO: Silene €€€
Contemporary **Map** D4
Località Pescina, 58038
Tel *0564 95 08 05* **Closed** *Sun*
dinner, Mon
Excellent food in a medieval *borgo*.
Dishes feature vegetables grown
in the owner's garden. Look out
for pumpkin soup served with
toasted seeds.

Elegant La Tenda Rossa, known for delicious pasta, in San Casciano Val di Pesa *(see p274)*

For more information on types of restaurants *see pp258–9*

SHOPS AND MARKETS

Shopping in Florence is a unique experience. Shops are scattered throughout its ancient and medieval streets, and many boutiques are run by families, or sell traditional regional crafts. Few cities of comparable size can boast such a profusion and variety of high-quality goods. Walking around the city, you will find shops selling Italian fashion, antiques, leather and jewellery. Tuscany is dwarfed by Florence when it comes to shopping possibilities. However, the rich traditions of many outlying towns and villages boast a variety of local crafts and specialities. These range from ceramics and hand-woven materials to the region's many gastronomic delicacies. *(See also pp34–5.)*

A colourful shop display of elegant leather handbags

When to Shop

Generally, shops open at around 9am and close at 1pm. In the afternoon, they re-open from 3:30pm to 7:30pm, though food shops tend to open earlier in the morning and remain closed from 1pm to 5pm. Most shops are shut on Monday morning, but food stores are closed on Wednesday afternoon.

Almost all shops close on Saturday afternoon in summer, and shops and markets tend to close for two or three weeks around 15 August, the national holiday *(ferragosto)*.

How to Pay

Major credit cards are usually accepted in larger shops, but smaller ones prefer cash. Traveller's cheques are now rarely accepted for goods and services.

Shopkeepers and market stallholders should, by law, give you a receipt *(ricevuta fiscale)*. If a purchased item is defective, most shops will change the article or give you a credit note, as long as you show the till receipt. Cash refunds are uncommon.

VAT Exemption

Visitors from non-EU countries can reclaim the 20 per cent sales tax (IVA) on purchases from the same shop exceeding €160. Ask for an invoice *(la fattura)* when you buy the goods, and inform the shop of your intention to reclaim the tax. You will need to show your passport, and the shop will fill out and stamp a form that can be taken to the relevant office at the airport.

Shopping in Florence

The centre of Florence is packed with shops selling everything from designer clothes to second-hand books. It is compact and easy to get around, as many streets are pedestrianized. It is also worth exploring the streets away from the centre – around Piazza di Santa Croce, Piazza dei Ciompi and Piazza di Santo Spirito – for furniture and gift

Window shopping in the Via de' Tornabuoni, in Florence

shops where craftsmen are busy at work. The best time for bargains is during the January and July sales *(saldi)*.

Department Stores

The city's main chain store is **Coin**, a popular independent department store with branches in Montecatini Terme and Livorno. This store stocks mid-range casual clothing, shoes, toiletries, children's clothing and toys, and a huge range of fashion accessories, including hosiery, sunglasses, bags and scarves. It also has an extensive home collection.

Rinascente, in Piazza della Repubblica, has designer clothing, lingerie, household items and a rooftop bar with direct views of the Duomo. **Principe** has classic menswear and women's and children's clothes, as well as upmarket home accessories.

Clothing

In Florence, the big names in Italian fashion – **Gucci**, **Armani**, **Ferragamo**, **Versace**, **Prada** and **Roberto Cavalli** – are mostly found in Via de' Tornabuoni *(see p109)*. This elegant street is also home to **Hermès**, at the top of the street in Piazza Antinori. Opposite the imposing Palazzo Strozzi is **Louis Vuitton**, with its impressive collections of footwear, clothing and luggage; **Dolce & Gabbana** is in Via degli Strozzi nearby, and **Valentino** is in Via dei Tosinghi.

On Via degli Strozzi, you will find designer underwear at **La Perla**, while younger styles can be found at **Gioel** and **Intimissimi**.

Luisa Via Roma and **Raspini** stock top designer clothing and shoes, while **Eredi Chiarini** and **Matucci** have more casual styles. **Emilio Pucci** *(see p92)*, famous for his extravagant 1960s print clothes, is in Via de'Tornabuoni.

There are opulent hand-woven fabrics, fine silks and vintage fabrics at **Casa dei Tessuti**, and embroidered linen can be found at **Taf**. Those looking for discounts on Italian designer clothing and shoes should venture out to **The Mall** or **Barberino Designer Outlet**. Both these outlets are located approximately 30 minutes away from Florence. A shuttle bus leaves regularly from the main railway station.

Classic leather goods at Beltrami

Shoes

Italy is renowned worldwide for its shoes and, with the local Tuscan tanneries, there is nowhere better than Florence to find footwear for all tastes. Some shops design and make classic shoes by hand in-store, while others stock huge collections of new styles for each season.

At the top end, the refined finishing and elegance of **Ferragamo**'s shoes are sought after by Hollywood stars, and **Gucci** and **Prada** are both meccas for admirers of designer Italian shoes. If you prefer more classic styles, then head to **Francesco**, a tiny shop that sells simple handmade shoes and

Trendy sandals at Ferragamo

sandals, or **Quercioli**, for high-quality, hand-stitched leather shoes for both men and women. The mid-priced range is well represented by **Romano**, which stocks collections of shoes and boots in good-quality leather. For more casual and sporty styles, try the reasonably-priced **Peluso**. Alternatively, stroll down Via de'Cerretani, which houses many affordable shoe shops, including the popular **Divarese**.

Leather Goods

Piazza di Santa Croce *(see p75)* and the adjoining streets are filled with leather shops and workshops. Inside the cloisters of the church itself is the **Scuola del Cuoio**, where leather craftsmen work in front of customers. Classic leather bags and gifts are sold at **Bojola**, **Il Bisonte** and **Beltrami**, and more contemporary styles can be found at **Coccinelle** and **Furla**. **Peruzzi** stocks leather clothing and accessories for men and women. The best place to buy gloves is **Madova**. For good-value bags, belts and leather jackets, try the Mercato Centrale *(see p92)* or the market stalls in Via Pellicceria *(see p279)*.

Toiletries

For toiletries and beauty products, head to a *profumeria* (perfumery), such as **Aline**, **Profumeria Inglese** or **Le Vanità**, which also has a beauty centre and solarium. *Erboristerie* (herbalists) sell a range of natural products. Try the **Erboristerie Spezierie di Palazzo Vecchio** *(see p79)* for unique handmade perfumes. The **Erboristerie Inglese**, on Via de'Tornabuoni, dispenses natural remedies and tisanes, and stocks natural beauty products, perfumes and gifts. Also worth a visit is the **Farmacia di Santa Maria Novella**, a frescoed apothecary selling products from the elixirs of the Camaldoli monks to perfumes, herbal remedies and sweets.

Jewellery

Florence has always been noted for its gold and silversmiths. Go to **Torrini**, whose family has produced jewellery for six centuries, and to **Pomellato**'s stunning shop on Via de'Tornabuoni, for its famous chunky white gold rings with huge semiprecious gems. **Bulgari** is on the same street, and so is **Parenti**, which has beautiful Baccarat rings and unique antique jewels. Try **Aprosio & Co** for decorative jewellery made from precious metals and tiny glass stones.

The tiny wooden shops on the Ponte Vecchio *(see pp110–11)* are all jewellery shops, some with beautiful antiques from Italy and abroad, others with high-quality new Italian gold pieces.

A vibrant array of fabrics in Casa dei Tessuti, in Florence

Typical antiques shop in Florence

Art and Antiques

Florence has always been a centre of artistic excellence. This heritage has translated into a wealth of antiques and fine-art shops. The antiques shops are mostly clustered around Via dei Fossi *(see pp116–17)*, Via Maggio *(see p122)* and Via dei Serragli.

For top-quality antiques go to **Antichità dei Bardi** or the nearby **Cei**. **Romanelli** has bronze statuary and works encrusted in semiprecious stones, while **Ducci** has an exquisite selection of handmade boxes, prints and sculpture in marble and wood. For lovers of modern art, there is **Galleria Tornabuoni**, while modern-art objects and gifts can be found at **Armando Poggi**. **Ugo Poggi** has a selection of household objects, including elegant porcelain.

Ugolini and **Mosaico di Pitti** create tables and framed pictures using the age-old technique of marble inlay. **Arredamenti Castorina** has a wonderful selection of picture frames, mouldings, brassware and intricate intarsias. More contemporary styles are at **Mirabili**, which showcases furniture and interior designers.

Gifts

Florence is a treasure trove for unusual gifts and souvenirs. Via de'Guicciardini and the area between Piazza di Santa Croce and Piazza della Signoria are good places to look for gifts.

Housed in a converted wine cellar, **Signum** has postcards, posters and prints, and items such as miniature shop models and tiny packs of cards. **Mandragora**, in Piazza del Duomo, has a wide choice of gifts based on famous artworks in the city, while the renowned **Pineider** has up-market stationery and office gifts in leather, linen and paper.

For locally made terracotta and decorative glazed ceramics, visit **Sbigoli Terracotte**. **La Bottega dei Cristalli** has Murano glass kitchenware, chandeliers and decorative objects. **Passamaneria Valmar** sells decorative key and curtain tassels, tapestries and soft furnishings in silks and wools, while **Lisa Corti Home Textile Emporium** has hand-printed cotton throws, bedcovers and cushions, as well as a range of children's clothes and pottery.

Books and Paper

The main bookshop in Florence is **Feltrinelli**, and at its main store in Via de Cerratani, you'll find publications in numerous languages. The offshoot bookstore **RED Feltrinelli** boasts a restaurant selling panini and light meals. **Paperback Exchange** has an extremely wide selection of new and second-hand books in English.

Typical Florentine crafts include bookbinding and hand-made marbled paper, which is used to decorate a variety of gift objects. These are easily available at **Giulio Giannini**, **Il Papiro** and **Il Torchio**; it's worth going to the latter just to see bookbinding in action, as you can watch it being done in the balcony workshop.

Feltrinelli International bookshop

Food and Wine

Those shopping for food should go to **Pegna**, a mini-supermarket in the heart of Florence that stocks fresh, as well as vast selection of gourmet, foods. The **Bottega dell'Olio** has shelves of extra-virgin Tuscan olive oils, spice-flavoured oils and gifts. For typically British items, such as teas and speciality foods, go to **Old England Stores**.

Dolceforte sells chocolate souvenirs in the shape of the Duomo and the statue of David. A huge selection of biscuits and chocolates fills the front half of **Alessi**, while at the back and in the cellar are fine wines, spirits and liqueurs. Another good place to buy wine is **Zanobini**, where you can mix with the locals and sample the wines. At **Procacci**, in Via de'Tornabuoni, shoppers

Fresh vegetables at a Florentine market stall

can stop for a glass of wine and a canapé while choosing between pots of black and white truffles and other delicacies to take away.

Florence's Markets

The covered **Mercato Centrale** is the city's main food market *(see p92)*. Touristy stalls selling leather goods, t-shirts and souvenirs line the streets and the square just to the north of the *mercato*. The **Mercato di**

Sant'Ambrogio has fresh fruit and vegetable stalls, as well as clothing and household goods. Beneath the 16th-century Loggia del Porcellino is the **Mercato Nuovo**, or Straw Market, which sells leather goods and souvenirs *(see p116)*. On Tuesday mornings, there is an enormous market at the **Parco delle Cascine**, with cheap clothing, shoes and food. The **Mercato delle Pulci** is a flea market selling antiques and

bric-a-brac. Garden enthusiasts might want to check out the **Mercato delle Piante**, held on Thursday mornings under the porticoes of Via Pellicceria, selling flowers, house plants and herbs.

Occasional markets spring up in Piazza Santa Croce and Piazza Santa Maria Novella, notably the German gift market in the weeks before Christmas and the monthly antiques market in **Piazza Santo Spirito**.

DIRECTORY

Department Stores

Coin
Via dei Calzaiuoli 56r.
Map 6 D3.
Tel 055 28 05 31.

Principe
Via delle Belle Donne 1/9r–15r.
Map 1 C5 (5 C2).
Tel 055 29 27 64.

Rinascente
Piazza della Repubblica 1.
Map 1 C5 (6 D3).
Tel 055 21 91 13.

Clothing

Armani
Via de'Tornabuoni 48/50r.
Map 1 C5 (5 C2).
Tel 055 21 90 41.

Barberino Designer Outlet
A1 Firenze–Bologna, exit Barberino di Mugello.
Map 2D.
Tel 055 84 21 61.

Casa dei Tessuti
Via de'Pecori 20–24r.
Map 1 C5 (6 D2).
Tel 055 21 59 61.

Dolce & Gabbana
Via degli Strozzi 12–18r.
Map 1 C5 (5 C3).
Tel 055 28 10 03.

Emilio Pucci
Via de'Tornabuoni 22r.
Map 1 C5 (5 C3).
Tel 055 265 80 82.

Eredi Chiarini
Via Roma 16r.
Map 3 C1 (6 D2).
Tel 055 28 44 78.

Ferragamo
Via de'Tornabuoni 14r.
Map 1 C5 (5 C2).
Tel 055 29 21 23.

Gioel
Via Porta Rossa 43r.
Map 3 C1 (6 D3).
Tel 055 28 79 19.

Gucci
Via de'Tornabuoni 73r.
Map 1 C5 (5 C2).
Tel 055 26 40 11.

Hermès
Piazza Antinori 6r.
Map 1 C5 (5 C2).
Tel 055 238 10 04.

Intimissimi
Via dei Calzaiuoli 97.
Map 3 C1 (6 D3).
Tel 055 21 21 47.

Louis Vuitton
Piazza degli Strozzi 1.
Map 3 C1.
Tel 055 26 69 81.

Luisa Via Roma
Via Roma 19r–21r.
Map 3 C1 (6 D2).
Tel 055 21 78 26.

The Mall
Via Europa 8, Leccio Reggello.
Tel 055 865 77 75.

Matucci
Via del Corso 71r.
Map 3 C1 (6 D3).
Tel 055 239 64 20.

La Perla
Via degli Strozzi 24/r.
Map 3 B1 (5 C3).
Tel 055 21 52 42.

Prada
Via de'Tornabuoni 67r.
Map 1 C5 (5 C2).
Tel 055 28 34 39.

Raspini
Via Roma 25r-29r.
Map 3 C1 (6 D2).
Tel 055 21 30 77.

Roberto Cavalli
Via de'Tornabuoni 83r.
Map 1 C5 (5 C3).
Tel 055 239 62 26.

Taf
Via Por Santa Maria 17r.
Map 3 C1 (6 D4).
Tel 055 239 60 37.

Valentino
Via dei Tosinghi 52r.
Map 1 C5 (6 D2).
Tel 055 29 31 42.

Versace
Via de'Tornabuoni 13-15r.
Map 1 C5 (5 C2).
Tel 055 28 26 38.

Shoes

Divarese
Piazza del Duomo 47r.
Map 3 C1 (6 D2).
Tel 055 21 31 68.

Francesco
Via di Santo Spirito 62r.
Map 3 B1 (5 A4).
Tel 055 21 24 28.

Peluso
Via del Corso 5-6r.
Map 3 C1 (6 D3).
Tel 055 26 82 83.

Quercioli
Via Calzaiuoli 18/20r.
Map 3 C1 (6 D2).
Tel 055 21 40 57.

Romano
Via Porta Rossa 14r.
Map 1 C5 (5 C3).
Tel 055 28 96 88.

Leather Goods

Beltrami
Via Panzani 11/r.
Map 1 C5 (5 C1).
Tel 055 21 26 61.

Il Bisonte
Via del Parione 31r.
Map 3 C1 (5 C3).
Tel 055 21 57 22.

Bojola
Via de'Rondinelli 25r.
Map 1 C5 (5 C2).
Tel 055 21 11 55.

Coccinelle
Via Calzaiuoli 28r.
Map 3 C1 (6 D3).
Tel 055 274 08 91.

Furla
Via dei Calzaiuoli 47r.
Map 3 C1 (6 D3).
Tel 055 238 28 83.

Madova
Via dei Giucciardini 1r.
Map 3 C2 (5 C4).
Tel 055 239 65 26.

Peruzzi
Borgo de'Greci 8–20r.
Map 4 D1 (6 E4).
Tel 055 28 90 39.

Scuola del Cuoio
Piazza di Santa Croce 16.
Map 4 E1 (6 F4).
Tel 055 24 45 33.

DIRECTORY

Toiletries

Aline
Via dei Calzaiuoli 53r.
Map 3 C1 (6 D3).
Tel 055 21 74 01.

Erboristerie Inglese
Via de'Tornabuoni 19.
Map 1 C5 (5 C2).
Tel 055 21 06 28.

Erboristerie Spezierie di Palazzo Vecchio
Via Vacchereccia 9r.
Map 3 C1 (6 D3).
Tel 055 239 60 55.

Farmacia di Santa Maria Novella
Via della Scala 16.
Map 1 A4 (5 A1).
Tel 055 21 62 76.

Profumeria Inglese
Piazza dell'Olio 4.
Map 3 C1 (6 D2).
Tel 055 28 97 48.

Le Vanità
Via Porta Rossa 55r.
Map 1 C5 (5 C3).
Tel 055 29 01 67.

Jewellery

Aprosio & Co.
Via della Spada 38r.
Map 3 B1 (5 B2).
Tel 055 29 05 34

Bulgari
Via de'Tornabuoni 61r.
Map 1 C5 (5 C3).
Tel 055 239 67 86.

Parenti
Via de'Tornabuoni 93r.
Map 1 C5 (5 C2).
Tel 055 21 44 38.

Pomellato
Via de'Tornabuoni 89r–91r.
Map 1 C5 (5 C2).
Tel 055 28 85 30.

Torrini
Piazza del Duomo 10r.
Map 2 D5 (6 D2).
Tel 055 230 24 01.

Art and Antiques

Antichità dei Bardi
Via dei Fossi 11.
Map 1 B5 (5 B3).
Tel 055 21 56 88.

Armando Poggi
Via dei Calzaiuoli 103–116r.
Map 6 D3.
Tel 055 21 17 19.

Arredamenti Castorina
Via di Santo Spirito 15r.
Map 3 B1 (5 A4).
Tel 055 21 28 85.

Cei
Via dei Fossi 17.
Map 1 B5 (5 B3).
Tel 055 239 60 39.

Ducci
Lungarno Corsini 24r.
Map 3 B1 (5 B3).
Tel 055 21 91 37.

Galleria Tornabuoni
Borgo San Jacopo 53r.
Map 3 C1 (5 C4).
Tel 055 28 47 20.

Mirabili
Lungarno Giucciardini 24r.
Map 3 B1 (5 A4).
Tel 055 294 257.

Mosaico di Pitti
Piazza de' Pitti 23r.
Map 3 B2 (5 B5).
Tel 055 28 21 27.

Romanelli
Borgo San Frediano 70.
Map 3 A1 (5 A3).
Tel 055 239 66 62.

Ugo Poggi
Via degli Strozzi 26r.
Map 1 C5 (5 C3).
Tel 055 21 67 41.

Ugolini
Lungarno degli Acciaiuoli 66–70r.
Map 3 C1 (5 C4).
Tel 055 28 49 69.

Gifts

La Bottega dei Cristalli
Via dei Benci 51r
Map 4 D1 (6 F4).
Tel 055 234 48 91.

Lisa Corti Home Textile Emporium
Piazza Ghiberti 33r.
Map 4 F1.
Tel 055 200 18 60.

Mandragora
Piazza del Duomo 9.
Map 2 D5 (6 D2).
Tel 055 29 25 59.

Passamaneria Valmar
Via Porta Rossa 53r.
Map 1 C5 (5 C3).
Tel 055 28 44 93.

Pineider
Map 3 B1 (5 B3).
Tel 055 28 46 56.

Sbigoli Terracotte
Via Sant'Egidio 4r.
Map 6 F2.
Tel 055 247 97 13.

Signum
Borgo dei Greci 40r.
Map 3 C1 (6 E4).
Tel 055 28 06 21.

Books and Paper

Feltrinelli
Via de'Cerretani, 30/32r.
Map Map 1 C5 (6 D2).
Tel 055 21 95 24.

La Feltrinelli RED
Piazza della Repubblica 27r.
Map 1 C5 (6 D3).
Tel 055 293 78 11.

Giulio Giannini
Piazza de'Pitti 37r.
Map 3 B2 (5 B5).
Tel 055 21 26 21.

Paperback Exchange
Via delle Oche 4r.
Map 2 D5 (6 E2).
Tel 055 29 34 60.

Il Papiro
Piazza del Duomo 24r.
Map 2 D5 (6 D4).
Tel 055 28 16 28.

Il Torchio
Via de'Bardi 17.
Map 3 C2 (6 D5) (6 D4).
Tel 055 234 28 62.

Food and Wine

Alessi
Via delle Oche 27r.
Map 3 C1 (6 D2).
Tel 055 21 49 66.

Bottega dell'Olio
Piazza del Limbo 2r.
Map 3 C1 (5 C4).
Tel 055 267 04 68.

Dolceforte
Via della Scala 21.
Map 1 B5 (5 B2).
Tel 055 21 91 16.

Old England Stores
Via de'Vecchietti 28r.
Map 1 C5 (5 C2).
Tel 055 21 19 83.

Pegna
Via dello Studio 26r.
Map 6 E2.
Tel 055 28 27 01.

Procacci
Via de'Tornabuoni 64r.
Map 1 C5 (5 C2).
Tel 055 21 16 56.

Zanobini
Via Sant'Antonino 47r.
Map 1 C5 (5 C1).
Tel 055 239 68 50.

Florence's Markets

Mercato Centrale
Via dell'Ariento 10–14
Map 1 C4 (5 C1).

Mercato Nuovo
See p112.
Map 3 C1 (6 D3).
Open 9am–7pm daily (Nov–Mar: Tue–Sat).

Mercato delle Piante
Via Pellicceria.
Map 6 D3.
Open Thu am.

Mercato delle Pulci
Piazza dei Ciompi.
Map 4 E1.
Open 9am–7:30pm daily (Nov–Mar: Tue–Sun).

Mercato di Sant'Ambrogio
Piazza Sant'Ambrogio.
Map 4 F1.
Open 7am–2pm Mon–Sat.

Parco delle Cascine
Piazza Vittorio Veneto.
Open 8am–2pm Tue.

Piazza Santo Spirito
Map 3 B2 (5 B5).
Open 8am–12:30pm Mon–Fri. Antiques market 2nd Sun of month.

Shopping in Tuscany

Small towns throughout Tuscany have a multitude of shops selling a range of handicrafts, foods and some of the best wine in Italy. These are invariably displayed in small shops or at the frequent markets, seasonal fairs and local celebrations *(see pp38–43)*, which are such an integral part of Tuscan rural life.

A Tuscan delicatessen

Display of local pottery

Gifts and Souvenirs

Characteristic ceramics are found throughout the region, from the famed raw terracotta of Impruneta to the decorated glazed pottery of Montelupo and Siena. In San Gimignano, look out for shops selling artistic ceramics *(see p34)* and hand-woven fabrics.

The best in marble can be found in Pietrasanta and Carrara *(see p176)*. The famous white marble of the Alpi Apuane still serves local craftsmen, who make busts and replicas of sculpted works of art, as in Michelangelo's day.

The Etruscans mastered the art of working alabaster, and today the tradition lives on in Volterra, where many shops sell a range of souvenirs *(see p170)*. The Etruscans also had knowledge of the minerals and precious stones typical of the volcanic Colline Metallifere, Maremma and Elba, the latter famous for its quartz and opals *(see pp238–9)*.

For textiles, Lucca lays claim to a rich tradition of silk manufacture, as well as embroidery and hand-woven fabrics, reflecting the strong rural craft tradition of the nearby Garfagnana area. Rustic crafts are common in the Mugello and Casentino.

Food and Wine

Excursions into Tuscany should be accompanied by visits to a local vineyard where wine is sold directly from the cellars. The Chianti region is studded with farms producing their own wines *(see p233)*. Greve has several good wine outlets, and during the third week of September there is the annual wine festival, the Rassegna del Chianti Classico *(see p40)*.

The excellent Vernaccia, a white wine, is typical of the San Gimignano area. The vineyards around Montalcino produce some of the best wine in Italy *(see p228)*.

Tuscany's rich gastronomic tradition is reflected in the profusion of local products. The main streets of towns such as Greve, Montalcino, San Gimignano and Pienza have a range of food shops.

Sheep's cheese *(pecorino)*, produced around the area of Crete, can be bought directly from the farm or from shops in local towns. In Pienza, shop shelves are laden with local cheeses *(see p230)*, cured meats, wines and grappas. In Grosseto, you will find truffles.

Siena is renowned for its *panforte*, a dark cake spiced with cloves and cinnamon, which has been produced since the Middle Ages. Biscuits include *cavallucci* (ground walnuts and aniseed) and *ricciarelli*, made from almonds, orange peel and honey.

Markets in Tuscany

Markets are aplenty throughout the region. Particularly famous is the Mercato dell'Antiquariato, which sells goods from antique furniture to bric-a-brac. It takes place in Arezzo on the Piazza Grande on the first weekend of each month, in Pisa on the Ponte di Mezzo on the second weekend, and in Lucca in Piazza San Martino on the third weekend.

The Mercato dell'Antiquariato on the Piazza Grande in Arezzo

ENTERTAINMENT

There is plenty going on in Florence and Tuscany by way of entertainment throughout the year. The warm summer months see a concentration of events from traditional festivals, classical concerts and dance performances to open-air films and live music in alfresco bars. The areas of Santo Spirito in Oltrarno and Santa Croce are home to lively bars and restaurants, while clubs tend to be situated on the edge of town. Opera lovers will not be disappointed; Florence's Teatro del Maggio, one of Italy's best, hosts some fine operas and concerts, while Tuscany plays host to the celebrated Puccini Opera Festival.

Practical Information

Local newspapers, such as *La Nazione* and the Florence section of *La Repubblica*, carry entertainment listings. The monthly magazine *Firenze Spettacolo*, with a short section in English, lists local events, entertainment venues and places to eat and drink. Look out, too, for the free, bilingual, *Concierge Information*, which is a useful source of listings, and the twice-weekly English newspaper *The Florentine*. Websites detailing events in the region include www.firenze.net, www.comune.firenze.it and www.turismo.toscana.it.

Booking Tickets

Box Office is a ticket agency for concerts, opera and ballet nationwide. Tickets for performances at the **Teatro del Maggio** can also be purchased at the on-site box office and online. It is advisable to buy tickets for opera in advance, but for other events, tickets are generally available on the door.

Facilities For The Disabled

Most major concert halls and music venues in Tuscany are now fully wheelchair accessible. However, churches, villas and gardens that hold occasional performances are unlikely to be so well equipped. If in doubt, always check in advance. There is a booklet published by the Province of Florence that is available at tourist offices, which details the accessibility of many outdoor venues in the area.

Opera and Classical Music

The most important musical event in Tuscany is the annual Maggio Musicale festival *(see p38)*, held at **Teatro del Maggio** in Florence between late April and late June, and features opera, concerts and ballet. The theatre also puts on a year-round programme, while Orchestra della Toscana gives several concerts a month at its base in **Teatro Verdi**. From October to April, the wonderful 18th-century **Teatro della Pergola** in Florence hosts world-class chamber-music concerts. **Estate Fiesolana** organizes opera, dance and music events from July to August in Fiesole's atmospheric amphitheatre.

The rest of Tuscany also celebrates the arts. Puccini's lakeside villa on the shores of Lago di Massaciuccoli makes a spectacular setting for the **Puccini Opera Festival**, held every July to August. The Opera Barga festival showcases little-known works in the restored **Teatro dei Differenti** *(see p178)*. In July and August, Siena hosts the **Estate Musicale Chigiana** in the magnificent abbeys of San Galgano, Monte Oliveto Maggiore and Sant'Antimo. The **Incontri in Terra di Siena** festival is known for its excellent chamber music, and the **Tuscan Sun Festival**, based in Cortona, has an exciting music and arts programme.

Film, Theatre and Dance

Films in English are shown three times a week at the **Odeon Original Sound** in Florence, and several other Tuscan towns now cater for the huge number of foreign visitors by screening English-language films.

Theatre has a long and distinguished history in Tuscany, but performances in English are rare, and as such, the genre

Fiesole's Roman amphitheatre is the setting for opera and dance events

Contemporary dance performance

is staged in the **Sala Vanni**, while several bars regularly hold live-jazz sessions.

Big-name rock concerts are mostly held at the 7,000-seater **Nelson Mandela Forum** or at the city's football stadium. For smaller, more intimate venues, go to clubs such as **Auditorium Flog**, **Tenax** or **Saschall**. *Firenze Spettacolo* has a detailed list of bars and clubs hosting live music.

In summer, Florence's piazzas and gardens become the venues for alfresco bars and live music. Summertime also sees open-air jazz and rock concerts taking place all over the region.

Blues fans should look out for **Pistoia Blues**, a mid-July weekend jamboree of open-air blues concerts, which attracts well-known names.

Open-Air Entertainment

Unique to Tuscany are the many traditional festivals celebrated through the year, the most famous being the Palio in Siena *(see p226)*. Others range from large events attended by thousands of spectators to tiny little village *sagre*. Commonly

defined by food, drink and music, these events are a great way to see the Tuscans at play.

Children's Entertainment

While Florence and Tuscany are extremely child-friendly, child-orientated entertainment is lacking, so parents need to be inventive. As far as museums are concerned, only the Museo dei Ragazzi in Palazzo Vecchio *(see pp82–3)* has a specific programme for children, but several other museums, such as Museo Galileo *(see p78)* and Museo "La Specola" *(see p123)*, are fun, too. For children below ten years, **Mondobimbo Inflatables Parterre** has bouncy castles and **Giardino di Boboli** is good for a run-around.

Outside Florence, there's a small zoo in Pistoia *(see p191)* and **Parco Preistorico**, with its gigantic model dinosaurs, is near Pisa. **Pinocchio Park** at Collodi *(see 187)*, is dedicated to one of Tuscany's most-loved characters, and **Parco Giochi Cavallino Matto** is a huge funfair with plenty of rides to keep the kids amused.

attracts few non-Italian speaking visitors. However, Tuscany's 300 local theatres – many of them now restored – are worth a visit.

Dance is popular throughout the region and several festivals, including the **Florence Dance Festival**, feature classical and contemporary dance.

Jazz, Blues and Rock

Florence is a great place for jazz fans. A busy season of progressive jazz concerts, often featuring international names,

DIRECTORY

SPECIALIST HOLIDAYS AND OUTDOOR ACTIVITIES

Nowhere is the Italian motto for good living, *la dolce vita*, more in evidence than in Tuscany. Sitting outside a café in a Tuscan village, you can glimpse original Renaissance art or take in the sight of well-tended olive groves and vineyards terraced into the steep hillsides. No wonder the gentle pace of an activity holiday here, which in many cases means painting the stunning countryside or sipping vintage wines, is so appealing. For those more interested in energetic pursuits, the region has plenty of sporting activities on offer, from horse riding to water sports. For educational courses see p290.

Art

Those of an artistic persuasion can enrol at art school and try their hand at sculpture, art restoration or painting the beautiful countryside. **Centro d'Arte Verrocchio**, a residential art school in the hilltop village of Casole d'Elsa, offers courses in drawing, painting and sculpture. Students can work on the terrace in stunning surroundings. For city-based courses, try **Lorenzo de'Medici Art Institute of Florence**. The semester and summer-school programmes include sketching, watercolour, fine art, painting, print-making, restoration and art history.

Cookery and Wine Tasting

Tuscany offers many gastronomic delights, from pecorino cheese to porcini mushrooms. The regional cuisine values quality of ingredients rather than complex technique, and recipes are handed down from one generation to the next. There are plenty of cookery courses where you can learn Italian food traditions – some of which are listed on **Nonna Lina's Kitchen** website.

Originally a medieval Benedictine abbey, **Badia a Coltibuono** *(see p233)* is a prestigious Chianti wine-producing estate. Courses on offer here range from brief wine and olive-oil tastings, to five-day residential cookery courses with tours of the vineyards, olive mills and wine-making cellars at Monti in Chianti.

La Cucina del Garga cookery school and restaurant, also in Florence, teaches recipes with a modern flourish. It holds one-day classes in the city and four- to eight-day gastronomic excursions in Tuscany.

Vineyards offer wine tastings by appointment. **Chianti Classico** promotes stays at vineyards in the Chianti Classico region, while **Consorzio del Vino Brunello di Montalcino** has information on visits to the Brunello region. Specialist *enoteca* (wine bars) and shops, including **Millesimi** near Santa Spirito, also arrange wine

Students learning Italian recipies

tastings by appointment. **Frontier Wine Tours** offer week- or day-long chauffeured vineyard tours throughout Tuscany.

Walking, Cycling and Horse Riding

Tuscany's scenery can be best enjoyed at walking pace. Several holiday companies offer walking itineraries, some through the landscape of forested hills and olive groves, while others wend their way through the medieval hilltop towns, taking in cultural landmarks along the way. **Ramblers Holidays** and **Sherpa Expeditions** are two such companies, and **Club Alpino Italiano** runs guided mountain treks.

Another great way to see the Tuscan countryside is by bike. For cycling holidays, contact **Cicloposse**, which deals in both guided and self-guided bike tours. The Maremma, in southern Tuscany, is famous for its wild horses and *butteri* (cowboys), and there are plenty

Painting the beautiful Tuscan countryside

of riding schools in the region. **Vallebona** in Pontassieve organizes trekking holidays and guided tours on horseback and **Rendola Riding Stables** at Montevarchi offers riding lessons.

Spa Holidays

Spa holidays are enjoying a renaissance, with many hotels offering a pool, gym and massage treatments, but Tuscany also has the real thing. Try the thermal pools at **Terme di Saturnia** in the Maremma, or bathe in the warm sulphurated waters of Cascate del Gorello *(see p242)* close by. You can purchase a day pass to experience the therapeutic waters of **Montecatini Terme** *(see pp188–9)*, with its nine spas.

A vast array of fantastic health and beauty treatments is also available here.

Water Sports

Tourists on the Ponte Vecchio *(see pp110–11)* can watch canoes gliding through the inky waters of the river Arno. **Società Canottieri Firenze** offers keen rowers visitor membership for a nominal sum.

In summer, many locals travel to the coast to escape the city heat. Those who can't do that head for one of the open-air swimming pools. **Costoli** is open summer and winter, and **Piscina Bellariva** has indoor and outdoor pools.

For the more adventurous, there is diving off the coast of Elba *(see pp238–9)* through **Spiro Sub Diving Club**.

Mountain Sports

Skiing in the Appennines is a possible day trip from Florence because, rather than being isolated in Alpine resorts, the slopes at **Abetone**, near Pistoia, are only 80 km (50 miles) away. Weekly as well as daily ski passes are available.

Ufficio Guide organise summer mountaineering courses, but single-minded climbers can go rock climbing independently at **Le Cave di Maiano** at Fiesole.

Golf

Combine a few rounds of golf at **Ugolino Golf Course** with sightseeing in Florence, or enjoy a golfing holiday at **Punta Ala Golf Club** overlooking the coast, at Grosseto *(see p242)*, an hour from Pisa airport.

DIRECTORY

Art

Centro d'Arte Verrocchio
Casole d'Elsa.
w verrocchio.co.uk

Lorenzo de'Medici Art Institute of Florence
Via Faenza 43.
Map 1 C4.
Tel 055 28 31 42.

Cookery and Wine Tasting

Badia a Coltibuono
Gaiole in Chianti.
Tel 057 77 44 81.
w coltibuono.com

Chianti Classico
Via Sangallo 41. Loc. Sanbuca, Tavarnele Val di Pesa. **Tel** 05 58 22 85.
w chianticlassico.com

Consorzio del Vino Brunello di Montalcino
Piazza Cavour 8, Montalcino.
Tel 0577 84 82 46.
w consorziobrunellodi montalcino.it

La Cucina del Garga
Via San Zanobi 33.
Map 2 D3. **Tel** 055 47 52 86. w garga.it

Frontier Wine Tours
Lucca.
Tel 33 86 08 56 34.
w frontierwine tours.com

Millesimi
Borgo Tegolaio 35r.
Map 5 B5.
Tel 055 265 46 75.
w millesimi.it

Nonna Lina's Kitchen
w nonnalinas kitchen.com

Walking, Cycling and Horse Riding

Cicloposse
Via I Maggio 27, Pienza.
Tel 0578 749 983.
w cicloposse.com

Club Alpino Italiano
Via del Mezzetta 2.
Tel 055 612 04 67.
w caifirenze.it

Ramblers Holidays
Tel 01707 33 11 33.
w ramblersholidays. co.uk

Rendola Riding Stables
Montevarchi.
Tel 055 970 70 45.
w rendolariding.it

Sherpa Expeditions
Tel 020 857 7 27 17.
w sherpa-walking-holidays.co.uk

Vallebona
Via di Grignano 32, Pontassieve.
Tel 055 839 72 46.

Spa Holidays

Montecatini Terme
Viale Verdi 41, Montecatini Terme.
Tel 0572 7781.
w termemontecatini.it

Terme di Saturnia
Saturnia (Grosseto). **Tel** 0564 60 01 11. w terme-di-saturnia.info

Water Sports

Costoli
Viale Paoli, Florence.
Tel 055 623 60 27.

Piscina Bellariva
Lungarno Aldo Moro 6, Florence.
Tel 055 67 75 21.

Società Canottieri Firenze
Lungarno Luisa dei Medici 8. **Map** 6 D4.
Tel 055 28 21 30.
w canottierifirenze.it

Spiro Sub Diving Club
La Foce 27, Marina di Campo, Elba.
Tel 0565 97 61 02.

Mountain Sports

Abetone
Tel 0573 602 31 (tourist info). **Tel** 0573 600 01 (ski info).

Le Cave di Maiano
Via delle Cave 16, Fiesole.
Tel 055 59 133.

Ufficio Guide
Libreria Stella Alpina, Via Corridoni 14b/r.
Tel 055 41 16 88.
w ufficioguide.it

Golf

Punta Ala Golf Club
Punta Ala, Grosseto.
Tel 0564 92 21 21.
w puntaala.net/golf

Ugolino Golf Course
Via Chiantigiana 3, Grassina.
Tel 055 230 10 09.
w golfugolino.it

SURVIVAL
GUIDE

PRACTICAL INFORMATION

Visitors have been coming to Tuscany for centuries, drawn by its slendid art and architecture, landscape and cuisine. These may all seem overwhelming at first, so plan carefully to make the most of this beautiful region. Start your day early and take time over lunch: most sights and shops close for several hours and reopen in the late afternoon. Try to have a relaxed attitude to your sightseeing – opening hours can be erratic and may vary depending on the season. Most Italians take their holiday in August, so some places may be shut. If your stay in Florence is limited, you could take a city tour. For a longer stay, consider a study course, offered throughout the year by colleges and language schools.

When to Go

Tuscany is great to visit year-round and has four distinct seasons. There is a pleasant, long spring, making April and May the best months to visit. September and October are generally warm. July and August tend to be very hot and crowded, especially in Florence. It rains a lot in winter, with cooler temperatures, but the region is much less crowded. Coastal areas are best visited from May to September; the mountains are good for snow sports in December through to March. In winter, many towns at high altitudes may be hard to reach without snow tyres (see p304).

Visas and Passports

All visitors need a valid passport. European Union (EU) residents and visitors from the US, Canada, Australia and New Zealand do not need visas for stays of up to three months. A visa is required for longer stays; apply at your local embassy or consulate. All visitors to Italy must, by law, register with police within three days of arrival. Most hotels will register visitors when they check in, although this is a formality and very rarely enforced. For a longer stay, you are responsible for registering yourself in person at the **Questura**.

Customs Information

Duty-free allowances are as follows: non-EU residents can bring in either 200 cigarettes, 50 cigars, 100 cigarillos or 250 grams of tobacco; 1 litre of alcohol above 22% vol; 4 litres of wine; 50 grams of perfume. Allowances for EU residents are almost unlimited, providing that the goods are for personal use only. Beware that random checks are often made to guard against drugs traffickers.

Non-EU residents who spend €160 in a single establishment that displays a tax-free sign are entitled to a partial refund for Valued Added Tax, known as IVA (see p276). Ask the cashier to fill out the form for you, and when departing the country, take the goods and receipts in your carry-on luggage for approval at the airport office. Ask for credit to be added to your credit card for faster processing.

Tourist Information

Florence, Pisa and Siena have several **Uffici Informazioni Turistiche** (tourist offices) offering information about tourist sights and authorized guides throughout the region. The "Tourist Rights Protection" desk in the main tourist office in Florence is specifically for making serious, written complaints against service providers. Tourist offices in small towns tend to give details only on their particular town.

The official tourist authorities – the **Italian Tourism Board** and **Turismo in Toscana** – run useful, informative websites that are worth perusing (see p291).

Entertainment Information

The best guide for entertainment is the monthly magazine *Firenze Spettacolo*, which has restaurant and café guides, as well as comprehensive details of concerts, exhibitions, museums and sporting events. For select event and exhibition listings, pick up a free copy of *The Florentine* English-language newspaper, or visit www.thetuscanmagazine.com. During summer evenings, fêtes with local bands are held throughout Tuscany, all listed at www.saimicadove.it.

Etiquette and Smoking

Italians act conservatively in public: they do not sit on the ground or eat while walking, and they tend to drink in moderation with meals. Smoking, though banned in indoor public spaces, is still common and you will see many people smoking on the street.

It is traditional to greet and thank shop staff when entering and exiting stores; if you enter a small store, say *buon giorno* (good morning), then *grazie* when you leave.

Tourist-information office on a Florence street

◄ Rural roads outlining farmers' fields near Pienza

Visitors in Santa Maria Novella, Florence

Visiting Churches

Churches enforce a strict dress code: knees and shoulders must be covered when entering any church. Women should carry a shawl to cover up, while men should avoid wearing shorts. Hemlines at the knee or below are usually fine.

Language

Italian is the only official language in Italy, though English is taught in schools. Young people and those in the tourist industry all speak some English, while the elderly and those in small towns will be less likely to know other languages. Any effort to speak a few words of Italian is always appreciated.

Opening Hours

Opening times tend to vary widely, though in general most museums are closed on Mondays. There are three main museum types: state, city and private, and each has its own opening hours. You'll need to plan your day to avoid turning up at small museums during lunch closure. Many museums have extended hours in the summer. Last admission time is often 45 minutes before closing.

Generally, state museums – such as the Uffizi, Galleria dell' Accademia and Palazzo Pitti –

tend to open Tue–Sun, 8:15am–6:50pm. Others, such as the Bargello, are open mornings only, with occasional Monday openings. City museums are open 9am–7pm daily and private museum hours vary. In the country, most diocese museums (next to each town's *duomo*) close at noon and reopen late afternoon.

Admission Prices

Admission costs for museums average €6–10. Some churches also charge a small entrance fee. Booking in advance is advisable for the **Accademia** and **Uffizi** via the official website or by phone *(see p291)*. **Amici dei Musei** offers an annual pass for state museums. The **Firenze Card**, valid for 72 hours, provides free access to all the major attractions in Florence, as well as free use of public transport.

Public Conveniences

Gabinetto means public toilet, though signs often say WC. There are toilets at almost all museums and cafés. In a bar, it is polite to make a small purchase before using the facilities.

A small fee may be charged at the Duomo and train stations, but elsewhere toilets are usually free. Small towns often have a

toilet near the main parking area. Carrying tissues and hand sanitizer is recommended.

Taxes and Tipping

A 22 per cent tax is included in the price of goods and services. In restaurants, there is usually a €1–3 *coperto* (cover charge), so leave extra only for superb service. It is not necessary to tip a taxi driver, although they often expect the fare to be rounded up to the next euro.

Travellers with Special Needs

Facilities for the disabled traveller visiting Florence and Tuscany are limited. Pavements are often narrow and difficult to navigate with a wheelchair. Always request an accessible hotel room in advance. Package-tour representatives can arrange assistance at airports and hotels. **Accessible Italy** is a specialized non-profit organization that can help you plan your trip and arrange the help you need on-site.

Trenitalia provides passenger assistance for all trains. Many Italian stations have a *Sala Blu* (Blue Hall), which is an assistance point for disabled travellers – there is one in Florence Santa Maria Novella Station *(see p300)*. You may reserve services in advance by email or phone.

Tourists and buskers outside the Uffizi

Travelling with Children

Italians love children, and while hotels and restaurants may not be completely equipped for young visitors, they will be happy to accommodate them. Most restaurants have high chairs and will serve children basic meals, such as pasta with olive oil or tomato sauce.

It's best to request cribs or cots at your hotel in advance. Most hotels do not have a kettle or other food-preparation facilities for newborns; short-let apartments (see pp248–51) are an excellent solution if you need kitchen access. Negotiating narrow pavements can be difficult with pushchairs. Buses in cities have a reserved seating area for people with pushchairs; enter the bus by the wide centre doors. Most sights offer a discounted entry rate for children.

Senior Travellers

Special services or discounts for seniors are few in Tuscany. EU citizens over 65 can get into state museums for free and receive a 25% discount on entry fees to city museums (valid photo ID must be shown), but seniors from outside the EU are not eligible. There is no discount on bus tickets. A train ticket discount of 15% is given to holders of the *Carta Argento*, an annual card you can apply for at train stations. It costs €30 for over 60s, so is only worthwhile if you're planning a lengthy stay in Tuscany. It is free for the over 75s.

Gay and Lesbian Travellers

Certain areas of Tuscany are particularly favoured by GLBT travellers, although the scene remains discreet. Most popular are the seaside resorts of Viareggio and Torre del Lago, which have many gay bars, and certain beaches in Torre del Lago and Maremma. There are numerous gay-friendly B&Bs in Tuscany, especially in Florence.

The oldest gay bar (men only) in Italy is Tabasco in Florence's Piazza della Signoria. There are few organized venues for women, but Florence's Piccolo Café, on Borgo Santa Croce, and Yag, on Via de' Macci, are open to both men and women.

Florence hosts the Queer Festival, dedicated to the arts and film, each November (www.florencequeerfestival.it), and Pitti Immagine fashion events also attract a large gay crowd. The **Arcigay** and **Ireos** associations provide further information (mostly in Italian).

Student and Budget Travellers

Travellers on a budget will find reasonably priced lodging and meal options throughout Tuscany, but there are very few free activities. Some small churches may be free to visit, and students with International Student Identity Cards (ISIC) are usually able to claim a discount on admission fees at museums and other attractions. The ISIC card also gives access to a 24-hour telephone helpline that provides general advice and information.

The student travel agency **CTS Viaggi** has branches throughout Italy and Europe. CTS can issue student cards and offers reasonably priced car hire. They are also able to organize holidays, excursions and courses.

Some traditional *trattorie* have inexpensive set menus, and lunchtime menus tend to be cheaper. There are numerous hostels and budget hotels in Florence and around Tuscany. Camp sites on the outskirts of some towns (see p251) are a good option, while those looking for something a little different could opt to stay in a convent. Bear in mind that convents are likely to have curfews and rules about unmarried couples staying together. Facilities vary from basic to luxurious, with corresponding cost.

Educational Courses

There are many language and art schools in Tuscany. The **British Institute in Florence** is one of the better known, and **The Learning Center of Tuscany** offers TEFL certificate courses. The **Palazzo Spinelli Istituto per l'Arte e il Restauro** offers courses on art, drawing, ceramics and painting. The **Centro Internazionale Dante Alighieri** or the **Università per Stranieri** in Siena have courses on Italian culture, history and cooking. A list of schools in Tuscany is available from the Uffici Informazioni Turistiche.

Tuscan Time

Tuscany is 1 hour ahead of Greenwich Mean Time (GMT). The time difference between Tuscany and other cities is as follows: London: -1 hour; New York: -6 hours; Perth: +7 hours; Auckland: +11 hours; Tokyo: +8 hours. These figures may vary for brief periods in the summer, with local changes. For all official purposes, the Italians use the 24-hour clock (eg 10pm = 22.00 hrs).

Student relaxing in the sun in Gaiole in Chianti

Electrical Adaptors

Electrical current in Italy is 220V AC, with two-pin, round-pronged plugs. It is probably better to buy an adaptor before leaving for Italy. Most hotels with three stars and above have electrical points for shavers.

Responsible Tourism

There are many ways to travel more sustainably in Tuscany, thanks to the region's respect for tradition. In the countryside, consider staying at an *agritourismo (see pp248–51)* and learn about what they produce, or visit local organic farms and wine producers. Tasty local produce can be purchased at markets in both towns and cities; small-town markets are often biweekly, so ask your host for dates. Buy your souvenirs at local artisan workshops. Tuscany is known for hand-decorated paper, ceramics and leather. In Florence, **Context Travel** offers an Oltrarno Artisan tour to meet and learn about these craftspeople.

Local market produce

Italy has an excellent recycling system. There are large coloured bins on many street corners. Use the blue bins for glass and plastic, white for paper, brown for food waste, and silver or black bins for non-recyclable rubbish.

Conversion Table

The metric system is used in Italy. Some basic conversions from metric to imperial are:
1 centimetre = 0.4 inches
1 metre = 3 feet, 3 inches
1 kilometre = 0.6 miles
1 gram = 0.04 ounces
1 kilogram = 2.2 pounds
1 litre = 1.8 pints

DIRECTORY

Immigration Information

Questura
Via Zara 2 (police office), Florence.
Map 2 D3.
Via della Fortezza, 17 (immigration office), Florence.
Map 1 C3.
Tel 0554 97 76 02.
Via del Castoro, Siena.
Tel 0577 20 11 11.
Via Lalli 4, Pisa.
Tel 050 58 35 11.
w questure.polizia distato.it

Embassies and Consulates

Australia
Via Antonio Bosio 5, Rome. **Tel** 06 85 27 21.
w italy.embassy.gov.au

New Zealand
Via Clitunno 44, Rome.
Tel 06 853 75 01.
w nzembassy.com

UK
Lungarno Corsini 2, Florence. **Map** 3 B1 (5 B3).
Tel 055 28 41 33.
w ukinitaly.fco.gov.uk

USA
Lungarno Amerigo Vespucci 38, Florence.
Map 1 A5 (5 A2).
Tel 055 26 69 51.
w florence. usconsulate.gov

Tourist Information

Italian Tourism Board
w italia.it

Tourism Florence
Via Alessandro Manzone 16, Florence.
Map 2 F5.
Tel 055 23 32 0.
Via Cavour 1r, Florence.
Map 2 D4 (6 D1).
Tel 055 29 08 32.
w firenzeturismo.it

Tourism Pisa
Piazza del Duomo, Pisa.
Tel 050 56 04 64.
w pisaunicaterra.it

Tourism Siena
Piazza del Campo 56, Siena.
Tel 0577 28 05 51.
w terresiena.it

Turismo in Toscana
w turismo.intoscana.it

Admission Prices

Amici dei Musei
w amicidei museifiorentini.it

Booking Line (Uffizi and Accademia)
Tel 055 294883.

Firenze Card
w firenzecard.it

Firenze Musei
Tel 055 29 48 83 (tickets).
w firenzemusei.it
w museicivicifiorentini. comune.fi.it

Travellers with Special Needs

Accessible Italy
Tel +378 94 11 11.
w accessibleitaly.com

Trenitalia
Tel 199 30 30 60.
w trenitalia.com

Gay Travellers

Information
w arcigay.it
w ireos.org

Student and Budget Travellers

Accommodation
w ostellofirenze.it
w monasterystays.com

CTS Viaggi
Borgo La Croce 42/r, Florence. **Tel** 055 28 95 70.
Via Bandini 21, Siena.
Tel 0577 28 50 08.
w cts.it

Educational Courses

British Institute
Lungarno Guicciardini 9, 50125 Florence. **Map** 3 B1 (5 B3). **Tel** 055 267 78 270.
w britishinstitute.it

Centro Internazionale Dante Alighieri

Via Tommaso Pendola 36, 53100 Siena.
Tel 0577 495 33.

The Learning Center of Tuscany

Viale Corsica 15c, 50134 Florence.
Tel 055 051 50 35.
w learningcenter tuscany.com

Palazzo Spinelli Istituto per l'Arte e il Restauro

Borgo Santa Croce 10, 50122 Florence.
Map 4 E1 (6 F4).
Tel 055 24 60 01.
w palazzospinelli.org

Università per Stranieri

Via Pantaneto 45, 53100 Siena.
Tel 0577 24 01 11.
w unistrasi.it

Responsible Tourism

Context Travel
Via Baccina 40, Rome.
Tel 06 97 62 52 04.
w contexttravel.com

Personal Security and Health

Tuscany and its cities are generally safe, as long as common-sense precautions are taken. Reports of serious crimes are rare, but petty theft and pickpocketing are common problems in the crowded tourist areas of Florence and Pisa. Ensure that you have adequate travel insurance before leaving for Italy, as it is very difficult to obtain once you are in the country.

Police

The *vigili urbani*, or municipal police *(see p305)*, wear blue uniforms in winter and white during summer. They are most often seen on the streets, regulating traffic. The *carabinieri* are the military police. They dress in black trousers with a red stripe on the leg and deal with a variety of offences, from theft to speeding. *La polizia* (the state police) wear grey trousers with a magenta stripe. They specialize in serious crimes. While uniforms differ, in an emergency the first officer on the scene is responsible and will help you.

A team of *carabinieri* on duty in Florence

What to be Aware of

When looking after your personal safety, use common sense as you would in any large city. Pickpocketing takes place on public transport and in crowded piazzas, markets and queues. Italian women tend to keep one hand on the closure of their handbag at all times (zip closures are best), while men put a hand over the pocket in which they keep their wallet. Theft from cars can be a problem, so never leave anything of value in your hire car.

Women should not walk home alone late at night. Always use official taxis, which clearly display their licence number. When you call for a taxi, you will be given the car number, for example Napoli 37, which will be visible on a sticker on the side of the taxi.

In an Emergency

The telephone number for medical emergency services is **118** and the operator should be able to assist you. Report all serious crime to the police, through dialling **112**.

Lost and Stolen Property

Avoid being a victim of theft in Tuscany in the same way as you would at home: lock doors, keep valuables in a safe and never leave anything in plain view inside a car. In the case of robbery, you must report the theft to the police within 24 hours and obtain a statement (*denuncia*) in order to make an insurance claim. Ask your hotel reception for assistance in doing this.

Lost property may be difficult to recover. Lost items on trains can sometimes be located by asking customer services. In some stations, lost bags will be put in a safe deposit box and you will have to pay to collect them.

Minor Hazards

Inoculations are not necessary for Tuscany. Mosquitoes are an irritation. Equip yourself with mosquito repellent as these insects are common, especially in the centre of Florence, and screens on windows are rare.

Alternatively, use an electrical device (referred to as *vape*, from the brand name), which works by heating mosquito repellent in tablet or liquid form. *Vape* can repel mosquitoes for up to 12 hours. These small devices are available in grocery stores and houseware shops (*mesticheria*). For a longer stay, you might prefer to use a temporary window net or to place a mosquito net over your bed. Both are available from a *mesticheria*.

Do not underestimate the strength of the sun – drink plenty of water and use a high-factor sunscreen. Although Italians prefer the taste of bottled water, tap water is perfectly safe in the cities. Many rural homes use water from a well – visitors may prefer to drink bottled water.

Hospitals and Pharmacies

If you are in need of urgent medical attention, you should go at once to the *Pronto Soccorso* (outpatients/emergency) department of the nearest main hospital.

If you have a medical problem during the night or at the weekend, but it is not an emergency, the **Guardia Medica** service in Florence is a fast and easy solution, similar to a walk-in medical clinic. It is open through the night and at weekends, and may charge a small fee for treatment.

In the summer, major tourist areas (including Florence and Siena) set up a Tourist Medical Centre, which operates during daytime hours.

Outside a typical pharmacy (*farmacia*) in Florence

Police car patrolling Campo dei Miracoli, in Pisa

In Florence and Siena, the **Associazione Volontari Ospedalieri** has interpreters who can help with medical matters. The service is free and available in English, French, German and Spanish.

If you need a dentist during your stay in Tuscany, ask for a recommendation at your hotel or look for an English-speaking dentist in the English yellow pages (www.insidersabroad. com/englishyellowpages).

Pharmacies in Tuscany have a night and weekend rota *(servizio notturno)* posted on their doors.

The **Farmacia Comunale 13,** at Florence's Santa Maria Novella station, is open 24 hours a day, as is the **Farmacia Molteni** in Via dei Calzaiuoli. Pharmacies do not usually accept prescriptions from other countries.

The Misericordia is one of the world's oldest charitable lay institutions and arranges many ambulance services in Tuscany. Most of the staff are volunteers, but there is also a fully qualified medical team. The traditional black cassock is for formal parade only; volunteers do not wear it during medical emergencies.

Travel and Health Insurance

Visitors from the EU are officially entitled to reciprocal state medical care in Italy. Before you travel, pick up a European Health Insurance Card (EHIC), which covers emergency medical treatment.

It is available online (www. dh.gov.uk) or at the post office. The EHIC does not cover repatriation costs or additional expenses, such as accommodation or flights, for anyone travelling with you. Purchasing additional travel insurance before leaving home is always recommended.

Visitors from outside the EU should take out a comprehensive travel-insurance policy before travelling.

Fleet of ambulances run by the Misericordia at a Florence hospital

DIRECTORY

Emergency Numbers

Ambulance
Tel 118.

Automobile Club d'Italia
Tel 116.
W aci.it

Fire
Tel 115.

General SOS
Tel 113.

Medical Emergencies
Tel 118.

Police (Carabinieri)
Tel 112.

Medical Service Firenze
Via Roma 4, Florence.
Map 1 C5 (6 D2).
Tel 055 47 54 11.

Traffic Police
Florence
Tel 055 506 81.
Pisa
Tel 050 31 39 21.
Siena
Tel 0577 24 62 11.

Questura (Police Offices)

Florence
Via Zara 2, Florence.
Map 2 D3.
Tel 055 497 71.

Siena
Via del Castoro, Siena.
Tel 0577 20 11 11.

Pisa
Via Lalli 4, Pisa.
Tel 050 58 35 11.

24-Hour Pharmacies

Farmacia Comunale 13
Santa Maria Novella station, Florence.
Map 1 B4 (5 B1).
Tel 055 21 67 61.

Farmacia Molteni
Via dei Calzaiuoli 7r, Florence.
Map 6 D3.
Tel 055 28 94 90.

Hospitals

Arcispedale di Santa Maria Nuova
Piazza di Santa Maria Nuova 1.
Map 6 F2.
Tel 055 275 81.

Associazione Volontari Ospedalieri
Florence
Tel 055 234 45 67.
Siena
Tel 0577 24 78 69.

Azienda Ospedaliero-Universitaria Careggi
Via delle Oblate 1, Florence.
Tel 055 794 111.

Guardia Medica
Piazza Del Duomo 20, Florence.
Tel 055 28 77 88.
Via Sant Agostino 6, Oltrarno.
Tel 055 21 56 16.

Meyer Children's Hospital
Viale Gaetano Pieraccini 24.
Tel 055 566 21.

Pisa Hospital
Ospedale di Santa Chiara, Via Roma 67.
Tel 050 99 21 11.

Siena Hospital
Policlinico Le Scotte, Viale Bracci 16.
Tel 0577 58 61 11.

Lost Credit Cards

American Express
Tel 06 722 82.

Diners Club
Tel 800 86 40 64 (freephone).

VISA
Tel 800 87 72 32 (freephone).

Lost Traveller's Cheques

American Express
Tel 800 87 20 00 (freephone).

Banking and Currency

Visitors to Tuscany have a number of options available to them for changing money. Banks and ATMs tend to give more favourable rates than bureaux de change, hotels and travel agents, but the paperwork when using a bank is usually more time consuming. When changing money you will need to show some form of identification, such as a passport. Alternatively, credit cards can be used for purchasing goods. Traveller's cheques are no longer frequently used.

A typical ATM point in the centre of Florence

Entering and leaving a bank through an electronic double door

Banks and Bureaux de Change

Major banks are usually open from 8:30am to 8pm Monday to Friday and from 8:30am to 1pm on Saturdays. They close on Sundays and for public holidays *(see p41)*. Exchange offices have long opening hours, but in general their rates are less favourable than those at banks.

In Florence, the exchange office behind the railway station is open from 8am till late evening, depending on the season. In Pisa, the exchange offices in Piazza del Duomo and at the railway station are open until the evening and at weekends. To change money at a bank, bring your passport

and be prepared to fill out numerous forms. As procedures vary from branch to branch, it may be worth asking staff for help.

For security reasons, most Italian banks have electronic double doors. Press the button to open the outer door, then wait for it to close behind you. The inner door then opens automatically. Metal objects may set off emergency detectors as you enter. You may be asked to deposit your belongings in lockers outside the secured area.

ATMs

The most convenient way to access your cash in Italy is to make withdrawals using an ATM. To avoid complications, check which cards the ATM accepts before inserting your card. Travelling with more than one debit (and credit) card is recommended in case one is not accepted. Most ATM machines accept VISA or MasterCard for cash advances, but be aware that interest is payable as soon as the money is withdrawn.

Italian ATMs dispense a maximum daily amount (approximately €300), so if

you need to make a larger cash payment you should plan ahead and make withdrawals from cash machines over more than one day.

Before your trip, be sure to tell your bank that you are travelling to Italy. They should remove any flags or limits on your bank and credit cards to avoid having them blocked. Ask your bank if you need a different PIN number for use in Italy: if you have a 6-digit PIN it may not work, as Italian ATMs usually accept 4- or 5-digit PINs only.

Credit Cards and Traveller's Cheques

Credit cards are widely accepted throughout Italy, and it is worth bringing one, or more, with you. VISA and MasterCard are the most popular, while American Express and Diners Card are rarely accepted. To avoid problems using your card during a trip you should inform your credit card company before travelling.

Some restaurants, cafés and shops may require a minimum expenditure to accept credit card payment. Be aware that some petrol stations do not accept credit cards, only cash. Always make sure you have some cash in case your card is not accepted.

Traveller's cheques are no longer in common use. Few stores will accept them (or even know what they are) although hotels may accept them for payment or exchange. If a bureau de change does accept traveller's cheques, be aware that there is a minimum commission charge, which may make changing small sums of money uneconomical.

A branch of Banca Toscana, seen widely across the region

The Euro

The euro (€) is the common currency of the European Union. It went into general circulation on 1 January 2002, initially for 12 participating countries. Italy was one of those 12 countries, and the lira was phased out in February 2002. EU members using the euro as their sole official currency are known as the Eurozone. Several EU members have opted out of joining this common currency.

Euro notes are identical throughout the Eurozone, each one including designs of fictional architectural structures and monuments. The coins, however, have one side identical (the value side), and one side with an image unique to each country. Both notes and coins are exchangeable in each participating country.

Euro Bank Notes

Euro bank notes have seven denominations. The €5 note (grey in colour) is the smallest, followed by the €10 note (pink), €20 note (blue), €50 note (orange), €100 note (green), €200 note (yellow) and €500 note (purple).

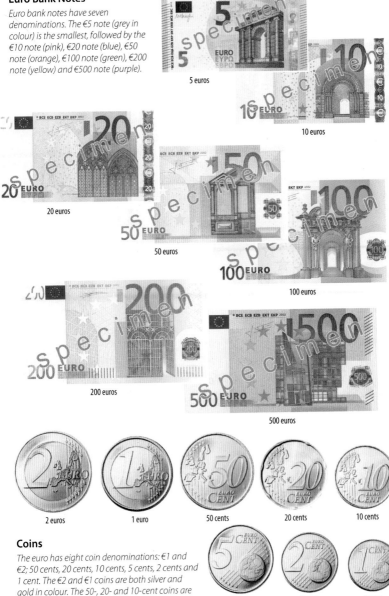

5 euros

10 euros

20 euros

50 euros

100 euros

200 euros

500 euros

2 euros

1 euro

50 cents

20 cents

10 cents

Coins

The euro has eight coin denominations: €1 and €2; 50 cents, 20 cents, 10 cents, 5 cents, 2 cents and 1 cent. The €2 and €1 coins are both silver and gold in colour. The 50-, 20- and 10-cent coins are gold. The 5-, 2- and 1-cent coins are bronze.

5 cents

2 cents

1 cent

Communications and Media

Payphones are few and far between in Italy, as access to Internet services and the use of mobile phones have increased. Pre-paid long-distance telephone cards are also now increasingly used by visitors. The postal service in Italy, once dogged by slow service, is much improved and also offers relatively fast courier services. Italians produce a lot of magazines (though fewer newspapers), and international and foreign-language print material can be found in areas catering to large numbers of tourists.

Reaching the Right Number

- City dialling codes are: Florence 055; Siena 0577; Pisa 050; Viareggio 0584; Arezzo 0575; Lucca 0583; Pistoia 0573.
- Mobile dialling codes begin with 3 (no 0).
- International operator assistance is on 170. You can place reverse-charge and credit-card calls on this number.
- *See also* Emergency Numbers, *p293*.

International and Local Telephone Calls

The growing use of mobile phones in Italy has caused a cutback in public-telephone services. Telecom Italia no longer has telephone offices, although there are some privately operated calling centres offering international phone services. Payphones are rare on the street, although there should be working payphones at train stations and airports. To use a public payphone, you need to purchase a Telecom Italia *scheda telefonica* card at any *tabacchi* or newsagent. Insert the card before making a call. You can also use a pre-paid long-distance calling card in public payphones (without using a Telecom *scheda*), also available from *tabacchi*. These have an 800 number on the back and a scratch-off code.

When dialling locally, city landline numbers start with a 0. To make a long-distance call, dial 00, followed by the country code and area code, before dialling the number. If using a long-distance calling card, use the 800 number provided, dial the country and area codes (without the 00 prefix), and then dial the number.

You can usually make land-line phone calls from your hotel, although these are expensive – ask for a price list if it is not displayed. You can also use long-distance calling cards with hotel phones – it should be free to connect. Most private apartment rentals

Telephone company logo

and *agriturismi* do not have phones in guest rooms. Faxes can be sent from post offices, copy centres, *cartolerie* (paper/office stores) and Internet points.

Mobile Phones

The cost of mobile phones and services has reduced to such an extent that it can now make sense to buy a mobile phone in Italy if you are visiting for more than a week and intend to use your phone a lot. Two major providers, **TIM** and **Vodafone**, sell basic phones for around €30, including a SIM card with €5 credit. Phones can also be bought from super-markets or electrical-supply shops and you can purchase additional credit from any *tabacchi*, newsagent or phone store (be sure to specify the carrier name). To buy a phone, you will need a copy of your passport. However, it is possible to buy an unlocked Italian mobile phone and SIM online before your trip. The SIM usually expires one year from your last top up.

If you have an unlocked phone from the UK or Europe, you can purchase an Italian SIM and use it in your phone. Alternatively, set up a roaming agreement with your provider, although these can be prohib-itively expensive. Keep in mind

Public-payphone sign

that charges for checking mes-sages and Internet usage while roaming ramp up quickly – connect to Wi-Fi where you can.

If you are travelling from North America, Australia or New Zealand, a tri-band/GSM phone should, technically, work in Italy. Check with your phone operator about roaming charges.

When using an Italian mobile phone, note that calls between phones using the same provider may cost less than calls to mobile phones serviced by other providers, depending on the package you signed up to. Long-distance rates are usually high, but you can use a long-distance calling card with your mobile phone – calls will still cost more than from a landline, however.

Internet and Wi-Fi

Increasing numbers of hotels and businesses are providing free or paid Internet services to their customers, and some Italian cities plan to offer free Wi-Fi for residents and tourists. You will be required to complete a brief registration process to use any Internet service in Italy.

If your hotel Internet service is fast, Skype calls via your laptop will be perfectly viable; calls to landlines will require a small cash credit. Skype also allows you to make calls to toll-free numbers in the US and UK (convenient if you need to contact your bank or credit card company), though you will be charged at the standard rate for these calls.

For those without a laptop, there are also many privately operated Internet points in Tuscany. In small towns, these may be located at the back of a store or bar. **Internet Train** (www.internettrain.it) has 25 stores in Tuscany (with eight in Florence); you simply buy a charged magnetic card that can be used across their network.

Newspaper kiosk stocking all major newspapers and magazines

Postal Services

To send letters or postcards, purchase stamps *(francobolli)* at any *tabacchi*. There is usually a red mailbox right outside. Mailboxes have two slots: the one designated *per la città* is only for destinations within the city; *altri destinazioni* is for everywhere else.

For oversized letters or packages, go to the post office. Sub-post office hours are usually 8:30am–2pm Mon–Sat. Main offices stay open until 8pm. Post offices also provide banking services, so for the postal desk you must follow the correct procedure. Take a number from the yellow machine with the green envelope symbol by the entrance. The letter "P", combined with your number, will be called out.

Priority mail *(posta prioritaria)* now designates regular airmail. Delivery time is somewhat variable, ranging from four days to six weeks worldwide. However, the post office

also offers a well-priced international and national courier service *(paccocelere)* for tracked, on-time mail. Fedex and UPS are the main consumer courier services. Check www.fedex.com and www.ups.com for offices in Tuscany. **Mailboxes Etc.** also ships mail using either courier; they have five stores in Florence and one in each of Siena, Arezzo and Pisa.

Addresses

Florence has a confusing dual-address system. Each street has a double set of numbers: a red number indicates a shop, restaurant or business, while a blue or black number refers to a hotel or domestic resi-dence. When writing to a business, insert an "r" after the number to distinguish it from a residential address. Each set of numbers has its own sequence, so business premises at, say, No. 10r may well be next to a residential address at No. 23.

Newspapers and Magazines

Most Italian newspapers, such as *La Repubblica* and *La Nazione*, publish supplements with a regional focus. Daily European and American newspapers, such as *USA Today* and the *Financial Times*, are widely available. The regional magazine for Tuscany in English is *The Tuscan Magazine*.

Television

There are a dozen Italian TV channels, including two music channels (MTV and DeeJay). Many hotels have satellite TV with BBC and CNN news in English, as well as German and French channels.

DIRECTORY

Mobile Phones

TIM
Via dei Lamberti 12, Firenze.
Via Salicotto 11, Siena.
W **tim.it**

Vodafone
Via de'Martelli 31, Firenze.
Via del Paradiso 30, Siena.
W **vodafone.it**

Main Post Offices

Pellicceria 3, Florence. Map 6 D3.
Tel 055 273 61.
Piazza Matteotti 37, Siena.
Tel 0577 21 42 95.
Piazza Vittorio Emanuele II, Pisa.
Tel 050 51 95 14.

Couriers

Mailboxes Etc.
Florence: Via San Gallo 61r;
Corso Tintori 39r. W **mbe.it**

Busy main hall at Florence's central post office

TRAVEL INFORMATION

Tuscany is easily reached by air, with airports in both Florence and Pisa. Amerigo Vespucci (Peretola) airport in Florence offers connections with all major European cities, although it does not accommodate long-haul flights. Pisa airport (Galileo Galilei) receives scheduled and low-cost flights, including a direct international New York JFK–Pisa flight daily in summer.

The city of Florence is also well connected by train and coach from most European cities. Train and coach travel, although slower and not necessarily cheaper, is a greener alternative to flying or driving.

Check-in area at Florence airport

Green Travel

Getting to Tuscany from mainland Europe without flying is possible due to Italy's excellent train network, which serves major towns and cities, including Florence, Pisa and Arezzo. Small discounts are available if travelling by train in a group of 10 or more. For information on train travel *see pp300–1*.

For those areas of Tuscany that are badly served by train, such as Siena and the coast, you may need to rent a car – look for economical diesel-engine models that use less fuel. If you want to explore the rolling hills of Tuscany without a car, two options are worth considering: **ATAF** *(see p307)* offers an inexpensive coach tour of the Chianti area, while a tourist steam train *(see p301)* runs occasional scenic day trips to seasonal fairs. Most towns and cities can be explored on foot or using local buses *(see p302)*. Electric minibuses are used on some routes in Florence's city centre.

Arriving by Air

There are numerous daily arrivals at both Florence and Pisa airports from all major airlines, including **Alitalia** and **British Airways**. Some of the low-cost airlines serve the region through Pisa's airport, Galileo Galilei; **Ryanair** flies from numerous airports in the UK and Ireland, while **easyJet** flies from London Gatwick and Luton, north of London.

Although direct intercontinental flights to Pisa airport are increasing, you may have to consider flying to Rome and taking the train up to Florence. The journey is approximately 1 hour 25 mins. Alternatively, you could hire a car in Rome and drive to Tuscany. Alitalia flies direct to Rome from Los Angeles, Chicago, Montreal, Toronto, Perth and Melbourne, and other airlines offer worldwide connections via Rome and other European capitals.

Florence Airport (FLR)

Florence's Amerigo Vespucci airport, often known as Peretola, is small, with relatively few shops and bars. The shuttle bus **VolaInBus** goes to and from the airport every 30 minutes 6am–8pm and hourly 9–11pm. The bus to the city centre leaves from in front of the airport building, while the bus to the airport departs from Florence's Santa Maria Novella train station. The evening buses (from 9pm) leave from Piazza dell'Unità. The journey takes 20 minutes and tickets may be purchased from the driver. Line 2 of the tramway system will link the airport to Santa Maria Novella train station and Piazza Libertà. It is currently under construction and will hopefully open in 2016.

Only take a taxi from the official taxi rank. Drivers will charge a supplement for coming from the airport, plus a supplement for any luggage. There is also an extra charge on Sundays and holidays. Fares start at €20 for the journey to/from the airport. Check that the meter is switched on at departure.

Modern exterior of Florence's Amerigo Vespucci airport

Entrance to Pisa's Galileo Galilei airport

Pisa Airport (PSA)

Pisa airport has several shops, bars and restaurants. There are no money-changing facilities in the baggage hall, so take some euros with you in order to hire a trolley.

There is a taxi rank at the front of the airport and good public-transport links. Trains run directly from Pisa's airport to Florence's Santa Maria Novella station. To reach the trains, turn left as you leave the airport arrivals hall. Train tickets must be bought from the information kiosk at the airport. The journey to Florence takes 1 hour and the service generally runs once an hour, but is less regular in the early morning and evening. There is also an infrequent train serving Lucca and Montecatini. The train to Florence stops at Pisa Centrale and Empoli, where you can change on to the local line serving Siena.

Terravision runs a shuttle bus from Pisa Airport to Florence Airport and SMN railway station near Florence's city centre. Book tickets in advance online or buy them at the airport.

On the platform at Pisa airport's train station

The No. 3 bus runs from Pisa airport to the town centre, tickets cost around €2. Buy tickets before you get on the bus from the airport information kiosk.

Air Tickets and Fares

It is worth shopping around for the lowest air fares online. There is no rule as to when the best prices may come up; if fares seem high when you start looking, try a few days later and you may be pleasantly surprised. A good way to start is by comparing online prices at Expedia and Travelocity, and looking at the airlines' own websites. Signing up for email alerts or special offers is another way of getting a good deal.

Package Holidays

Package holidays incorporating a stay in Florence with nights in Rome and Venice are often available. Compare prices online and look at websites for major hotel resellers, such as Expedia. Whilst convenient, package deals are not always a cheaper option. Through contacting a hotel directly, it may be possible to negotiate a lower rate than those found online. This is also a good way to support local hoteliers, as they will receive payment direct from the customer.

Car Rental

All the major car-rental firms have rental offices at both Florence and Pisa airports. However, it is cheaper to make

DIRECTORY

Airline Information

Alitalia
Tel 06 22 22.
W alitalia.it

British Airways
Tel 199 71 22 66.
W britishairways.com

EasyJet
W easyjet.com

Ryanair
Tel 050 50 37 70 or
899 67 89 10.
W ryanair.com

Airport Information and Transfers

Florence
Tel 055 306 13 00.
W aeroporto.firenze.it

Pisa
Tel 050 84 93 00 &
050 84 91 11.
W pisa-airport.com

Terravision
W terravision.eu

VolaInBus
W ataf.net

Airport Car Rental

Avis
Florence Airport: Tel 055 31 55 88.
Pisa Airport: Tel 050 420 28.
W avis.com

Hertz
Florence Airport: Tel 055 30 73 70.
Pisa Airport: Tel 050 491 87.
W hertz.com

Maggiore
Florence Airport: Tel 055 31 12 56.
Pisa Airport: Tel 050 425 74.
W maggiore.it

rental arrangements before your departure (see p305).

Leaving Pisa airport by car, it is straightforward to get on to the dual carriageway linking Pisa and Florence. At Florence airport, turn right to get on to the A1 highway (Rome–Bologna). It is not advisable to drive into the centre of Florence (see p304).

Travelling by Train

Travelling overland can be a pleasurable way of getting to, and travelling around, Tuscany. Italy's state railway (Trenitalia) has a train for every type of journey, from the quaintly slow *regionale* (local trains) through various levels of rapid intercity service to the luxurious, super-fast Frecciarossa, which rushes between Italian cities at a speed to match its ticket price. The network between large cities is good, but journeys to towns on branch lines may be quicker by coach *(see p302)*.

Frecciarossa (red arrow) train at
Santa Maria Novella station

Arriving by Train

Florence is a major arrival point for trains from Europe, including the Galilei from Paris and the Italia Express from Frankfurt. Passengers from London have to change in Paris or Lille. From Florence, there is a direct train link with Pisa's airport *(see p299)*.

Trains from all over Italy arrive at, and depart from, Pisa Centrale and Florence's Santa Maria Novella stations. Trenitalia's high-speed train Frecciarossa and privately run high-speed Italo both stop at Santa Maria Novella on their main rail link between Milan and Rome via Bologna. The high-speed trains also run to Venice, Naples and Turin.

Some intercity and regional trains stop at Florence's other two (smaller) stations; from here, you can take a regional train to Santa Maria Novella for free, or it may be quicker to take a local bus to your final destination *(see p306)*.

Santa Maria Novella Station, Florence

Santa Maria Novella *(see p117)* is Florence's central railway station. It is always crowded and attracts some unsavoury characters, so you need to be vigilant and take care of your belongings. There is a taxi rank in front,

and local buses *(see p306)* depart from the side of the building.

Facilities include a left-luggage office, a pharmacy, a *sala blu* (for disabled-traveller assistance), a hotel-booking service and newspaper kiosks which also sell city-bus tickets. The nearest tourist information office is at Piazza della Stazione 4, across the street. Florence also has two other, smaller train stations – Campo de Marte and Rifredi – running some regional trains and intercity night trains.

Siena Station

Siena's train station is situated outside the city walls on Piazzale Carlo Roselli. It is quite small and about a 20-minute walk from the centre. Any bus from opposite the station goes to the city centre. The TRA-IN bus company *(see p307)* runs coaches to Montepulciano, Montalcino and Buonconvento. These depart from the front of the station. Tickets must be bought from the bus-ticket window or self-service machines before you board.

Pisa Centrale

Pisa's central station is quite large, with facilities including a restaurant and bar, newspaper kiosks selling bus tickets, a currency-exchange booth and left-luggage office.

Tourist information is at the front of the station. Most local buses, including to the Campo dei Miracoli *(see pp162–3)* and the airport, stop in front of the station. A bus-information and ticket office are close by. Pisa also has another train station at the airport *(see p299)*.

Tickets and Fares

Fares vary by train type (the slowest trains cost the least) and class (first and second). Fares and timetables for **Trenitalia** and **Italo** trains are listed online. Fast trains have obligatory seat booking, while regional trains do not have reserved seats.

There are often special offers online for certain trains or destinations, as well as online price variations for fast trains (Eurostar, Frecciarossa and Italo). You can get a 15–30 per cent discount on advance bookings for the Frecciarossa, but such tickets come with limited flexibility if you need to change your booking later; you can also pay a 20 per cent surcharge in order to have total flexibility.

Trenitalia offers a Travelcard for one week, two weeks or a month on the route and train type of your choice, offering 1,000 km (620 miles) of travel during the specified period. Travelcards can be purchased online or at train stations.

Logo on an intercity train

Buying Tickets

Always buy a ticket before you travel, otherwise you will be charged the price of a full-fare ticket plus a €50 fine. If the ticket office is busy, try one of the self-service ticket machines found at most stations. You must validate your ticket before every trip by stamping it in one of the yellow machines situated at the entrance to most platforms. If you forget to stamp your ticket, write the time and date on the edge of the ticket and explain your error to the inspector in order to avoid paying a fine.

To purchase Trenitalia tickets online, you must first register at www.trenitalia.com. American Express is not accepted. You can download and print your ticket in PDF form or show the reservation number to the agent on the train. Tickets bought online do not need to be validated. When booking tickets online, make sure you are aware of any limitations on flexibility – most tickets purchased online can only be amended online, and sometimes a penalty will be incurred. If you think you may want to change your ticket later, wait to purchase it at the train station once you are in Italy. In most cases, a few days' advance purchase will be sufficient to get the train of your choice, except on or around major holidays.

Some regional trains allow you to bring a bicycle on board; these are indicated by a bicycle symbol on the train timetable. Tickets for bicycles (valid for all trips within a 24-hour period) can only be purchased at the train station; stamp both sides before boarding and attach half to the bicycle itself.

Rail Passes

Europe-wide train passes, such as EurRail (US) or InterRail for those under 26 (Europe), are accepted on the FS network – supplements are payable on fast trains and there are restrictions on private lines. A senior railcard, offering a 15 per cent fare reduction, is available *(see p290)*.

Tourist Trains

Ferrovie Turistiche offers day trips on historic steam trains for tourists. A popular trip is to Marradi, a delightful mountain town bordering Tuscany and Emilia-Romagna that hosts a chestnut festival each November and a Christmas fair in December.

Machines for Trenitalia Rail Tickets

Ticket machines at main stations have a multi-language touch screen and accept credit and bank cards, as well as cash. Regional stations may be unmanned and often have rather basic ticket machines that take cash only and do not issue change. If you put in too much cash, you will be issued with a paper receipt – you need to take this to the nearest main station for a refund.

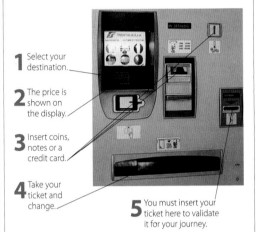

1 Select your destination.

2 The price is shown on the display.

3 Insert coins, notes or a credit card.

4 Take your ticket and change.

5 You must insert your ticket here to validate it for your journey.

Italy's Principal Rail Network

The Italian State Rail Network operates various types of service. Check fares and timetables at www.trenitalia.com. All trains have facilities for disabled travellers *(see p289)*.

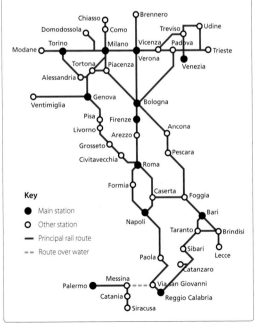

Key

● Main station
○ Other station
— Principal rail route
-- Route over water

Travelling by Bus and Coach

Florence is linked by coach to most major European cities, and local companies operate an extensive network of services within Tuscany. Coaches are considered to be quicker where there is no direct train link, particularly in the countryside. Although trains are faster for long journeys, coaches may be a cheaper option. The coach companies' main offices, usually situated near city railway stations, stock timetables and route maps to help you plan your journey. This information is also provided online, but due to the complexity of schedules, it is usually more helpful to consult a local travel agent.

A ticket office in Pisa, selling Lazzi and CPT tickets

Arriving by Coach

Santa Maria Novella railway station in Florence is Tuscany's main arrival and departure point for all long-distance coach journeys, and the hub of the extensive local coach network. The **Lazzi** company runs coach services to major European cities from Florence and sells tickets for Eurolines coaches. Tickets can be booked at their office by Santa Maria Novella station. There are express services from Florence to Rome, run by Lazzi, and from Florence to Siena, run by **TRA-IN** or **SITA**.

The Network

Florence has four main coach companies. Lazzi serves the region north and west of Florence and SITA serves the southern and eastern regions (including Siena, San Gimignano and Volterra). The **COPIT** bus company connects the city with the Abetone/Pistoia region and **CAP** links it to the Mugello area, north of the city. All of these companies have ticket and information offices near Santa Maria Novella railway station.

Siena's main bus and coach company is TRA-IN, which runs local and regional services. Local services leave from Piazza Antonio Gramsci and regional buses from Piazza San Domenico. There is a ticket office in both squares. TRA-IN runs buses to most of Tuscany, including a direct coach to Rome twice daily.

In Pisa, the city bus company **CPT** serves the surrounding area, including the towns of Volterra, Livorno, San Miniato and Pontedera. These buses leave from Piazza Sant'Antonio. Lazzi runs a service to Viareggio, Lucca and Florence from Pisa, departing from Piazza Vittorio Emanuele II, where there is a Lazzi ticket office. Arezzo's **La Ferroviaria Italiana** bus lines connect to all the small towns nearby, including Cortona.

Tickets and Reservations

Coach tickets must be purchased at an authorized ticket reseller or at the bus company's office. It's worth discussing your requirements with a travel agent, who can help you understand the complex schedules and routes. On most routes, reserved seating is not available. Passengers need to line up before the bus departure time in order to get a seat. Expect a long wait around the holidays.

A SITA coach, serving southern and eastern Tuscany

Travelling by Ferry and River Boat

Tuscany has a long and beautiful coast that boasts seven islands, of which Elba, Giglio, Capraia and Giannutri are visitable. All are well served by the ferry companies Moby and Toremar, especially during the summer months. The mainland ports are Piombino, Santo Stefano and Livorno (Leghorn). The closest airport is Pisa, from which you can reach Piombino by a combination of bus and train, or by car. For Livorno, bus No. 101 from the airport arrives in Livorno city; from there, switch buses for the port.

Portoferraio, the main port on Elba

Arriving by Ferry

Tuscany can be reached by ferry from other regions of Italy. Livorno is connected to Sardinia (port of Cagliari) and Sicily (Palermo); Piombino connects to Sardinia (Olbia) and Corsica (Bastia). Livorno is also the major port for international cruise ships.

Ports

Tuscany's mainland ports are Livorno, Piombino and Porto Santo Stefano. On the islands, Elba's main port is Portoferraio, along with the smaller Rio Marina and Porto Azzurro. The other islands have only one tourist port.

  If you arrive at Stazione Marittima, at the port of Livorno, and wish to take a self-guided day trip to Florence, the train is your best option. It takes 1½ hours and there are trains every hour. Take the shuttle bus (€5 return) from the port to Piazza Grande, in front of the Duomo. From here, various city bus lines go to Livorno Centrale train station. Alternatively, Piazza Grande is about 10 minutes' walk from where ferries dock.

It will take longer to walk from other parts of the port used by major cruise lines, but taxis are available. From the port, there is also a bus service to Pisa Airport and Pisa train station, which takes around 35 minutes. The train to Pisa runs approximately every 20 minutes and the journey takes 15–20 minutes.

Travelling by Ferry

When driving to any port, follow signs for *Porto/Imbarchi* and then the sign for your chosen ferry company (**Moby** or **Toremar**).

  If you are taking your vehicle on the ferry, you will be directed to line up and turn off your engine in a numbered lot to await the boat. There is also short- and long-term parking available at Livorno and Piombino.

  Washrooms are scarce at ports, but services on board are available and reasonably clean. Ferries have both indoor and outdoor seating and a snack bar. There is limited shade outdoors so be sure to wear a hat.

Ferries from Piombino to Elba and Porto Santo Stefano to Isola del Giglio take approximately 1 hour. Livorno to Capraia is nearly 3½ hours on the ferry or 1½ hours on the fast boat (passengers only, no vehicles). Ticket costs vary depending on what vehicle you take and the number of passengers you are travelling with. Toremar tends to be the cheaper option.

Tickets

Tickets for all ferries can be purchased directly from the ferry company. It's also worth checking their websites, which may have special offers. Avoid resellers who may charge extra. Advance booking is strongly recommended if you are travelling with a vehicle; for travel in August, you will need to book a few weeks in advance. Individuals travelling without a vehicle can usually get tickets on the day of travel.

River-Boat Tours

From June through to September, the **Renaioli Association** in Florence offers inexpensive 1 hour boat tours on the Arno, departing from near Ponte alle Grazie. Boats seat up to 16 people, with a minimum of six people per group. It is possible to reserve a tour guide to accompany you on the tour. Price varies by number of guests and use of guide.

DIRECTORY

Ferry operators

Moby
Tel 02 76 028 132 (from abroad).
Tel 199 30 30 40 (from Italy, toll).
W moby.it

Toremar
Tel 02 26 302 803 (from abroad).
Tel 892 123 (from Italy, toll).
W toremar.it

River-Boat Tours

Renaioli Association (Arno tour) and Tickets
Tel 347 7982 356.
W renaioli.it
W info@renaiolo.it

Driving in Florence and Tuscany

There are certain areas of Tuscany, such as tiny hill towns and authentic *agritourismo* locations, which are best reached by car. However, heavy traffic in some areas and narrow roads in others can make driving difficult, and it is unwise to drive without someone to help navigate. Train and coach travel *(see pp300–2)* are good options for reaching larger towns and cities. It is best to avoid having a car if you intend to stay in the cities of Florence or Siena; both cities restrict car traffic and parking is difficult and expensive.

Country road in the mountainous Garfagnana region of Tuscany

Arriving by Car

The main *autostrada* (toll highway) that services Tuscany (between Rome and Bologna) is the A1, also known as *Autostrada del Sole. Autostrada* signage is green. The Firenze–Mare (A11) goes to Pisa, Lucca and the coast. There are two *superstradas* (four-lane highways): the Firenze–Siena and the "Fi–Pi–Li", short for the cities it serves (Firenze, Pisa and Livorno). *Superstrada* signage is blue. Both types of highway have large service stations with good facilities, including restaurants and shops selling everything from *prosciutto* to DVDs.

Drivers from the UK need a Green Card for insurance purposes, and the vehicle's registration document. EU nationals who intend to stay for more than six months and do not have the standard pink licence will need an Italian translation of their licence (IDP: International Drivers' Permit), available from most motoring organizations and Italian tourist offices.

SOS columns on the road allow instant access to emergency services. In a rental car, call the 800 number provided by the agency. The **ACI (Automobile Club d'Italia)** will tow anyone for free and offers free repairs to members of affiliated associations, such as the AA or RAC in the UK.

Rules of the Road

Drive on the right, use the left lane only for passing, and give way to the right. Seat belts are compulsory in the front and back. You must carry a warning triangle in case of breakdown and a fluorescent safety vest, which you must wear if you exit the vehicle on the highway. In winter, it is obligatory to fit snow tyres or carry snow chains in the car. Speed limits for cars are: 50 km/h (30 mph) in town centres; 70 or 90 km/h (43/55 mph) on roads outside cities; 90/110 (55/70 mph) on the *superstrada* as indicated, and 130 km/h (80 mph) on the *autostrada*.

Driving in Towns and Cities

City centres are usually fraught with one-way systems, limited traffic zones and moped drivers, who weave through traffic. You must be constantly vigilant and aware of other road users in order to avoid accidents. In Lucca, Siena and San Gimignano, only residents and taxis may drive inside the city walls, while Pisa has limited traffic zones around the Arno. Visitors may go in to unload at their hotel, but must then park outside the residents' area.

Florence has an extensive pedestrian zone around the Duomo, so that not even taxis or buses may use the roads connecting major sights in that area. Inside the *viali* (ring road), there is a strict *zona a traffico limitato* (ZTL), with electronic gates barring traffic when the ZTL sign is red. The fine for an infraction is steep. The light is green only on Sundays and late at night. If you stay in a hotel in the ZTL you will be given a temporary access permit so that you can unload your luggage, but then you must park elsewhere.

Parking

Street parking in the centre of Florence (and in most of Tuscany) is indicated by blue or white lines on the pavement. White lines indicate residents' parking only. Visitors must park in the designated areas marked by blue lines and pay at the meter. Insert the amount of money for the time you need, and leave the receipt visible on the dashboard.

Sign for specified parking times

There are three large underground car parks in central Florence: at Santa Maria Novella station; below the Mercato Centrale; and at the Fortezza da Basso. Slightly further out, and less costly (€1.50 per hour, €18 daily rate), are the Parterre northeast of Piazza della Libertà, and the ultra-modern Alberti car park near Via Aretina. Some hotels offer their own parking, while others have agreements for reduced rates with private garages.

In Tuscany, one day a week is set aside for street cleaning, when parking is forbidden.

Parking signs show a small symbol (which looks a little like a tractor) with a day and time, indicating when cleaning takes place each week.

If you park illegally, your car could be towed away. If this happens, phone the **Vigili**, the municipal police, to find out where it has been taken.

Road signs in Gaiole in Chianti, central Tuscany

Driving in the Countryside

Driving on Tuscan country roads offers incredible views, but there are hairpin bends. Sound your horn when approaching a blind bend (flash your lights at night). If using GPS, always check the route on a printed map and avoid impossibly convoluted white roads; they are likely to be poorly paved, narrow and steep. Avoid driving in unfamiliar areas of the countryside at night.

Tolls and Fuel

Autostradas are toll highways; you are issued with a ticket on entry, and pay as you exit. At the toll exit, signs above each lane indicate the payment method available – either an attendant who will accept cash or a machine that accepts

credit cards. The yellow lane is reserved for electronic "Telepass" holders.

Fuel stations are regularly spaced on *autostradas*, but less so on *superstradas*. In the countryside, they can be found in, or just outside, most towns. Small fuel stations close for a long lunch, but most operate 24 hours with automatic machines – insert banknotes into the machine, select the tank number, then begin pumping fuel. Don't put in more money than is needed to fill your tank, as the machine does not give change. Instead, a receipt is issued that you can use to get change when the fuel station is open. The machines do not take credit cards. Unleaded fuel is *senza piombo*; diesel is *gasolio*.

Car Rental

Car rental in Italy is expensive and, ideally, should be booked online or through a tour operator before travelling. To rent a car, you must be over 21, and have held a licence for at least a year. Visitors from outside the EU need an International Drivers' Permit (IDP). Make sure the rental package includes collision damage waiver, breakdown service and insurance against theft *(casco)*.

Moped and Bike Rental

Moped (scooter) rental is available across Tuscany. It is not advisable for visitors to ride a moped in cities due to heavy traffic, but touring the countryside is very pleasant. Helmets are mandatory.

Bicycle rental is available in most towns and is a sustainable and inexpensive way to get around or to explore the countryside. Helmets are also mandatory for children.

DIRECTORY

Breakdown

Automobile Club d'Italia
Viale G. Amendola 36, Florence.
Map 4 F1. **Tel** 055 248 61.
Via Cisanello 168, Pisa.
Tel 050 95 01 11.
Viale Vittorio Veneto 47, Siena.
Tel 0577 490 01.
Emergency toll-free number:
Tel 803 116.
W **aci.it**

Towing Away

Vigili (Municipal Police)
Florence: **Tel** 055 328 33 33.
Pisa: **Tel** 050 91 08 11.
Siena: **Tel** 0577 29 25 50.

City Car Rental

Avis
Borgo Ognissanti 128r,
Florence. **Map** 1 A5 (5 A2).
Tel 055 21 36 29.
c/o de Martino Autonoleggi,
Via Simone Martini 36, Siena.
Tel 0577 27 03 05.

Hertz
Via Maso Finiguerra 33r,
Florence. **Map** 1 B5 (5 A2).
Tel 055 239 82 05.

Maggiore
Via Maso Finiguerra 31r,
Florence. **Map** 1 B5 (5 A2).
Tel 055 21 02 38.

Moped and Bike Rental

Automotocicli Perozzi
Via dei Gazzani 16, Siena.
Tel 0577 28 83 87.
W **perozzi.it**

DF Bike
Via Massetana Romana 54, Siena.
Tel 0577 27 19 05.
W **dfbike.it**

Florence by Bike
Via San Zanobi 91r.
Map 2 D3.
Tel 055 48 89 92.
W **florencebybike.com**

A moped rider crossing the river Arno in Florence

Getting Around Towns and Cities in Tuscany

Tuscan cities are compact enough to get around reasonably comfortably on foot, and the city buses are relatively cheap, regular and wide-ranging. A one-way ticket takes you 15 km (10 miles) out of town, making the bus ideal for trips from the city centre to outlying areas of Florence, Pisa or Siena.

One of Florence's city buses driving near Santa Maria Novella

Walking

Sightseeing on foot in Tuscan cities is made all the more pleasurable by the fact that there are plenty of squares in which to rest and watch the world go by, or cool churches to pop into when the heat gets too much. Most towns have pedestrian zones, including the area around Florence's Duomo and almost all of Siena, in which walking is very pleasant. On streets where traffic does have access, pavements tend to be narrow and crowded.

Be sure to cross the street at the white pedestrian crossings, which are sometimes accompanied by traffic lights. Although required to by law, not all drivers will stop voluntarily at crossings so proceed with caution. It helps to make eye contact with drivers and then step out slowly but confidently. Some very large streets have pedestrian underpasses.

Signs for sights and landmarks have brown backgrounds. In Florence, use the Duomo and river as orientation points. A gentle stroll around the main sights of Florence can take just a couple of hours.

The main sights in Pisa are all in the same square. Siena is compact but hilly, so be sure to wear comfortable shoes.

The cities can be unbearably hot in summer. Plan your day so that you are inside for the hottest part. Recuperate Italian-style with a leisurely lunch followed by a siesta. Shopping is more pleasant in the early evening, when it is cooler and the streets start to come alive.

Cycling

Bicycles can be rented in all towns and cities. Lucca is a great town for cycling as it is flat and has a bike path along the city walls. Florence has some bike paths on the *viali* (tree-lined avenues), but otherwise bikes share the road with other vehicles. Tour companies, such as **Florence by Bike**, offer bike tours departing from Florence and Siena. They take a pleasant route into the countryside and provide bikes, helmets, water and food.

No Pedestrian Access sign

Guided Tours

Tours and private guides can be arranged through tourist offices (*see p288*) or a travel agent. For guided walks around the city, contact **ArtViva** or **Context Travel**. **Citysightseeing Firenze** offers a hop-on hop-off bus service (complete with audioguide) to all the major sights in the city. Segway tours of Florence and Pisa are arranged by **Segway Firenze**. The Florence tour is limited to the historic centre due to the number of narrow streets.

City Buses

Florence's city bus company is called **ATAF**, Pisa's is **CPT**, and Siena's **TRA-IN**. City buses in most cities are bright orange. Most lines run frequently until around 9:30pm, after which they tend to run hourly. There are designated night bus lines offering services through the night, but these are very infrequent.

Florence does not have a main terminus, but most buses can be picked up alongside Santa Maria Novella station or in Piazza San Marco. Buses run near most major sights: normal bus routes, indicated by numbers and names, are supplemented by electric minibuses, indicated by letters C1, C2, C3 through to D, that serve the narrow streets in the very centre of town.

Pisa's buses also serve the main sights. Most buses stop at the railway station and Piazza Vittorio Emanuele II. In Siena the main bus stops are Piazza Antonio Gramsci and Piazza San Domenico. There are bus information kiosks at all these points, but they are not always open. Tourist information offices can usually help, or consult the route maps online.

In all cases, enter the bus at the front or back and get off through the middle doors. The four low seats at the front of the bus are meant for the elderly,

Signs showing pedestrian routes to sights and landmarks in Florence

the disabled and people with children, although Italian etiquette calls for people to give up their seats for anyone in greater need than themselves.

Bus Tickets

Tickets for city buses must be bought before travel and validated (stamped) in the machines on the bus. They can be boughts at newsstands, bars displaying the bus company sign (ATAF, APT, TRA-IN), *tabacchi*, or at the bus terminus. If you are likely to make a few trips, buy multi-trip tickets that offer a slight discount. There are two- and four-trip paper tickets available; in Florence there is also the *Carta Agile* with an electronic chip loaded with €10, €20, or €30. Any of these multi-trip tickets can be used by people travelling together; just validate once for each passenger. Children under 1 metre in height travel free.

Ticket-stamping machine

If you are planning to stay longer in any one town, consider a multi-day ticket or monthly pass, which are non-transferable. Anyone wishing to claim a student discount must first purchase a student photocard.

Trams in Florence

There have been plans to run trams through Florence for several years. In 2010, Line 1 finally opened. This connects the suburb Scandicci to Santa Maria Novella train station. Line 2 from Florence airport to Santa Maria Novella train station and Piazza Libertà is under construction, as is a third line.

Tickets for the bus are also valid on the tram. Be sure to validate the ticket on whichever transport you use first, by stamping it in the machine found on board.

Taxis in Tuscany

Official taxis found in Tuscan towns and cities are white with a "Taxi" sign on the roof. Only take taxis at official ranks – ignore all offers from touts at the stations. There are supplements for baggage, for rides between 10pm and 7am, on Sundays and on public holidays, and for journeys to and from the airport. If you phone for a taxi, the meter starts to run from the moment you book it, so by the time it arrives you could already owe several euros. Generally, travelling by taxi is rather costly. Taxi drivers are usually honest, but make sure you know what any supplements are for. Italians give very small tips or nothing at all.

In Florence, there are ranks at Via Pellicceria, Piazza di Santa Maria Novella (near the station) and Piazza di San Marco. In Siena, taxis can be found in Piazza Matteotti and Piazza della Stazione; and in Pisa at the Piazza del Duomo, Piazza Garibaldi and Piazza della Stazione.

White taxis awaiting customers at a rank in Florence

General Index

Acknowledgments

Dorling Kindersley would like to thank the following people whose contributions and help have made the preparation of this book possible.

Main Contributor
Christopher Catling has been visiting Florence and Tuscany since his first archaeological dig there as a student at Cambridge University 25 years ago. He is the author of several guide books on the city and region.

Additional Photography
Jane Burton, Philip Dowell, Neil Fletcher, Steve Gorton, Michelle Grant, Frank Greenaway, Alexandra Korey, Neil Mersh, Rebecca Milner, David Murray, Ian O'Leary, Poppy, Rough Guides/James McConnachie, Clive Streeter, Christine Webb, Linda Whitwam.

Additional Illustrations
Gillie Newman, Chris Dorr, Sue Sharples, Ann Winterbotham, John Woodcock, Martin Woodward.

Cartography
Uma Bhattacharya; Colourmap Scannning Limited; Contour Publishing; Cosmographics; European Map Graphics; Suresh Kumar; Kunal Singh. Street Finder maps:ERA Maptech Ltd (Dublin), adapted with permission from original survey and mapping by Shobunsha (Japan).

Cartographic Research
Caroline Bowie, Peter Winfield, Claudine Zante.

Design and Editorial Assistance
Louise Abbott, Beverley Ager, Gaye Allen, Douglas Amrine, Sam Atkinson, Rosemary Bailey, Claire Baranowski, Kate Berens, Marta Bescos, Tessa Bindloss, Hilary Bird, Julie Bond, Lucia Bronzin, Ann-Marie Bulat, Carolyn Burdet, Julia Burdet, Jacob Cameron, Cooling Brown, Imogen Corke, Vanessa Courtier, Michelle Crane, Felicity Crowe, Federico Damonte, Surya Deogun, Nicola Erdpresser, Joy FitzSimmons, Sarah Fraser, Anna Freiberger, Natalie Godwin, Jackie Gordon, Katie Greenaway, Vinod Harish, Jacky Jackson, Annette Jacobs, Claire Jones, Emma Jones, Roberta Kedzierski, Steve Knowlden, Alexandra Korey, Kathryn Lane, David Lamb, Neil Lockley, Siri Lowe, Carly Madden, Georgina Matthews, Alison McGill, Rebecca Milner, Kamin Mohammadi, George Nimmo, Catherine Palmi, Reetu Pandey, Helen Partington, Susie Peachey, Alice Peebles, Marianne Petrou, Pamposh Raina, Ellen Root, Sands Publishing Solutions, Baishakhee Sengupta, Shailesh Sharma, Asavari Singh, Kate Singleton, Ellie Smith, Meredith Smith, Susana Smith, Jaynan Spengler, Nicky Swallow, Rachel Symons, Andrew Szudek, Dawn Terrey, Tracy Timson, Alka Thakur, Daphne Trotter, Nick Turpin, Glenda Tyrrell, Janis Utton, Conrad van Dyk, Alastair Wardle, Lynda Warrington, Alex Whittleton, Fiona Wild, Stewart J. Wild, Sophie Wright.

Special Assistance
Antonio Carluccio; Sam Cole; Giuseppe de Micheli and Moira Barbacovi at the Museo dell'Opera di Santa Croce; Julian Fox, University of East London; Simon Groom; Signor Tucci at the Ministero dei Beni Culturali e Ambientali; Museo dell'Opificio delle Pietre Dure; Signora Pelliconi at the Soprintendenza per i Beni Artistici e Storici delle Province di Firenze e Pistoia; Prof. Francesco Villari, Direttore, Istituto Italiano di Cultura, London.

For special assistance in supplying the computer- generated image of the Gozzoli frescoes in the Palazzo Medici Riccardi: Dr Cristina Acidini, Head of Restoration, and the restorers at Consorzio Pegasus, Firenze; Ancilla Antonini of Index, Firenze; and Galileo Siscam SpA, Firenze, producers of the CAD Orthomap graphic programme.

Photographic Reference
Camisa I & Son, Carluccio's, Gucci Ltd.

Photography Permissions
Dorling Kindersley would like to thank the following for their permission to photograph:
Florence: Badia Fiorentina; Biblioteca Mediceo-Lau-renziana; Biblioteca Riccardiana; Centro Mostra di Firenze; Comune di Firenze; Duomo; Hotel Continentale; Hotel Hermitage; Hotel Villa Belvedere; Le Fonticine; Museo Bardini; Museo di Firenze com'era; Museo Horne; Museo Marino Marini; Museo dell'Opera del Duomo di Firenze; Ognissanti; Palazzo Vecchio; Pensione Bencistà; Rebus; Santi Apostoli; Santa Croce; San Lorenzo; Santa Maria Novella; Santa Trinità; Soprintendenza per i Beni Amb-ientali e Architettonici delle Province di Firenze e Pistoia; Tempio Israelitico; Trattoria Angiolino; Ufficio Occupazioni Suolo Pubblico di Firenze; Villa La Massa; Villa Villoresi.
Tuscany: Campo dei Miracoli, Pisa; Collegiata, San Gimignano; Comune di Empoli; Comune di San Gimignano; Comune di Vinci; Duomo, Siena; Duomo, Volterra; Museo della Collegiata di Sant'Andrea, Empoli; Museo Diocesano di Cortona; Museo Etrusco Guarnacci, Volterra; Museo Leonardiano, Vinci; Museo dell'Opera del Duomo, Pisa; Museo dell'Opera del Duomo, Siena; Museo delle Sinopie, Pisa; Opera della Metropolitana di Siena; Opera Primaziale Pisana, Pisa; Soprintendenza per i Beni Ambientali e Architettonici di Siena; Soprintendenza per i Beni Artistici e Storici di Siena; Soprintendenza per i Beni Ambientali, Architettonici, Artistici e Storici di Pisa.

Picture Credits
Key: a-above; b-below/bottom; c-centre; f-far; l-left; r-right; t-top.
Works of art have been reproduced with the permission of the following copyright holders: *Cavaliere* (1943) Marino Marini © DACS, London 2011 108tc.
The publisher would like to thank the following individuals, companies and picture libraries for permission to reproduce their photographs:
4Corners: SIME/Pietro Canali 154bl, 234; SIME/Massimo Ripani 64. **dF Aeroporto di Firenze S.p.A.:** 298br, 298cla; **Alamy Images:** Alvey & Towers Picture Library 306tr; Gary Cook 261tl; CuboImages srl 10cl; CuboImages srl/Nico Tondini 139tr; Eye Ubiquitous 155br, 210, 9; Tim Graham 270tr; imageBROKER 154c, 156, 259br, 271br; JTB MEDIA CREATION, Inc. 2–3; Scenics & Science 75t; Stock Italia 294bl; Sebastian Wasek 154cla, 172; Dave Zubraski 14br; **Archivi Alinari, Firenze:** 108bl; **The Ancient Art and Architecture Collection:** 81tl; **Archivio Fotografico Enciclopedico, Roma:** Giuseppe Carfagna 42tr, 43br, 207tr, 207ca; Claudio Cerquetti 37bl; K & B News Foto /B. Kortenhorst 25tc; B. Mariotti 43cb; S. Paderno 27tl, 43tl; G. Veggi 38c; **AWL Images:** Walter Bibikow 286–7; Nadia Isakova 152–3; **Belmond Hotels:** Villa San Michele 249tl; **The Bridgeman Art Library, London:** Archivio dello Stato, Siena 51clb; Bargello, Firenze 72ca, 73tc; Biblioteca di San Marco, Firenze/K & BNews Foto 101ca; Biblioteca Marciana, Venezia 48crb; Galleria dell'Accademia, Firenze 98bl; Galleria degli Uffizi, Firenze 31cr, 49br, 47cla, 51ca, 84clb, 85tl, 85tc, 87tc, 87crb; Musée du Louvre, Paris/Lauros-Giraudon, 109ca; Museo di San Marco, Firenze 57tc, 101br; Museo Civico, Prato 192tr; Palazzo Pitti, Firenze 125tc; Sant'Apollonia, Firenze 93tr (d), 96clb (d); Santa Croce, Firenze 76b; Santa Maria del Carmine, Firenze 131bl (d); Santa Maria Novella, Firenze 115cra; © **The British Museum:** 46br. **Caffe Cibreo:** 264bc; **Foto Carfagna & Associati:** 277cl, 278tr; **Casa Dei Tessuti:** 277br; **Castello di Vicarello:** 248br, 256bl; **Cibrèo Ristorante:** 265tr; **Bruce Coleman:** N. G. Blake 37br, Hans Reinhard 37cla, 37cra; **Corbis:** Ric Ergenbright 261c; Eye Ubiquitous/Paul Seheult 138bc; Owen Franken 260cla; David Lees 62–3, 155tr, 194; Massimo Listri 277tc; **Joe Cornish:** 36–7,

40cra, 41ca, 41br, 209tc, 231tl; **Giancarlo Costa, Milano**: 49tc, 59clb, 60cla, 60bl. **Il Dagherrotipo**: Salvatore Barba 139bc, 141br; Marco Cerruti 140cla; Maurizio Leoni 140bc; Paolo Marini 138cla; Giovanni Rinadli 141tr; **Dreamstime.com**: A1977 92bl; Jennifer Barrow 246–7; David Carillet 132; Miloslav Doubrava 15bc; Frenta 104; Jakobradlgruber 12bl; Jaysi 11br; Jborzicchi 176tc; Konstik 11tl; Ladiras81 14tr; Uros Mitrovic 159tr; Prillfoto 12tc; Dave Stabley 13tr; Raluca Tudor 307bl; Rudy Wong 69tc; Dmitriy Yakovlev 15tr.
ECB: 295 all; **Mary Evans Picture Library**: 50cl, 52br, 54bl (Explorer), 59bc, 78cr, 183c, 200c.
Ferrovie Dello Stato S.p.A.: 300cr, 300cla; **Florence Dance Festival**: Rambert Dance Company/Swamp 283tl.
Getty Images: De Agostini 88; De Agostini/G. Dagli Orti 8–9; Sami Sarkis 22; **Jackie Gordon**: 61cb, 278tl, 301cra; **La Grotta**: Giovanni Baldini 258br; **Il Guelfo Bianco/Il Desco**: 252bc, 266tr.
Alison Harris: Museo dell'Opera del Duomo, Firenze 31bc, 71t, 71cl; Palazzo Vecchio, Firenze/Comune di Roma/Direzione dei Musei 4t, 56cb(Sala di Gigli), 57clb, 83tl; San Lorenzo, Firenze/ Soprintendenza per i Beni Artistici 95cr; Santa Felicità, Firenze 123tl (d); Santo Spirito, Firenze 122bl; 120cla; **Pippa Hurst**: 187cr.
The Image Bank: C. Place 112bl; **Impact Photos**: Brian Harris 23b; **Index, Firenze**: 190bc, 190crb (d), 191tl; Galileo Siscam, S.p.A, Firenze 60–1; P. Tosi, 70cr; **Istituto e Museo di Storia della Scienza di Firenze**: 78br, 79c; www.italiancookerycourse.com: 284cra. www.landscapepainting.com: Daria Insalaco 284bl; **Frank Lane Picture Agency**: R. Wilmshurst 37crb; **Locanda dell'Amorosa**: 250tl; **Lungarno Hotels**: Borgo San Jacopo 269tr; Continentale 249br, 253tr; Gallery Art Hotel 248cla; Hotel Lungarno 255tr.
The **Mansell Collection**: 51br; **Marka, Milan**: Globe 25br; F Pizzochero 35cla. **Mercato Centrale, Florence**: Federica di Giovanni & Enrica Quaranta 92tr; **Misericordia Ambulance Service**: 293cra; **Un Mondo di Sapori**: 274tc; **Museo dell'opificio delle Pietre Dure, Firenze**: 99tc.
Grazia Neri, Milano: R. Bettini 40br; Carlo Lannutti 61bl; **Peter Noble**:176br, 226tr, 226cra, 292cl. **Oliviero**: 267br; **Il Osteria Personale**: 268bc; **Oxford Scientific Films**: Stan Osolinski 240tr. **Palazzo Magnani Ferone**: 251bl, 254bl; **Roger Phillips**: 206cra, 206crb; **Photolibrary**: Bertrand Gardel 305bl; **Andrea Pistolesi, Firenze**: 228br, 282br; **La Porta**: 259t, 272bc; **Poste Italiane**: 297bl; **Le Potazzine**: 273tr; **Emilio Pucci S.r.l, Firenze**: 61ca. **Relais Campo Regio**: 251tr, 257tc; **Retrograph Archive, London**: © Martin Breese 177cl, 189bc, 263bl; **Royal Collection**: © Her Majesty Queen Elizabeth II: 59t (d). **SAT Societa Aeroporto Toscano SpA./Pisa Airport**: 299tl; **Photo Scala, Firenze** courtesy of the Ministero Beni e Att. Culturali : Abbazia, Monte Oliveto Maggiore 215tr; Galleria dell'Accademia, Firenze 96br, 98t, 99cla; Badia, Fiesole 53clb; Badia, Firenze 74br; Bargello, Firenze 4tr; 47bl, 48bl, 50bc, 53ca, 53br, 55cr, 58br, 70tr, 72bl, 73cla, 73cra, 73clb, 113cb; Battistero, Pisa 162ca; Biblioteca Laurenziana, Firenze 94cl; Camposanto, Pisa 160br; Cappella dei Principi, Firenze 94cla; Cappelle Medicee, Firenze 95tc; Casa del

Vasari, Arezzo 203t (d); Chiesa del Carmine, Firenze 130–1, (130t, 130b, 131br all details); Cimitero, Monterchi 32cl; Collegiata, San Gimignano 216clb; Corridoio Vasariano, Firenze 110tr; Duomo, Lucca 184bc; Duomo, Pisa 163tc; Duomo, Prato 32tr (d), 33tr(d), 33crb (d), 33bl (d), 32–3; Galleria Comunale, Prato 192br; Galleria d'Arte Moderna, Firenze 58cb, 125tl; Galleria Palatina, Firenze 59crb, 126–7 all; Galleria degli Uffizi, Firenze 47c, 47br, 52clb, 54cl, 54br, 55tr, 55cl, 55br, 56cl, 56b (Collezione Giovanna) 85crb, 84cla, 85bl, 86cra, 86b, 87clb (d); Loggia dei Lanzi, Firenze 81ca; Musée Bonnat, Bayonne 73br; Musei Civici, San Gimignano 44, 217br, 219b; Museo Archeologico, Arezzo 203cr; Museo Archeologico, Firenze 46cl, 47clb, 47bl, 97crb, 103tl, 103bl, 244bl; Museo Archeologico, Grosseto 244c; Museo Civico, Bologna 52tr; Museo degli Argenti, Firenze 57bl, 58tr, 58cla, 124br; Museo dell'Accademia Etrusca, Cortona 47tc, 48cla; Museo dell'Opera del Duomo, Firenze 51tc, 67t (d); Museo dell'Opera Metropolitana, Siena 30tr; Museo di Firenze com'era, Firenze 129tl, 169b; Museo Diocesano, Cortona 208br; Museo di San Marco, Firenze 100cla, 100bl, 101cr, 101bl; Museo Mediceo, Firenze 54tr; Museo Nazionale di San Matteo, Pisa 161tl; Necropoli, Sovana 245crb; Palazzo Davanzati, Firenze 107cra (Sala dei Pappagalli), 113tr; Palazzo Pitti, Firenze 124cla, 125bl; Palazzo Pubblico, Siena 50–1, 223t; Palazzo Vecchio, Firenze 56–7 (Sala di Clemente VII), 82tr (Sala dei Gigli); Pinacoteca Comunale, Sansepolcro 201bl; Pinacoteca Comunale, Volterra 170ca; San Francesco, Arezzo 204–5, (204tr, 204b, 205tc, 205b all details); San Lorenzo, Firenze 31tr; Santa Maria Novella, Firenze 30c, 50cb (d), 53t (d), 114bl; Santa Trinità, Firenze 106cla; Santissima Annunziata, Firenze 102br; Tomba del Colle, Chiusi 46clb, 232tl; Tribuna di Galileo, Firenze 58–9; Vaticano 45b (Galleria Carte Geographica); **SITA Bus**: 302bl; **SuperStock**: 293tl; LOOK-foto 118; Marka/Giovanni Mereghetti 13bl; **Sygma**: G. Giansanti 226cl, 226cb, 226bl; Keystone 61tl. **La Tenda Rossa**: 275br; **Telecom Italia**: 296ca; **The Travel Library**: Philip Enticknap 98cr, 222cr.

Map cover
Robert Harding Picture Library: Paul Seheult

Jacket
Front and spine top: **Robert Harding Picture Library**: Paul Seheult.

Front Endpaper
4Corners: SIME/Pietro Canali Lbr; SIME/Massimo Ripani Rcr; **Alamy Images**: Eye Ubiquitous Rbc; imageBROKER Lcb; Sebastian Wasek Lcla; Corbis: David Lees Rcrb; **Dreamstime. com**: Frenta Rtl; **Getty Images**: De Agostini Rtr; **SuperStock**: LOOK-foto Rca.

All other images © Dorling Kindersley. For further information see **www.dkimages.com**

Phrase Book

In An Emergency

Help!	Aiuto!	eye-**yoo**-toh
Stop!	Fermate!	fair-**mah**-teh
Call a.	Chiama un	kee-**ah**-mah oon
doctor	medico	**meh**-dee-koh
Call an	Chiama un'	kee-**ah**-mah oon
am-ambulance.	ambulanza	boo-**lan**-tsa
Call the	Chiama la	kee-**ah**-mah lah
police.	polizia	pol-ee-**tsee**-ah
Call the fire	Chiama i	kee-**ah**-mah ee
brigade.	pompieri	pom-pee-**air**-ee
Where is the	Dov'è il telefono?	dov-**eh** eel teh-**leh**-
telephone?		foh-noh?
The nearest	L'ospedale	loss-peh-**dah**-leh pee-
hospital?	più vicino?	oo vee-**chee**-noh?

Communication Essentials

Yes/No	Sì/No	see/noh
Please	Per favore	pair fah-**vor**-eh
Thank you	Grazie	**grah**-tsee-eh
Excuse me	Mi scusi	mee skoo-zee
Hello	Buon giorno	bwon jor-noh
Good bye	Arrivederci	ah-ree-veh-**dair**-chee
Good evening	Buona sera	**bwon**-ah **sair**-ah
morning	la mattina	lah mah-**tee**-nah
afternoon	il pomeriggio	eel poh-meh-**ree**-joh
evening	la sera	lah **sair**-ah
yesterday	ieri	ee-**air**-ee
today	oggi	**oh**-jee
tomorrow	domani	doh-**mah**-nee
here/there	qui/là	kwee/lah
What?	Quale?	**kwah**-leh?
When?	Quando?	**kwan**-doh?
Why?	Perchè?	pair-**keh**?
Where?	Dove?	**doh**-veh

Useful Phrases

How are you?	Come sta?	**koh**-meh stah?
Very well,	Molto bene,	**moll**-toh **beh**-neh
thank you.	grazie.	**grah**-tsee-eh
Pleased to	Piacere di	pee-ah-**chair**-eh dee
meet you.	conoscerla.	coh-noh-shair-lah
See you soon.	A più tardi.	ah pee-oo tar-dee
That's fine.	Va bene.	va **beh**-neh
Where is/are ...?	Dov'è/Dove sono ...?	dov-eh/doveh **soh**-noh?
How long does	Quanto tempo ci	**kwan**-toh **tem**-poh
it take to get to ...?	vuole per	chee voo-**oh**-leh pair
	andare a ...?	an-**dar**-eh ah...?
How do I ?	Come faccio per	koh-meh **fah**-choh
get to ...	arrivare a ...?	pair arri-**var**-eh ah...?
Are you		
getting off?	Scende?	**Shen**-deh?
Do you speak	Parla inglese?	par-lah een-**gleh**-zeh?
English?		
I don't	Non capisco.	non ka-**pee**-skoh
understand.		
Could you speak	Può parlare	pwoh par-**lah**-reh
more slowly,	più lentamente,	pee-**oolen**-ta-**men**-teh
please?	per favore?	pair fah-**vor**-eh
I'm sorry.	Mi dispiace.	mee dee-spee-**ah**-cheh

Useful Words

big	grande	**gran**-deh
small	piccolo	**pee**-koh-loh
hot	caldo	**kal**-doh
cold	freddo	**fred**-doh
good	buono	**bwoh**-noh
bad	cattivo	kat-**tee**-voh
enough	basta	**bas**-tah
open	aperto	ah-**pair**-toh
closed	chiuso	kee-**oo**-zoh
left	a sinistra	ah see-**nee**-strah
right	a destra	ah **dess**-trah
straight on	sempre dritto	**sem**-preh **dree**-toh
near	vicino	vee-**chee**-noh
far	lontano	lon-**tah**-noh
up	su	soo
down	giù	joo
early	presto	**press**-toh
late	tardi	**tar**-dee
entrance	entrata	en-**trah**-tah
exit	uscita	oo-**shee**-ta
toilet	il gabinetto	eel gah-bee-**net**-toh
free, unoccupied	libero	**lee**-bair-oh
free, no charge	gratuito	grah-**too**-ee-toh

Making a Telephone Call

I'd like to place a	Vorrei fare	vor-**ray** far-eh oona
long-distance call.	una interurbana.	in-tair-oor-**bah**-nah
I'd like to make	Vorrei fare una	vor-**ray** far-eh oona
a reverse-charge	telefonata a carico	teh-leh-fon-**ah**-tah ah
call.	del destinatario.	**kar**-ee-koh dell dess-
		tee-nah-**tar**-ree-oh
I'll try again later.	Ritelefono più	ree-teh-**leh**-foh-noh
	tardi.	pee-oo**tar**-dee
Can I leave a	Posso lasciare	**poss**-oh lash-**ah**-reh
message?	un messaggio?	oon mess-**sah**-joh?
Hold on.	Un attimo,	oon **ah**-tee-moh,
	per favore	pair fah-**vor**-eh
Could you speak	Può parlare più	pwoh par-**lah**-reh
up a little please?	forte, per favore?	pee-oo **for**-teh, pair
		fah-**vor**-eh?
local call	la telefonata	lah teh-leh-fon-**ah**-ta
	locale	loh-**kah**-leh

Shopping

How much	Quant'è,	kwan-**teh**
does this cost?	per favore?	pair fah-**vor**-eh?
I would like ...	Vorrei ...	vor-**ray**
Do you have ...?	Avete ...?	ah-veh-teh...?
I'm just looking.	Sto soltanto	stoh sol-**tan**-toh
	guardando.	gwar-**dan**-doh
Do you take	Accettate	ah-chet-tah-teh **kar**-teh
credit cards?	carte di credito?	dee **creh**-dee-toh?
What time do	A che ora apre/	ah keh or-ah
you open/close?	chiude?	**ah**-preh/kee-**oo**-deh?
this one	questo	**kweh**-stoh
that one	quello	**kwell**-oh
expensive	caro	**kar**-oh
cheap	a buon prezzo	ah bwon **pret**-soh
size, clothes	la taglia	lah **tah**-lee-ah
size, shoes	il numero	eel **noo**-mair-oh
white	bianco	bee-**ang**-koh
black	nero	**neh**-roh
red	rosso	**ross**-oh
yellow	giallo	**jal**-loh
green	verde	**vair**-deh
blue	blu	bloo
brown	marrone	mar-**roh**-neh

Types of Shop

antique dealer	l'antiquario	lan-tee-**kwah**-ree-oh
bakery	la panetteria	lah pah-net-tair-**ree**-ah
bank	la banca	lah **bang**-kah
bookshop	la libreria	lah lee-breh-**ree**-ah
butcher's	la macelleria	lah mah-chell-eh-**ree**-ah
cake shop	la pasticceria	lah pas-tee-chair-**ee**-ah
chemist's	la farmacia	lah far-mah-**chee**-ah
delicatessen	la salumeria	lah sah-loo-meh-**ree**-ah
department store	il grande	eel **gran**-deh
	magazzino	mag-gad-**zee**-noh
fishmonger's	la pescheria	lah pess-keh-**ree**-ah
florist	il fioraio	eel fee-or-**eye**-oh
greengrocer	il fruttivendolo	eel froo-tee-**ven**-doh-loh
grocery	alimentari	ah-lee-men-**tah**-ree
hairdresser	il parrucchiere	eel par-oo-kee-**air**-eh
ice-cream parlour	la gelateria	lah jel-lah-tair-**ree**-ah
market	il mercato	eel mair-**kah**-toh
news-stand	l'edicola	leh-**dee**-koh-lah
post office	l'ufficio postale	loo-**fee**-choh pos-**tah**-leh
shoe shop	il negozio di	eel neh-**goh**-tsioh dee
	scarpe	**skar**-peh
supermarket	il supermercato	su-pair-mair-**kah**-toh
tobacconist	il tabaccaio	eel tah-bak-**eye**-oh
travel agency	l'agenzia di viaggi	lah-jen-**tsee**-ah dee
		vee-**ad**-jee

Sightseeing

art gallery	la pinacoteca	lah peena-koh-**teh**-kah
bus stop	la fermata	lah fair-**mah**-tah
	dell'autobus	dell **ow**-toh-booss
church	la chiesa	lah kee-**eh**-zah
	la basilica	lah bah-**seel**-i-kah
closed for the	chiuso per la	kee-**oo**-zoh pair lah
public holiday	festa	**fess**-tah
garden	il giardino	eel jar-**dee**-no
library	la biblioteca	lah beeb-lee-oh-**teh**-kah
museum	il museo	eel moo-**zeh**-oh
railway station	la stazione	lah stah-tsee-**oh**-neh
tourist	l'ufficio	loo-**fee**-choh
information	turistico	too-**ree**-stee-koh

Staying in a Hotel

Do you have any vacant rooms?	**Avete camere libere?**	ah-**veh**-teh kah-mair-eh lee-bair-eh?
double room	**una camera doppia**	oona **kah**-mair-ah **doh**-pee-ah
with double bed	**con letto matrimoniale**	kon **let**-toh mah-tree-moh-nee-**ah**-leh
twin room	**una camera con due letti**	oona **kah**-mair-ah kon **doo**-eh **let**-tee
single room	**una camera singola**	oona **kah**-mair-ah **sing**-goh-lah
room with a bath, shower	**una camera con bagno, con doccia**	oona **kah**-mair-ah kon **ban**-yoh, kon **dot**-chah
porter	**il facchino**	eel fah-**kee**-noh
key	**la chiave**	lah kee-**ah**-veh
I have a reservation.	**Ho fatto una prenotazione.**	oh **fat**-toh oona preh-noh-tah-tsee-**oh**-neh

Eating Out

Have you got a table for …?	**Avete un tavolo per …?**	ah-**veh**-teh oon **tah**-voh-loh pair …?
I'd like to reserve a table.	**Vorrei riservare un tavolo.**	vor-**ray** ree-sair-**vah**-reh oon **tah**-voh-loh
breakfast	**colazione**	koh-lah-tsee-**oh**-neh
lunch	**pranzo**	**pran**-tsoh
dinner	**cena**	**cheh**-nah
Enjoy your meal.	**Buon appetito.**	bwon ah-peh-**tee**-toh
The bill, please.	**Il conto, per favore.**	eel **kon**-toh pair fah-**vor**-eh
I am a vegetarian.	**Sono vegetariano/a.**	**soh**-noh veh-jeh-tar-ee-**ah**-noh/nah
waitress	**cameriera**	kah-mair-ee-**air**-ah
waiter	**cameriere**	kah-mair-ee-**air**-eh
fixed price	**il menù a prezzo fisso**	eel meh-**noo** ah **pret**-soh **fee**-soh
menu	**il menù a prezzo fisso**	
dish of the day	**piatto del giorno**	pee-**ah**-toh dell **jor**-no
starter	**antipasto**	an-tee-**pass**-toh
first course	**il primo**	eel **pree**-moh
main course	**il secondo**	eel seh-**kon**-doh
vegetables	**ilcontorno**	eel kon-**tor**-noh
dessert	**il dolce**	eel **doll**-cheh
cover charge	**il coperto**	eel koh-**pair**-toh
wine list	**la lista dei vini**	lah **lee**-stah day **vee**-nee
rare	**al sangue**	al **sang**-gweh
medium	**al puntino**	al **poon-tee**-noh
well done	**ben cotto**	ben **kot**-toh
glass	**il bicchiere**	eel bee-kee-**air**-eh
bottle	**la bottiglia**	lah bot-**teel**-yah
knife	**il coltello**	eel kol-**tell**-oh
fork	**la forchetta**	lah for-**ket**-tah
spoon	**il cucchiaio**	eel koo-kee-**eye**-oh

Menu Decoder

l'abbacchio	lah-**back**-kee-oh	lamb
l'aceto	lah-**cheh**-toh	vinegar
l'acqua	lah-kwah	water
l'acqua minerale	lah-kwah mee-nair-ah-leh	mineral water
gasata/naturale	**ah**-leh gah-**zah**-tah/ nah-too-**rah**-leh	fizzy/still
l'aglio	lahl-yoh	garlic
al forno	al **for**-noh	baked
alla griglia	ah-lah **greel**-yah	grilled
l'anatra	lah-nah-trah	duck
l'aragosta	lah-rah-**goss**-tah	lobster
l'arancia	lah-**ran**-chah	orange
arrosto	ar-**ross**-toh	roast
la birra	lah **beer**-rah	beer
la bistecca	lah bee-**stek**-kah	steak
il brodo	eel **broh**-doh	broth
il burro	eel **boor**-oh	butter
il caffè	eel kah-**feh**	coffee
il carciofo	eel kar-**choff**-oh	artichoke
la carne	la **kar**-neh	meat
carne di maiale	**kar**-neh dee mah-**yah**-leh	pork
la cipolla	lah chee-**poll**-ah	onion
i fagioli	ee fah-**joh**-lee	beans
il formaggio	eel for-**mad**-joh	cheese
le fragole	leh **frah**-goh-leh	strawberries
frutta fresca	froo-tah **fress**-kah	fresh fruit
frutti di mare	froo-tee dee **mah**-reh	seafood
i funghi	ee **foon**-gee	mushrooms
i gamberi	ee **gam**-bair-ee	prawns
il gelato	eel jel-**lah**-toh	ice cream
l'insalata	leen-sah-**lah**-tah	salad
il latte	eel **laht**-teh	milk
i legumi	ee leh-**goo**-mee	vegetables

lesso	**less**-oh	boiled
il manzo	eel **man**-tsoh	beef
la mela	lah **meh**-lah	apple
la melanzana	lah meh-lan-**tsah**-nah	aubergine
la minestra	lah mee-**ness**-trah	soup
l'olio	**loll**-yoh	oil
l'oliva	loh-**lee**-vah	olive
il pane	eel **pah**-neh	bread
il panino	eel pah-**nee**-noh	roll
le patate	leh pah-**tah**-teh	potatoes
patatine fritte	pah-tah-**teen**-eh **free**-teh	chips
il pepe	eel **peh**-peh	pepper
la pesca	lah **pess**-kah	peach
il pesce	eel **pesh**-eh	fish
il pollo	eel **poll**-oh	chicken
il pomodoro	eel poh-moh-**dor**-oh	tomato
il prosciutto cotto/crudo	eel pro-**shoo**-toh **kot**-toh/**kroo**-doh	ham cooked/cured
il riso	eel **ree**-zoh	rice
il sale	eel **sah**-leh	salt
la salsiccia	lah sal-**see**-chah	sausage
secco	**sek**-koh	dry
succo d'arancia/ di limone	**soo**-koh dah-**ran**-chah/ dee lee-**moh**-neh	orange/lemon juice
il tè	eel **teh**	tea
la tisana	lah tee-**zah**-nah	herb tea
il tonno	**ton**-noh	tuna
la torta	lah **tor**-tah	cake
l'uovo	loo-**oh**-voh	egg
l'uva	**loo**-vah	grapes
vino bianco	**vee**-noh bee-**ang**-koh	white wine
vino rosso	**vee**-noh **ross**-oh	red wine
il vitello	eel vee-**tell**-oh	veal
le vongole	leh **von**-goh-leh	baby clams
lo zucchero	loh **zoo**-kair-oh	sugar
gli zucchini	lyee dzo-**kee**-nee	courgettes
la zuppa	lah **tsoo**-pah	soup

Numbers

1	**uno**	**oo**-noh
2	**due**	**doo**-eh
3	**tre**	treh
4	**quattro**	**kwat**-roh
5	**cinque**	**ching**-kweh
6	**sei**	**say**-ee
7	**sette**	**set**-teh
8	**otto**	**ot**-toh
9	**nove**	**noh**-veh
10	**dieci**	dee-**eh**-chee
11	**undici**	**oon**-dee-chee
12	**dodici**	**doh**-dee-chee
13	**tredici**	**tray**-dee-chee
14	**quattordici**	kwat-**tor**-dee-chee
15	**quindici**	**kwin**-dee-chee
16	**sedici**	**say**-dee-chee
17	**diciassette**	dee-chah-**set**-teh
18	**diciotto**	dee-**chot**-toh
19	**diciannove**	dee-chah-**noh**-veh
20	**venti**	**ven**-tee
30	**trenta**	**tren**-tah
40	**quaranta**	kwah-**ran**-tah
50	**cinquanta**	ching-**kwan**-tah
60	**sessanta**	sess-**an**-tah
70	**settanta**	set-**tan**-tah
80	**ottanta**	ot-**tan**-tah
90	**novanta**	noh-**van**-tah
100	**cento**	**chen**-toh
1,000	**mille**	**mee**-leh
2,000	**duemila**	**doo**-eh **mee**-lah
5,000	**cinquemila**	**ching**-kweh **mee**-lah
1,000,000	**un milione**	oon meel-**yoh**-neh

Time

one minute	**un minuto**	oon mee-**noo**-toh
one hour	**un'ora**	oon **or**-ah
half an hour	**mezz'ora**	medz-**or**-ah
a day	**un giorno**	oon **jor**-noh
a week	**una settimana**	oona set-tee-**mah**-nah
Monday	**lunedì**	loo-neh-**dee**
Tuesday	**martedì**	mar-teh-**dee**
Wednesday	**mercoledì**	mair-koh-leh-**dee**
Thursday	**giovedì**	joh-veh-**dee**
Friday	**venerdì**	ven-air-**dee**
Saturday	**sabato**	**sah**-bah-toh
Sunday	**domenica**	doh-**meh**-nee-kah

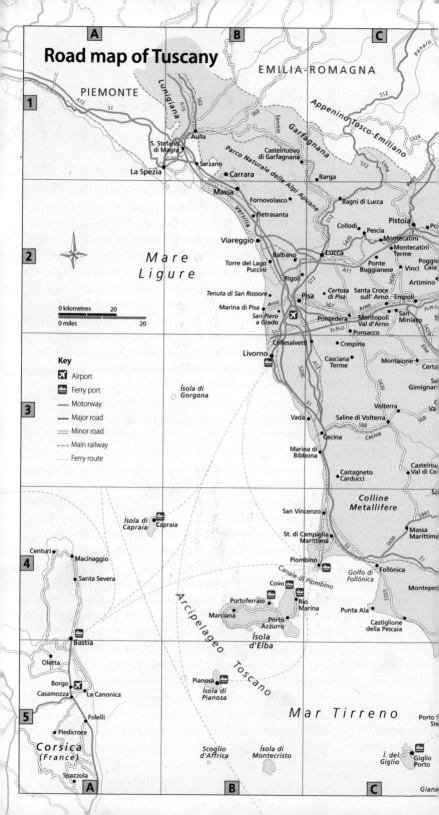